A Note from the Authors

If you are holding this book in your hands, you are most likely a high school student searching for a way to have world history make sense. Perhaps AP World History is your first exposure to the Advanced Placement program and the demands of college-level work. Perhaps you are overwhelmed by the prospect of studying the history of 10,000 years for a 3-hour exam. Many of us who teach AP World History also have been overwhelmed with the awesome scope of this course.

Remember that thousands of high school students have already gained college credit for AP World History since the first exam in 2002, and most have been sophomores. Their success can be your success if you master the skills and themes of world history. Kaplan review books have provided students an edge on AP exams for many years. The practical strategies for success on the AP World History exam provide the focus for this book. The AP World History course is like no other, and this review book is tailored to its specific demands.

This year you will most likely spend many hours reading, writing, and studying world history. You are to be commended for rising to this challenge. Years from now, you will understand the world better from having studied its past. Despite all of the hard work, do not lose sight of what makes people love world history: the fascinating stories of people much like us doing extraordinary things during extraordinary times.

Best of luck,

Jennifer Laden

Patrick Whelan

RELATED TITLES

AP Biology

AP Calculus AB & BC

AP Chemistry

AP English Language & Composition

AP English Literature & Composition

AP Macroeconomics/Microeconomics

AP Physics B & C

AP Psychology

AP Statistics

AP U.S. Government & Politics

AP U.S. History

SAT Subject Test: Biology E/M

SAT Subject Test: Chemistry

SAT Subject Test: Literature

SAT Subject Test: Mathematics Level 1

SAT Subject Test: Mathematics Level 2

SAT Subject Test: Physics

SAT Subject Test: Spanish

SAT Subject Test: U.S. History

SAT Subject Test: World History

Test Prep and Admissions

AP® World History

2006 Edition

Jennifer Laden and Patrick Whelan

Simon & Schuster
NEW YORK · LONDON · SYDNEY · TORONTO

AP® is a registered trademark of the College Entrance Examination Board, which neither sponsors nor endorses this product.

Kaplan Publishing
Published by SIMON & SCHUSTER
Rockefeller Center
1230 Avenue of the Americas
New York, NY 10020

Copyright © 2006 by Kaplan, Inc.
All rights reserved. No part of this book may be reproduced or transmitted in any form or by any means, electronic or mechanical, including photocopying, recording, or by any information storage and retrieval system, without the written permission of the Publisher. Except where permitted by law.

Kaplan® is a registered trademark of Kaplan, Inc.

SIMON & SCHUSTER and colophon are registered trademarks of Simon & Schuster, Inc.

Contributing Editor: Jon Zeitlin
Editorial Director: Jennifer Farthing
Project Editor: Ruth Baygell
Production Manager: Michael Shevlin
Content Manager: Patrick Kennedy
Interior Page Layout: Renée Mitchell
Cover Design: Mark Weaver

Manufactured in the United States of America.
Published simultaneously in Canada.

10 9 8 7 6 5 4 3 2 1

January 2006

ISBN-13: 978-0-7432-7436-4
ISBN-10: 0-7432-7436-9

For information regarding special discounts for bulk purchases, please contact Simon & Schuster Special Sales at 1-800-456-6798 or business@simonandschuster.com.

Table of Contents

About the Authors vii
Kaplan Panel of AP Experts ix

PART ONE: The Basics
Chapter 1: Inside the AP World History Exam 3
    Overview of the Test Structure 4
    How the Exam Is Scored 7
    Registration and Fees 9
    Additional Resources 10

Chapter 2: Strategies for Success: It's Not Always How Much You Know 11
    How to Approach the Document-Based Question 12
    How to Approach the Change-Over-Time Question 29
    How to Approach the Comparative Question 37
    Stress Management 44
    Countdown to the Test 44

PART TWO: Diagnostic Test
    Diagnostic Test 49
    Answers and Explanations 55
    How to Make This Book Work for You Based on the Results of Your Diagnostic 58

PART THREE: AP World History Review
Chapter 3: Foundations (8000 BCE to 600 CE) 61
    The Big Picture 61
    Why This Periodization? 63
    Development of Agriculture 65
    The First Civilizations 67
    Development and Spread of Religion 71
    Classical Societies 77
    Role of Trade in Classical Societies 85
    Spread of Disease 86
    Movement of Peoples 86
    Fall of Classical Empires 87
    Review Questions 89
    Answers and Explanations 98

Chapter 4: 600 to 1450 103
    The Big Picture 103
    Why This Periodization? 105
    Post-Classical Political Developments 105
    Nomadic Empires 115
    Impact of Interaction 118
    Recovery and Renaissance in Asia and Europe 124
    American Civilizations 126
    Review Questions 128
    Answers and Explanations 137

Chapter 5: 1450 to 1750 141
   The Big Picture 141
   Why This Periodization? 142
   Impact of Interaction—The Development of a Global Economy 143
   State-Building 146
   Systems of Forced Labor 152
   Cultural and Intellectual Changes 154
   Review Questions 157
   Answers and Explanations 167

Chapter 6: 1750 to 1914 173
   The Big Picture 173
   Why This Periodization? 175
   Revolutions and Independence Movements 175
   Nationalism and the Nation State 178
   Industrialization 179
   Reform and Reaction 181
   Imperialism and Its Impact 186
   Emancipation 188
   Cultural Influences 189
   Review Questions 191
   Answers and Explanations 199

Chapter 7: 1914 to Present 205
   The Big Picture 205
   Why This Periodization? 207
   Global Conflict 207
   Independence and Nationalist Movements 214
   Revolutions 217
   Political Reform and Economic Changes 220
   Demographic and Environmental Issues 222
   Societal Changes 223
   Review Questions 226
   Answers and Explanations 235

PART FOUR: Practice Tests
   How to Take the Practice Tests 242
   How to Compute Your Score 243

Practice Test 1 245
   Answer Key 262
   Answers and Explanations 263

Practice Test 2 271
   Answer Key 290
   Answers and Explanations 291

Glossary 299

ABOUT THE AUTHORS

Jennifer Laden has taught global and world history at Fox Lane High School in Bedford, New York since 1996, where she developed the AP World History program. She has been a reader and table leader for the AP World History exam since its inception in 2002 and a consultant for the College Board.

The author wishes to thank her AP World History students at Fox Lane High for their inspiration and insight; her co-author Patrick Whelan for his encouragement and guidance; and her husband Tom Murphy for his limitless support.

Patrick Whelan has taught history at Saint Stephen's Episcopal School in Bradenton, FL since 1988, where he helped develop the AP World History program. He has been a reader and table leader for the AP World History exam and a consultant for the College Board since 2002.

The author would like to acknowledge all of the teachers and students who have so enriched his life: his parents, who taught him that his worth is more than what can be measured on a test, his wife and sons, who continue to demonstrate the importance of love, and his co-author, Jennifer Laden. His AP World History class of 2005 was also of great assistance, having reminded him of why he enjoys teaching high school history so very much.

TEACHERS AND STUDENTS—GO ONLINE!

FOR TEACHERS ONLY:
HOW TO USE THIS BOOK IN YOUR CLASSROOM

simonsaysteach.com

Visit our resource area for teachers. We've provided ideas about how this book can be used effectively in and outside of your AP classroom. Easy to implement, these tips are designed to complement your curriculum plans and help you create a classroom full of high-scoring students.

FOR STUDENTS AND TEACHERS

kaptest.com/publishing

The material in this book is up-to-date at the time of publication, but the College Board may have instituted changes in the test since that date. Be sure to carefully read the materials you receive when you register for the test. If there are any important late-breaking developments—or any changes or corrections to the Kaplan test preparation materials in this book—we will post that information online at kaptest.com/publishing.

FEEDBACK AND COMMENTS

kaplansurveys.com/books

If you have comments and suggestions about this book, we invite you to fill out our online survey form at kaplansurveys.com/books. Your feedback is extremely helpful as we continue to develop high-quality resources to meet your needs.

Kaplan Panel of AP Experts

Congratulations—you have chosen Kaplan to help you get a top score on your AP exam.

Kaplan understands your goals, and what you're up against—achieving college credit and conquering a tough test—while participating in everything else that high school has to offer.

You expect realistic practice, authoritative advice, and accurate, up-to-the-minute information on the test. And that's exactly what you'll find in this book, as well as every other in the AP series. To help you (and us!) reach these goals, we have sought out leaders in the AP community. Allow us to introduce our experts:

AP World History Expert

Jay Harmon has taught world history for the past 22 years at Catholic High School in Baton Rouge, LA. He has been a table leader for the AP World History exam since 2002, and also serves on the test development committee.

AP Biology Experts

Larry Calabrese has taught biology for 36 years, and AP Biology for 19 years at Palos Verdes Peninsula High School in CA. He also teaches Anatomy and Physiology at Los Angeles Harbor College in Wilmington, CA. He has been an AP Biology reader since 1986, and a table leader since 1993. For the past 10 years, he has taught College Board workshops.

Cheryl G. Callahan has been teaching biology for over 20 years, first at the college level and now at the high school level at Savannah Country Day School, Savannah, GA. She has been an AP Biology reader and table leader since 1993. She also moderates the AP Biology Electronic Discussion Group.

AP Calculus Expert

William Fox has been teaching calculus at the university level for over 20 years. He has been at Francis Marion University in Florence, SC since 1998. He has been a reader and table leader for the AP Calculus AB and BC exams since 1992.

AP Chemistry Experts

Lenore Hoyt teaches chemistry at Idaho State University. She has done post-doctoral studies at Yale University, and holds a Ph.D. from University of Tennessee. She has been a reader for the AP Chemistry exam for 5 years.

Lisa Zuraw has been a professor in the Chemistry Department at The Citadel in Charleston, SC for 13 years. She has served as a faculty reader for the AP Chemistry exam as well as a member of the AP Chemistry Test Development Committee.

AP English Language & Composition Experts

Natalie Goldberg recently retired from St. Ignatius College Prep in Chicago, IL, where she helped develop a program to prepare juniors for the AP English Language and Composition exam and taught AP English Literature. She was a reader for the AP English Language and Composition exam for 6 years, and has been a consultant with the Midwest Region of the College Board since 1997.

Ronald Sudol has been a reader of AP English Language and Composition for 20 years and a workshop consultant for 12. He is Professor of Rhetoric at Oakland University in MI, where he is also Acting Dean of the College of Arts and Sciences.

AP English Literature & Composition Experts

Mitchell S. Billings has taught for 35 years and began the AP program at Catholic High School in Baton Rouge, LA 12 years ago. He has been an Endorsed College Board Consultant for 12 years. He has also been a reader for the AP exam for 10 years, and for the Alternate AP exam for 2 years.

William H. Pell has taught AP English for the past 20 years, and chairs the Language Arts Department at Spartanburg High School in Spartanburg, SC. He has been an adjunct instructor of English at the University of South Carolina Upstate, and has been active in many programs for the College Board, including the reading, workshops, institutes, conferences, and vertical teams.

AP Macroeconomics/Microeconomics Experts

Linda M. Manning is a visiting professor and researcher in residence at the University of Ottawa in Ontario, Canada. She has worked with the AP Economics Program and the Educational Testing Service as a faculty consultant for almost 15 years, and served on the test development committee from 1997–2000.

Bill McCormick has been teaching AP Economics at Spring Valley High School and Richland Northeast High School in Columbia, SC for the past 26 years. He has served as a reader of AP Macroeconomics and Microeconomics exams for the past 8 years.

Peggy Pride has taught AP Economics at St. Louis University High School in St. Louis, MO for 15 years. She served for 5 years on the AP Economics Test Development Committee, and was the primary author for the new AP Economics Teacher's Guide published by College Board in the spring of 2005.

AP Physics B & C Experts

Jeff Funkhouser has taught high school physics since 1988, and since 2001 has taught AP Physics B and C at Northwest High School in Haslet, TX. He has been a reader and table leader for the AP Physics B & C exams for the past 3 years.

Martin Kirby has taught AP Physics B and tutored students for Physics C at Hart High School in Newhall, CA for the last 18 years. He has been a reader for the AP Physics B & C exams and a workshop presenter for the College Board for the past 10 years.

AP Psychology Experts

Ruth Ault has taught psychology for the past 26 years at Davidson College in Davidson, NC. She was a reader for the AP Psychology exam from 1998–2001 and has been a table leader since 2001.

Nancy Homb has taught AP Psychology for the past 7 years at Cypress Falls High School in Houston, TX. She has been a reader for the AP Psychology exam since 2000, and began consulting for the College Board in 2005.

AP Statistics Experts

Lee Kucera has been teaching Statistics at Capistrano Valley High School in Mission Viejo, CA for 12 years, where she has been a teacher for 26 years. Lee has also been a reader for the AP Statistics exam since its inception in 1997.

Mary Mortlock has been teaching statistics since 1996, beginning at Thomas Jefferson High School for Science & Technology in Alexandria, VA, and continuing on to her current position at Cal Poly State University, CA, where she has taught since 2001. Mary has also been a reader for the AP Statistics exam since 2000.

AP U.S. Government & Politics Expert

Chuck Brownson teaches AP U.S. Government & Politics and AP Economics at Stephen F. Austin High School in Sugar Land, TX. He is currently a graduate student working on his Master's Degree in Political Science at the University of Houston. He has been teaching AP U.S. Government & Politics and AP Economics classes for 2 years.

AP U.S. History Experts

Steven Mercado has taught AP U.S. History and AP European History at Chaffey High School in Ontario, CA for the past 12 years. He has also served as a reader for the AP U.S. History exam, and as a reader and table leader for the AP European History exam.

Diane Vecchio has taught in the History Department at Furman University in Greenville, SC since 1996. She has been Chief Faculty Consultant for the AP U.S. History exam for the past four years, and also served as a member of the AP U.S. History Test Development Committee.

| PART ONE |

The Basics

Chapter 1: Inside the AP World History Exam

"World History"—even the title of the course seems overwhelming. At first glance, it seems like a course on the entire world for all of recorded time. Anyone teaching a world history course, therefore, must decide what to include and what to leave out.

The people writing the AP World History exam face the same dilemma. As a student studying for the AP exam, you need to know how to separate the important stuff to know from the not-so-important stuff.

The content sections of this review book go into the specifics of what you should know. This first chapter deals with the organization of the test itself and the major themes and skills that will be tested. Together these sections will tell you how to manage 10,000 years of world history and succeed on the AP exam. In addition, a short Diagnostic test and two full practice tests will get you well acquainted with the types of questions you'll see on the real exam.

You should know that this course has a completely different approach than the typical history course. AP World History deals more with the **connections** between issues in history than the facts of everything that has happened in world history. The **"big picture"** is much more important than the small details. In some ways, this organization makes your job easier; in others, it makes your job more difficult.

OVERVIEW OF THE TEST STRUCTURE

The material tested on the exam is divided into five chronological periods of approximately equal weight:

Time Period	Weight on the Exam
8000 BCE to 600 CE	19–20%
600 CE to 1450 CE	22%
1450 to 1750	19–20%
1750 to 1914	19–20%
1914 to the Present	19–20%

The College Board uses the designation BCE **(before the common era)** and CE **(common era)** instead of BC and AD. The dates themselves otherwise correspond; 1492 CE is the same as 1492 AD. This abbreviation system is not difficult to understand but might be confusing if you have never seen it before.

The last 90 or so years of history are as important as the first 8600 years. Often, teachers speed through the 20th century in a rush to finish the material before the exam date. In your review, you may want to emphasize more modern history to compensate.

You may also notice that the exam covers material up to the present. In case you think that your studying should also include reading the newspaper for the past few months, do not worry. The exam is written a few years before it is administered to students. You will *not* need to know any specific material that has occurred in the *very recent past*.

Regions Tested on the Exam

Almost all parts of the world are covered on the AP World History exam, though some areas are covered more extensively than others. Asia, for instance, receives much more attention than Australia.

The College Board offers an AP European History exam and does not want to duplicate exam coverage. For this reason, the overwhelming majority of the World History exam deals with those areas outside of Europe, such as Asia, Africa, and Latin America. The questions that address European history account for at most 30% of the exam.

In addition, U.S. History is not emphasized on the World History AP exam, except when it involves relationships with other areas of the world and with issues that involve larger global processes.

Exam Format

Multiple-Choice	70 questions	55 minutes	50% of the exam
Free-Response Essays	3 questions	130 minutes	50% of the exam

Question Types

There are two types of questions on the exam: multiple-choice and free-response (essays).

Multiple-Choice Questions

The multiple-choice questions have five possible responses (A through E). The 70 questions are arranged in chronological clusters or groups. You don't need to shift your mind from African prehistory to the Cold War to the Mongol invasions for consecutive questions. Some of the questions will cover material that crosses chronological boundaries.

Some questions will contain visual materials, such as maps, charts, graphs, illustrations, and pictures.

Free-Response Questions

There are three types of free-response essay questions. Each essay allows for the same amount of writing time and counts the same for the final score. Note, however, that there are **no mandatory stop times for each essay**. If you spend 90 minutes on the Document-Based Essay, your other two essays are bound to be sloppy. Bring a watch, and consciously budget your time.

Essay Type	Time Allotted	Scoring Weight
Document-Based Essay	10 minutes reading 40 minutes writing	33.3% of the essay section; 16.7% of the whole test
Change-Over-Time Essay	40 minutes writing	33.3% of the essay section; 16.7% of the whole test
Comparative Essay	40 minutes writing	33.3% of the essay section; 16.7% of the whole test

Unlike the other AP history exams, AP World History does not provide you with a choice among several questions. You must answer the question provided. You do, however, have some flexibility within each question: You may be able to answer an essay question by using information about two regions of the world out of six regions that are listed.

World History Themes

In defining what the AP exam should include, the College Board highlights six specific themes in world history—all dealing with the "big picture" of world history. These themes form the building blocks of the course, and they help the College Board decide what to put into the test. Knowing these themes will help you focus on certain areas for studying.

Theme 1
Patterns and effects of interactions among major societies and regions: trade, war, diplomacy, and international organizations

> In other words: **What happens when people come in contact with each other?**

Theme 2
The dynamics of change and continuity across the world history periods covered in this course, and the causes and processes involved in major changes of these dynamics

> In other words: **Why do some things change while other things stay the same?**

Theme 3
The effects of technology, economics, and demography on people and the environment (population growth and decline, disease, labor systems, manufacturing, migrations, agriculture, weaponry)

> In other words: **How does the development of new technology and movement of people affect the world?**

Theme 4
Systems of social structure and gender structure (comparing major features within and among societies and assessing change and continuity)

> In other words: **How do societies organize themselves socially and what roles do men and women play?**

Theme 5
Cultural, intellectual, and religious developments and interactions among and within societies.

> In other words: **How do people identify themselves and expresses themselves culturally and intellectually?**

Theme 6
Changes in functions and structures of states and in attitudes toward states and political identities (political culture), including the emergence of the nation-state (types of political organization)

> In other words: **How do people govern themselves?**

Almost every question on the exam will deal with at least one of these themes. All six themes are important for each of the five time periods covered by the exam, and each theme should receive about equal weight in your preparation.

"Habits of Mind" Skills

In addition to the six major themes of world history, the College Board has identified seven thinking skills that are tested on the exam. They call these skills "habits of mind."

General History Skills
1. Constructing and evaluating arguments by using evidence
2. Using documents to analyze point of view
3. Assessing issues of change and continuity over time
4. Handling a diversity of interpretations through analysis of context and frame of reference

Specific World History Skills
5. Seeing global patterns and being able to connect localized issues to the big picture
6. Comparing within and among societies especially reacting to global processes
7. Assessing claims of universal standards and putting culturally diverse ideas into historical context

How can you apply this list of skills to your studying? It comes down to understanding the exam better. A multiple-choice question might use a quotation to test how you are able to analyze point of view; another question might ask you to identify the correct statement comparing two cultures. Both of these types of questions assess your ability with the habits of mind.

The free-response essay section uses the habits of mind even more than the multiple-choice section. All of the essays, for example, ask you to construct arguments, which is the first habit of mind. One essay deals specifically with change and continuity over time, and another deals specifically with making comparisons among societies. The document-based essay heavily emphasizes point of view, diversity of interpretations, and putting diverse ideas into historical context. Knowing why the questions are written helps you decode what is being asked.

HOW THE EXAM IS SCORED

The multiple-choice and free-response sections each count for 50% of your total exam grade. The actual grading process and formula are more complicated.

Multiple-Choice Section

The first thing you should know is there is a penalty for answering a question incorrectly: $\frac{1}{4}$ of a point is subtracted for every wrong answer. No points, however, are deducted for leaving a question blank. This design is intended to discourage students from randomly filling in answers to questions.

Leaving too many answers blank is a bad idea. Often you can use the process of elimination to rule out at least one of the five possible responses. The odds are more in your favor if you can narrow it down to two or three responses. Use your best judgment, make an educated guess, and move on quickly to the next question.

The answers for the 70 multiple-choice questions are scored by machine. A weighted score for this first section comes from subtracting the number of correct responses by $\frac{1}{4}$ of the number wrong, then multiplying the result by 0.8571. The weighted scores range from 0 to 60. Any score less than zero is rounded up to zero.

[Number Correct – ($\frac{1}{4}$ × number wrong)] × 0.8571 = Multiple-Choice Section Score

Free-Response Section

The essays are scored by hand, meaning that real people read and evaluate them. World History teachers come together to a central reading site, and are guided through the specific standards for each essay question. A great deal of effort is taken to ensure consistency so that all essays are scored fairly and with the same set of standards.

Each essay is scored on a 10-point system, from 0 to 9. Each essay score is multiplied by 2.2222; all essay scores are then added together to get a total weighted free-response score between 0 and 60.

(Question 1 score × 2.2222)
+
(Question 2 score × 2.2222)
+
(Question 3 score × 2.2222)
} = Free-Response Section Score

Final AP Score

For your composite score, the scores from both sections of the exam are added together.

Multiple-Choice Section Score (out of 60 points)
+
Free-response Section Score (out of 60 points)
} = Composite Score (out of 120 points)

Neither you nor your school will ever see your composite score, however. That score is converted into a scale of 1 through 5. The primary factors for these grades are as follows.

AP Grade	Recommendation	2005 AP World History Grade Distribution
5	Extremely well qualified	10.2
4	Well qualified	17.1
3	Qualified	25.2
2	Possibly qualified	23.4
1	No recommendation	24.0

How do these scores convert to college credit? That depends. Each college department sets its own AP policy. Grades of 3, 4, and 5 are accepted for college credit at the majority of American colleges and universities, yet the most competitive schools accept only grades of 4 or 5.

You may be accustomed to tests that score on a straight percentage basis. In other words, on a 25-question test, five wrong would be an 80% or a B-. Ten wrong out of 25 would be barely passing with 60%.

Part One: The Basics
Inside the AP World History Exam

The AP exams do *not* work this way. For one thing, you probably noticed that the questions tend to be much more difficult than non-AP questions. Even very well-prepared students find it difficult to achieve percentage scores above 90%.

The difficulty of the multiple-choice questions depends on the options presented. On some questions, it can be quite difficult to make a distinction between two, even three answer choices. Thus, the process of eliminating clearly incorrect responses is critical. On the most difficult questions, if you can get down to two possibly correct answers, you are doing well. On the AP exam, many of the questions that you get right will be educated guesses.

You may also notice that the types of questions are different from other kinds of tests, as well. Very few questions ask for the detailed recall of specific events, dates, or people. Even the testing of historical vocabulary is done within the context of higher-level, thought-provoking questions. The questions tend to come from the world history themes and habits of mind discussed earlier. Questions concerning technology, social structure, and the impact of interactions among societies receive greater emphasis on the World History AP exam than they might in other kinds of history classes.

REGISTRATION AND FEES

If you are taking an AP World History course at your high school, registering for the AP exam is easy. Just talk with your teacher and your school's AP coordinator about signing up. Make sure that your name is on the AP exam order list that your AP coordinator sends in March.

If you are home schooled or not in a school that offers AP courses, you can still take the exam. Call AP Services at (609) 771-7300 or (888) 225-5427 by March 1st for a list of schools in your area where you can take the exam. Then contact the AP coordinator at one of the schools identified by the College Board for a place on the exam day.

The College Board makes accommodations if you have a documented disability. These may include extended time, large-print exams, use of a word processor, and other necessary accommodations. If you have a need for these sorts of special accommodations, see your AP coordinator.

At the date of printing, the cost of the exam was $82. If you have financial need, you may petition for a fee reduction. Many states and school districts also provide subsidies to encourage students to take the AP exams.

For more information on the AP Program and the World History Exam, contact:
AP Services
P.O. Box 6671
Princeton, NJ 08541–6671
Phone: (609) 771–7300 or (877) 274–6474
Email: apexgrams@info.collegeboard.org
Website: www.collegeboard.com/student/testing/ap/about.html

ADDITIONAL RESOURCES

The best starting place to find information about the AP World History and the AP exams in general is at the official College Board AP website: **www.apcentral.collegeboard.com**.

The major world history textbook companies also run valuable websites that can be used for review and getting additional information.

Pearson Longman *World Civilizations*
wps.ablongman.com/long_stearns_wcap_4

McGraw Hill *Traditions and Encounters*
highered.mcgraw-hill.com/sites/0072424354/student_view0/

Prentice Hall *The World's History*
cwx.prenhall.com/bookbind/pubbooks/spodek2/

Houghton Mifflin *The Earth and Its People*
college.hmco.com/history/world/bulliet/earth_peoples/2e/students/

Chapter 2: **Strategies for Success: It's Not Always How Much You Know**

The essay section inspires the most dread in the minds of students taking the AP World History exam. Knowing the structure, and especially, how the essays will be scored can give you a substantial advantage.

The three essays are written together during the second part of the exam. All of the essays go into the same pink booklet. Your proctor will *not* tell you to move from one essay to the next—you must do this on your own. A total of 130 minutes is the time allotted for reading, organizing, and writing all three questions.

The three essays can be done in any order. Almost everyone chooses to write the Document-Based question (DBQ) first. The second question is an essay that asks a Change-Over-Time Question (COT); the third is a Comparison question (COMP). Depending on your comfort level with the specific questions, you may want to do the last two essays in a different order than they are listed on the exam.

Pace yourself during this section, so you do not rush through the essays too quickly or, even worse, run out of time. Plenty of students write full and detailed responses to the first essay but are able only to put down a few sentences for the last essay. Partial essays, not surprisingly, do not receive high scores.

HOW TO APPROACH THE DOCUMENT-BASED QUESTION

The first of the three essays is the Document-Based Question (DBQ). This essay **asks you to be a historian**; it will ask a specific question, provide a bit of historical background, and then present 4–10 related documents. Essentially, you are the historian who will take these sources and draw conclusions based on your skills of historical analysis. The DBQ evaluates historical understanding at its purest: the task is not to remember facts but to organize information in an analytical manner.

Many students panic once they see the DBQ because they do not know much about the topic—the question and the documents often cover something well outside of the mainstream of their high school class. The test writers do this on purpose. Outside knowledge is not needed for the DBQ. You may bring in outside information if you wish, but there is no need to mention facts other than those found in the documents provided. (This approach is different than the DBQ task on the AP U.S. History exam.)

The other two essays on the exam will evaluate your knowledge of history, but the DBQ evaluates your proficiency with historical material. Consequently, writing the DBQ is a skill that can be learned much like any other skill.

Organizing Your Essay in 10 Minutes

The entire 130-minute essay time is divided into two parts: the first 10 minutes is reading and organizing time, during which you may not write in the pink essay booklet, and the last 120 minutes is the essay writing period. Spend that first 10 minutes working solidly on the DBQ, since that is the essay which requires the most reading and preparation time.

First, read the question. Underline the words that are most related to your task. Let's look at a sample question:

> "For the period 1876–1908, analyze how the Ottoman government viewed ethnic and religious groups within its empire. Explain what additional kind of document(s) would help you analyze the views of the Ottoman government."

All of the documents that follow will relate to the time period and the place, so you do not need to underline 1876–1908 or Ottoman government. You are being asked how the Ottoman government **viewed ethnic and religious groups** within its empire. An essay that dealt with how the groups viewed the Ottoman Empire would miss the point.

In the DBQ, you will always be asked to provide and explain examples of additional kind of documents. The words **additional kind of document(s)** will most likely be in bold letters—a sign to you that this task is important.

Second, read the historical background. Since the College Board does not expect you to bring in outside information, the background paragraph sets the historical scene so that you understand the most basic aspects of the topic before you begin. Perhaps you know a great deal about late Ottoman imperial history. More likely, you will need a few sentences to bring you up to speed before you start looking at the documents themselves.

Be careful, though. Quoting from the historical background paragraph in your essay is not recommended. Essays that have material from the historical background repeated in the first paragraph tend to do poorly. The task of the DBQ is to answer the question by using the documents—not by using the historical background.

> Historical background: In the middle of the 19th century, the Ottoman Empire instigated a series of liberal reforms that granted civil rights to subjects of their empire. These reforms culminated in the new constitution of 1876. In the same year Sultan Abdulhamid II came to power after a military revolt. His rule of the Sublime State (what the Ottoman Empire called itself) included a diverse set of groups including large Christian communities of Bulgarians, Greeks, Armenians, and Serbo-Croatians. Many Muslims within the empire practiced forms of Islam that varied from the official Sunni-Hanefi version favored by the imperial court. In 1908, an uprising by a group of nationalist reformers known as the Young Turks created a new style of government; Sultan Abdulhamid II stepped down the next year.

Third, read the documents. Most of the first 10 minutes of the writing period will be used looking at the documents and organizing them into groups for analysis. Each of the 4 to 10 documents will have a number above a box. Inside the box will be information on the source of the document, which is very important as you will see later, and the document itself.

Documents can be of many different sorts. Written documents are usually excerpts of much longer pieces that have been edited specifically for the exam. They could be from personal letters, hidden journals, official decrees, public speeches, or propaganda posters. Obviously, the nature of the source should guide you in how you analyze the document. Documents can also be pictures, photographs, maps, charts, and graphs, which will identify the source.

Often students have a harder time analyzing visual and graphic sources than the written sources. Even so, use all of the documents in your essay, treating the non-written sources with the same attention as the written ones.

Feel free to write notes in the green question booklet as you read the documents. Nothing in the green booklet is read as part of the essay scoring. Feel free to underline important words in both the source line and the document itself. Use the generous margins for notes that will help you group the documents with other documents and discuss their points of view.

While taking notes, write the following about the authors of the document in the margins: social class, education, occupation, and gender. On the bottom of the document, write a short phrase that summarizes the basic meaning of the document, the purpose (why it was written), and possibly, a missing piece of evidence that relates to the document. If the document is a speech, the missing evidence could be the perception of those listening to the speech. If the document is a government declaration, the missing evidence could be information about how effectively the declaration was carried out.

Once you have finished reading and have made short notes of all of the documents, **reread the question**. Note again what the question asks. If you have not done so already, mark which documents address the different issues that the question asks. Group the documents by their similarities. Can you draw enough conclusions at this point to organize an analytical thesis?

At the end of the 10-minute reading period, the proctor will announce that students may open their pink booklets and begin writing the essays. If you have not yet finished reading and organizing the essay, take a few more minutes to finish up. A few students might be ready to write before the end of the 10-minute reading period, but most find that 10 minutes is just about right.

Core Point Scoring

For fairness and ease of scoring, the essays for AP World History are evaluated using what is called a "core scoring method" that comes from scoring rubrics. Each essay is scored on a 10-point system from zero to 9, with 9 being the best.

With the DBQ, the first 7 points are awarded for the completion of specific tasks. These are called the "basic core" points. Up to an extra 2 points ("expanded core" points) may be awarded after all of the essential core points are met.

For the DBQ, the basic core points are as follows:

Points	Task
1	Has an acceptable thesis
1	Understands the basic meaning of documents (may misinterpret one document)
2	Supports thesis with appropriate evidence from all or all but one of the documents
(1)	Supports thesis with appropriate evidence from all but two documents
1	Analyzes point of view in at least 2 documents
1	Analyzes documents by grouping them in two or three ways
1	Identifies and explains the need for an appropriate additional document or source
7	Subtotal for all basic core points
2	Possible expanded core points
9	Total possible points for the DBQ

Your goal for the DBQ is to get all 7 basic core points. If you make all of your core points, you will have a much better chance of doing well on the whole exam.

Expanded core points reward excellence in those essays that have met all of their basic core points. More on the expanded core later. First, let's look at an example of a DBQ before learning how to earn your basic core points.

> For the period 1876–1908, analyze how the Ottoman government viewed ethnic and religious groups within its empire. Explain what **additional kind of document(s)** would help analyze the views of the Ottoman Empire.
>
> <u>Historical Background</u>: In the middle of the 19th century, the Ottoman Empire instigated a series of liberal reforms that granted civil rights to subjects of their empire. These reforms culminated in the new constitution of 1876. In the same year Sultan Abdulhamid II came to power after a military revolt. His rule of the Sublime State (what the Ottoman Empire called itself) included a diverse set of groups including large Christian communities of Bulgarians, Greeks, Armenians, and Serbo-Croatians. Many Muslims within the empire practiced forms of Islam that varied from the official Sunni-Hanefi version favored by the imperial court. In 1908, an uprising by a group of nationalist reformers known as the Young Turks created a new style of government; Sultan Abdulhamid II stepped down the next year.

Document 1

Source: Adapted from Abdolonyme Ubicini and Pavet de Courteille, *The Present State of the Ottoman Empire*, a guide concerning the Ottoman Empire published in Western Europe, 1876

FIGURES ON NATIONALITIES WITHIN THE OTTOMAN EMPIRE

Ethnic Group (Total population) Percentage of Empire	Subgroup	Subgroup Population
Turkish group (14,020,000) 49.1%	Ottoman Turks Turkomans Tatars	13,500,000 300,000 220,000
Greco-Latin group (3,520,000) 12.3%	Greeks Kutzo-Vlachs Albanians	2,100,000 220,000 1,200,000
Slavic group (4,550,000) 15.9%	Serbo-Croatians Bulgarians Cossacks Lipovans	1,500,000 3,000,000 32,000 18,000
Persian group (3,620,000) 12.7%	Armenians Kurds Other Persians	2,500,000 1,000,000 120,000
Semites (1,611,000) 5.6%	Jews Arabs Other Semites	158,000 1,000,000 453,000
Other groups (1,232,000) 4.3%		

Total Population of the Ottoman Empire: 28,553,000

Document 2

Source: The Ottoman Constitution, 23 December 1876

Art. 1. The Ottoman Empire comprises present territory and possessions, and semi-dependent provinces. It forms an indivisible whole, from which no portion can be detached under any pretext whatever.

Art. 4. His Majesty the Sultan, under the title of "Supreme Caliph," is the protector of the Muslim religion. He is the sovereign and emperor of all the Ottomans.

Art. 8. All subjects of the empire are called Ottomans, without distinction whatever faith they profess; the status of an Ottoman is acquired and lost according to conditions specified by law.

Art. 9. Every Ottoman enjoys personal liberty on condition of non interfering with the liberty of others.

Art. 11. Islam is the state religion. But, while maintaining this principle, the state will protect the free exercise of faiths professed in the Empire, and uphold the religious privileges granted to various bodies, on condition of public order and morality not being interfered with.

Document 3

Source: Mr. Owen Davis, from a lecture at a British Congregational Church "Those Dear Turks," 1st November 1876.

"Unfortunately for the peace of mankind, it has happened that the Turks is placed in a position where it is impossible to ignore him, and almost equally impossible to endure him; while by his origin, habits, and religion, he is an Asiatic of Asiatics, he is by irony of fate established in a position where his presence is a ceaseless cause of misery to millions of Christian people."

Document 4

Source: Hagop Mintzuri, an Armenian baker's apprentice, from his book *Istanbul Memoirs 1897-1940*, commenting about the military guards accompanying the sultan's arrival at a mosque for ceremonial prayers at the end of the fast of Ramadan.

"First the Albanian guards, dressed in violet knee-breeches, who were not soldiers or police and did not speak Turkish, would fill the upper part of our market square. Then would come the Arab guards of the sultan, dressed in red salvar and adorned with green turbans. These too, did not speak Turkish and they would fill the road. Finally the Palace Guard of the sultan, chosen exclusively from Turks who were tall, sporting their decorations on their chests, would take up their positions as an inner ring in front of the Albanians and Arabs."

Document 5

Source: Suleyman Husnu Pasha (Pasha is a title of distinction within the Ottoman Empire), former high adviser to the sultan and in political exile in Iraq, commenting on the ethnic and religious diversity in Iraq, 7 April 1892.

"The elements belonging to the official faith and language of the state are in a clear minority whereas the majority falls to the hordes of the opposition."

Document 6

Source: Ahmed Cevdet Pasha, respected Ottoman statesman and historian, undated official memorandum

"the Sublime State rests on four principles. That is to say, the ruler is Ottoman, the government is Turkish, the religion is Islam, and the capital is Istanbul. If any of these four principles were to be weakened, this would mean a weakening of one of the four pillars of the state structure... The Sublime State is a great structure made up of various peoples and strata, all of these constituent elements are held together by the sacred power of the Caliphate. Because the only thing uniting Arab, Kurd, Albanian, and Bosnian is the unity of Islam. Yet, the real strength of the Sublime State lies with the Turks. It is an obligation of their national character and religion to sacrifice their lives for the House of Osman until the last one is destroyed. Therefore it is natural that they be accorded more worth than other peoples of the Sublime State."

Document 7

Source: Proclamation by the Young Turks, 1908

3. It will be demanded that all Ottoman subjects having completed their twentieth year, regardless of whether they possess property or fortune, shall have the right to vote.

9. Every citizen will enjoy complete liberty and equality, regardless of nationality or religion, and be submitted to the same obligations. All Ottomans, being equal before the law as regards rights and duties relative to the State, are eligible for government posts, according to their individual capacity and their education. Non-Muslims will be equally liable to the military law.

Do You Have a Thesis?

You have one chance to make a good first impression. Usually, an AP reader can tell within the first few sentences whether or not an essay is going to be strong. A few essays recover after a poor start, but first impressions matter. Consequently, nothing is more important in the first paragraph than the clear statement of an analytical thesis.

Different kinds of writings demand different types of opening paragraphs. In English class you may learn a style of essay writing that asks for general background information in a first paragraph. On a DBQ, however, you do not have much time. The reader is most interested in seeing a strong thesis as soon as possible.

Your thesis can be more than just one sentence. With the compound questions often asked by the DBQ, two sentences might be needed to complete the idea. To count for the basic core point, the thesis needs to include specific information that responds to the question. Many students think they have written a thesis but actually have not; their opening paragraphs are just too general and unspecific.

The thesis is that part of your essay which 1) specifically addresses the terms of the question and 2) sets up the structure for the rest of your essay. Let's use a specific question.

> "For the period 1876–1908, analyze how the Ottoman government viewed ethnic and religious groups within its empire."

Thesis Statements That Don't Work

This statement below is not an acceptable thesis; it is far too bland. It says very little about how the essay is structured.

> "There were many ways in which the Ottoman government viewed ethnic and religious groups."

This next statement paraphrases the historical background and does not address the question. It would not receive credit for being a thesis.

> "The Ottoman government brought reforms in the constitution of 1876. The empire had a number of different groups of people living in it, including Christians and Muslims who did not practice the official form of Islam. By 1908 a new government was created by the Young Turks and the sultan was soon out of his job."

This next sentence gets the question backward: You are being asked for the government's view of religious and ethnic groups, not the groups' view of the government. Though the issue of point-of-view is very important, this statement would not receive a basic core point.

> "People of different nationalities reacted differently to the Ottoman government depending on their religion."

The following paragraph says a great deal about history but it does not address the substance of the question. It would not receive a basic core point based on irrelevancy.

> "Throughout history, people around the world struggled with the issue of political power and freedom. From the harbor of Boston during the first stages of the American Revolution to the plantations of Haiti during the struggle to end slavery, people have battled for power. As Marxism became an ideology sweeping the world, people became more radicalized. Even in places like China with the Boxer Rebellion, people were responding against the issue of westernization. Imperialism made the demand for change even more pronounced, as European powers circled the globe and stretched their influences to the far reaches of the known world. In the Ottoman Empire too, people demanded change."

Thesis Statements That Do Work

Now we turn to thesis statements that do work. The two sentences below address both the religious and ethnic aspects of the question. They describes *how* these groups were viewed.

> "The Ottoman government took the same position on religious diversity as it did on ethnic diversity. Minorities were servants of the Ottoman Turks, and religious diversity was tolerated as long as Islam remained supreme."

This statement answers the question in a different way, but is equally successful.

> "Government officials in the Ottoman Empire were able to send out the message that all people in the empire were equal regardless of religion or ethnicity, yet an underlying reality was that the Turks and their version of Islam were superior."

Do You Understand the Documents Properly?

With the core point system of scoring, the readers award points based on what the essays accomplish. They do not remove points if an essay is off-task, written poorly, or wrong. There is one exception, however. In the DBQ, you must demonstrate that you understand the documents being used. If your essay makes more than one major misinterpretation, the basic core point cannot be earned.

A major misinterpretation is one that misses the basic intent of the document. If you wrote that the Proclamation of the Young Turks was a movement away from ethnic and religious equality, then that misinterpretation would be a major error.

If, instead, you wrote that the Ottoman Empire survived for decades after the Proclamation of the Young Turks in 1908, the statement would be wrong (the Ottoman Empire collapsed after World War I) but would not be a misinterpretation of the document. All of the documents could still count as being understood properly.

Be careful, especially, with visual and graphic documents. Students tend to misinterpret these non-written documents more than traditional written documents.

Do You Use Evidence to Support Your Thesis?

These core points strike at the basic idea of the DBQ. The documents present a case for answering the question. Your ability to use those documents to answer the question is the focus of the essay. Use the documents to analyze, and you will earn this basic core point.

If the essay supports the thesis with appropriate evidence from all or all but one of the documents, then the essay earns 2 basic core points. If it uses evidence from all but two of the documents, then 1 basic core point is earned.

As you are writing your essay, check off the document in your green booklet when you use each document. Writing under time pressure, you may forget to mention one or two. Also remember to include the documents that are in graphic or visual formats. Students often forget to analyze these to the same degree that they do written sources.

To receive this core point, the documents need to be used as part of the analysis. In other words, if a document is only mentioned in a list, it will not count for this point. For example, "The Ottoman Empire looked down on ethnic and religious minorities, as seen in documents 3, 4, and 5." If documents 3, 4, and 5 were not analyzed further, this essay would not receive the basic core points for supporting the thesis with appropriate evidence.

How should essays refer to the documents? Any of the following ways could count for the evidence core points. Your essay could:

1. Refer to the document number directly in the sentence: "As shown by document 7, the Young Turks believed that all ethnic and religious groups should be treated equally."

2. Refer to the document within parentheses at the end of the sentence: "The Young Turks believed that all ethnic and religious groups should be treated equally (doc. 7)."

3. Refer to information presented in the line of source attribution: "As shown by The Proclamation of the Young Turks in 1908, the Young Turks believed that all ethnic and religious groups should be treated equally."

4. Combine the last two techniques: "As shown by The Proclamation of the Young Turks in 1908, the Young Turks believed that all ethnic and religious groups should be treated equally (doc. 7)." **(best option)**

5. Give no attribution: "The Young Turks believed that all ethnic and religious groups should be treated equally." **(worst option)**

Merely summarizing the documents is the easiest way to miss these basic core points. You must link the document to the question, not just repeat what the document says. For example, the following paragraph would not count as evidence in support of the thesis:

> "Document 1 is a chart with numbers for the different nationalities within the Ottoman Empire. Turks are 49.1% of the population. There are a lot of other groups listed too. The total population is about 28 million people. In document 2 the constitution says that the Sultan is the religious authority and the sovereign. It also says that Islam is the state religion and that, 'the state will protect the free exercise of faiths professed in the Empire, and uphold the religious privileges granted to various bodies.'"

This summary does not provide any analysis. It states simply *what* the documents say; it does not describe *how* the documents show government views toward ethnic and religious groups. The task of the essay is to answer the question by analyzing.

The following paragraph would earn the basic core point for evidence in support of the thesis:

> "Document 1 is a chart that clearly demonstrates the ethnic diversity of the Ottoman Empire at the time of the new constitution. The Turks were a minority at 49.1% of the population, even though they controlled the government of the Ottoman Empire. The Constitution of 1876 (doc 2) also reinforces the idea that the empire was formed of various ethnicities and religions. It formally states that all people are granted equality, and that all religions answer to the same law. However, this document reflects the law from the point of view of high government officials. It therefore demonstrates only the legal rules, rather than the day-to-day reality in the empire."

Another easy way to miss core points is by not having a strong thesis. How can you use document evidence to support the thesis if the thesis itself is weak? Your essay should be organized enough so that the reader can see how each document fits into the analysis presented in the thesis. Using the same terms that are mentioned in the thesis is a good way to make the links between the evidence and the thesis more apparent.

Do You Discuss the Point of View of the Documents?

More essays do not get point of view (POV) than any other basic core point. So be warned: POV is the most important and difficult task. It will separate the mediocre essays from those that do very well. As with any of the other basic core qualities, if an essay does not contain point of view, the highest score it can earn is 6. Your goal is to earn a 7 or above.

Your essay will need to mention aspects of POV for at least two documents in order to receive the basic core point for POV.

So what is point of view? Essentially, POV is the analysis of why a certain person composed the material for the document. What is the author's (or the document's) "angle"? Comments in your essay that delve into the motivations for the documents often count as POV. In addition, comments relating to the reliability of a source relate to that source's POV.

Ask these questions in order to earn the core point for POV:

1. Does the occupation of the author give the document more reliability?

2. Does the class, religion, national background, or gender of the author influence what is mentioned in the document?

3. Does the type of document influence the content of what is said? A journal entry or private letter might be more candid about a topic than a public address that is meant to be persuasive. A political cartoon by definition is exaggerated and meant to convey a certain message, whereas a photograph may accurately represent what was in front of the camera for a shot, but could be staged and framed to only capture a certain perspective.

4. Does the timing of the document influence the message? Recollections and memoirs written long after an event may not have the same reliability as first-hand materials done immediately afterward.

5. Does the intended audience can skew the message of a source? If a document is meant to be read by the sultan, it has a different POV than one written for a European audience.

6. Describing the tone of the document can also count for POV—if the document is sarcastic, triumphant, haughty, etc. This issue can be more subtle and is best used with other descriptions of POV.

Merely attributing the document's source by repeating the source material from the document is not enough to earn the POV point. The source material, however, gives you clues as to what you could say relating to POV.

Using our sample DBQ on the Ottoman government's view of ethnic and religious groups, let's examine different examples of POV. You may want to go back to review the documents in the sample DBQ shown above. The following statements may all count for point of view:

For Document 1:

- "The census of national groups within the Ottoman Empire was compiled for Western European readers, which may make it more reliable in counting ethnic minorities than one published for a Turkish distribution." (Intended audience and reliability)
- "The figures on nationalities provide a detailed picture of the population at the beginning of the sultan's reign but does not show how the population groups changed over time." (timing of the document)
- "Ubicini and Courteille took care to list the numbers for even the very small ethnic groups in the Ottoman Empire, like the Cossacks and Lipovans. They apparently wanted an accurate and detailed listing of national groups." (reliability)
- "The numbers in these census figures might be inexact because of the difficulty of counting widely dispersed people over a hundred years ago. The numbers seem rounded and may be educated guesses." (reliability)

For Document 2:

- "The Constitution of 1876 reflects the official governmental laws and may not accurately represent the reality within the empire." (type of document)
- "The Constitution was most likely written by high government officials, who may have wanted the Ottoman Empire to seem more enlightened than it actually was." (background of the authorship)
- "The protection of the rights of non-Turkish people in the Ottoman Empire may not be a move of tolerance but may be an effort to bring stability to the Empire at a tumultuous time." (timing)

For Document 3:

- "Mr. Davis's speech demonstrates anti-Muslim sentiment among Christians and the perception that Christians were persecuted within the Ottoman Empire." (background of author and tone)
- "This speech given to a Christian group far away from the Ottoman Empire may be biased against the Ottoman government since the Ottomans were not in the mainstream of Western European society." (audience and reliability)
- "As a speech given in a British church, this document may have exaggerated the problems the of Ottoman government's treatment of Christians for dramatic effect." (type of document)

For Document 4:
- "As an Armenian, Mintzuri was very aware of the different ethnic groups representing the sultan's guard." (background of the author)
- "Since this recollection was published in Mintzuri's memoirs years after the event, the details may be inexact." (type of document)
- "As a lower-class baker's apprentice, Mintzuri may have had strong feelings about his low position in society and consequently recorded the arrangement of guards as a ranking based on status." (occupation of author)

For Document 5:
- "Suleyman Husnu Pasha, who had a title of distinction, was a former advisor to the sultan. Husnu's occupation had an effect on his opinion since he probably knew more about the conditions of the empire." (occupation of the author)
- "Since Suleyman Husnu Pasha was in political exile at the time of this document, he may have been more open about the situation in Iraq since he was not officially a part of the government." (background of the author)
- "Suleyman Husnu Pasha seems to hold a bias against the ethnic and religious minorities in Iraq, calling them 'hordes of the opposition.' This bias may have come from Husnu's loyalty to the official version of Islam and the Turkish language." (tone and background of author)

For Document 6:
- "As a respected Ottoman statesman, Ahmed Cevdet Pasha was representing the official government views towards the different ethnic groups in the empire." (occupation of the author)
- "Since Cevdet's comments were the form of an official memo, this document reveals the view of someone close to the power center of the Ottoman Empire." (type of document)
- "Most likely Ahmed Cevdet Pasha was a Turk and a Muslim and therefore would look more favorably on the role of Muslims and Turks within the Ottoman Empire." (background of author)

For Document 7:
- "The Young Turks, as a revolutionary group of reformers, wanted the support of ethnic minorities. Consequently, they demanded complete liberty and equality in this proclamation to the people." (type of document, intended audience, and authorship)
- "The Young Turks wanted a new style of government. As a result they called on values different from those that had been practiced by the Ottoman officials." (background of authors)
- "Since this proclamation came in 1908 at the end of the sultan's rule, the message is more democratic and progressive than seen previously." (timing of document)

Some of the statements seem more sophisticated than others. Some of the statements may actually contradict each other. Even so, describing point of view is a skill that must be demonstrated for at least two documents.

Essays that use POV in a sophisticated manner and use it consistently are rewarded with expanded core points, if every other basic core point has been earned.

Do You Group the Documents Together in your Analysis?

Historians analyze material by pulling together evidence, and in writing your DBQ, so should you. The documents naturally come together into groups for analysis. Within each of your body paragraphs, group the documents. Essays that successfully have two or three groupings, depending on the question, earn this core point.

Do not work with documents in isolation. A group cannot have just one document; each document should be discussed with reference to others. A common mistake is for students to describe each document in order, by paraphrasing what it says. This "listing" format is deadly to good performance on the DBQ.

Earlier you may have read two paragraphs that served as examples of how to use and how not to use evidence to support your thesis. Let's look at these paragraphs again to see how effectively they group documents.

- "Document 1 is a chart with numbers for the different nationalities within the Ottoman Empire. Turks are 49.1% of the population. There are a lot of other groups listed too. The total population is about 28 million people. In document 2 the constitution says that the Sultan is the religious authority and the sovereign. It also says that Islam is the state religion and that, 'the state will protect the free exercise of faiths professed in the Empire, and uphold the religious privileges granted to various bodies.'"
- "Document 1 is a chart that clearly demonstrates the ethnic diversity of the Ottoman Empire at the time of the new constitution. The Turks were a minority at 49.1% of the population, even though they controlled the government of the Ottoman Empire. The Constitution of 1876 (doc 2) *also reinforces* the idea that the empire was formed of various ethnicities and religions. It formally states that all people are granted equality, and that all religions answer to the same law. However, this document reflects the law from the point of view of high government officials. It therefore demonstrates only the legal rules, rather than the day-to-day reality in the empire."

In example 1, the documents are discussed independently. In example 2, they are discussed together.

How you group documents is a matter of personal opinion. Typical groupings include:
- Chronological timing of the documents (grouped by time periods of the documents)
- Class, gender, occupation and ethnicity of the documents' authors
- Purpose or intended audience of the documents (grouped by who was supposed to read the document)
- Attitude and tone of the documents (favorable or unfavorable to a certain issue or group)
- Aspects covered by the documents (economic, political, social, or religious)
- Geographic areas represented by the documents
- Type of documents (pictures, charts, written documents, transcripts of speeches)

For our sample essay, you could group the documents in the following ways:

By document type and intended audience

    Official proclamations/constitutions (document two and seven)

    Ottoman internal correspondence (documents four and five)

    Documents intended for non-Ottoman audiences (documents one and three)

By attitudes toward ethnic and religious minorities

    Documents that show inclusion (documents two, four and seven)

    Documents that show division (documents three, four, five, and six)

By focus on types of groups

    Documents that focus on religious groups (documents two, three, five, six, seven)

    Documents that focus on ethnic groups (documents one, four, six, seven)

One document can be used in more than one grouping. Document 4, which makes comments about the guards accompanying the sultan's arrival, could show inclusion or division. In the document, Arabs and Albanians were described as included in the sultan's official military guards, which is a pretty high honor. But they were also separated by ethnic group and occupy a lower position. Using the document to show inclusion or separation (or both) would be acceptable. Document 6, because it describes attitudes toward both ethnic and religious minorities, could be placed in both sets for analysis.

Do You Suggest and Explain the Need for an Additional Document?

When doing research, historians continuously ask the question, where else could valuable information be found on this topic? Historians are in constant search of new areas of inquiry and new sources to explain the past. Since the DBQ is the essay that asks you to be a historian, you need to provide in your essay suggestions for additional documents that could be useful in answering the question. These suggestions should not be types of documents that are *already* present in the DBQ, but rather the "missing voice" not already included in the list of documents.

For this task, you do not need to be very specific; you do not even need to mention a specific document. All you need to do is mention a type of document that could be useful. The readers of the AP essay do not expect that high school students would have knowledge of hidden documents in some archive that might shed light on this topic. General statements involving hypothetical types of documents would be fine, *even if* they do not really exist.

Just as important as mentioning a potentially useful additional type of document is describing *why* it would be useful. To earn this basic core point, therefore, you need to include mention of an additional document and an explanation about why it would be useful in analyzing the question.

For our sample DBQ, examples of additional documents could be:
- A document from the sultan himself since he represents the central power of the Ottoman Empire
- Official orders from the Ottoman government on how to treat different ethnic and religious subjects since such a document could show how the government implemented its policies
- A chart showing statistics of religious diversity within the empire would help describe the position of the official faith within the empire
- A speech or article from a Young Turk on his attitude toward the Ottoman government would help show the differences in thought between reformers and officials
- A document from a religious leader within the Ottoman Empire would provide a sense of how official religious policies were perceived by the religious communities themselves
- A map showing the distribution of different ethnic groups within the Ottoman Empire would help illustrate the divisions faced by this multi-ethnic country

Any of these responses or any combination of these would receive a basic core point for the additional document(s). Other potential responses would also be counted if their importance could be explained.

Be careful: Mentioning a type of document that already exists disqualifies the statement. For our sample DBQ, mentioning a document from a person outside of the Ottoman Empire would not count since document 3 is written from a British perspective. Nor would mentioning a document from an ethnic or religious minority within the Ottoman Empire count, since document 4 is written by an Armenian in Istanbul. To make sure that you get this basic core point, you may want to mention two or three different types of additional documents and why each would be useful.

Typically, students mention an additional document at the end of the essay; however, that is not required. Discussion of the additional document can take place anywhere in the essay.

Do You Go Beyond the Basic Requirements?

Your goal for the DBQ is to earn all 7 basic core points. Students who earn scores of 7 are well on track for success. But what about the additional 2 points—the expanded core points—which would elevate your essays even further above the norm? For those, you must first have earned all 7 of the basic core points.

Earning expanded core points is not as straightforward as earning basic core points. For the basic core, either your essay has a thesis or it does not. Either your essay analyzes documents through grouping or it does not. And so on.

For the expanded core, several indicators of excellence may come into play. For instance, an essay that earns expanded core points might:

- Have a highly sophisticated thesis
- Show deep analysis of the documents
- Use documents persuasively in broad conceptual ways
- Analyze point of view thoughtfully and consistently
- Identify multiple additional documents with sophisticated explanations of their usefulness
- Bring in relevant outside information beyond the historical background provided

Expanded core points are awarded to essays that do the tasks of the basic core really well. Instead of just having an acceptable thesis or just 2 references to point of view, an essay would have an outstanding thesis and refer to point of view with almost every document.

Knowledge of outside information is not required for the DBQ. If you have some basic knowledge of the period, however, incorporate that information into your essay. For our sample DBQ, you may know that one of the leaders of the Young Turks was Mustafa Kemal Attaturk, who later became the leader of the Republic of Turkey. Or you may know that officials of the Ottoman Empire committed mass murder against the Armenians during World War I. Neither of these ideas needs to be mentioned in order to do well on the DBQ, yet if they were included, your essay would be set apart from the rest and would likely earn extra expanded core points (as long as your essay met the other basic core point criteria).

Readers have the option of awarding 2, 1, or zero expanded core points. Even essays that earn the highest score of 9 might not be perfect, but they have done the tasks of the DBQ very well.

Final Notes on How to Write the DBQ

The following list of items applies specifically to the DBQ. More general essay writing hints appear later in this chapter.

Do:

- Take notes in the margins during the reading period relating to the background of the speaker and his or her possible point of view
- Assume that each document provides only a snapshot of the topic—just one perspective
- Look for connections between documents for grouping
- Mark off documents that you use in the green booklet so that you do not forget to mention them
- Refer to the authorship of the documents as you are writing, not just the document numbers
- Mention additional documents and the reasons why they would help further analyze the question

Don't:

- Repeat information from the historical background in your essay
- Assume that the documents are universally valid rather than a single perspective
- Avoid visual and graphic information in those kinds of documents
- Spend too much time on the DBQ rather than moving on to the other two essays
- Write the first paragraph before you have a clear idea of what your thesis will be
- Ignore part of the question
- Structure the essay with just one paragraph
- Write in the present tense
- Underline or highlight the thesis (this may be done as an exercise for class, but on the test it looks juvenile)

HOW TO APPROACH THE CHANGE-OVER-TIME QUESTION

The Change-Over-Time (COT) question **asks what has changed and what has not**. Here, you must be as detailed as possible with your knowledge of the material. Being good at historical interpretation is not enough; you also need to know history.

Organizing Your Essay in 5 Minutes

COT questions include a definite timespan for analysis. The timespan may have the same division dates as the main structural periods for the course: 8000 BCE, 600 CE, 1450 CE, 1750 CE, 1914 CE, and the present. In your green question booklet, you will want to sketch a quick timeline, and fill in some notes about what happened. Think about breaks in this stretch of time that represented departures from what happened before. Also think about what has *not* changed.

Start by reading the question. Underline the parts that are most important for your essay. Let's look at an example:

> Choose ONE of the areas listed below and analyze the changes and continuities in social structure that occurred between 1914 and the present. In your analysis, be sure to mention the reasons for the changes and continuities.
>
> - Russia
> - China

For this example, you may want to underline the term *social structure* and the dates *1914 to the present*. To adequately answer this question, you need to have a good handle on what "social structure" actually means. Vocabulary is not tested on the AP exam, but knowing how to define terms can make a big difference in interpreting the questions. You would be in trouble with this question if you did not know what social structure meant.

For world history, **social structure** refers to the ways in which a society might organize relations between people. Such structures might include different gender roles for women and men, different ways that social classes interact, and different patterns for family and work. One of the themes of the AP course is "social structure and gender structure." As these themes form the building blocks for the course, fluency with these ideas and their applications will help you decode what the questions are asking.

Continuity refers to those aspects that remained the same during the entire stretch of the time period. In this way, it is the *opposite* of the word **change**.

The best way to organize your thoughts for the COT question is to construct a crude timeline in the green question booklet. Remember that the readers do not look at the green booklet when scoring—they look only at the pink answer booklet. Putting together a timeline might take a minute or two, but it is helpful. Let's look at a sample timeline for the Russian response.

```
1914                                                                    present
|---------|---------------|---------------|-----------------------------|
Late Czarist   Communist         Stalin's         Fall of USSR
Period         Revolution (1917) Dictatorship     (1990s)
```

As is, this timeline is inadequate. Though it mentions some of the great division points in 20th century political history, it does not address social structure. A discussion of social structure is the main point of the essay, so if your essay response included only political issues, you would be responding to a question that had not been asked. In that case, your score would drop dramatically.

In your timeline notes, you will want to write about social changes that happened. How did gender, family, work, and class structures change? You may remember that communism brought about huge changes in women's legal status and equality, or that many people were persecuted because of their social class, especially during Stalin's dictatorship. Collective farming and the changes in work patterns coming from the forced industrialization under Stalin would also be good information to note, especially since they represented a sharp change from the peasant labor system from before the revolution. Recent changes after the collapse of the USSR involved capitalist work patterns and social structure modeled on western ideas.

Your timeline and notes might start out as follows, but you would add information as you think of them.

```
1914                                                                        present
|---------|---------------|---------------|-----------------------------|
Late Czarist      Communist          Stalin's          Fall of USSR
Period            Revolution (1917)  Dictatorship      (1990s)

Peasant labor    Women's equality   Labor thru collectives   Capitalist labor
for rich landlords and revolutionary Persecution by           Western influence
                 involvement        social class
```

So far, the notes have provided several examples of changes, but nothing yet for continuity. **Do not forget to mention what has stayed the same.** Jot down at least two ideas for continuities throughout this time period—perhaps that Russian and Soviet society did not allow women to rise to the highest positions of power, and that common working-class people suffered low standards of living during that time.

Core Point Scoring

The COT Essay uses a 7-point basic core point system, with an additional expanded core of 2. The 7 points of the basic core are divided among 5 tasks: two of the tasks count for 2 core points, with a partial credit of 1 point awarded in some instances.

Points	Task
1	Has acceptable thesis
2	Addresses all parts of the question
(1)	(Addresses most parts of the question)
2	Substantiates thesis with appropriate historical evidence
(1)	(Partially substantiates thesis with appropriate historical evidence)
1	Uses global historical context effectively to explain COT and/or continuity
1	Analyzes the process of change over time and/or continuity
7	Subtotal for all basic core points
2	Possible number of points earned for the expanded core
9	TOTAL possible points for the COT

As for the DBQ, the goal for your performance on the COT should be to meet all of the core points. Excellent essays may earn points beyond the basic core, but those that earn seven points are very good indeed.

Do You Have a Thesis?

Your initial task is to present a clear thesis statement. Do not simply restate the question; you must state, instead, the specifics about change and continuity. A strong thesis will deal both with what changed and what stayed the same. Let's continue with our sample question.

> Choose ONE of the areas listed below and analyze the changes and continuities in social structure that occurred between 1914 and the present. In your analysis be sure to mention the reasons for the changes and continuities.
>
> - Russia
> - China

Thesis Statements That Don't Work

As common as it may be, the statement below is worthless as a thesis. It lacks the specificity required to set up the analysis in the essay.

> "There are many ways that Russia changed between 1914 and the present and many things that stayed the same."

The phrase, *There are many* is a terrible way to start an essay; it indicates weak writing and weak analysis. Avoid this kind of sentence construction like the plague.

The three-way divided thesis we present next is typically a good way to structure the analysis of an AP essay, yet here, it fails on two counts: It mentions neither social structure nor continuities. It would likely not receive credit as a thesis.

> "Russia changed most dramatically as a result of the Communist Revolution, the dictatorship of Stalin, and the collapse of the Soviet Union."

This next thesis is simply incorrect. The communist period in the Soviet Union did not bring perfect equality or prosperity to its people, despite what the old Soviet propaganda said. To count as a thesis, the statement must be correct. In addition, the claim that "no continuities exist" is a cop-out. You should find at least one major social issue that stayed the same.

> "Russian society changed from a country of horrible poverty during the Czarist time to one of perfect equality and general prosperity under the rule of Stalin. Nothing remained the same, so no continuities exist during this time period."

The next thesis deals with changes and continuities outside of the time period from 1914 to the present. Serf emancipation occurred in Russia in 1861, and Czarist rule ended in 1917.

> "With the emancipation of the serfs, Russian society shifted from one based on forced labor to one based on modern wage labor. Strict Czarist rule remained the same."

Although this next statement would receive credit as a thesis, the essay would likely be headed for problems. Stick to material on either Russia or China—not both.

> "Social structure in both China and Russia changed most dramatically from 1914 to the present because of the role of Communism. The plight of lower class workers, however, remained the same in both China and Russia."

Thesis Statements That Do Work

A successful thesis statement has specific information on both changes and continuities:

> "Three aspects of society changed dramatically in Russia between 1914 and the present: gender roles, work patterns, and class structure. An important continuity would be the plight of the working class."

Do You Address All Parts of the Question?

The COT often requires the analysis of change and continuity. If an essay neglects one of these two aspects—almost always, *continuity* is the one left out—then it may not receive the full 2 points. Neglecting to mention **what stays the same** may be a tragic pitfall.

To correctly analyze continuity, you must consider the entire timespan of the question. In our example, that would be from 1914 to the present. The continuities mentioned in the essay must apply for the whole period. The thesis statement below, for instance, does not address continuity for the periods 1914 to 1917, and 1991 to the present.

> "During the time of the Soviet Union, a continuity would be that the government officially proclaimed social equality. The reality, however, was social inequality."

Our sample essay question is divided into two parts: one part asks for the analysis of the changes and continuities, while the other asks for the reasons why they occurred. If you provided several examples of how social structure changed and stayed the same in Russia but didn't explain the reasons behind all of that, you would earn 1 point only.

Our sample question asks only for the analysis of social structure. If it had asked instead, "analyze the changes and continuities in social and *political* structure," then you would need to address both items to receive the full 2 points. COT questions often ask for 2, even 3, areas of analysis. Remember to cover them all.

Also important is the issue of setting chronological boundaries. Each COT essay has a starting date and an ending date. A description of the background situation for a given area at the time of the starting date is crucial for understanding how things later change. For our sample question, a paragraph on Russian social structure in 1914 would frame the discussion that followed.

> "Russian society in 1914 existed much as it had for centuries. The largest social class was the enormous peasant class, who toiled on land owned mostly by landlords. The Czar was at the top of the social structure, followed by the nobles. The Russian Orthodox Church provided the social glue that held all of the classes together. On the eve of World War I, factories were beginning to change the social dynamics of urban areas, where the working-class was heavily exploited. Within Russian society women had few rights and almost no ability to demonstrate political leadership."

This discussion would work best as a second paragraph, directly following the thesis/introductory paragraph. It sets up the analysis that is to come later about the changes and continuities of Russian society. Similarly, a paragraph near the end of the essay about the situation at *present* would serve as a sophisticated balance to the whole essay.

Do You Use Enough Facts to Support Your Thesis?

For the DBQ, no outside knowledge is required. For the COT, however, this is not the case. A strong essay must have facts. If it has several facts, it will earn 2 basic core points. If it has a few facts, it will earn 1 point.

How many facts are needed and what counts as a fact completely depends on the question. For our sample question, material must relate to social structure. Facts on politics, the revolutions, or the economy would not count unless they were linked to a discussion of social structure. In addition, the facts must be correct and within the chronological boundaries of the question.

Many people think of *historical facts* as names, dates, and events of history—"Columbus sailed the ocean blue in 1492." Though these things indeed count as facts, specific statements that relate to the question count as well. For example:

"Women participated in many aspects of the Communist Revolution."

"Workers received little to no material benefits from Stalin's drive to industrialize the Soviet Union."

"The Orthodox Church lost its position of prominence in Russian society when the Communists took control."

"In recent years, Russian society has been structured with more capitalist values."

All of these statements are correct and relevant to the question; they all deal with social structure. As such, they would count as facts.

Statements that are incorrect certainly do not help your score, but neither do they count against you in terms of core points. As with information outside of the time boundaries or statements that don't address the precise question, errors don't necessarily count against your score. Even essays that earn the top score of 9 may have small factual errors. Avoid errors, to be sure, but understand that a factual misstatement won't sink your chances at a decent score.

Do You Discuss the Global Context of the Changes and Continuities?

On the COT, you must explain how events in one area relate to the big picture; that is, you need to discuss the global context of the changes and continuities.

The global context point can be earned by effectively showing:
- Comparisons to other regions
- Connections to global processes
- Interactions among regions

A simple statement is all that is required to earn this basic core point. Any of the following statements would be considered accurate:

> "After World War II, the Soviet Union forced Eastern European countries to adopt the same Communist social structure."

(Interaction among regions)

> "Women in the Soviet Union did not have the same chances at high political positions as compared to women in the rest of Europe."

(Comparison to other region)

> "Social roles in the former Soviet Union changed dramatically during the early 1990s as part of a worldwide movement away from Communism."

(Connection to global process)

At some point during your essay, you must **think big**. The COT is designed to focus on large global issues such as trade, technology, culture, social systems, and migrations. Making connections to global processes may come as a natural part of writing about the topic.

Do You Analyze the Changes Over Time and the Continuities?

Analysis is a critical skill when writing college-level essays. Analysis means asking *why* the changes and continuities occurred. The skill it requires involves a deeper kind of thinking than simply remembering facts to support a thesis.

Analysis works best when it is integrated into the body paragraphs. Readers do not typically look to the thesis statement for the analysis core point, though a strong thesis should indeed have some analysis.

For our question on the changes and continuities of Russian or Chinese social structures, think about *why* some conditions changed and why others stayed the same. Since analysis asks *why*, your essay should include the word *because*: "This is significant because…." "This changed over time because…."

Following are some examples of analysis:

> "Social structure changed the most in Russia after the Russian Revolution because the new Soviet leaders adopted many of the ideas of sexual equality and class equality found in Karl Marx's writings. The social structures changed again at the end of the twentieth century when the Soviet Union collapsed, and Russian society rapidly rushed towards free-market capitalism."

> "The working class in Russia and the Soviet Union had low standards of living throughout the twentieth century because any economic gains were focused elsewhere, such as on the military and the ruling elite. Even after the collapse of the Soviet Union, the working class was still poor because of the underdeveloped Russian economy."

> "Rapid industrialization was the major cause of why Soviet society changed so much in the middle decades of the 20th century."

(This sentence does not include *because*, but it does explain the cause of industrialism.)

Do You Go Beyond the Basic Requirements?

Once a COT essay has met all 7 basic core points, it is eligible for up to 2 additional points. These points are awarded for excellence above the basic core point standards. Indicators of excellence might include the following:

- A clear and analytical thesis
- An abundance of evidence
- Particularly sophisticated connections to global processes
- Clear chronology with the use of dates associated with events
- Links to a rich variety of events, ideas, and trends
- Deep and even coverage of all parts of the question
- A thorough discussion of continuity in addition to change

Final Notes on How to Write the COT

Do:

- Read the question several times so that you understand the tasks required
- Draw a quick timeline in order to organize your thoughts
- Write a thesis statement that uses the terms of the question while providing analysis
- Describe in a paragraph the situation at the starting point of the timespan
- Focus on continuities, not just changes
- Make sure the continuities cover the entire timespan of the question
- Bring in a discussion of the big picture context of these changes through global processes
- Mention facts—remember, content is king

Don't:
- Discuss events that are not related to the question
- Include long sections of material outside the timespan of the question
- Focus only on changes and not on continuities
- Include continuities that apply only to one part of the timespan

HOW TO APPROACH THE COMPARATIVE QUESTION

By the last essay of this exam, most students are exhausted. At best, their hands are tired. At worst, they have not managed their time well and have only a few minutes to complete a task that counts for one-sixth of their entire grade.

As a result, the third essay is often the weakest of the group. It does not need to be this way. The Comparative question (the COMP) **asks what is the same and what is different**. It requires a task familiar to historians and non-historians alike: analyzing similarities and differences. As a student, you should be used to making comparisons—whether it is comparing teachers, to comparing Coke and Pepsi. Unlike the COT, which focuses on changes and continuities across time, the COMP focuses on similarities and differences between regions.

By the time you reach the COMP, take a deep breath, stretch out your arms, wiggle your fingers, and dive into it with the best that you have. Your handwriting may be messier than it was on the DBQ, but fortunately AP readers are accustomed to reading all sorts of handwriting. Consequently, don't take the time to rewrite an essay to make it look more presentable—an essay cannot earn points for neatness, and cannot lose points for sloppiness.

Even so, try to make your essay as neat as possible: If you have sloppy handwriting, don't abbreviate words. If you are a poor speller, do not disguise the problem by writing difficult words with a few letters at the beginning and then a scribble. Moreover, don't include too many arrows that point to inserted sentences elsewhere in the essay—they just make the whole essay less readable.

Organizing Your Essay in 5 Minutes

The COMP asks you to analyze a broad historical issue or issues in at least two regions of the world. Several regions are listed.

So once you read the question, you will be faced with a choice: Which regions to compare? Pick those regions you know the most facts about that relate to the question.

As always, underlining and note taking are important. Even a few notes jotted down in the green booklet can make your essay more focused. Let's look at an example:

> Compare and contrast the use of technology and the dynamics of trade in TWO of the following regions for the periods mentioned:
>
> - China during the Qin and Han Dynasties (3rd century BCE to 3rd century CE)
> - The Mediterranean during the Roman Empire (1st century BCE to 4th century CE)
> - Mesoamerica during the Maya Empires (4th century CE to 11th century CE)
> - South America during the Inca Empire (13th century CE to 16th century CE)

This is a complex question. You are being asked for similarities and differences between two regions in the areas of technology and trade. Not all COMP questions are this complex. Some might just ask you to compare one aspect. Others might just present one region.

Yet other questions might not provide categories of comparison as this one does with trade and technology. In those cases, you will need to create your own categories of comparison. Think broadly and brainstorm about 3 aspects for comparison. Good categories for analysis might include political, economic, social, technological, cultural, intellectual, and artistic aspects.

Core Point Scoring

The COMP is scored in much the same way as the COT—up to 7 basic core points in 5 task areas. Though the essays are fundamentally different, several of the tasks are the same.

Points	Task
1	Has acceptable thesis
2	Addresses all parts of the question
(1)	(Addresses most parts of the question)
2	Substantiates thesis with appropriate historical evidence
(1)	(Partially substantiates thesis with appropriate historical evidence)
1	Makes at least one or two relevant, direct comparisons between or among societies
1	Analyzes at least one reason for the similarities or differences
7	Subtotal for all basic core points
2	Possible number of points earned for the expanded core
9	TOTAL possible points for the COT

Do You Have a Thesis?

A thesis must compare technology and trade for two regions. Ideally, it should provide both similarities and differences. Our example again:

> Compare and contrast the use of technology and the dynamics of trade in TWO of the following regions for the periods mentioned:
>
> - China during the Qin and Han Dynasties (3rd century BCE to 3rd century CE)
> - The Mediterranean during the Roman Empire (1st century BCE to 4th century CE)
> - Mesoamerica during the Maya Empires (4th century CE to 11th century CE)
> - South America during the Inca Empire (13th century CE to 16th century CE)

Thesis Statements That Don't Work

The statement below discusses technology without mentioning trade. It most likely would not receive a basic core point for the thesis. Even so, the facts are good.

> "In Maya culture the elites used elaborate astronomical observatories and highly complex calendars, and in Inca society the government elites used a complex method of knot tying called Quipu to keep records."

The next statement uses all 4 regions instead of selecting 2 of the 4. It demonstrates wasted effort. In addition, it discusses only trade dynamics; technology is omitted.

> "In both the Maya and Inca societies, trade occurred mostly within their empire by land. For the Chinese and Roman societies trade occurred by land with the Silk Road, but also by water."

Thesis Statements That Do Work

The thesis statement does not need to be sophisticated. It just needs to cover differences and similarities for both regions in trade and technology.

> "Trade dynamics in the Roman Empire centered around the Mediterranean Sea. In China, they also used rivers for trade. For technology, the Romans built huge projects like roads. The Chinese built huge project too. They also invented paper."

You will notice that this statement is four sentences long. If a thesis is usually defined as one sentence, you may ask how can this count as the thesis? For the purposes of scoring COMP essays, the readers know that a question of this complexity might require a long thesis (though 4 sentences is a bit long).

This next example answers the question with greater sophistication and discusses the reasons behind the similarities and differences.

> "The greatest similarity between the Han and the Roman Empires involved trade since both were linked by the Silk Road and both used the structures of empire to support transportation projects. The greatest difference was in the area of technology since the Romans advances were in architectural technology and the Chinese advances were in aspects such as paper that would appeal to the new scholarly officials."

Does You Address All Parts of the Question?

To earn the full 2 basic core points, an essay on our sample question should do all of the following. To earn 1 point, it should do two of the three items.

- Address the issue of technology for both regions
- Address the issue of the dynamics of trade for both regions
- Provide an accurate similarity and an accurate difference between the two areas

The biggest challenge with earning the points for this task is **mentioning similarities**. Remember that, for the purposes of the AP World History exam, the term *compare* means **both** similarities and differences.

You may want to make a checklist so that all of the tasks of the question are addressed. A list for our sample question might look like this:

- Tech. for Maya
- Tech. for China
- Trade for Maya
- Trade for China
- Similarities for trade
- Differences for trade
- Similarities for tech.
- Differences for tech.

Making this kind of list will help guide you to answering the question thoroughly. The information you provide, however, needs to be accurate. Also, the material that you provide to support the thesis may not count again for this task.

Do You Use Enough Facts to Support Your Thesis?

Knowing facts about your topic is critical for scoring well on the COMP. Two points are awarded if an essay mentions several correct facts about both regions. One point may be earned if the facts are minimal or deal almost entirely with one region.

Information that is incorrect obviously does not receive credit as facts. And material not pertaining to the question does not receive credit. For our sample question, the essay's information would need to concern trade dynamics and/or technology in order to count as a fact.

The following would count as facts for the sake of the basic core scoring:
- The Inca road system facilitated trade from one region of the empire to another.
- The Roman's built elaborate aqueducts to carry water to cities. These aqueducts used a new innovation: the arch.
- Maya city states traded among each other for mostly elite items such as feathers and slaves.
- One of the biggest technological discoveries in China was paper.

If you mentioned the Chinese innovation of gunpowder, the statement would not receive credit as a fact—gunpowder was developed around the 10th century in China, significantly later than the time of the Han Dynasty. Since the question is specific in its time frame, the facts need to fit.

Likewise, mention of political accomplishment—a unified China under one dynasty, let's say—would not count unless it was related to a larger discussion of trade dynamics.

Do You Make a Solid Comparison Between the Societies?

This basic core point should be easy to earn. In writing a comparative essay, you should be making plenty of direct comparisons. Essays that make at least one relevant and substantial direct comparison between the two societies earn this basic core point. To earn the point, the comparison cannot be found in the thesis.

Many students, however, write essays in which the comparisons are indirect. Their essays start with an introductory thesis paragraph, are followed by paragraphs about the first region, and are followed by entirely separate paragraphs about the second region. Perhaps these essays have plenty of facts and even address most parts of the question, but they never get around to making a substantial direct comparison.

The way to avoid that kind of organizational problem is to **weave comparisons within each paragraph**. For our sample question, have paragraphs on technology in which both regions are discussed—similarities and differences. Same with trade dynamics. When both areas are addressed simultaneously, the essay is more likely to make direct comparisons.

You should also use plenty of comparative words as **logical connections** between the regions. Such words include:

- also
- as well as
- furthermore
- likewise
- on the other hand
- however
- to the contrary

Good essays have sentences and paragraphs that are connected together. Unsuccessful essays discuss regions in isolation.

Do You Analyze the Reasons for the Similarities and Differences?

Analysis is crucial for building a sophisticated COMP essay. One basic core point is awarded to essays that state clear reasons why the similarities or differences existed. This analysis must go beyond simply listing the items in common or the differences.

The following statements may earn the basic core point for analysis on the COMP:

"The vast expanse of both the Roman and Incan Empires required the technological innovations of elaborate roads to bring the area together."

"Rome was located on the Mediterranean Sea, consequently its trade was water-based to a great extent. The Aztec Empire differed since its location within Mesoamerica meant that its trade was not as focused on water travel."

"The Aztec religion created a need for technological innovations related to calendars and astronomy, whereas Chinese religions were not the prime motivator for why they arrived at so many practical innovations."

Do You Go Beyond the Basic Requirements?

Most COMP essays do not earn all 7 basic core points. Those that do are eligible for up to 2 expanded core points. Essays that earn those expanded points may include some or all of the following indicators:

- A clear and analytical thesis
- An abundance of evidence
- Comparisons related to larger global processes
- Clear mention of similarities as well as differences
- Explanations for the reasons why the differences and similarities existed
- Frequent and consistent direct comparisons between regions
- Comparisons made within regions in addition to between regions

These indicators show a kind of sophistication that separates the truly great essays from the merely acceptable ones.

Final Notes on How to Write the COMP

Do:

- Treat the COMP question with the same degree of focus as the other two essays. All three essays are worth the same number of points.
- Use all of the 130 minutes for organizing and writing the essays.
- Select regions for which you have the most factual information.
- Write a thesis that addresses all aspects of the question.
- Make a checklist of tasks that must be completed.
- Include both similarities and differences between the two regions.
- Use comparative words to join ideas together.
- Write paragraphs in which both regions are discussed together.
- Mention plenty of facts for both regions.

Don't:

- Rewrite complete essays—rarely is the extra time investment worth it.
- Favor one region to the exclusion of the other.
- Mention facts that are not focused on the topic of the question.
- Discuss each region in isolation.

STRESS MANAGEMENT

The high school AP program is intended to provide rigorous, college-level course material. AP World History, in particular, deals with high-level analytical connections between different places and times. This is hard work.

But what if your AP class is not up to par? Maybe it is overenrolled with more students than the teacher can effectively teach. Maybe the textbook resources are not at the college level or do not reflect the topics covered on the exam. What if your teacher is not thoroughly trained for teaching AP World History?

Certainly, if you are in this situation, you are at a disadvantage. But this does not mean that you cannot succeed. Thousands of students succeed with the AP exams despite having sub-par AP classes—or no AP class at all.

You, too, can succeed, but it will take extra work and diligence. Much of this work will need to be done through your own independent study.

You have already taken the first step already. The review book in your hands provides detailed information about the exam and the course. Read over its chapters several times, especially those chapters that cover unfamiliar aspects of the course. Take the Diagnostic test and full practice tests and analyze the results. This book should not be considered as a replacement for a rigorous AP course, but it can certainly help solidify content knowledge and skills.

Second, you will need a quality college-level textbook. A good one will have about 1,000 densely packed pages of writing, documents, and illustrations.

Third, you can use the resources of the internet to help you connect to the class websites of top college professors of world history. Often college professors will post their lecture notes and assignments online. Following these notes can help you supplement a less-than-perfect situation in your own classroom. You can also learn more about the AP World History exam by examining **www.apcentral.collegeboard.com**.

Finally, you may want to create a study group with other students who are in the same situation as you. Divide the review tasks and help share review notes. Use the world history themes and chronological periods listed in chapter 1 to help organize responsibilities. Have a fixed agenda when the group meets so that the gatherings will be more productive.

COUNTDOWN TO THE TEST

Preparation for the AP World History exam should be an on-going process from the beginning of your class to the day before the exam. **Six weeks before** the exam—which is about the time for Spring Break for most high school students—review should begin in earnest. Spend one week on each of the five sections in chapter 3 that correspond to the five chronological divisions of the course.

The **week or two before** the exam, fill the gaps in your preparation. Perhaps the material at the start of the course has faded from your memory. Perhaps you never had a solid grasp of gender structure among different societies. Perhaps you did not cover the history of Latin America thoroughly the first time. Find your weaknesses and make them your strong points. This review book, along with your textbook, will help provide the missing content.

Chart out a plan of attack. Be realistic, however, and don't overextend yourself. Your review will not be as effective if you are losing a great deal of sleep studying for the AP World History exam. Certainly, part of your strategy before test day should be to practice exam questions. Use the questions in this book to become more confident with the concept of pacing. You will also want to work ahead on projects for classes other than AP World History so that your schedule is clear as possible right before the test.

The day before the exam, shift your studying strategy. Instead of reading content, you may want to look over the pictures, maps, and illustrations in your textbook. Or you may want to read over the guidelines for the essay questions listed earlier in this review book.

Retire early the night before the exam. Sleep well—but don't get more sleep than normal. Eat healthy food for dinner and for breakfast the next morning. Follow a normal routine. In the morning read a few pages of a favorite piece of literature to get your mind moving in a thoughtful direction.

On the day of the exam, avoid unnecessary anxiety: arrive early. Most likely the exam will not be in the same place as your classroom. Know where the room is located and when the test is starting.

Keep your distance from other students who are freaked out; they will only make you more anxious.

If you have a cell phone, keep it far away from the exam room. The Educational Testing Service has strict policies prohibiting the use and even the possession of cellular telephones during the AP exam and during the break. New advances in text messaging and photo messaging have created problems with test security and cell phones. Perhaps nothing would increase your anxiety more than having your exam score disqualified for a breach of the rules.

You will not be allowed to drink or eat during the exam. A short break is set up between the multiple-choice and essay sections. This break would be a good time for a light snack.

Make sure to bring the following items:
- a watch or other timepiece (without an alarm)
- a number 2 pencil with a good eraser
- a dark pen (black is best)
- an extra pencil and pen
- photo ID
- your social security number (or other government-issued identification number)

Right before you step into the exam room, you may want to stretch your muscles. The increased blood flow will help you think better, and the more limber muscles will make sitting in a chair for three hours more comfortable.

Pacing During the Test

The AP World History exam is a timed test. Your strategy during the exam should be to use all available time without leaving anything out. During the exam you should be very aware of the passage of time. On the multiple-choice section, do not linger over any questions. Either guess after using the process of elimination, or circle the question and leave it for later. Check frequently as you bubble in answers so that the numbers for the questions and the numbers for the answers match.

Also be sure during the multiple-choice section that you don't rush through the questions without reading or thinking about them thoroughly. Nobody can leave the exam room before the full 55-minute session, and no advantage is gained by being the first person done. Likewise, don't be distracted by people who seem to be finishing faster. You have 55 minutes; use the time to its best potential.

Pacing is equally important on the essay section. The first 10 minutes is dedicated as a "reading period," in which you may not write in the pink answer booklet. Use this time for reading and organizing your DBQ.

The three essays can be done in any order. All three call for an equal amount of time and have equal weight in the final score. Shoot for 40 minutes on each. Spending much less than 40 minutes writing the DBQ is not advised; it is so complex that it requires the full amount of time. The COT and the COMP can also be very complex. Rushing through these often leads to incomplete essays and lower scores.

If you finish a few minutes before the end of the multiple-choice section, go back to review those questions that you left blank. But be careful: most students run into problems when they change answers from an earlier hunch. Your first intuition is more likely to be correct.

If you think you won't have time to finish the multiple-choice section, don't randomly fill in bubbles. You are penalized for incorrect answers. An educated guess is fine—even going with your hunch on a few questions can be a good idea. But filling in bubbles in a mad dash is counter-productive.

If you have time remaining, read over the essay questions again to make sure that you have answered every aspect of the questions. Only when you have written all that you can should you go back and read over your essays. Spelling errors and grammatical problems do not lower an essay's score. Even so, you should correct any problems that you encounter. A simple cross-out is fine; blotting out errors with lots of ink just looks messy.

The last piece of advice deals with…conclusions. Both English and history teachers emphasize the importance of conclusions for strong essay writing. Strong, sophisticated conclusions certainly leave AP readers with good impressions of the essays just before they mark the score. A thoughtful conclusion can never hurt an essay.

On the other hand, many conclusions don't help AP World History essays nearly as much as one might expect. Your most important task when writing these essays is to have all of the indicators for the basic core scoring. If you have only a few minutes remaining, spend the time writing a solid body paragraph of factual analysis. The last paragraph should not rehash what has been said earlier in the essay. Such conclusions are not all that valuable since an idea can only receive credit once.

The most valuable conclusions are those that include analysis that was lacking in the rest of the essay: a DBQ conclusion that mentions two possible additional documents; the COT conclusion that makes a solid point about continuities across the time period; the COMP conclusion that has a direct relevant comparison between societies. You might be able to tie the whole essay together for the first time at the very end. These conclusions are extremely useful.

| PART TWO |

Diagnostic Test

Part Two: Diagnostic Test | 49

Diagnostic Test

The Diagnostic test is a brief multiple-choice exam to help you identify your strengths and weaknesses in the area of AP World History. The goal is to help you determine the areas that you should focus on while studying. The questions are drawn from all areas covered on the actual AP World History exam.

To score your Diagnostic, go through the answers once you have completed the exam. Add up the number of questions you answered correctly and those you answered incorrectly.

If you score well, you are in terrific shape. Keep doing what you are doing. If you didn't score that high, you have some studying to do. This book should help a great deal.

Diagnostic Test Answer Grid

To Score Your Diagnostic

1. Count up the number of questions you missed, and multiply $\frac{1}{4}$ by that number.
2. Count up the number of questions that you got correct.
3. Do not count any questions that you may have left blank.

Number Correct $- (\frac{1}{4} \times$ Number Wrong$) =$ Diagnostic Test Score

Test Score	Result
25–16.25	Excellent
16–13	Very good
12.75–9	Good
8.75–5.5	Fair
5.25–0 or less	Poor

1. Ⓐ Ⓑ Ⓒ Ⓓ Ⓔ
2. Ⓐ Ⓑ Ⓒ Ⓓ Ⓔ
3. Ⓐ Ⓑ Ⓒ Ⓓ Ⓔ
4. Ⓐ Ⓑ Ⓒ Ⓓ Ⓔ
5. Ⓐ Ⓑ Ⓒ Ⓓ Ⓔ
6. Ⓐ Ⓑ Ⓒ Ⓓ Ⓔ
7. Ⓐ Ⓑ Ⓒ Ⓓ Ⓔ
8. Ⓐ Ⓑ Ⓒ Ⓓ Ⓔ
9. Ⓐ Ⓑ Ⓒ Ⓓ Ⓔ
10. Ⓐ Ⓑ Ⓒ Ⓓ Ⓔ
11. Ⓐ Ⓑ Ⓒ Ⓓ Ⓔ
12. Ⓐ Ⓑ Ⓒ Ⓓ Ⓔ
13. Ⓐ Ⓑ Ⓒ Ⓓ Ⓔ
14. Ⓐ Ⓑ Ⓒ Ⓓ Ⓔ
15. Ⓐ Ⓑ Ⓒ Ⓓ Ⓔ
16. Ⓐ Ⓑ Ⓒ Ⓓ Ⓔ
17. Ⓐ Ⓑ Ⓒ Ⓓ Ⓔ
18. Ⓐ Ⓑ Ⓒ Ⓓ Ⓔ
19. Ⓐ Ⓑ Ⓒ Ⓓ Ⓔ
20. Ⓐ Ⓑ Ⓒ Ⓓ Ⓔ
21. Ⓐ Ⓑ Ⓒ Ⓓ Ⓔ
22. Ⓐ Ⓑ Ⓒ Ⓓ Ⓔ
23. Ⓐ Ⓑ Ⓒ Ⓓ Ⓔ
24. Ⓐ Ⓑ Ⓒ Ⓓ Ⓔ
25. Ⓐ Ⓑ Ⓒ Ⓓ Ⓔ

Diagnostic Test

Time: 20 Minutes
25 Questions

1. Which of the following aspects did the Harrapan, Shang, and Sumarian civilizations have in common?

   (A) Horse-drawn plows
   (B) River-based settlements
   (C) Urban centers of over 100,000 people
   (D) Pastoral-based economy
   (E) Pyramid-shaped ceremonial centers

2. Which of the following represents the greatest change in the Chinese political state during the reign of Emperor Qin Shihuangdi (3rd century BCE)?

   (A) Creation of elaborate sculpture for tombs
   (B) Use of Confucian principals
   (C) Acceptance of Buddhism
   (D) Establishment of the civil service exams
   (E) Centralization of rule

3. Both early Christianity and Mahayana Buddhism shared which of the following religious ideas?

   (A) Personal salvation
   (B) Sacramental worship
   (C) Sacrificial offerings
   (D) Physical reincarnation
   (E) Transubstantiation

4. Cross-Asian trade of the first two centuries of the Common Era (CE)

   (A) used sleds to cross frozen areas of northern Asia.
   (B) linked Polynesian islands to the urban centers of the Near East.
   (C) relied on cowry shells as mediums of exchange.
   (D) linked the Roman Empire with Chinese textile producers.
   (E) dealt mostly with food items such as rice.

5. The biggest environmental problem for ancient Mesopotamia was

   (A) Rising sea levels
   (B) Deforestation
   (C) Polluted drinking water
   (D) Volcanic eruption
   (E) Loss of soil fertility

The Swahili language illustrates which of the following aspects of African civilization during the 1200s and 1300s CE?

   (A) Lack of linguistic diversity in Africa
   (B) Growth of West African empires
   (C) Connection to Arab and Asian trade routes
   (D) Continuity of Egyptian culture
   (E) Influence from Mediterranean culture

GO ON TO THE NEXT PAGE

7. In which of the following regions did the Mongols remain as a political force more than 200 years following their conquest?

   (A) Persia
   (B) Russia
   (C) China
   (D) Northern India
   (E) Mesopotamia

8. The Gothic movement in European architecture required which of the following medieval technological innovations?

   (A) Concrete molds
   (B) Pointed arches
   (C) Wooden scaffolding
   (D) Glass blowing
   (E) Quarry mining

9. The main factor for the population drop of both Egypt and China during the mid 1300s was

   (A) Foreign invasion
   (B) Desertification
   (C) Famine
   (D) Disease
   (E) Religious war

10. The greatest territorial expansion of the Muslim religion occurred

    (A) during Mohammed's life.
    (B) within the first 100 years after Mohammed death.
    (C) in areas that had been previously Christian.
    (D) along a north-south geographic orientation.
    (E) as a result of wars with followers of animist religions.

11. How did Aztec religious expression in the late 1400s differ from the religious expression of earlier Mesoamerican civilizations, such as the Toltec and Maya?

    (A) The Aztec worship focused on fertility gods whereas Toltec and Maya worship focused on gods of creation and destruction.
    (B) Missionaries converted the Aztecs to Christianity but had not been active among the Toltec and Maya.
    (C) The Aztecs expanded the role of human sacrifice from what the Maya had previously practiced.
    (D) The Aztecs were monotheistic, worshipping only Quetzalcoatl, whereas the Toltec and Maya were polytheistic.
    (E) The Aztecs worshipped an entirely different set of animist gods than the Toltec and Maya civilizations.

12. The majority of African slaves taken from Africa in the 1600s and 1700s were shipped to

    (A) Western Europe
    (B) British and French colonies in North America
    (C) British and French colonies in the Caribbean
    (D) Spanish and Portuguese colonies in Central and South America
    (E) Arabian Peninsula

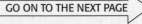
GO ON TO THE NEXT PAGE

13. Which of the following events created economic conditions that motivated Christopher Columbus's voyage in 1492?

    (A) The fall Constantinople's trade routes to the Turks
    (B) The voyages of Vasco DaGama to India
    (C) The expulsion of Jews and Muslims from Spain
    (D) The adoption of silver currency in Spain
    (E) The creation of sugar plantations off the African coast

14. The majority of people living in Russia in the 1600s were

    (A) Free Peasants
    (B) Boyars
    (C) Mongols
    (D) Serfs
    (E) Muslim

15. The French Revolution and the American Revolution were similar in that both

    (A) involved a violent reign of terror against members of the upper class.
    (B) started because of anger over taxation.
    (C) had the lowest members of the working class attain political power.
    (D) changed the religious structure of the country.
    (E) supported the concept of one person, one vote.

16. In the later half of the 19th century, Jewish people were most persecuted in

    (A) Ottoman Empire
    (B) Northern Europe
    (C) North America
    (D) Russia
    (E) North Africa

17. The first large-scale industrial factories in Western Europe were established in order to produce

    (A) Refined food items
    (B) Ceramics
    (C) Textiles
    (D) Weapons
    (E) Glass

18. A Marxist historian would most likely see which of the following as a primary mover of historical events?

    (A) Technological innovation
    (B) Scholarship and intellectualism
    (C) Class conflict
    (D) Interaction among societies
    (E) Women's rights

19. The economic changes of the Meiji Restoration in Japan were most influenced by

    (A) Chinese merchants
    (B) German and British industrialists
    (C) Portuguese and Dutch traders
    (D) The increased power of the Samurai
    (E) The free market ideas of Adam Smith

GO ON TO THE NEXT PAGE

Justice

20. The cartoon shown above from the British magazine *Punch* (1857) relates to which of the following ideas?

   (A) Women's ability to serve in the military
   (B) The inferiority of Africans as compared to the British
   (C) The importance of female modesty for British women
   (D) The need to retaliate against the Sepoy Rebellion in India
   (E) The high disease rates in British colonies

21. Which of the following types of countries were *excluded* from permanent membership on the security council of the United Nations?

   (A) Defeated countries of World War II
   (B) Non-Christian countries
   (C) Communist countries
   (D) Non-industrialized countries
   (E) Non-European countries

22. Over the last four decades of the 20th century, the political structure of most Latin American countries changed

   (A) from democracy to communism.
   (B) from communism to military dictatorship.
   (C) from European colonial rule to independence.
   (D) from dictatorship to democracy.
   (E) from anarchy to one-party rule.

23. Cambodia in the 1970s and Rwanda in the 1990s both experienced

   (A) Communist revolution
   (B) Genocidal violence
   (C) European invasion
   (D) Hyperinflation
   (E) High rates of AIDS infection

24. The technology for the jet engine originated

   (A) from Chinese sources.
   (B) in Nazi-controlled Germany
   (C) within 20 years after the first manned airplane flight.
   (D) as part of the Cold War space race.
   (E) first with naval applications.

25. What impact did the Chinese Communist revolution of 1949 have with regard to gender roles?

   (A) Women reached high positions of leadership as generals of the Red Army.
   (B) Husbands and wives were told to share responsibilities of childrearing and housekeeping.
   (C) Women were encouraged to marry at a younger age.
   (D) Men became more prominent as a result of communist ideology.
   (E) Foot binding and arranged marriages were eliminated.

IF YOU FINISH BEFORE TIME IS CALLED, YOU MAY CHECK YOUR WORK. **STOP**

ANSWERS AND EXPLANATIONS

1. B

Many AP World History questions will ask you to pick out similarities among several different societies. In this case, early civilizations developed around rivers so that the water could be used for irrigating fields: the Yellow (Huang He) River for the Shang, the Tigris and Euphrates Rivers for the Sumerians, and the Indus for the Harrapans. Since each of these early civilizations was agricultural, they did not have pastoral economies. Horses were not used regularly as plow animals until proper yokes were created much later. Only the Sumerian civilization had urban centers approaching 100,000 people. Sumerian ziggurats were pyramid-shaped temples, but they were not common architectural forms for the Indian Harrapans or Chinese Shang.

2. E

Emperor Qin Shihuangdi, who established the Qin Dynasty, is famous for his self-proclaimed title of "first emperor" of China. Emperors had actually existed before but none had established extensive centralized rule, with aspects of law, military defense, and even written script becoming more regulated by the central government. Qin Shihuangdi created an extensive burial complex for himself, but people of prominence had elaborate tombs with sculpted items before. He ruled using a philosophical system called Legalism, which is considerably different from both Confucianism and Buddhism. The civil service exam came later.

3. A

Mahayana Buddhism, known as the "greater vehicle," places special emphasis on the greater accessibility of salvation for its followers. Early Christianity, though different in its beliefs and practices, also shared this personal sense of salvation. Early Christians believed in resurrection, not reincarnation, unlike Buddhists. Early Christians also emphasized the role of sacraments in worship, especially the real presence of Christ in the Eucharist, which is known as transubstantiation.

4. D

The Silk Roads of the first centuries of the Common Era involved both land and sea trade from the Han Empire to the west, reaching as far as the eastern end of the Roman Empire. The primary items traded by the Chinese included silk and spices. In exchange they received finished goods and other luxury items.

5. E

Any major early civilization relies on the fertility of the soil in order to achieve its population density. With the type of farming practices and irrigation used by the Mesopotamians, the soil lost its fertility over time, especially since the evaporating water from irrigation left behind salt residue that dramatically reduced soil fertility over time.

6. C

Swahili developed as a blended language in the cities on the east coast of Africa that traded with Arabs merchants and others who participated in the Indian Ocean trade system. Its development shows the connection that Africa had with the rest of the Indian Ocean basin. Africa had a huge amount of linguistic diversity. A common tongue facilitated trade.

7. B

All of the areas listed were conquered by Mongol troops. The Golden Horde of Russia, however, had some loose political influence in Russia until 1480 CE when Ivan the Great stopped paying tribute to the Mongols. By that time Mongol influence in other regions had long past.

8. B

The design of gothic architecture needed pointed arches in order to transfer the weight of the roof and ceiling from the walls to supporting buttresses. With the weight off of the walls, taller structures could be built with stained glass windows. All of the other technologies listed had been around since at least the classical age.

9. D

The bubonic plague, otherwise known as the Black Death, was a world-wide pandemic of the mid-1300s. It caused the population of China, Egypt and Western Europe to fall dramatically. Although the time period also experienced warfare and famine neither had the demographic impact as did disease.

10. B

By the early 700s CE, the span of Islam reached from the Iberian Peninsula of modern day Spain and Portugal in the west to the Indus River in the east. At the time of Muhammad's death in 632 CE, the Islamic areas were limited to Arabia. Many of the areas that were converted were Christian, but the majority of the population was to the east, which was not primarily Christian.

11. C

Aztec religion was highly influenced by the earlier Toltec and Maya religions. All three of them practiced polytheism with gods of fertility as well as gods of creation and destruction. Indeed many of the gods were the same. The Aztecs, however, took the previous religious practice of human sacrifice to another level, making blood sacrifice to a much larger degree than either the Toltec or Maya had.

12. D

The largest portion of people who traveled on the Middle Passage from Africa went to Brazil (about 40%). Other major areas include Spanish colonies on the mainland and Spanish and French colonies the islands of the Caribbean. North American accounted for less than 5% of the total African slave immigrants to the Americas. Slavery to Arab regions was significant during this time, but not as much when compared to the numbers involved in the Middle Passage.

13. A

The prime economic motive for Christopher Columbus's initial voyage was to discover a new route to the East Asian spice markets. Trade routes that had previously existed had traveled overland through Byzantine territories. After the conquest of Constantinople in 1453, the supply of Asian trade goods in Western Europe declined sharply. Interest in using the New World as a place for silver mining and sugar plantations occurred after Columbus's initial voyage to what he thought was Asia. Vasco DaGama traveled to India in 1494, after Columbus's trip. Jewish and Muslims people had been expelled from Spain just before Columbus's 1492 voyage. This resulted in greater religious unity in Spain but not the prime economic motive for exploration.

14. D

Russian society was structured around large agricultural estates run by the nobility, who were known as boyars, and the Russian Orthodox Church. The estates were farmed by the forced labor of serfs, who accounted for the vast majority of the population. Free peasants became a big factor in Russia after the emancipation of the serfs in 1861.

15. B

The initial motive for the American Revolution involved what the revolutionaries considered intolerable taxation through the Stamp Act, the Townshend Act, and the Tea Act. A primary grievance for the Third Estate in France involved the unequal tax burden due to the exemption of the First and Second Estates. Political power especially in the American Revolution did not flow to the working class, and many men without property were denied the right to vote until many years after the revolution. The American Revolution did witness violence against people loyal to Britain, but this terror was not directed specifically to aristocrats. In fact the American Revolution was instigated by the wealthiest classes. In the United States following the revolution, the vote was extended to men of the propertied classes, not members of the working class according to a one-person, one-vote system.

16. D

Jewish people in the villages of western Russia suffered vicious attacks known as pogroms in the last decades of the 1800s. Often these anti-Semitic raids were officially sanctioned by the Russian authorities. Anti-Semitism existed elsewhere, but did not take on the ruthless violence that existed in Russia.

17. C

The first factories of Britain in the 1700s were created to spin thread and yarn and then later weave textiles. Mills had been set up in the Caribbean to refine sugar before, but the needs of production meant that sugar could not be refined in Britain.

18. C
According to Karl Marx and Frederick Engels, history follows a path determined by the struggle of social classes. Their theory of dialectical materialism dictates that all history comes from the struggle between competing social classes. Class conflict will end only after revolution and the establishment of communism.

19. B
Japan came out of isolation and pursued a rapid course of industrialization and westernization starting in the 1860s. During this time the Meiji officials hired a large number of consultants from Germany and Britain. The Samurai lost power. Much of the economic activity was directed by the government officials, contradicting the free market ideas of Adam Smith.

20. D
This illustration shows the female figure "Justice," as seen by the title and the scales on her shield, slaying dark-skinned people. The *Punch* cartoon corresponds to the time of the Sepoy Mutiny. In 1857 native troops of the British army in India mutinied and killed many British soldiers, East India Company officials and their families. The reaction in Britain was outrage. Thousands of British troops were deployed to northern India to regain control, and the British government took a more direct form of colonial rule.

21. A
In 1945 the five permanent members of the United Nations were based on the victorious countries of World War II: United States, Soviet Union (now Russia), China, United Kingdom, and France. The Soviet Union was communist, and China was non-Christian and non-industrialized. Germany, Japan, and Italy were excluded from permanent membership at that time.

22. D
In 1960 most Latin American countries had some form of dictatorship. Democracy, where it existed, was not complete or fully expressed. Only Cuba was forming what would become a communist-style government. In 2000 almost all countries in the western hemisphere, with the notable exception of Cuba and Haiti, had a functioning democracy. Most European colonial control in Latin America ended in the early 1800s.

23. B
The Khmer Rouge rule by the dictator Pol Pot led to the systematic murder of about two million people in Cambodia during the mid-1970s. In 1994 one million people in Rwanda were murdered systematically in violence directed towards ethnic Tutsis. Although AIDS was killing vast numbers of Africans in the 1990s, it did not become a global epidemic until the 1980s.

24. B
Germany scientists perfected jet aircraft technology as a result of the military demands of World War II. Propeller planes had been used previously. The first manned flight took place by the Wright Brothers in 1903; jet airplanes first appeared in the late 1930s. The Cold War space race took place in the 1960s.

25. E
Revolutionary time periods generally involve great changes in women's social roles. In no place is this truer than in China. The Chinese communist revolution of Mao Zedong eliminated force marriages, granted equal rights to divorce, and made footbinding illegal. Women were encouraged to become active leaders in the Communist Party, but they did not become army generals. Official concepts of equal rights often did not translate into more equitable roles within the household.

HOW TO MAKE THIS BOOK WORK FOR YOU BASED ON THE RESULTS OF YOUR DIAGNOSTIC

First, you should know that only one-half of the composite score for the AP World History exam will be multiple-choice. The three essays are equally important and potentially easier to master with preparation. No matter what your results on the diagnostic test, you should review the essay exam format and expectations carefully.

How you interpret your diagnostic score depends on your situation. How soon is the exam? If you took the diagnostic test the in the fall or winter, you are likely to score lower than if you took the test in early May. Analyze the types of questions that you missed.

The diagnostic is arranged into five equal chronological periods that match the five periods covered on the exam: 8000 BCE to 600 CE, 600 to 1450, 1450 to 1750, 1750 to 1914, and 1914 to the present. If you missed a bunch in one or two chronological periods, you may want to focus your preparation on that time period. Also, if a certain type of question tripped you up, for example questions on technology or social structures, then you may want to focus your preparation on that theme.

This review book can help. Part Three breaks down each of the chronological periods and reviews the content by topic. Look over these sections, paying special attention to your weaknesses. Each chronological period covered in chapter Three is followed by practice questions to sharpen your understanding.

Part Four provides more testing practice: two complete exams with 70 multiple-choice questions and three essays. You will be ready to take these full exams after the bulk of your review. Set a time and a place for taking these full practice exams under test-like conditions without interruptions or distractions.

| PART THREE |

AP World History Review

For each time period of the course, you need to **think like a world historian**, You should be able to identify the "big picture ideas." Imagine you where looking down upon the earth and could physically see the global developments.

You could see the increase in trade, the growth of empires, the spread of religions, or the movement of people.

What would these visible changes look like? Those are your **big picture ideas**. For each time period, try to focus in on 5 to 10 big picture ideas. Before you answer any multiple choice or essay questions dealing with that time period, first go through the list of big picture ideas in your head. Then tackle the question.

For the sample essay questions, feel free to use additional paper. For all three of those questions on the real test, you will be given 16 pages of paper.

Part Three: AP World History Review | 61

Chapter 3: Foundations (8000 BCE to 600 CE)

- The Big Picture
- Why This Periodization?
- Development of Agriculture
- The First Civilizations
- Development and Spread of Religion
- Classical Societies
- Role of Trade in Classical Societies
- Spread of Disease
- Movement of Peoples
- Fall of Classical Empires

THE BIG PICTURE

This period is called *Foundations* for a reason. Most of the core developments that shape our world today began during this time period: government, religion, trade, and social structure just to name a few.

1. Patterns and effects of interactions among major societies and regions: trade, war, diplomacy, and international organizations

    In other words: **What happens when people come in contact with each other?**

Trade: From the simplest barter system to long journeys along the Silk Roads, the exchange of goods and ideas shaped this period and led to further change throughout the world. To respond to this growth in trade, systems of currency were developed. As a result of this interaction, religions, ideas, and technology spread from one area to another.

2. The dynamics of change and continuity across the world history periods covered in this course, and the causes and processes involved in major changes of these dynamics

    In other words: **Why do some things change while other things stay the same?**

Be aware of the *reasons why* change occurs and not just that things change. Also, do changes occur because of interaction with other societies or because of independent innovation or a combination of the two? A major change, for example, was the development of agriculture. A major continuity was the use of non-representative type governments throughout the world.

3. The effects of technology, economics, and demography on people and the environment (population growth and decline, disease, labor systems, manufacturing, migrations, agriculture, weaponry)

    In other words: **How does the development of new technology and movement of people affect the world?**

Farming: The Neolithic Revolution was a world-altering event. With the discovery of agriculture, people's lives began to change at a more rapid pace. Alternatively, people living in the steppes developed pastoral nomadism.

The use of metals: From the development of copper to bronze and then to iron, the use of metallurgy allowed humans to develop stronger and more efficient weapons and tools.

4. Systems of social structure and gender structure (comparing major features within and among societies and assessing change and continuity)

    In other words: **How do societies organize themselves socially and what roles do men and women play?**

Social Stratification: The accumulation of a food surplus allowed some members of society to do things other than farm. This led to job specialization and the beginnings of social class structures based on economic roles, i.e., aristocrats, artisans, peasants.

Gender Roles: As humans organized themselves in families, gender roles emerged. With the development of agriculture, the division of labor further deepened these divisions. In some cultures, women had some protective rights, but in others, patriarchal societies emerged. This patriarchy was often reinforced by organized religion.

5. Cultural, intellectual, and religious developments and interactions among and within societies.

    In other words: **How do people identify themselves and expresses themselves culturally and intellectually?**

Religions: People always had questions that could not be answered and religion played the role of the answer man. During this period, major world religions developed and spread, which shaped the civilizations they encountered.

Writing: As civilizations developed, so did the need to keep records and further communicate systems of writing.

Artistic Expression: Around the world, man expressed themselves through the arts: from the earliest cave paintings to great works of architecture.

6. Changes in functions and structures of states and in attitudes toward states and political identities (political culture), including the emergence of the nation-state (types of political organization)

In other words: **How do people govern themselves?**

Cooperation: Along with agriculture, humans began to settle down in larger groups, and this facilitated the need to cooperate and get along with each other.

Cities: Once a surplus of food could be grown, not all people needed to farm their own food, and those surpluses needed to be protected. This enabled the rise of cities, in which job specialization could occur and larger populations could be maintained.

Civilizations: From these first cities, civilizations emerged which had organized governments, complex religions, social structures, job specialization, public works, systems of writing, and arts and architecture. Over time, these early civilizations grew larger and more complex.

Governments: Most early governments were non-representative monarchies or oligarchies. Representative forms of government such as democracies and republics were uncommon.

Empires: Many civilizations expanded their original area of one state and conquered surrounding neighbors to build an empire.

Study Suggestion: As we look at more specific information for this unit, be aware of the theme the information is addressing. Also note changes and continuities and why the change or continuity occurred.

WHY THIS PERIODIZATION?

It is important to understand why historians view history through the use of periodization and to understand that there is not one right way to organize history. From the purposes of our course, world history has been divided into five chronological units: the first starting in 8,000 BCE.

Around 8,000 BCE, the development of farming began to emerge, and gradually spread to major parts of the world. This development kicks off a period of major change and development. By 600 CE, many of the classical empires of the world had collapsed. The recovery from this collapse will kick off our next unit (600 to 1450 CE).

BCE and CE

AP World History qualifies dates as BCE (**Before the Common Era**) and CE (**Common Era**). BCE refers to the same time as BC (Before Christ) and CE refers to the same time as AD (Anno Domini, "in the year of our Lord.") World historians believe it is important to use terminology that does not apply the standards of one society to all others, so the terminology BCE and CE has arisen to be more inclusive.

Geographic Regions: Where in the World Am I?

You will not be asked on the AP exam to fill in a blank map of the world, so don't worry, but you should know your basic geographic regions and hemispheres. Also, it is important to develop a sense of geography.

Study suggestion: When you are reading about a given situation, try to visualize where in the world those developments are taking place. Alternatively, reproduce a blank world map and take notes as you read in the proper geographic region.

North America
Historic example: British and French colonies
Modern Example: Canada, United States, Mexico

Latin America
Historic example: Incan empire
Modern example: South America, i.e. Brazil and the Caribbean, i.e. Haiti

Western Europe
Historic example: Charlemagne's Carolingian Empire
Modern example: England, France, Spain, Italy

Eastern Europe
Historic example: parts of the Byzantine Empire
Modern example: Poland, Western Russia

West Asia or Middle East
Historic example: Ottoman Empire
Modern example: Iran, Iraq

South Asia
Historic example: Gupta empire
Modern example: India, Pakistan

Central Asia
Historic example: Tamerlane's Empire
Modern example: Kazakhstan, Uzbekistan

East Asia
Historic example: Han dynasty
Modern example: China, Japan, Korea

Southeast Asia
Historic example: Malay sailors
Modern example: Vietnam, Indonesia

Oceania
Historic example: Polynesian Migration
Modern example: Australia, New Zealand

Sub-Saharan Africa
Historic example: Kingdom of Mali, Swahili City–States
Modern example: Zaire, Kenya

Western Hemisphere
The Americas

Eastern Hemisphere
Europe, Asia, Africa, Oceania

DEVELOPMENT OF AGRICULTURE

The Neolithic Revolution: An Experiment with Seeds Leads to Farming

Early man lived for thousands of years hunting animals and gathering roots and plants. Around 8,000 BCE, a dramatic breakthrough in human history called the **Neolithic Revolution** changed the way people lived their lives. It might have been called the Neolithic *transition*, though, since it took hundreds, if not thousands, of years of change before an agricultural economy took hold.

The discovery of agriculture, most likely made by women who were experimenting with seeds they had gathered, allowed people to change the way they lived. The first farmers used **slash-and-burn agriculture**, in which they would slash the bark and burn the trees to the ground. The problem with this was that although the land was initially very fertile, it lost much of that fertility after a few years. This caused people to migrate to new areas, helping to facilitate the spread of agriculture to new areas. A second great discovery was the **breeding of animals**. With these tools, people could now remain in one place.

More Stability = More People

Now that humans had settled, many changes could occur. Even though farming was a lot more work (the average hunter and gatherer only worked 4 hours a day to find food), it was also a lot more stable. With stability comes population increase. Hunters and gatherers had very small families, but now that the moving had stopped, families could be larger. Just look at the numbers below.

Time	World Population
10,000 BCE	4 million
5,000 BCE	5 million
3,000 BCE	14 million
2,000 BCE	27 million
1,000 BCE	50 million
500 BCE	100 million

Life in a Neolithic Village

Early farmers began to organize themselves in a more permanent way through the formation of villages. This permanence allowed for the development of new technologies: farming tools such as the hoe, for instance. As farmers experimented, they began to develop a **surplus** of food, and once a surplus was developed, **job specialization** was required. Not everyone needed to be a farmer; other jobs such as blacksmith, miller, brewer, trader, and priest provided services for the farmers—and the farmers could provide them food.

With the beginning of privately owned land, a wealthier class emerged. The ownership of this land equaled economic power. This land was kept in the families hands, and passed down from generation to generation and with this social class emerges. It was the wealthiest in the community who desired luxury items which could be traded for with other communities.

For the Neolithic people, nature meant life or death. They had to learn the changes of the seasons, the position of the sun, moon, and stars. Religiously, their main goal was to ensure fertility—both theirs and the lands. Religious beliefs centered on the life cycle of birth, growth, death, and regenerated life. Clay figurines of gods and goddesses have been unearthed that reflect this better.

The Neolithic Revolution also had consequences on **gender roles.** Men were working in the fields and herding the animals, which required them to be outside the home. On the other hand, women performed such jobs as caring for the children, weaving cloth, and making cheese from milk, which required them to be in the home. Over time, the work outside the home was perceived as more important, and men began to take a more dominant role in the gender relationship.

Early Inventions in Metal and Transportation

In Neolithic villages, three main craft industries developed and became essential elements of almost all human agricultural societies: pottery, metallurgy, and textiles. The earliest metal made was **copper** for jewelry and simple tools. It was later heated to become more workable and was made into knives, axes, hoes, and weapons. Copper was the foundation for the later developments of gold, bronze, and iron.

Around 3,000 BCE, Mesopotamian metalworkers began to alloy copper and tin and developed a harder and stronger metal called **bronze**. Bronze was made into weapons such as swords, spears, axes, shields, armor, and bronze-tipped plows for farming. Sometime around 1,000 BCE, **iron** tools and weapons were first developed. Metalworkers discovered that when carbon was added to iron, it became much stronger. This knowledge spread throughout Mesopotamia, Anatolia, Egypt, and Africa.

The exact origin of the **wheel** is unknown, but we do know that Sumerians used wheeled carts for several centuries before they were more formally organized around 3,200 BCE. The wheel allowed for the transport of heavier loads and much longer distance travel and trade. This important technology spread like wild fire and within a few centuries was the standard means of overland transport.

An Alternative Way of Life—Not Everyone Becomes a Farmer

Pastoral nomadism was another alternative lifestyle that developed at this time. Pastoral nomads depended on their herd for survival and traveled to find grassland or **steppe** land required for their herds to graze. (**Steppe** was a tall feathery grass that grew in areas where there was not much rainfall, something ideal for animal grazing.)

Pastoral nomadism was not a step toward a life of farming; it was quite unique. It was a complicated and advanced lifestyle in which nomads literally lived off their animals. Geography usually determined who would be a pastoralist and who would be a nomad.

Life could be quite difficult for these early pastoralists, and in response, they developed fighting skills, using both offensive and defensive military tactics to defend their herds. It was the interaction between the pastoralists and the settled people that caused much of the development in this and other time periods.

THE FIRST CIVILIZATIONS

Farming communities often developed along river banks. As the river banks flooded and carried silt onto the land, the land became more fertile. The river also allowed for transportation and communication.

Living near these large rivers required a larger amount of cooperation, because the flooding had to be controlled. Flood control and irrigation projects were soon developed. Such cooperation among these first civilizations led to the development of the first urban centers or cities. These large, densely populated, permanent settlements shared many common characteristics:

- Diverse people
- Specialization—people with different jobs
- Social stratification—some people had more status than others
- Trade

Like the development of farming, the development of cities was a gradual process. Early cities were larger than Neolithic towns and villages, had more intense specialization, professional craftsman, professional managers (such as governors and tax collectors), and professional cultural specialists (priests, etc.). Cities had a large economic center called the **marketplace**, which was extremely influential to the surrounding regions. The marketplace became the center of political, military, and economic control.

These cities often led to the growth of more complex societies. These societies often had the following in common:

- Surplus
- Cities
- Specialization
- Trade
- Social stratification
- Organized government
- Complex religions
- Written language
- Arts/architecture

Mesopotamia

The "land between the waters" in southwest Asia is part of the **Fertile Crescent**, which helped to encourage the earliest farming communities. Small-scale irrigation started in Mesopotamia around 6000 BCE. That caused an increase in the amount of food production, which led to an increase in population. By 3000 BCE, **Sumer** (as it came to be known) had a population of 100,000. Temples, public buildings, defensive walls, and irrigation systems were built by laborers recruited by government authorities. By 3000 BCE, the cities had kings with absolute authority, each ruling their own city–state.

These hereditary kings were at the top of the social order, followed closely by the priests and priestesses who were often younger relatives of the rulers. A third group was called the **free commoners**, who worked as peasants, builders, craftsmen, or professionals. The **dependent clients** owned no property, and worked only on the estates of others. Both of these groups paid taxes with surplus or labor. At the bottom of the social pyramid were the **slaves**, who were agricultural laborers or domestic servants.

Mesopotamia had its share of important technological and artistic achievements. The writing system **cuneiform** dates back to 2900 BCE. These graphic symbols were used to represent sounds, syllables, ideas, and physical objects. Knowledge of astronomy and math helped with the development of a calendar (based on 12 months) and harvest planning. The *Epic of Gilgamesh* dates back to 2000 BCE. This reflection writing recounts the experiences of Gilgamesh, king of Uruk.

Over time, these city–states grew into a regional empire. The most famous emperor was the Babylonian, **Hammurabi**, who ruled from 1792 to 1750 BCE. Hammurabi used an organized central bureaucracy and regular taxation to rule his empire. He is most famous for his legal code and laws, which he borrowed from his predecessors; it was the first documented attempt in ancient history to detail crimes and punishments. The laws had a high standard of behavior backed up with strict punishments. The death penalty was given for crimes such as murder, theft, and adultery. There were also **civil laws**, which regulated prices, martial relations, and the condition of slavery. The idea was that offenders should suffer punishment that resembled their crimes. Hammurabi's society was patriarchal with a strict social structure. Peasants and the upper class received different punishments for similar crimes. Men were clearly the head of the household; they had the power to sell their wives and children into slavery to pay off a debt. Women, however secondary, were protected by some of these laws.

Egypt

The Nile River was truly a gift to Egypt. It gave Egypt the life blood of its civilizations. Around 5000 BCE, experimentation with agriculture began in this area. The people learned to plant crops such as barley and wheat after the floods had receded. They soon built dikes to protect the fields from the floods. By 4000 BCE, villages had developed irrigation systems.

Egypt also was protected by its geography. The Nile, of course, protected it from invasion, but so did the Red Sea, Mediterranean Sea, and Sahara Desert.

By 3100 BCE, the leader Menes extended authority throughout Egypt. He built a centralized state ruled by **pharaohs** or kings. These rulers of Egypt were considered gods living on earth in human form. It was under the leadership of these godly rulers that Egypt built the pyramids. The most famous are the pyramids of Giza, which, it is estimated, took 84,000 laborers 20 years to build.

The Egyptians excelled in making bronze weapons and were skilled in mathematics, medicine, and astronomy. The solar calendar of 365 days that we use today was first devised in ancient Egypt. Around 3100 BCE, the Egyptians developed their own written language made up of pictographs, or **hieroglyphics.**

For obvious reasons, the pharaoh was at the top of the social class structure, followed by priests, commoners, and slaves. Egypt had professional military forces and a bureaucracy of administrators and tax collectors. The way to get ahead in society was to be close to the pharaoh. Service to him meant higher status.

As far as the issue of death was concerned, for the **polytheistic** Egyptians, death was not an end, but a transition to a new existence. To accommodate the transition, **mummification** was developed.

Indus

The Indus is a civilization with much mystery even today. This urbanized civilization was discovered only in the early 20th century. It developed between 3000 BCE and 2500 BCE and had declined by 1500 BCE. Its language is still not understood, but we do know that its **polytheistic** religious belief system centered on a strong concern for fertility. The entire area was approximately 500,000 square miles, larger than both Mesopotamia and Egypt.

Large Indus cities have been uncovered in recent years: The two largest ones have been named **Harappa** and **Mohenjo-Daro.** These walled cities, designed in a grid pattern, featured broad streets, marketplaces, temples, assembly halls, baths, and uniform housing. There were even rich and poor sections of town. The wealthiest people even had private bathrooms with showers and toilets that drained into city sewage systems.

Technologically and economically speaking, Indus had a lot going for it: it traded pottery, tools, and decorative items; it obtained gold, silver, and copper from Persia; and it obtained wool, leather, and olive oil from Mesopotamia. Metal tools of bronze and copper have been found, as well as jewelry made of precious stones. Cotton was cultivated in this area before 5000 BCE.

The writing system, however, has yet to be deciphered. It is still a mystery today. We do know that it used approximately 400 symbols to represent sounds and words. These symbols have been found on clay seals and copper tablets.

Sometime after 2000 BCE, the Indus civilization was on the decline. A combination of environmental factors might have caused this, and by 1500 BCE, the civilization had collapsed.

Aryans

The Aryans, a nomadic people of Indo-European origin, entered the subcontinent through the Khyber Pass around 1700 BCE. They quickly dominated the inhabitants of the Indus valley, and established a racial mix in what is now **India**.

Few artifacts were left behind by the Aryans, so much about them is unknown. What we do know is from a collection of sacred hymns, songs, prayers, and rituals known as the **Vedas**. They reveal a hierarchical, male-dominated society. The Aryans were polytheistic with many gods connected to nature. The social structure had probably the largest impact on India; it developed gradually and became the basis for the **caste system**. People were divided into four **varnas** based on occupation: brahmins (scholars and priests), ksatriyas (ruling and warrior class), vaisyas (professional class), and shudras (servant class). The lower class of untouchables (outcastes) was incorporated into the system later. Aryans tried to prohibit intermarriage between the varnas, but this was difficult to enforce, and over the years a blending of Aryan and indigenous people took place.

Shang and Zhou

The first river valley civilization in China developed along the **Huang He** or **Yellow River.** This river got its name from the light-colored **loess** soil that caused the river to appear yellow. Despite its fertile land, the river's devastating floods earned it the nickname "China's Sorrow." This dynasty is called the **Shang**, which ruled a northern territory in what today is called China from 1766 to 1122 BCE. Major archeological evidence used to prove the existence of the Shang dynasty is found in "**oracle bones**." Questions about—and predictions of—the future were written on these bones, so we have a type of written record. The development of written Chinese (pictograph) characters is traced back to the Shang. These pictures evolved into symbols, or ideographs. Additionally, the Shang developed **bronze metallurgy**, which aided in its rise as a military state.

The next and longer dynasty, the **Zhou** (1122 to 256 BCE), further cemented important Chinese traditional foundations. The most notable tradition was the concept of the **Mandate of Heaven,** meaning power to rule was granted from heaven. Since this power was divinely given, there was a direct connection between ruler and god. This power could be taken away, however, if justice and order were not maintained. Signs from the gods such as floods, earthquakes, and peasant rebellions were indications that the end was near for the dynasty.

Culturally and religiously, the Zhou placed great emphasis on the **veneration of ancestors**, and the family unit was the most important organizational structure. The belief was that if everyone honored their responsibilities toward the family, society would function smoothly. The Zhou had a strong ruling elite class, reinforced by hereditary aristocrats. A small class of free artisans and craftsmen, a large class of peasants, and slaves completed the social class structure. Additionally, during the Zhou period, **iron metallurgy** spread to China.

Even with all of this, the Zhou lost control of the western half of the empire as early as 771 BCE. The last two centuries were known as the "**Era of Warring States**."

Mesoamerica and South America

In the Americas, agriculture developed around the same time as in our other civilizations, but the civilizations there did not develop in river valleys. Around 1500 BCE, the **Olmecs** settled in the coastal plain near the **Gulf of Mexico** along river banks. The periodic flooding left the land fertile for agriculture. The first important settlement was **San Lorenzo**, which was the religious, political, and economic center for the large population. Later, **La Venta** served as an important center, and with its abundant rainfall, there was no need to build an extensive irrigation system. Olmec artisans carved masks and human figurines out of jade, which they imported from a neighboring area. Social status was often indicated by the type of clothing and ornaments a person wore. The more elaborate the dress and decoration, the higher the social class.

One of the great mysteries of the Olmecs is the **Colossal Heads** they built, which are 6-feet high and weigh between 16 to 18 tons each. It is believed that they are carvings of the leadership, but no one knows for sure. What we do know is that it took a lot of organization and labor to construct such things, especially since there were no draft animals to help with the work. The society was most likely authoritarian, in which the lower class performed the biddings of the upper class. The decline and fall of the Olmecs is also a bit of a mystery. The ceremonial centers were destroyed and abandoned, but no one knows why.

In South America, urban centers developed in isolation from those in Mesoamerica, but at about the same time. Around 2500 BCE, cultivation of such crops as beans, peanuts, and sweet potatoes was occurring in the **Andean heartland**. Around 1000 BCE, an important religious cult—the **Chavin**—gained influence and the society became more complex. Chavin de Huantar was the most important ceremonial center and had several large temple platforms. Artisans worked with ceramics, textiles, and gold. Both Mesoamerica and South America constructed religious shrine centers. These early American civilizations would leave their mark on the civilizations and empires to develop later.

DEVELOPMENT AND SPREAD OF RELIGION

Since the earliest times, man has struggled with the unanswerable questions, "Why am I here?" "Who made me?" and "What happens after I die?" Religions developed around the world to address these questions.

Early civilizations were mostly polytheistic: Often gods or goddesses were associated with nature, and sacrifices were made to these gods to ensure things such as good harvests. Over time, religions became more complex.

Around 600 BCE, major religions and philosophies emerged to address some new questions or concerns that the previous traditions may not have been sufficiently answering. Philosopher Karl Jaspers calls this time period the **Axial Age**. The axial represents the core ideas around which a society revolves. Great philosophers emerged during this period, with new answers to difficult questions. These "axial" ideas went on to make indelible marks on the civilizations in which they developed.

Hinduism

The religion of Hinduism originated in India, but we cannot link a specific time or person to its creation. There was no "Mr. Hindu." It is a belief system that evolved over time. It actually refers to a wide variety of beliefs and practices that developed in South Asia. Hinduism is often described as not just a religion, but a way of life, because of the important impact it has on its followers.

At the most basic level, Hindus believe that they have a **dharma** or duty to perform in life. If all follow their dharma, the world works smoothly. Only when dharma is violated do things seem to be out of sync. This dharma is determined by birth and one's stage in life. If one follows his dharma, he will get good **karma.** It is the accumulation of this good karma (the sum of all good and bad deeds performed) that allows someone to move up in the level of **samsara** in the next life.

Hindus believe that they will be **reincarnated** (reborn) after death. The new position they assume in the next life will depend on how well they performed their dharma in the past life. The ultimate goal for Hindus is to end the cycle of reincarnation by finally reaching **moksha** or oneness with the universe. Hinduism is a polytheistic religion that believes in **Brahma**, the creator god, and his various incarnations including: Vishnu, Shiva, and Devi. Bhatki is a popular practice in which followers have a personal devotion to a particular deity.

The social structure known as the **caste system** has had an enormous impact on the followers of Hinduism. The four varnas are the basis for the caste system. They are **Brahmins** (priests and scholars), **ksatriyas** (warriors and ruling class), **vaisyas** (farmers and businessmen), and **shudras** (servants). A fifth group at the bottom of society became known as the **untouchables**.

The caste system is based on the concepts of purity and pollution. This includes pure foods, sounds, and sights. Jobs are ranked because purity is associated with those who work with their minds, and pollution is associated with those come in contact with polluted things such as sweat or human excrement. To ensure this purity, people should only marry members of their own caste.

Hinduism remains important in India and a few areas in southeast Asia to which it spread, but the core ideas of Hinduism were reformed into the religion of Buddhism, which soon become a worldwide religion.

Buddhism

Siddhartha Gautama, who lived from approximately 563 BCE to 483 BCE, became an important axial-age thinker in India. He was raised as a prince in a small state near present day Nepal. After living a sheltered life, he decided to leave the palace in search of answers to such questions as: "Why is there so much suffering in the world?" "Is there a way out of suffering?" After meditating under a bodhi tree, the prince reached enlightenment and became known as the **Buddha (enlightened one)**.

The Buddha made a crucial decision that helped to transform his ideas from the thoughts of one man into a world religion: He decided to teach what he had learned to others. The Buddha taught that there were four noble truths.

1. All life is suffering.
2. Suffering is caused by desire.
3. There is a way out of suffering.
4. The way out of suffering is to follow the Eightfold Path.

The **Eightfold Path** includes right understanding, purpose, speech, conduct, livelihood, effort, awareness, and concentration. The idea was that if you want to stop suffering, you must stop **desiring**, and if you want to stop desiring, you must live in a righteous manner by following the Eightfold Path.

Buddhism took the central ideas of Hinduism such as dharma, karma, and samara, but then altered them significantly. According to Buddhism, people did not need the rituals of the Brahmins. Gods and goddesses are not necessary—everyone can seek enlightenment on her own, and no one is an outcast by birth (challenging the caste system, very important in India). There is, it espouses, complete equality among all believers.

Buddhism was a religion that "hit the road." The followers of the Buddha acted as **missionaries** spreading his message. These ideas particularly appealed to low caste Hindus as well as women.

The Mauryan emperor **Asoka** actively encouraged the spread of Buddhism. Back at home in India, however, some Buddhist beliefs were absorbed into Hinduism, which remained the dominant religion. Buddhism traveled to Asia, however, along the Silk Roads, where it met with great success. It later went on to influence Central Asia, China, Japan, Korea, and Southeast Asia. As it spread, it would blend with the native ideas of the lands it encountered (syncretism). It was its flexibility and its message of universal acceptance that helped make Buddhism a major world religion.

Axial Age in China

From 441 to 221 BCE, no strong central government control existed in China. This was a time of constant fighting and disorder, and is referred to as the **Era of Warring States**. It is within this time that three important philosophies emerged in China: **Confucianism**, **Daoism**, and **Legalism**. All attempted to end the fighting and restore order, but in different ways.

Confucianism

Confucius (551 to 479 BCE) was a philosopher who believed that his answers could bring an end to the existing warfare. The key to ending the chaos and to bringing back peace, he felt, was to find the right kind of leadership to rule China.

His two most important concepts were **ren** (appropriate feelings) and **li** (correct actions), which must be used together in order to have any effect. Additionally, **filial piety** or respect for one's parents was a key concept.

Confucius taught that order would be achieved when people knew their proper role and relationship to others. Rulers would rule by **moral example** and people would learn to behave properly through the example of those superior to them. There are **five key relationships**:

1. Ruler to subject
2. Father to son
3. Husband to wife
4. Older brother to younger brother
5. Friend to friend

Confucianism became the most influential philosophy in China. During the Han dynasty, Confucian ideas were used (in addition to some Daoism and Legalism) to bring peace and order. These ideas left a permanent mark on China and were continually used by subsequent dynasties throughout China's history. These ideas also spread to Korea and Japan, where they became very influential.

Daoism

Some claim that the Chinese sage **Laozi** founded the Daoist school of thought around the 6th century BCE, around the same time as Confucius, but the ideas go back further in Chinese history. The **Daodejing**, a collection of Daoist wisdom, is attributed to Laozi. These ideas represent a protest movement during the troubled times of the Era of Warring States.

The literal translation of the Dao is the **way**, the **way of nature**, or the **way of the cosmos**. According to Daoism, all life is interdependent, and human beings should exist in harmony. Its advice is to relax and get in harmony with the Dao. In order to solve the problems of the day, Daoists taught the concept of **wu wei**, which means *act by not acting*. Do nothing and problems will solve themselves, like nature. Be like water—soft and yielding—but at the same time, very naturally powerful.

Daoists believed it was useless to try to build institutions to govern men, because institutions (or anything that rewarded knowledge) were dangerous. Institutions lead to competition and eventually, to fighting. The less government the better; the ideal state is a small, self-sufficient town. The ultimate goal should be to cultivate the virtues of patience, selflessness, and concern for all.

You might wonder how a philosophy like this could bring an end to the Era of Warring States. In reality, it couldn't, but the idea of it was a rejection of some strict guidelines in society, and a way to find an alternative way of life. In Chinese society, it provided an escape from the proper behavior of Confucianism—it encouraged people to take time off, relax, just let things happen. It allowed the Chinese to be Confucian at work and Daoist while not at work.

Daoism's attitude toward war was that it should be used only for defensive purposes. The Han followed this idea by stationing its troops along the Great Wall to maintain the safety of trade routes. Laozi gained many disciples in China, though some mixed his ideas with magic and attempted to search for immortality.

Comparative Close-up: Social Hierarchy and Religion

Religion	Social Hierarchy
Hinduism	Brahmins (Scholars/Priests) Ksatriyas (Warrior/Ruling class) Vaisyas (Professional class) Shudras (Servant class) Untouchables (Outcastes)
Confucianism	Scholar Gentry Peasants Merchants

Legalism

The philosophy of Legalism was based on the principle that man was inherently evil and needed strict laws and punishment to behave properly. Additionally, a strong central government with an absolute leader and heavy taxes would ensure a more stable society.

Judaism

The Hebrews were a nomadic people who migrated from the Arabian Peninsula sometime between 2000 and 1000 BCE. By 1700 BCE, many Hebrews had migrated into Egypt. Some of them may have been employed as administrators and advisors, yet most, over time, were enslaved by the Egyptians. Sometime after 1300 BCE, Moses led the Hebrews out of Egypt in a flight that became known as the **Exodus**.

The Hebrews believed that they were protected by their own god **YHWH** (what may have been pronounced *Yahweh*, but was considered too holy a word to say aloud). They believed that they had a special relationship with this god. According to the Bible, the **Ten Commandments** were given to Moses by God, and at that time, it was revealed that the Hebrews were God's chosen people.

As a result, the Hebrews entered into a **Covenant** with God; they were forbidden from worshipping any other god and were obligated to follow the Ten Commandments. Some of these commandments included honoring your mother and father, not killing, and not committing adultery. The Hebrews believed that if they honored the Ten Commandments, YHWH would lead them to the promised land. Most important, the Hebrews (who became known as Jews) established a **monotheistic tradition**, which claims there is one creator (God) who made the world and all life.

The Hebrews returned to the "Promised Land" on the eastern shores of the Mediterranean, and the kingdom of **Israel** was established, led by a monarchy. The height of Israelite power came during the reigns of King David and his son Solomon around 1000 BCE. Later, the Assyrians invaded, destroyed the temple, and scattered part of the population. The Babylonians then finished the job. The temple was rebuilt, but the former kingdom of Israel was swallowed up by the Greek and Roman empires after 330 BCE.

The Jews remained determined to preserve their culture. Uprisings against the Romans in 66 and 135 CE were suppressed with large military campaigns. Many Jews were killed and the temple was leveled. In 135 CE, the Romans drove the Jews out of their homeland, causing them to scatter. This scattering of the Jews is referred to as the **Diaspora**. Jews survived in scattered communities around the Mediterranean.

As a monotheistic religion, Judaism would go on to influence the development of Christianity and Islam.

Christianity

Jesus was born to Jewish parents about 4 BCE in the area know as **Judea** (today the country of Israel), which was part of the Roman Empire. At the time, there was tension between Rome and its Jewish subjects.

Jesus taught devotion to God and love for fellow human beings. He earned a reputation of wisdom and the power to perform miracles, i.e., heal the sick. His message of the **Kingdom of God** alarmed Roman authorities, however, and to quell a potential rebellion, they had him executed on a cross in the early 30s CE.

Jesus had been concerned with the growing cosmopolitan nature of Jewish society and preached a simple message of love and compassion. These ideas appealed to the lower class, the urban population, and women. Men and women were considered spiritually equal before God. For many, this message gave them a sense of purpose. The faithful would experience **eternal life** in heaven with God.

The death of Jesus was just the beginning of this story. His followers believed that he rose from the dead and that he was the son of God. As such, they compiled a body of writings about his life and his messages; this became the **New Testament**.

The earliest followers of Jesus (Christians) were all Jews, but in the mid-first century CE, Paul began to spread the message to non-Jews, or gentiles. He and other missionaries used the Roman roads and sea lanes to spread this new religion. However, Christians, much like the Jews, refused to honor the state cults or to worship the emperor as a god, and as a result, were often subject to campaigns of persecution.

Even so, the religion continued to spread throughout the empire, until Emperor Constantine issued the **Edict of Milan**, making Christianity legal in the Roman Empire. Emperor Theodosius went on to make it the official religion of the empire.

Christianity also spread to Mesopotamia, Iran, and even parts of India. Over time, the Southwest Asian Christians and the Western (or Roman) Christians grew apart. Southwest Asian Christians followed a form of the religion called **Nestorian Christianity**. This form of Christianity continued to spread across the Silk Roads into Central Asia, India, and China.

Comparative Close-up: Role of Women in Religion

Religion	Role of Women
Buddhism	Women could achieve nirvana. An alternative lifestyle was available for women as nuns in a monastery.
Christianity	Men and women were equal in eyes of god. Women could go to heaven. Many early converts were women. Women could live in convents.
Confucianism	Men were superior to women. One of five key relationships is that of husband to wife.
Hinduism	Men were superior to women. Women were not allowed to read the sacred prayers, the Vedas. In order to reach moksha, one must be a male Brahmin.

CLASSICAL SOCIETIES

The political and cultural beginnings in the four classical societies of Greece, India, Rome, and China laid the foundations for future development. It was these four societies that left a large imprint on these areas in which future civilization would copy or revise. Greece and India left a political imprint that was primarily decentralized based on local identity, while Rome and China's imprint was that of an imperial centralized state.

Greece

Political Development

Greece's political identity revolved around the concept of the **polis** or city–state. Greece's geography of mountainous terrain helped in the development of this decentralized political structure. Different city–states took on different forms, and they emerged independently. A few functioned as monarchies, but most were based on some form of collaborative rule.

The two most famous city–states were **Sparta** and **Athens**. Sparta used military strength to impose order, though Athens used democratic principles to negotiate order. Athens's government was a direct democracy that relied on its small size and the intense participation of its citizens. Those citizens were free adult males. (This meant no women, foreigners, or slaves could be citizens.)

The Spartans, on the other hand, lived life with no luxuries, where distinction was earned through discipline and military talent. Boys began their rigorous military training at age 7, and girls received physical education to promote the birth of strong children.

Over time, population pressures led to the establishment of colonies along the Mediterranean Sea, yet a centralized state was not created. These colonies relied on their own resources and took their own course. They did, however, facilitate trade throughout the region.

Greek cities in Anatolia (modern-day Turkey) resented what they viewed as the oppressive rule of the Persian Empire and revolted. The revolt started the **Persian War** (500–470 BCE). Athenians, too, sent their own troops in support. Though Athens was burned by Persians, two important victories at Marathon and Salamis helped the Greeks to defeat the Persians. For the Greeks, it was a moral victory, with the independently minded city–state overtaking the big, evil empire. For the Persians, it was more of a minor conflict and annoyance.

The alliance of the Greeks against the Persians led to the formation of the **Delian League**, of which Athens served as the leader. However, this leadership soon caused resentment by other parts of the Greek world. The conflict came to a head during the **Peloponnesian War** (431–404 BCE). Sparta and Athens each led the two conflicting camps, and though Sparta was victorious, the internal conflict weakened Greece and left it vulnerable to domination by a stronger power.

That stronger power came from Macedonia, a frontier state north of the Greek peninsula. **King Philip II** (359–336 BCE) consolidated control of his kingdom and moved into Greece, and by 338 BCE, the region was under his control.

His next move was to conquer Persia, but that job would be left to his son, **Alexander**. Alexander, a skilled military commander and strategist, successfully conquered Persia by 330 BCE and went on to conquer the most northwest regions of the Indian subcontinent. But his troops had had enough, and they refused to go any further. By 323 BCE, at the age of 33, Alexander the Great was dead. What he left behind was the creation of a **Hellenistic Empire and Era**. The empire was divided among three of his generals: Antigonid (Greece and Macedonia), Ptolemaic (Egypt), and Seleucid (Persia).

Economic Developments

The Greek world relied heavily on trade as the cornerstone of its economy. The Mediterranean Sea linked its communities through this trade, and created a larger Greek community. During the Hellenistic Era, caravan trade flourished from Persia to the West, and sea lanes were widely traveled throughout the Mediterranean Sea, Persian Gulf, and Arabian Sea. This trade created a cosmopolitan culture.

Social Structure and Gender Roles

Overall, Greece was a **patriarchal** society with fairly strict social divisions. Women were under the authority of their fathers, husbands, and then, sons. Most women owned no land and often wore veils in public. Their one public position could be that of a priestess of a religious cult. Literacy, however, was common among upper-class Greek women, and Spartan women took place in athletic competitions.

Slaves in Greek society were acquired because they had debt, were prisoners of war, or were traded. The treatment of slaves varied widely, depending of the needs and temperament of the owner.

Culture, Arts, Science, and Technology

Culturally, the Greeks stressed a central importance on human life and a growing appreciation of human beauty. This is seen through religion, philosophy, art, architecture, literature, athletics, and science. **Polytheistic**, the Greeks believed that their gods were personifications of nature. Each city-state had its own patron god or goddess for whom rituals were performed.

The great philosopher **Socrates**, who posed questions and encouraged reflection, said, "the unexamined life is not worth living." His student **Plato** wrote *The Republic*, in which he described his ideal state ruled by a philosopher king. Plato's student **Aristotle** wrote on biology, physics, astronomy, politics, and ethics. In literature, the great epic poems attributed to Homer, the *Iliad* and the *Odyssey*, convey the value of the hero in Greek culture. In architecture, the Greeks built temples using pillars or columns, and they developed a realistic approach to sculpture. The Olympic games were held regularly to demonstrate athletic excellence.

The Greeks also made great strides in anatomy, astronomy, and math, including the medical writings of Galen and the mathematics of Archimedes.

India

Political Development

Following the invasions of the Aryans, India developed by the 6th century BCE into **small regional kingdoms** that often fought each other. Though there were periods of centralized rule, the subcontinent remained **decentralized** through most of its history.

One significant example of that centralized rule was that of the **Mauryans**. In the 320s BCE, **Chandragupta Maurya** made his move to fill the power-vacuum left after Alexander of Macedonia withdrew from the region. Maurya successfully dominated the area and set up a bureaucratic administrative system to rule his empire. His grandson, **Ashoka**, continued his grandfather's conquering ways until the bloody campaign to conquer Kalinga. This bloodbath convinced Ashoka to stop using a conquering approach and instead rule by moral example. He used his *Rock Edicts* (announcements carved into cliffs and in caves) to get his message out to people. During his reign, Ashoka set up a tightly organized bureaucracy that collected taxes and was made up of officials, accountants, and soldiers. He built roads, hospitals, and rest houses which facilitated trade. After Ashoka's death, the Mauryan Empire declined and India returned to a land of large regional kingdoms, but order and stability was maintained with an increase in trade.

It was not until 320 CE that India would again be united under imperial rule. Chandra Gupta (no relation to the other one) established the **Gupta Empire** and conquered many of the regional kingdoms. The south, however, remained out of his control. Instead of setting up an organized bureaucracy, the Guptas left the local government and administration in power. Their rule continued until the invasion of the White Huns severely weakened the empire and India returned to regional rule.

Economic Development

India's economy benefited from the expansion of agriculture and the increase in trade throughout the Foundations period. Ashoka encouraged agricultural development through irrigation, and encouraged trade by building roads, wells, and inns along those roads. Agricultural surplus led to an increase in the number of towns; these towns maintained marketplaces and encouraged trade. Long-distance trade increased with China, Southeast Asia, and the Mediterranean basin. Overland trade via the **Silk Roads** connected India with China through Central Asia.

Indian sailors mastered the technique of riding the monsoon (seasonal) winds, and they sailed to Indonesia and Southeast Asia. Their goods, such as cotton and black pepper, made it all the way to Rome.

Social Structure and Gender Roles

Like Greece, India developed into a **patriarchal** society with a strict social structure. Women were forbidden from reading the sacred prayers (the Vedas), and under Hindu law, they were legally minors and subject to the supervision of their fathers, husbands, and then sons.

In order to marry well, a woman's family needed a large dowry. Women were not allowed to inherit property, and a widow was not permitted to remarry. The social structure became dominated by the power of the Brahmins and the caste system. **Caste**—something that could not be changed—determined one's job, diet, and marriage. These restrictions were reinforced by the ruling class. As the Brahmins became more powerful, especially during the rule of the Guptas, caste distinctions grew more prominent.

Culture, Arts, Science, Technology

During the Foundations period, India's culture thrived, as did its advancements in the arts, math and science. The Mauryan emperor Ashoka became a devout Buddhist around 260 BCE, after the battle at Kalinga, and changed the way he ruled his empire. He rewarded Buddhists with land, and encouraged the spread of the religion by building monasteries and stupas. He even sent out missionaries, who facilitated the spread of **Buddhism** to Central Asia, East Asia, and Southeast Asia. But through political support, **Hinduism** gradually eclipsed the influence of Buddhism. The Guptas gave land grants to Brahmins, supported education that promoted Hindu values, and built great temples in urban centers.

Unlike Greek art, Indian art during this time stressed symbolism rather than accurate representation. Math and science flourished in areas such as geometry and algebra. The circumference of the earth and the value of *pi* were calculated. Additionally, the concept of zero, the decimal system, and the number system we use today called "Arabic" numbers was developed.

China

Political Development

China's political development during this time period laid the foundation for what was to endure over 2,000 years. What kind of system can have that kind of lasting power?

It all started during a period referred to as the **Era of Warring States** (403–221 BCE). During this time of turmoil and warfare, three important philosophies emerged (the **Three Schools of Thought**) to address the problems of the day and attempt to end the fighting: Confucianism, Daoism, and Legalism. Legalism offered the firmest solution to China's problems, preaching a practical and ruthless approach to state rule. The foundation of a state's strength, it proposed, was in its agricultural production and its military, and strict laws and punishments were required to maintain order.

The first Chinese emperor thought these Legalist ideas might be the solution to China's problems. In 221 BCE, the first emperor, **Qin Shihuangdi** ended the Era of Warring States and started China's tradition of centralized imperial rule under the **Qin dynasty**. He had a centralized bureaucracy and divided the land into administrative provinces. For protection, he sponsored the building of defensive walls throughout the empire, which were the predecessor to China's **Great Wall**. Laws, currencies, weights, measures and the Chinese script were standardized. As the emperor was not a fan of Confucianism, he had most of those books burned and had 460 scholars buried alive. His rule and dynasty lasted only 14 years, but he established the precedent for centralized imperial rule in China, which would last for 2,000 years. When the emperor died in 207 BCE, revolts broke out and a new dynasty—the Han—was established.

The **Han dynasty** (206 BCE–220 CE) was much longer than the Qin dynasty, and it also learned from the Qin's mistakes. The Han used what worked—such as centralized imperial rule and a strong bureaucracy—but lessened the Legalist hard edge of the rule. The most prominent emperor **Wu Di** (141–87 BCE) built roads and canals, and established an imperial university with Confucianism as the basis for the curriculum. The university was the basis for the **civil service exams**, which became the entry test for government jobs. The Han emperors still exerted absolute control, but they used the Confucian ideas about their authority over the empire in the same way that a father has authority over his family and home. During the Han dynasty, a foreign policy of expansion was pursued, and North Vietnam, Korea, and Central Asia came under its control.

Economic Development

China's economy was based on agriculture, and it flourished during this period with the increase in long-distance trade. Iron metallurgy was introduced, which led to an increase in agriculture. That, in turn, allowed for an increase in trade and an increase in the military strength of the empire. With the military expansion of the Han, overland trade could increase because peace and order were maintained.

It was during the Han dynasty that the trade route known as the **Silk Roads** began to flourish. The route was a series of roads that allowed trade to connect the Han Empire with Central Asia, India, and the Roman Empire.

The Han also followed a **tributary system of trade**. Officially, the policy was that the Han did not need to trade with their inferior neighbors, so instead, they demanded tribute from neighboring groups. These neighboring groups would visit the court, bringing tribute, and the Chinese would give trade goods in return. In addition, the Han often sent gifts to nomad groups so as to prevent any possible invasion.

Social Structure and Gender Roles

China, like the other classical civilizations, had a **patriarchal** society with a set social structure. A woman's most important role was to make a proper marriage that would strengthen the family's alliances. (Widowed women were, however, permitted to remarry.) Upper-class women were often tutored in writing, arts, and music, but overall, women were legally subordinate to their fathers and their husbands.

Socially, the highest class was that of the **scholar–gentry**. These landlord families were often the only ones able to take the civil service exam, because preparation was very expensive. Most Chinese were peasants who worked the land. Merchants, who gained great wealth during this period with the increase in trade, were considered socially low because they did not produce anything, but rather lived off the labor of others.

Culture, Arts, Science, Technology

In China, the family became the most important cultural and organizational unit in society. The **family** consisted both of its living members and its **ancestors**. Confucius's **filial piety**, respect or reverence for one's parents, was also very important. The family always provided for its own members.

Daoism's emphasis on being close to nature also had a lasting impact on China. This reverence for nature became a central value of the Han people. This was also a time of great invention and innovation. Agriculture was aided by the wheelbarrow, while horse collars and watermills were created to grind grain. The sternpost rudder and compass aided sea travel. Possibly most important was the invention of **paper**, which increased the availability of the written word.

Rome

Political Development

Rome's political history is one of change and evolution. In 509 BCE, the Roman nobility overthrew the Etruscan king, and what had been a monarchy became a **republic**—a government in which the people elect their representatives. The republic consisted of two consuls who were elected by an assembly that was dominated by the wealthy class, known as the **patricians**. The Senate, made up of patricians, advised these consuls.

This system of leadership created tension between the patricians and the common people, known as the **plebeians**. Eventually, the patricians granted the plebeians the right to elect tribunes, who had the right to veto. When a civil or military crisis occurred, a dictator was appointed for 6 months.

Things began to change as Rome expanded throughout the Italian peninsula and then the Mediterranean. It encountered a fierce competitor in the city of Carthage in North Africa, which had gained wealth through the thriving trade in the Mediterranean Sea. This economic competition led to the Punic Wars, which took place between 264 and 146 BCE. By the end of the conflict, Rome had sacked the city of Carthage, solidifying its domination of the Mediterranean. Rome was also expanding east, into the former empire of Alexander.

As Rome expanded, it transitioned from a **republic** to an **empire**. The wealth and power of conquest led to a growth in problems, most notably, the unequal distribution of land and class tension. The wealthy had amassed large plantations using slave labor and the small farmers could not compete. Also, the growth of cities led to a growth in the urban lower class and an increase in poverty.

The Roman general **Julius Caesar** led the Roman army in its conquest of Gaul, and in 46 BCE, made himself dictator for life. He centralized military and political functions, and initiated large-scale building projects which gave jobs to the poor. But the senators feared Caesar was becoming a tyrant and assassinated him. His nephew, Octavian, took over, and in 27 BCE, was given the title Augustus. During his 45-year rule, Rome was a monarchy disguised as a republic. He centralized political and military power, but preserved the traditions of the republic. The continued expansion of the empire stimulated the growing economy and cities emerged throughout. As such, the next two and a half centuries were called the **Pax Romana**, or Roman Peace.

Rome's system of law had begun in 450 BCE with the **Twelve Tables**. As the empire spread, the laws went with it. Such laws as "a defendant is innocent until proven guilty" and "a defendant has the right to challenge his accuser before a judge" originated in Rome.

Height of the Roman Empire, 116 CE

Economic Development

The key to the Roman Empire's economic success was its extensive system of **roads**. The 60,000 miles of roads linked the empire's 100 million people, linking all regions of the empire for trade and communication. This trade made the merchants very rich and created markets for the goods that the farmers produced, and as a result, the increase in tax revenue made the empire stronger. A **uniform currency** was used, and **Latin** became the common language of trade.

All of this trade made the empire very interdependent. Cities grew and so did their populations. The cities had access to fresh water through the use of aqueducts, sewage, plumbing, and public baths.

Social Structure and Gender Roles

Like other classical societies, Rome was **patriarchal**, where the eldest male, **pater familias**, ruled as father of the family. Roman law gave the pater familias authority to arrange marriage for the children, and the right to sell them into slavery—or even execute them. Women's roles were in supervising domestic affairs; laws put strict limits on their inheritances, though this was inconsistently enforced. As the wealth of the empire increased, new classes emerged, and these new wealthy merchants and landowners built very large homes. On the other side, the poor were often unemployed. **Slaves**, one-third of the population by the second century CE, worked on large estates in the countryside or in the cities as domestic servants.

Culture, Arts, Science, Technology

Much of Roman culture and achievements were inspired by the **Greek examples**. Romans were **polytheistic**, like the Greeks, and believed that the gods intervened directly in their lives. The empire tolerated the cultural practices of its subjects—it they paid their taxes, did not rebel, and revered the emperors and Roman gods. The **Jews**, strict monotheists, were considered a problem, however, and rebellions occurred between the third and first centuries BCE. They ultimately failed and were defeated by the Romans by 70 CE.

The **Christians**, originally a Jewish sect, were also seen as a threat to Roman rule, and were often persecuted. However, the number of Christians continued to grow throughout the empire. By 313 CE, Emperor Constantine issued the **Edict of Milan**, which legalized Christianity in the empire. By 380 CE, Emperor Theodosius proclaimed Christianity as the empire's official religion.

Rome was also heavily influenced by the Greeks in art and architecture. Roman architecture took its inspiration from Greece, making its columns and arches more ornate. Improvements in engineering allowed the Romans to build stadiums, public baths, temples, aqueducts, and a system of roads.

ROLE OF TRADE IN CLASSICAL SOCIETIES

Long-distance trade expanded greatly during the classical period, allowing for the movement of goods and ideas. There were a few factors: the Han Empire secured the trade routes through Central Asia; the Mauryan Empire had declined in India, but regional states were able to provide the necessary stability and security; and the Romans kept the Mediterranean Sea safe for trade and travel. This stability and security allowed for long-distance trade to thrive.

Silk Roads

The Silk Road trade originated during a diplomatic mission to Central Asian nomads during the Han Empire. Though the diplomatic mission failed, the silk brought as gifts were very popular, as were the horses that the diplomats brought from Central Asia. The trade route began in the east in Changan, went through Mongolia and Turkestan, and veered either north or south around the Taklamakan Desert. It branched southeast to India or through Central Asia, and finally to the eastern end of the Roman Empire.

Almost never did one merchant make the entire journey. Instead, the caravan routes were traveled in stages, from one oasis town to the next. Buddhism became quite popular in such oasis towns as Samarkand, Kashgar, and Dunhuang, where merchants rested, sold their wares at market, and often built monasteries.

Goods that Traveled East to West	Goods that Traveled West to East
Silk	Glassware
Spices	Jewelry
Cotton	Bronze goods
Pearls	Wool and linen
Coral	Olive oil
Ivory	Gold and silver bullion

Indian Ocean

The Indian Ocean is sometimes referred to as the sea lanes of the Silk Roads. This ocean trade went from Guangzhou in southern China through the South China Sea, through the islands of Southeast Asia, India, the Arabian Sea, and the Persian Gulf. The principal players in the trade were Malay and Indian sailors. Religion and culture also spread across the seas. Some merchants spread Buddhism to Southeast Asia, while others promoted the Hindu cults of Shiva and Vishnu.

Mediterranean Sea

The Mediterranean Sea is often referred to as the **Roman Lake**, because the Roman Empire surrounded the sea. Sea trade flowed from Syria to Spain to North Africa. The Romans kept their lake safe and free from pirates, which allowed the trade to thrive and grow, and transport goods from one part of the expansive empire to the other.

SPREAD OF DISEASE

During the second and third centuries CE, both the Han and Roman Empires suffered large-scale outbreaks of epidemic disease. From the trade and interaction that had taken place, the incidence of disease increased. Diseases such as smallpox, measles, and bubonic plague had a devastating effect on the population because people did not have the immunity or the medicine to combat them. In the second century in the Roman Empire, the population dropped by 25%, and it was even worse in the cities. The effects of these diseases caused great economic and social change. Trade within the empires declined, and economies become more regionally focused.

MOVEMENT OF PEOPLES

Bantu Migration

The migration of the Bantu people began around 2000 BCE, and by 1000 CE, the Bantu occupied most of sub-Saharan Africa. Resources were stretched to their limits as the population increased. As a result, groups of people began to leave the areas (in modern day Nigeria) to set up new agricultural settlements, and the process repeated itself slowly.

The Bantu people often intermarried with those they came in contact with, and these people often adopted the Bantu language and joined the Bantu society. Around 1000 BCE, the Bantus began to produce iron and iron tools, which enabled them to clear more land and expand agriculture. This led to an increase in population and more migration. Around 500 CE, the cultivation of bananas—which had made their way to African via the Indian Ocean trade—enabled the Bantus to expand into heavily forested regions and to continue the migration process. All of this migrating led to an increase in the overall population of Africa—from 3.5 million in 400 BCE to 22 million in 1000 CE—and the spread of agriculture throughout much of Africa. Today there are over 500 distinct (though related) languages that can be traced back to the Bantus.

Polynesian Migration

Humans migrated to Australia around 60,000 years ago via watercraft that could travel the low level seas. These people developed maritime technology and agricultural expertise, and eventually established settlements in the islands of the Pacific Ocean. Beginning around 2000 BCE, the movements which settled the Polynesian islands commenced to islands such as Vanuatu, Fiji, Samoa, and later Hawaii. Long-distance voyages were taken on double canoes with large triangular sails, which carried a platform between the two hulls for shelter.

Some scholars believe that the **settlement** was accidental by sailors being blown off course, while others believe it was a planned colonization. As the migration spread, so did the cultivation of new food crops such as yams, taros, breadfruit, and bananas, and the introduction of domesticated animals such as dogs, pigs, and chickens. The Polynesian islands developed into hierarchical chiefdoms in which leadership was passed down to the eldest son, and relatives served as the local aristocracy. Conflict between groups, as well as population pressure, often led to further migration to new areas. The cultures and languages of these widely dispersed islands often adapted and evolved differently.

FALL OF CLASSICAL EMPIRES

As the Foundations period drew to an end, the classical societies that helped to shape it were all suffering through periods of decline, for mostly similar reasons. The chart below outlines some of the reasons. The recovery from this decline shapes the beginning of our next chapter.

	Han	Western Rome	Gupta
Time of Fall	220 CE	476 CE	550 CE
Economic Reasons	Scholar officials were often exempt from taxes and peasants often fled from tax collectors to these estates. As a result, a severe reduction in tax revenue financially crippled the empire. Long-distance trade did decrease, but the Chinese were quite self-sufficient and were not severely hurt by this.	The rich landowning class often resisted paying their taxes and when the tax collectors did approach, they were driven away by the landowners private armies. Also the church land was not taxable. As the empire declined, so did the trade because of unsafe roads and because it relied on economic interdependence. The drop in tax revenue and inflation crippled Rome's economy.	The government had great difficulty raising enough taxes to pay the army to protect its borders.
Political Reasons	The government was unable to check the power of the large private estate owners. The emperor heavily relied on the advice of his court officials and was often misinformed for their personal gain.	The government had trouble finding bureaucrats who could enforce the laws. Power struggles for the throne plagued the empire. From 235 to 284 CE, 25 out of 26 emperors died a violent death. The division of the empire into two sections allowed the eastern portion to remain stronger, while the western portion weakened.	The regional powers of the Guptas allowed them to keep much of their administrative power. They eventually grew more powerful than the central government.
Social Reasons	The population increase led to smaller family plots and increased difficulty of the peasant class to pay taxes.	Plagues dramatically reduced the population, in particular the farming population.	
Role of Nomadic Invasions	The Xiongnu invaded, but only after the empire had already fallen. Nomadic invasions took place because the empire was no longer providing them with what they needed.	The Roman army could not defend against the movement of such nomadic groups as the Ostrogoths, Huns, and Visigoths. Rome was sacked by the Visigoths in 476 CE.	The government was too weak to defend against the nomadic invasions of the White Huns.

All the classical societies entered a period of recovery where they were all decentralized following their collapse, but the **western half of the Roman Empire (Western Europe) experienced the most severe collapse**. Why? A few possible reasons:

- Rome was economically interdependent and the decline in trade severely hurt the economy
- Continual waves of nomadic invasions made recovery difficult
- The spread of disease led to a decrease in population and a weakened empire

IF YOU LEARNED ONLY FIVE THINGS IN THIS CHAPTER....

1. From the simplest barter system to long journeys along trade routes, the exchange of good and ideas shaped this period and led to further change throughout the world. Important trade routes like the Silk Road, Indian Ocean, and Mediterranean Sea shaped development.

2. Once people began to settle and gradually organize into early civilizations, the discovery of agriculture began to change their lives at a more rapid pace.

3. As humans organized themselves in families, gender roles emerged. With the development of agriculture, the division of labor further deepened these divisions. These gender roles were reinforced by religious systems and governmental systems.

4. During this period, major world religions developed and spread, shaping the civilizations they encountered. Religions and belief systems such as Hinduism, Buddhism, Confucianism, and Daoism (Asia), and Christianity and Judaism (Europe, Asia) influenced large numbers of people throughout the period.

5. Civilizations emerged which had organized governments, complex religions, social structures, job specialization, public works, systems of writing, and arts and architecture. These civilizations grew into larger and more complicated governmental organizations such as empires, i.e. Rome, Han, and Gupta.

REVIEW QUESTIONS

1. The period 8000 BCE to 600 CE is characterized by all of the following EXCEPT

   (A) The development of agriculture
   (B) The growth in world population
   (C) The use of metal technology
   (D) The development of writing
   (E) The use of gunpowder technology

2. The change to an agriculturally based economy as a result of the Neolithic Revolution

   (A) was gradual as it took hundreds or thousands of years.
   (B) developed in one part of the world and spread from there.
   (C) was universally accepted throughout the world.
   (D) had little impact on the environment.
   (E) led to a decrease in population.

3. Which classical society was located in South Asia?

   (A) Roman
   (B) Han
   (C) Mauryan
   (D) Qin
   (E) Greek

4. The development of agriculture led to an increase in population because

   (A) farming was much less labor intensive than hunting and gathering.
   (B) the stable food source allowed for more permanent homes and larger families.
   (C) farming provided a healthier diet than hunting and gathering.
   (D) hunting and gathering was an extremely dangerous lifestyle.
   (E) the nomadic way of life ended worldwide.

5. Pastoral nomads are similar to settled farmers in that they both

   (A) Grow crops
   (B) Domesticate animals
   (C) Settle into larger communities
   (D) Have job specialization
   (E) Have a written language

6. The Neolithic Revolution influenced gender roles in that

   (A) men and women's economic roles were deemed equal.
   (B) work outside of the home was more highly valued.
   (C) women no longer worked.
   (D) men played the only significant economic role.
   (E) men continued to hunt, and women continued to gather.

7. All of the following are characteristics of early civilizations EXCEPT

   (A) Diverse people
   (B) Job specialization
   (C) Social stratification
   (D) Trade
   (E) Representative government

8. The phrases below describe what culture?

   • Used cuneiform as a writing system
   • Was organized into city–states
   • Used Hammurabi's Code as the system of law

   (A) Egypt
   (B) Indus
   (C) Mesopotamia
   (D) Huang He
   (E) Olmecs

9. The Egyptians were to the Nile as the Chinese were to the
   (A) Tigris
   (B) Euphrates
   (C) Yellow
   (D) Indus
   (E) Ganges

10. All of the early river valley civilizations were
    (A) City–states
    (B) Polytheistic
    (C) Law givers
    (D) Superstitious
    (E) In Europe

11. The Chinese system of Mandate of Heaven refers to
    (A) the power granted to the ruler from the heavens.
    (B) the belief that China was superior to the rest of the world.
    (C) the emperor's obligation to give laws to his people.
    (D) the never ending power of the emperor.
    (E) the belief in many gods.

12. The Indus civilization is still somewhat of a mystery to archeologists because
    (A) the Aryans destroyed all the remains of the civilization.
    (B) the writing system has not been deciphered.
    (C) the small size of the civilization makes it difficult to excavate.
    (D) its isolation from the rest of the world limited trade and diffusion.
    (E) their religious beliefs have no influence on religion in India today.

13. The period known as the "Era of Warring States" refers to
    (A) the nomadic invasions that brought an end to the Roman empire.
    (B) the period of disorder in China before the establishment of the Qin dynasty.
    (C) the transition from republic to empire in Rome.
    (D) the revolt that ended the reign of the first Emperor of China.
    (E) the period of rule in India during which only regional kingdoms maintained power.

14. What ideas do Hinduism and Buddhism have in common?
    (A) Universal salvation
    (B) Reincarnation
    (C) The caste system
    (D) Monotheism
    (E) Heaven and hell

15. Which of the following religions both used missionaries to spread their message?
    (A) Hinduism and Buddhism
    (B) Judaism and Christianity
    (C) Confucianism and Daoism
    (D) Buddhism and Daoism
    (E) Christianity and Buddhism

16. All of the following pairs of individuals influenced the same region EXCEPT
    (A) Confucius and Laozi
    (B) Ashoka and Siddhartha Gautama
    (C) Socrates and Alexander
    (D) Wu Di and Chandra Gupta
    (E) Constantine and Jesus

17. The social hierarchies of both Hinduism and Confucianism demonstrate the value of

    (A) Peasants
    (B) Landowners
    (C) Government officials
    (D) Scholars
    (E) Women

18. The Mauryan and Gupta Empires demonstrated India's

    (A) long and consistent history of imperial rule.
    (B) interruption in its political control marked by regional kingdoms.
    (C) large influence of Islamic rule and culture.
    (D) history of rule by nomadic invaders.
    (E) consistent imperial reinforcement of Hindu values.

19. Which statement most accurately compares the fall of the Han and Roman empires?

    (A) Both empires were severely hurt by the decrease in trade.
    (B) Nomadic invasions were more of a problem in Han than in Rome.
    (C) Regional authorities held more political power than imperial authorities.
    (D) Leaders were assassinated in both empires.
    (E) Large landowners successfully avoided tax collectors.

20. Long-distance trade flourished in the classical societies because

    (A) many merchants could travel the entire length of the Silk Road.
    (B) the Imperial powers kept trade routes safe and secure.
    (C) Chinese emissaries negotiated with Roman officials.
    (D) India remained centrally ruled throughout the period.
    (E) the use of the compass facilitated travel.

21. Which two religions gave women access to spiritual salvation?

    (A) Daoism and Christianity
    (B) Confucianism and Buddhism
    (C) Daoism and Confucianism
    (D) Buddhism and Christianity
    (E) Confucianism and Judaism

22. Both Greek and Chinese traditional societies had a(n)

    (A) Dependence on slavery for labor
    (B) Fluid social structure
    (C) Unbroken dynastic cycle
    (D) Authoritarian patriarchal family structure
    (E) Decentralized political structure

23. Which of the following is true of both the Qin and Han dynasties?

    (A) Confucianism was the philosophical basis of the government.
    (B) The merchant class was highly regarded.
    (C) The central government was strong.
    (D) Trade was discouraged.
    (E) Buddhism influenced each empire.

24. Which of the following civilizations was characterized by government participation by its citizens?
    (A) China
    (B) India
    (C) Persia
    (D) Egypt
    (E) Rome

25. Which of the following was NOT a factor in the Bantu migrations?
    (A) Population pressures
    (B) Use of iron tools
    (C) Cultivation of bananas
    (D) Spread of agriculture
    (E) Desertification

Document-Based Question

Directions: The following question is based on the accompanying Documents 1 to 4. (The documents have been edited for the purpose of this exercise.)

This question is designed to test your ability to work with and understand historical documents. Write an essay that:
- Has a relevant thesis and supports that thesis with evidence from the documents.
- Uses all of the documents.
- Analyzes the documents by grouping them in as many appropriate ways as possible. **Does not simply summarize the documents individually**.
- Takes into account the sources of the documents and analyzes the authors' points of view.
- Explains the need for at least one additional type of document.

You may refer to relevant historical information not mentioned in the documents.

Based on the following documents, analyze and describe the traditional role of women in China.

Document 1

Source: Liu Hsiang (first century BCE) a renowned scholar, editor, and author, *Biographies of Admirable Women*, this selection is about the mother of the great Confucian philosopher Mencius.

His mother answered, "A woman's duties are to cook the five grains, heat the wine, look after her parents-in-law, make clothes, and that is all! Therefore she cultivates the skills required in the women's quarters and has no ambition to manage affairs outside of her house. The *Book of Change* says, 'In her central place, she attends to the preparation of food.' The *Book of Poetry* says, 'It will be theirs neither to do wrong nor to do good,/ Only about the spirits and the food will they have to think.' This means that a woman's duty is not to control or to take charge. Instead she must follow the 'three submissions.' When she is young, she must submit to her parents. After marriage, she must submit to her husband. When she is widowed, she must submit to her son."

Document 2

Source: Ban Zhao, in the first century CE, China's foremost female scholar, imperial historian, poet, and tutor of an empress.

Womanly Qualifications

A woman (ought to) have four qualifications: (1) womanly virtue; (2) womanly words; (3) womanly bearing; and (4) womanly work. Now what is called womanly virtue need not be brilliant ability, exceptionally different from others. Womanly words need be neither clever in debate nor keen in conversation. Womanly appearance requires neither a pretty nor a perfect face and form. Womanly work need not be work done more skillfully than that of others.

To guard carefully her chastity; to control circumspectly her behavior; in every motion to exhibit modesty; and to model each act on the best usage, this is womanly virtue.

To chose her words with care; to avoid vulgar language; to speak at appropriate times; and not to weary others (with much conversation), may be called the characteristics of womanly words.

To wash and scrub filth away; to keep clothes and ornaments fresh and clean; to wash the head and bathe the body regularly, and to keep the person free from disgraceful filth, may be called the characteristics of womanly bearing.

Continued →

> With whole-hearted devotion to sew and to weave; to love not gossip and silly laughing; in cleanliness and order (to prepare) the wine and food for serving guests, may be called the characteristics of womanly work.
>
> These four qualifications characterize the greatest virtue of a woman. No woman can afford to be without them. In fact they are very easy to possess if a woman only treasures them in the heart. The ancient had a saying: "Is Love afar off?" If I desire love, then love is at hand!" So can it be said of these qualifications.

Document 3

> Source: Fu Xuan, 217–278 CE. A noted Chinese poet and philosopher of the Western Jin Dynasty
>
> How sad it is to be a woman:
> Nothing on earth is held so cheap.
> Boys stand leaning at the door
> Like Gods fallen out of Heaven.
> Their hearts brave the Four Oceans,
> The wind and dust of a thousand miles.
> No one is glad when a girl is born:
> By *her* the family sets no store.
> When she grows up, she hides in her room
> Afraid to look a man in the face.
>
> No one cries when she leaves her home—
> Sudden as clouds when the rain stops.
> She bows and kneels countless times.
> She must humble herself even to the servants.
> *His* love is distant as the stars in Heaven,
> Yet the sunflower bends toward the sun.
> Their hearts more sundered than water and fire—
> A hundred evils are heaped upon her.
> Her face will follow the years' changes:
> Her lord will find new pleasures.

Document 4

> Source: A Buddhist song. This text was found among the ancient Buddhist writing unearthed from the caves at Dunhuang
>
> At ten, like a flowering branch in the rain,
> She is slender, delicate, and full of grace.
> Her parents are themselves as young as the rising moon
> And do not allow her past the red curtain without a reason.
>
> At twenty, receiving the hairpin, she is a spring bud.
> Her parents arrange her betrothal; the matter's well done.
> A fragrant carriage comes at evening to carry her to her lord.
> Like Hsiao-shih and his wife, at dawn they depart with the clouds.
>
> At forty she is mistress of a prosperous house and makes plans.
> Three sons and five daughters give her some trouble.
> With her ch'in not far away, she toils always at her loom,
> Her only fear that the sun will set too soon.
>
> At fifty, afraid of her husband's dislike,
> She strains to please him with every charm,
> Trying to remember the many tricks she had learned since the age of sixteen.
> No longer is she afraid of mothers- and sisters-in-law.
>
> At sixty, face wrinkled and hair like silk thread,
> She walks unsteadily and speaks little.
> Distresses that her sons can find no brides.
> Grieved that her daughters have departed for their husband's homes.
>
> At seventy, frail and thin, but not knowing what to do about it,
> She is no longer able to learn the Buddhist Law even if she tries.
> In the morning a light breeze
> Makes her joints crack like clanging gongs.
>
> At eighty, eyes blinded and ears half-dead,
> When she goes out she cannot tell north from east,
> Dreaming always of departed loves.
> Who persuade her to charm the dying breeze.
>
> At ninety, the glow fades like spent lighting.
> Human affairs are no longer her concern.
> Lying on a pillow, solitary on her high bed,
> She resembles the dying leaves that fall in autumn.
>
> At a hundred, like a cliff crumbling in the wind,
> For her body it is the moment to become dust.
> Children and grandchildren will perform sacrifices to her spirit
> And clear moonlight will forever illuminate her patch of earth.

Change-Over-Time Question

Directions: You are to answer the following question: You should spend 5 minutes organizing or outlining your essay. Write an essay that:

- Has a relevant thesis and supports that thesis with appropriate historical evidence.
- Addresses all parts of the question.
- Uses historical context to show change over time and/or continuities.
- Analyzes the process of change over time/or continuity.

> Describe and analyze the spread, changes, and impact of a religion/belief system on a civilization, from the origin of the religion/belief system up to 600 CE. Be sure to discuss continuities as well as changes to the civilization as a result of that religion/belief system. Choose ONE from below:
>
> Hinduism: India
> Confucianism: China
> Christianity: Roman Empire

Comparative Question

Directions: You are to answer the following question: You should spend 5 minutes organizing or outlining your essay. Write an essay that:

- Has a relevant thesis and supports that thesis with appropriate historical evidence.
- Addresses all parts of the question.
- Makes direct, relevant comparisons.
- Analyzes relevant reasons for similarities and differences.

> Discuss the major similarities and differences between the collapses of TWO of the following empires:

Rome
Han
Gupta

_____
_____
_____
_____
_____
_____
_____
_____
_____
_____
_____
_____
_____
_____

ANSWERS AND EXPLANATIONS

1. E

The development of agriculture, growth in world population, use of metal technology, and writing all occurred in this period. However, the use of gunpowder technology did not begin until the time period 600 to 1450, during the Song dynasty.

2. A

The Neolithic Revolution was a gradual event that probably started with experimentation with seeds. Farming is something that developed gradually, over a long period of time.

3. C

The Mauryan dynasty was located in India, South Asia.

4. B

In hunting and gathering communities, populations remained low because of the scarcity of food and the need to move. The development of agriculture allowed these communities to develop permanent homes and have larger families.

5. B

Both pastoral nomads and settled farmers rely on the domestication of animals for their economic survival.

6. B

The development of farming led to a division of labor. Work that was conducted outside the home was deemed more valuable than work conducted inside the home.

7. E

Representative government was not a characteristic of early civilizations. Most of these civilizations were ruled by a small elite class.

8. C

Mesopotamia used cuneiform as a writing system; was organized into city–states; and used Hammurabi's Code as the system of law. (Hammurabi was an important ruler of the area.) Of the answer choices, this is the only culture that used cuneiform. Egypt used hieroglyphics.

9. C

Early Chinese civilization developed along the Yellow, or Huang He River. The Tigris and Euphrates were in Mesopotamia. The Indus River and the Ganges River are in India.

10. B

Though some of the early civilization such as Mesopotamia were organized into city–states, others such as Egypt were organized into kingdoms. All of the civilizations were, however, polytheistic.

11. A

The Mandate of Heaven is the belief that the gods have granted power to the ruler, but that power can also be taken away. Certain signs indicate the loss of the mandate such as floods, peasant revolts, and nomadic invasions.

12. B

Although the Indus civilization was discovered in the early 20th century, the writing system found on clay seals has yet to be deciphered.

13. B

The Era of Warring States was a period of hundreds of years when no one state could control China; instead the smaller states battled each other for control.

14. B

The rebirth of the soul or reincarnation is an essential belief of both Hindus and Buddhists, who both believe that it takes many lives to accumulate the necessary amount of karma to be released from the cycle of rebirth.

15. E

Both Christianity and Buddhism are considered universal religions, meaning that they are open to all people. Universal religions are also often associated with a missionary component, which spreads the belief to new converts.

16. D

Wu Di was an emperor of the Han dynasty in China (East Asia). Chandra Gupta was the first ruler of the Mauryan empire in India (South Asia).

17. D

In both Hinduism and Confucianism, scholars are highly regarded. The highest caste in Hinduism is the Brahmin class, which consisted of priests and scholars. Confucius taught that learning separated the inferior man from the superior man.

18. B

Most of India's history is characterized by a decentralized government of regional kingdoms. Both the Mauryan and Gupta empires were successfully able to centralize large parts of the Indian subcontinent.

19. E

Neither the Han nor the Roman empire was able to collect sufficient tax funds. In both cases, large landowners avoided paying taxes. In fact, they often protected peasants on their land who were attempting to escape the tax collectors.

20. **B**

If trade routes were safe and well maintained, long-distance trade flourished. Oftentimes, when imperial rule weakened, roads were not long maintained. Travel became unsafe, and trade would decline as a result.

21. **D**

Both Buddhism and Christianity preached that women and men had equal access to salvation, though their equality on earth was not guaranteed.

22. **D**

Both Greek and Chinese traditional societies were patriarchal: The man was considered the head of the household and the most respected member.

23. **C**

The Qin used a strict legalist philosophy to rule, while the Han placed a strong emphasis on Confucianism. However, in order to keep their empires organized, both societies used a strong central government with a powerful emperor.

24. **E**

In the early days of Rome, the government was a republic, which meant that the citizens chose representatives to rule for them. Rome had a senate, which passed laws and made decisions for its people, but as the city grew into an empire, the senate lost most of its power to an all-powerful emperor.

25. **E**

The use of agriculture led to population pressure, which contributed to the Bantu migration. Also, the use of iron tools allowed for more land to be available for cultivation, which in turn caused population growth. Finally, the cultivation of bananas allowed people to move into new areas.

Document-Based Question: Sample Response

The traditional role of women in China has been shaped by philosophical beliefs such as Confucianism. According to the documents, the traditional role of women has been inferior and subservient to men, but women were expected to conduct themselves with proper behavior and teach that behavior to their children. In the end, women held a special place in the family in which they would be respected and eventually worshipped as an ancestor.

In China's patriarchal society, a woman's traditional role was one of subservience. In the excerpt from Biographies of Admirable Women by Liu Hsiang, Mencius's mother describes the subservient role of women. She is always in a place of submission, whether to her parents, husband, or son. Liu Hsiang's purpose is to use the mother of Mencius, a Confucian scholar, to reinforce and promote the idea of proper Confucian behavior in women. In the poem, written by Fu Xuan, women's lives are described as sad and cheap compared to men. No one is glad when a girl in born, but everyone is elated when a boy is born. Unlike the birth of a boy, which is viewed as a wealth-gaining opportunity, the birth of a girl is seen as a burden to the family. This poem written by a noted Chinese poet and philosopher of the Western Jin dynasty expresses a generalized view of women and does not offer specific evidence to support these ideas, but the emotions of the poem communicate the author's pity for the plight of women. It would be helpful to know a Chinese woman's interpretation of the poem. Would a woman living in China during this time believe that her life was both sad and cheap? According to a Buddhist song, which expresses an ideal role of women, girls are protected at age 10 and rely on a proper marriage arranged by her parents, but as she grows up her role changes. This ancient Buddhist writing was unearthed from the caves at Dunhuang. It would be helpful to know if lower-class and higher-class women in China shared the feeling of this song, in order to judge if women's roles varied according to class.

Like other members of Chinese society, women were expected to behave in a proper way and set an example for others to follow. The excerpt from Biographies of Admirable Women states that the woman is to know her place and focus on cooking, looking after her parents-in-law, and making clothes, and that she should have no outside ambition. According to a Buddhist song, women were expected to serve as the mistress of the home and, as had been done for her, focus on arranging a proper marriage for her children. As a dutiful wife, she must continue to please her husband throughout the marriage, though as the cycle of life continues, her children leave home and her role continues to change. According to Ban Zhao, China's foremost female scholar in the first century CE, a woman must have certain qualifications which include virtue, words, bearing, and work. A woman must exhibit modesty, avoid any use of vulgar language, and speak only during appropriate times. She should focus on her work at home and keep a clean and orderly home. This document, written by a female who served as the imperial historian, poet, and tutor of an empress, expresses an idealized view of women whose purpose was to communicate the proper and ideal behavior desired by women in Chinese society. It would be helpful to also see a first-hand account of a woman's life in the form of a diary entry, to see if it agreed with Ban Zhao's view of the role of women. Additionally, knowing the views of women outside of China would serve as a helpful comparison: One could judge if the role of women in China was characteristic of the time or more particular to traditional Chinese beliefs.

The examination of a poem, a Buddhist song, and the writing of an imperial female scholar clearly communicate the traditional role of women in Chinese society. In China's patriarchal society, women were subservient to men, were expected to follow the model of an ideal female, and were expected to run the workings of the household. Reinforced by philosophical beliefs such as Confucianism, these traditional roles for Chinese women shaped the lives of women throughout most of history.

Change-Over-Time Question: Sample Response

Christianity had both a political and cultural impact on the Roman Empire from the birth of Christ to the fall of the empire because of its missionary thrust and its eventually political support. The religion also appealed to both the lower class and women remained throughout the period. Although Christianity was at first rejected by Roman authorities and the Christians were treated as scapegoats, it was eventually accepted by Roman authorities and gained a privileged status.

Around the turn of the millennium, the Roman Empire was culturally influenced by polytheistic beliefs. The emperor himself was to be worshipped as a god. Though the empire was culturally tolerant, the Jews, who were monotheistic, could not worship the Roman gods or the emperor. It was in this environment that Jesus was born. His message was one of forgiveness, love, and the promise of salvation for those who believed. The Roman authorities believed Jesus was a threat to their power, and he was sentenced to death. It was not until Jesus died, however, that his message began to spread widely. One follower, Paul, began to convert Jews as well as non-Jews to Christianity. This helped to make Christianity a universal religion. The Christians, a minority group, were often persecuted by Roman authorities and used as scapegoats, and as a result many became martyrs. It was this martyrdom that helped the religion to spread further. Christianity's message especially appealed to the lower class and women because of the promise of salvation for all who believe, not just wealthy men.

Christianity's fate drastically changed during the rule of the Roman emperor Constantine. The emperor's mother was a Christian and so he issued the Edict of Milan, making Christianity legal in the Roman Empire. This political acceptance transformed Christianity from a fringe, persecuted cultural and religious group to one that had the favor of the emperor himself. This political fortune of Christianity improved even more when Emperor Theodosius made Christianity the official religion of the Roman Empire. For those who wanted political acceptance, conversion to Christianity was the path to follow. Additionally, with government support, missionaries could travel to all parts of the Empire to spread the word. The Church became more organized and gained land from its government support. Some historians even argue that devotion to Christianity replaced devotion to Rome and the emperor, and may have contributed to the fall of the empire. Regardless, Christianity's political support allowed it to get organized, so much so, that when the empire did fall, the Church replaced it as the centralizing force in the region.

Christianity and the Roman Empire started with a less-than-favorable relationship. Jesus, with his idea of the kingdom of God, was viewed as threatening to the Roman power. But his message of peace, forgiveness, and salvation remained powerful and influential enough to attract many converts, despite the government persecution. The relationship, however, reversed toward the end of the Roman Empire, when Christianity received official government patronage. Christianity, like another universal religion-Buddhism-benefited from its missionary approach and most of all, the political patronage of the powers that be.

Comparative Question: Sample Response

The great classical empires of Rome and Han dominated much of Eurasia for hundreds of years. Their strength and stability allowed for great advancement and trade to flourish. Similar economic and political factors led the collapse of both empires, such as difficulty collecting taxes and government corruption. Yet the effects they saw from a decline in trade differed, as did their timing and involvement of nomadic invasions in their demise.

Both the Roman and Han Empires had great difficulty sustaining a strong tax collection system toward the end of their empires. In the Han Empire, scholar officials were often exempt from taxes, and peasants were subject to high taxes. As the empire was weakening, peasants often fled from the tax collectors to the estates of the scholar officials. The result was an unstable empire-financially unable to maintain its public works. Similarly in Rome, the rich landowning class often resisted paying their taxes. They were able to do this because of the private armies they had amassed to protect their land. Just like in the Han Empire, Roman peasants began to seek refuge from tax collectors on these estates. Additionally, Church land was not taxable and toward the end of the empire, the Church had amassed a great deal of land and power. Rome's inability to collect sufficient taxes led to a decline in the maintenance of its famous system of roads. This, in turn, led to a decline in trade. Rome had become economically interdependent with various parts of its empire, and this decline in trade further weakened the empire. The Han empire also had difficulty maintaining the safety and stability of its trade routes and roads. That, however, had less of an impact on the empire's fall because the Chinese economy was much more self-sufficient than that of Rome.

Politically, both governments had serious problems with corruption. In the Han Empire, the emperor began to rely on the advice of his court officials who often advised him in ways that promoted their own interests. Away in his palace, the emperor was quite isolated from his empire, and could not see for himself the poor advice he was being given. Throughout it all, though, the emperor did maintain his power. In Rome, being an emperor was a much more dangerous and short-lived job. From 235 to 284 CE, 25 of 26 emperors died a violent death. This constant change in leadership and the power struggles that ensued left the Roman government in disarray. Additionally, the empire had been divided into two sections: the eastern section remained strong, while the western section weakened significantly. In both empires, nomadic invasions damaged the political hold on the area. In the Han Empire, the Xiongnu invaded China, but only after the empire had already fallen. This occurred because the empire could no longer provide them with the goods they required. This set off a wave of nomadic migrations that would eventually make its way to the Roman empire. As nomads continued to migrate, they put pressure on other nomadic groups to move, often into settled land. The Roman army had great difficulty defending itself against the movement of such groups as the Ostrogoths, Huns, and Visigoths. The great city of Rome was eventually sacked by the Visigoths in 476 CE, bringing an end to the western portion of the empire.

As the great empires came to an end, it became clear that the key to maintaining a great empire is the ability to collect sufficient taxes to pay for the services needed by the population. Without sufficient tax revenue, the Han and Roman Empires could not sufficiently maintain their empires, protect their people, or continue to trade.

Part Three: AP World History Review | 103

Chapter 4: 600 to 1450

- The Big Picture
- Why This Periodization?
- Post-Classical Political Developments
- Nomadic Empires
- Impact of Interaction
- Recovery and Renaissance in Asia and Europe
- American Civilizations

THE BIG PICTURE

1. Patterns and effects of interactions among major societies and regions: trade, war, diplomacy, and international organizations

    In other words: **What happens when people come in contact with each other?**

This time period witnessed a tremendous growth in long-distance trade through the Silk Road, the Indian Ocean, Trans-Saharan trade, and the Mediterranean Sea. During the period known as Pax Mongolia, when peace and order was established due to the vast Mongol empire, trade and interaction were at their height.

2. The dynamics of change and continuity across the world history periods covered in this course, and the causes and processes involved in major changes of these dynamics.

    In other words: **Why do some things change while other things stay the same?**

The major changes that occurred in this time period were that the classical empires had fallen and new political units of organization developed globally to respond to new challenges. Additionally, the nomadic migrations of groups like the Turks and Mongols caused major change throughout the world. Some things remained the same. Religion continued to be important in societies and continued to spread. Trade routes established in the classical period continued to grow in importance and most societies had patriarchal gender structures.

3. The effects of technology, economics, and demography on people and the environment (population growth and decline, disease, labor systems, manufacturing, migrations, agriculture, weaponry)

   In other words: **How does the development of new technology and movement of people affect the world?**

Major technological developments shaped the development of the world including the compass, improved ship building technology, and gunpowder. The movement of people including the Bantus, Turks, Mongols, and Vikings greatly altered our world. One of the worst epidemic diseases in history, the Bubonic Plague (or Black Death), spread during this period due to the movement of people and the increase in interaction.

4. Systems of social structure and gender structure (comparing major features within and among societies and assessing change)

   In other words: **How do societies organize themselves socially, and what roles do men and women play?**

Although most societies continued to reinforce their patriarchal nature and strict social structure, the spread of universal religions had some effects. Religions such as Islam, Christianity, and Buddhism preached the equality of all believers and this seemed to be the case, at least, in the eyes of God. The monastic life of both Buddhism and Christianity offered an alternative path for women.

5. Cultural, intellectual, and religious developments and interactions among and within societies

   In other words: **How do people identify themselves and express themselves culturally and intellectually?**

The spread of religion during this time period often acted as a unifying force. For example, Christianity and the Church served as the centralizing force in Western Europe during most of this period. Also, the spread of Confucianism and Buddhism throughout East Asia solidified a cultural identity in those areas. The new religion of Islam created a new cultural world known as Dar al-Islam which transcended political boundaries.

6. Changes in functions and structures of states and in attitudes toward states and political identities (political culture), including the emergence of the nation-state (types of political organization)

   In other words: **How do people govern themselves?**

Following the fall of the classical empires, the political structures of many areas adapted and changed to the new conditions of the world. Centralized empires like the Byzantine, Arab Caliphates, and the Tang and Song dynasties built off the successful models of the past. Decentralized areas like Western Europe and Japan developed political organization that more effectively dealt with their unique issues. The movements of the Mongols altered much of Asia's political structure for a time. Finally, the recovery from the Mongol period introduced political structures that defined many areas for centuries to follow.

WHY THIS PERIODIZATION?

This unit begins in 600 CE after the great classical civilizations of the Foundations period fell and the world seemed to be in a period of recovery. Both China and Europe went through periods of decentralization in their recovery. China eventually reunited as an imperial empire, but the Roman Empire never successfully reunited in Europe, and regional kingdoms developed there instead.

The new player on the scene is Islam. This new religion and identity develops as the chapter begins, and will have far-reaching consequences culturally, politically, economically, and intellectually throughout the period. Additionally, the world is more integrated than ever—thanks to the movement of nomads like the Turks and Mongols, the increase in long-distance trade, and the continual spread of religion. As the period comes to a close in 1450 CE, the world shifts once again as Europeans look outward and explore the world, with the help of "southern" technology and ideas.

POST-CLASSICAL POLITICAL DEVELOPMENTS

"New" Empires

After the fall of the Han and Roman Empires, a form of political centralization will eventually return in part of the world: China, the former Eastern Roman Empire (now known as the Byzantine Empire, and a new player—the Islamic Caliphates.

Tang Dynasty (618 to 907 CE)

Political Development

Following the fall of the Han dynasty, China returned to regional small kingdoms for the next 400 years. It was not until 581 CE that the Sui dynasty reunited China. This short-lived but influential dynasty used Buddhism and the Confucian civil service system to establish legitimacy. In addition, it started the construction of the Grand Canal, and launched numerous military campaigns to expand the empire. Rebellions overthrew the empire in 618, but it had laid an important foundation for future dynasties to follow.

The Tang dynasty that followed was more focused on scholars than on soldiers. It did, however, expand its territory beyond China proper to Tibet and Korea. It also completed the Grand Canal and offered support to Buddhism, Daoism, and Confucianism. The capital, Changan, was a major political center, to which foreign diplomats visited from the Byzantine and Arab worlds. Confucian beliefs were further solidified into the Chinese government through the examination system.

In the middle of the 8th century, Tang power began to decline as higher taxation created tension within the population. Peasant rebellions led to more independent regional rule and to the abdication of the emperor. After this, there was a period of rule by regional warlords for the next 50 years.

Economic Developments

The dynasty established military garrisons as far out as Kashgar, which allowed for the protection and security of **Silk Road** trade. An **equal field system** was established, in which all peasants were given land in return for tax in grain and corvee, and at death they were to return it back to the government. Even with this system, however, the Tang had difficulty breaking the power of the large landowners.

Changan was a major trading center and cosmopolitan city. The West Market there flourished with Indian, Iranian, Syrian, and Arab traders and their goods. By 640, its population reached 2 million, making it the largest city in the world at that time.

Cultural Developments

Culturally, the Tang dynasty was heavily influenced by the spread of **Buddhism**. **Empress Wu**, originally the emperor's concubine, amassed her own personal power, and in 690 was given the title of Heavenly Empress. Concerned (or possibly obsessed) with any possible threat to her power, she had thousands of the emperor's concubines killed and had their sons banned from office. On a more positive note, she started a school dedicated to Buddhist and Confucian scholarship. Her support for Buddhism, and in particular its art, increased the religion's influence throughout China.

Buddhism experienced a serious backlash toward the end of the dynasty. This "foreign religion" was attacked for the economic and political power it had obtained. From 841 to 845 CE, an **anti-Buddhist campaign** destroyed many monasteries and seriously weakened the religion's influence on China. In the wake of this backlash, NeoConfucianism developed: Confucian scholars wanted a new form of Confucianism that would limit foreign influence. The result was an incorporation of Buddhist and Confucian ideas. Some ideas included individual self-improvement, the idea that human beings are good, and the goal to strive and perfect oneself.

Women's marriages during the Tang dynasty were arranged within their own social class, but upper-class women could own property, move about in public, and even remarry. If all other heirs had died, women could inherit property. Poetry flourished with such poets as **Li Bai** and **Du Fu**.

Influence

NeoConfucianism moved to the forefront of Chinese philosophy and was also very influential in Japan and Korea. Neighboring peoples became tributary states that had to pay honor to China. Delegations from the "outside," such as Japan or Siam, had to show great deference to the Chinese emperor and performed the kowtow—a prostrate bow during which one touches one's head to the ground multiple times—in the imperial presence. This furthered the Chinese self-perception of being superior to all foreigners.

Song Dynasty (960 to 1279 CE)

Political Development

By 960, the Song dynasty had reestablished centralized control over China. The civil service exam system retained great prominence during this period. It successfully checked the power of the landed aristocracy and developed alongside a powerful, moral elite. Upward mobility existed through the exam system, but it took place very rarely. The Song de-emphasized a military approach, and instead reestablished the **tribute system** with its nomad neighbors. This was a system of literally "paying off" the nomads with such gifts as bolts of silk to keep the peace.

The Song, however, experienced military and economic weakness. The scholar-controlled professional army was often ineffective, and too much paper money in circulation caused inflation. By 1126, they had lost the northern half of the empire to nomads. The Southern Song continued to flourish unitl 1274. However, military threats from the north continued, and finally the greatest of all northern groups invaded in the 1200s, absorbing the Song dynasty into the new Mongol Empire.

Economic Development

Historians often refer to the developments during the Song dynasty as an **economic revolution**. Rice production doubled due to the new fast-ripening rice from Champa. Internal trade from the Yellow Sea and Grand Canal flourished due to the increased number of merchants, the growth in population, and the capital of Kaifeng became a **manufacturing center** with its production of cannons, moveable type printing, water-powered mills, looms, and high quality porcelain. China had more per capita production than any other country in the world. Minted copper coins were used as cash and eventually replaced with paper currency. Officials collected taxes in cash—not goods—and letters of credit (known as flying cash) were used by merchants.

The Southern Song established their capital at **Hangzhou**, and though this smaller area had less taxable land, commerce soared. With their cotton sails and **magnetic compasses**, the Song had the most powerful navy in the world, and eventually, the availability of more goods for sale. As a result, the dynasty's power shifted from the north to the south, and the Song became the leaders in Afro-Eurasian trade. Song goods traveled to Southeast Asia, India, Persia, and East Africa.

Tang and Song Innovations

- The first use of the compass to aid maritime navigation
- A water-powered clock, demonstrating facility in mechanical engineering
- The invention of gunpowder—first demonstrated during the late 1000s CE, the explosive combination of sulfur and saltpeter would alter weapons technology forever and lead to the first cannons, rockets, and incendiary bombs
- Philosophy—neo-Confucian thought delved into the ancient texts and further codified traditional Chinese philosophy. It blended Confucianism with elements of Daoism and Buddhism.
- Urbanization, with some cities exceeding one million inhabitants
- A printing press with movable type
- Stylized and symbolic landscape painting
- Paper money
- Flying cash

Cultural Developments

During the Song dynasty, women were entitled to keep their dowries and had access to new jobs such as merchants, but they also were the subject of a practice called **footbinding**. The practice originated with the aristocratic class, copying the emperor's concubines or Turkish dancers at court, and was viewed as a sign of wealth and status. Girls as young as 6 or 7 had their feet bound to create "lily-like" feet in order to secure a better marriage. The result was an increase in the restriction of freedom of women.

Islamic Caliphates

Islam: The Religion

Prior to the introduction of Islam, Arabs lived in separate, loyal, tribal groups, and were often involved in overland and maritime trade. The city of Mecca was an important religious site with a large influx or traders and pilgrims. The **Kaaba**, a black meteorite placed in the Great Mosque by Abraham, was in the center of the city. Most people practiced an animist type of religion that involved the worship of idols.

Arabia

Mohammed was born in 570 CE in Mecca and later married a merchant widow named Khadija. Together, they traveled on caravans and met Jews, Zoroastrians, and Christians. When Mohammed was 40, the angel Gabriel appeared to him as he was sleeping in a cave and revealed that he had been selected to receive divine inspiration. The message was that there was only one all-powerful and all-knowing God, **Allah**. Mohammed, who claimed to have no supernatural powers himself, was to be God's messenger.

Mohammed preached that all people were to submit to Allah and that everyone was equal in the eyes of Allah. All would face a final day of judgment; those who had submitted to God would go to heaven, and those who had not would go to hell. Mohammed's message was not met with enthusiasm in Mecca, and he fled to Medina in 622, a journey known as the hegira.

Mohammed's message was quite popular in Medina, where he was viewed as a prophet and a political leader. Further organizing his new religion, he taught that he was the last of a long line of prophets from the Jewish and Christian scriptures that included Abraham, Moses, David, and Jesus. In 630, he and his followers returned to **Mecca**, captured the city, and destroyed the idols.

After his death, Mohammed's revelations were written down by his followers in the **Quran**, which is believed to be the actual words of God as revealed to Mohammed. The word *Islam* means "submission" to God's will.

Islam is based on five duties (called **Pillars**) that define the faith. These are:

1. There is no god but Allah, and Mohammed is his messenger.
2. Pray five times a day facing Mecca.
3. Give alms (charity) to the poor.
4. Fast during the holy month of Ramadan.
5. Make a pilgrimage or hajj to Mecca during one's lifetime if able.

Islam is a **universal religion** that is open to everyone. It promises salvation to all who believe and follow the rules, which are easy to understand. Islam appealed to women because they had equal status to men before God, they could keep their dowries as wives, and there was a prohibition on female infanticide. Like Christianity, Islam appealed to the poor and powerless, and it gave the community a strong sense of brotherhood.

Political Development

By the time of Mohammed's death two years later, almost all of Arabia was under Islamic control. There was disagreement, however, over his successor. One group, the Shia, believed that the leader should be a descendant of Mohammed. The other group, the Sunni, prefered that it be the wisest member of the strongest tribe.

After the first four caliphs, the **Umayyad clan** took control in 661 CE and transformed the caliphate into a hereditary monarchy, with its government centered in Damascus. They continued on to conquer Syria, Egypt, Persia, Byzantine territory in West Asia, North Africa, and Spain. Their military skills, the soldiers' commitment to Islam, and the promise of plunder helped them in these successful conquests. The Umayyad Caliphate set up a bureaucratic structure in which local administrators governed the areas. All cultures were tolerated as long as they obeyed the rules, paid their taxes, and did not revolt. Arabic became the language of administration, business, law, and trade.

The **Abbasid Caliphate** moved the center of the empire to Baghdad, a political and commercial center. At the time it was the second largest city in the world next to Changan. However, the Abbasid Caliphate's size made it difficult to control, and the use of slaves weakened the empire. These slaves, the Mamluks, served in the army and weakened Abbasid rule. By the mid-9th century, the Abbasid political authority had become only symbolic, and the caliphate was broken into smaller states. At the same time, the culture of Islam united the area. The term **Dar al-Islam**, or "all under Islam" refers to the areas that share a common Muslim culture as a basis for society.

Economic Developments

Trade flourished throughout the caliphate and beyond, as Muslim merchants relied on a common set of rules. Improved irrigation led to great production of agriculture and an increase in tax revenues. Artisans flourished in the cities as they became centers for manufacturing pottery, fabrics, and rugs. Paper was imported from China, and soon, paper mills were set up.

Cultural Developments

Mosques, hospitals, schools, and orphanages were built throughout the empire. Intellectual developments took place such as algebra, the concept of longitude and latitude, and the study of Greek philosophers such as Aristotle. **The House of Wisdom** built in Baghdad in 830 sought out Greek and Persian texts and translated them into Arabic. Universities were established in Cordoba, Toledo, and Granada. In art and architecture, the use of images was forbidden (remember the idol worship), so instead, the use of geometric shapes and calligraphy were used in their works.

Influence

Even though the Caliphate declined and ended with the Mongol invasions, the influence of Islam continued to spread throughout the period. Islam spread to West Africa through Trans-Saharan trade, to East Africa and Southeast Asia through Indian Ocean trade, to Central Asia and China through the Silk Road, and to India through the migrations of the Turks. By the conclusion of this period, Dar al-Islam had developed into one of the most dominant influences throughout the eastern hemisphere.

Byzantine Empire (4th century to 1453 CE)

Political Development

The Byzantine Empire, a continuation of the **Eastern Roman Empire**, was the only survivor from the classical age. The Roman Empire had officially been divided into east and west in 375 CE, with the western half severely weakened because the east produced the majority of grain and controlled the major trade routes.

The most famous emperor, Justinian, who ruled from 527 to 565 CE, tried unsuccessfully to reconquer Western Rome. His laws, however, were a success. His Body of Civil Law (**Justinian's Code**) was based on the Roman Twelve Tables of Law. Justinian controlled both political and religious power in his empire, and he also replaced Latin with Greek as the official language of the empire.

The strong central government was a hereditary monarchy. It made law, had an efficient military, oversaw effective land distribution, and had a bureaucracy that answered to the emperor. The emperor was considered a friend and imitator of Christ, and as the head of the Church, appointed the patriarch. The empire was divided into themes—or military districts—and military generals were appointed to rule. Free peasants were given land for military service.

Economic Developments

Its location on the Mediterranean Sea contributed to strong trade in the Byzantine Empire. Silk worms were smuggled out of China, which allowed a Byzantine silk industry to develop. Artisans produced glassware, linen, jewelry, gold, and silversmithing.

Cultural Developments

Most subjects spoke Greek, but it was not forced on people. In theory, there was social mobility through the bureaucracy, army, trade, or service to the Church, but in reality, mobility was rare. Constantinople was the political, commercial, and intellectual center, with libraries containing Greek, Latin, Persian, and Hebrew texts.

The Byzantine and Roman Christian churches had been growing apart since the fall of Rome, and a disagreement over the worship of icons—images of saints—seemed to be the final straw. The Pope and the Patriarch each excommunicated each other, and in 1054, the church officially split into the **Roman Catholic Church** and the **Eastern Orthodox Church**. This form of Christianity later spread to the Slavic people and Russia.

Decentralized States

Western Europe—Early Middle Ages (around 500 to 1000 CE)

Political Development

Compared to Byzantium, China, and the Islamic world, Western Europe was at this time considerably backward. Those other societies were able to build centralized governments supported by a bureaucracy, but Western Europe remained politically decentralized. The Franks came closest to reestablishing imperial control with the leadership of Clovis, and later, the Carolingian Empire of **Charlemagne**. Both leaders used the Church to strenghthen their legitimacy, but were unsuccessful in setting up a political structure that could outlast their rule.

Instead, Europe developed a **feudal system**, in which land was given to vassals in exchange for military service and loyalty. This allowed various lords and vassals to gain and compete for power, but left the central authority quite weak. The one centralizing power in this period was the Church and its ruler, the Pope, and by the 13th century, the Church owned one-third of all the land in Europe.

Economic Developments

The absence of a strong central authority led many peasants to seek protection on large estates. These peasants became **serfs**; they had the right to work a portion of the land and could pass that right onto their children, but they could not leave the land. They could keep a portion of what they grew, but the majority of their earnings went to the lord.

These estates became large walled **manors** that were economically self-sufficient. They maintained mills, bakeries, and breweries. They had their own private armies served by armor-clad knights. The introduction of the heavy plow led to an increase in agricultural production, but the surplus was not substantial enough to sustain cities and towns in the early Middle Ages.

Cultural Developments

Birth was the determining factor of one's status. Noblewomen had more power and authority than peasant women and could inherit land if widowed or if without sons. Marriage was the key to political power, and marital alliances were crucial to a family's continued success. Christian nunneries were a way for women to escape their traditional duties.

Beginning in the 12th century, the code of conduct called chivalry developed. It stressed honor, modesty, loyalty, and duty. As warfare decreased, it incorporated courtly romance and knight participation in tournaments to prove their skills.

Christianity was the principal source of religious, moral, and cultural authority throughout the period, and strong papal leadership contributed to this influence. Monasteries were the dominant feature in social and cultural life, and they often had large landholdings. Monks preserved classical knowledge by hand-copying great literature and philosophical works.

Comparative Close up: Political and Social Institutions in Western and Eastern Europe

	Western Europe	Eastern Europe
Political Institutions	Local authority of lord of manor. Central authority was weak.	Absolute power of emperor as centralizing authority supported by bureaucracy.
Social Institutions	Church as social and cultural unifier. Pope is spiritual head and strong centralizing figure. Latin is the language of the Church.	Emperor and Patriarch are co-heads of Church. Greek is the language of Church.

Japan (around 600 to 1000 CE)

Political Development

Japan's geography as a group of islands led to the development of small isolated, independent communities that were often self-sufficient. Clan members cooperated with each other much like a large, extended family. By the 600s, the Yamato clan gained religious and cultural influence on other clans, and wanted to copy China's model of empire-building and create a strong, stable state. Its leaders began to call themselves **emperors of Japan**. They were unsuccessful in creating a centralized state, however, and Japan remained divided by its clans. The Fujiwara clan, which dominated between 710 and 785 CE, sent emissaries to China and modeled their capital, Nara, on Changan. They could not, however, successfully introduce a Chinese-style bureaucracy, and a strict hereditary hierarchy developed instead.

During the Kamakura Shogunate, the emperor and his court kept their capital in Kyoto, yet a military dictatorship existed, ruled by powerful landholding clans. A Japanese form of **feudalism** developed in which the **Shogun**—supreme general—controlled the centralized military government and divided the land into regional units based on military power. The regional military leaders were the **daimyo**, and the warriors who fought for them were the **samurai**. Over the centuries, the samurai military class developed a strict warrior code called bushido.

The emperor remained in power throughout this period, but served only as a symbolic figurehead. Many Shoguns were overthrown, but the emperor was not.

Economic Development

Japan was a predominantly agrarian society with a local artisan class of weavers, carpenters, and ironworkers. Local trade was regulated by clan leaders. Trade and manufacturing developed more in the Kamakura Period, which focused on markets in larger towns and foreign trade with Korea and China.

Most people were peasants who worked on land that was owned by a lord or by Buddhist monasteries. Though their freedom was limited, peasants could keep what was left of their harvest after paying their tax quota. Those unable to pay their taxes became landless laborers known as **genin**, and could be bought and sold with the land. As slaves, they performed jobs such as burying the dead or curing leather.

Cultural Development

Japan adopted many foreign ideas, but remained culturally true to its own traditions. According to **Shinto,** the religion native to Japan, everything possessed a spirit, or, kami. Natural forces and nature were awe-inspiring, and shrines were built to honor kami. The first ruler from the Yamato clan claimed descent from the supreme Shinto deity, the Sun Goddess.

Japan was also strongly influenced by Korea and China. It adopted Chinese technology, written language, and Buddhism (though Japan developed its own version of Buddhism which added a strong aesthetic dimension known as **Zen Buddhism**). During the Heian period (794 to 1185), contact with China was cut off, and concentration was focused on expressing Japanese cultural values.

In a lavish court lifestyle, women dominated literature. *The Tale of Genji*, for instance, was written by Lady Murasaki. Wives inherited land from their husbands and often owned land, and priestesses dominated religious life. Over time, however, women began to lose power and influence.

NOMADIC EMPIRES

Vikings (Dates of influence—around 800 to 1100 CE)

The Vikings were a nomadic group who had settled in present day Scandinavia. In order to supplement their farm production, they conducted seasonal raids into Europe and ransacked towns. Using small and maneuverable boats, they raided and terrorized coastal communities in France, Scotland, Ireland, and England. The Vikings eventually evolved from plunderers into traders, and established communities in Scotland, northern France, and Eastern Europe.

These outstanding seafarers also traded actively throughout the North Sea and Baltic Sea. In the 800s, they colonized Iceland and Greenland, and around 1000, established a colony that lasted only a few decades in Newfoundland, modern Canada. The transplanted Viking settlements in France became known as Normans (or "**Northmen**").

In 1066, a Norman lord named William from northern France invaded England with his army. He defeated the Saxons and established Norman power in what is now Britain. Over time, the Normans and Vikings were Christianized and absorbed into the larger European feudal order.

Turks (Dates of influence—around 1000 to 1450 CE)

The Turks, a pastoral nomadic group from the **central Asian steppes** began to gradually migrate out of the steppes at the end of the first millennium. They were often hired by Muslim leaders as mercenaries, or hired soldiers. The **Seljuk Turks**, who had converted to Islam, invaded Abbasid territory and captured Baghdad in 1055. The caliph was left as the spiritual authority of the empire, but the Seljuk Sultan became the secular monarch. By 1071, they defeated the Byzantine Empire and took most of Anatolia (modern day Turkey).

The **Afghan Turks** were nomads from Afghanistan and began a series of raids into India in the 10th century. They looted cities for gold and jewels and destroyed Hindu temples and then left. It wasn't until the 12th century that they invaded and then started to govern. This started the **Delhi Sultanate**, which ruled northern India from 1206 to 1526.

Mongols (around 1200 to 1550 CE)

As the chapter began in 600 CE, it would have been difficult to predict that the Mongols, a pastoral nomadic group from the central Asian steppes, would create the world's largest empire. These nomadic herders' lives revolved around their sheep, goats, and yaks for food, clothing, and shelter, their camels for transportation, and their horses for mobility. This clan-based society was organized around bloodlines. The man born Temujin, later renamed **Genghis Khan**, successfully united the various Mongol tribes.

The Mongols' greatest strength was their **mobility**. In times of war, they had total male mobilization. Every male from 15 to 70 had to serve, and each was rewarded with captured goods. The military strategy was extremely effective. Often the Mongol armies would seem to retreat only to quickly turn around and resume the attack. They were also masters at psychological warfare. Genghis Khan is believed to have said, **"Submit and live. Resist and Die."**

A sharp decline in the mean annual temperature may have caused less and shorter grass to grow, and may have forced the Mongols to trade or raid the settled societies. Once united, Genghis led his troops into Central Asia, Tibet, Northern China, and Persia. In 1215, the Mongols attacked and destroyed present-day Beijing. The Mongol charge continued into Afghanistan and Persia, yet by 1227, the Great Khan died, and his empire was divided amongst his four sons.

China: The Yuan Dynasty

In 1279, Genghis Khan's grandson, **Kublai Khan**, defeated the Southern Song dynasty, and for the first time, China was under foreign rule. Khan created a Chinese-style dynasty, with a fixed and regular tax payment system and a strong central government. Foreigners, not Chinese, were employed in the bureaucracy, and the civil service exam was not used. The Chinese were subject to different laws and were consciously separated from the Mongols.

Connecting Beijing to Vienna was a communication system using horse relays and 1,400 postal stations. In time, overland and maritime trade flourished, and though the Mongols were not directly involved in the trade, they welcomed merchants and foreigners. Merchants converted their foreign currency to paper money when they crossed into China.

The Middle East: The Ilkhanates

In 1258, Kublai's brother, **Hulegu**, defeated the Abbasid Caliphate. The Mongols in the Middle East employed local bureaucrats in the government, and converted to Islam by 1295. The local rulers were permitted to rule, as long as they delivered the tax revenue and maintained order. Though they did not support agriculture, they did facilitate trade, and Mongol culture often mixed with that of the conquered people.

As the Mongols continued west, they met with their first and only major defeat. The armies of the **Mamluks**, a slave dynasty in Egypt, defeated the Mongols in 1260, and stopped the movement of the Mongols in that region.

Russia: The Golden Horde

The Mongol ruler **Batu** conquered and ruled Russia but kept a large number of the local rulers intact. The taxes on the peasants were heavy, but they were collected by Russian bureaucrats. Trade was supported, and although these Mongols were Muslim and conversion was encouraged, missionaries were allowed to visit.

Pax Mongolia

At the peak of Mongolian power, with huge areas of Asia and Europe under one rule, there was a period called the **Mongol Peace**. For about a century, Mongol rule united two continents and allowed for relatively safe trade and contacts between very different cultures. It did so by eliminating tariffs.

During this period, the **Silk Road trade** reached its greatest height. Paper money—a Chinese innovation—was used in many parts of the empire. It was also common for the Mongols to convert to or adopt the local religions, or at least be religiously tolerant.

Mongolian Conquests

Mongol Decline

In 1274 and 1281, the Mongols tried once again to expand their empire—they invaded Japan. Typhoon winds destroyed their fleet both times, however. The Japanese believed these "kamikaze," or "sacred winds," had protected them.

Despite great military accomplishment, the Mongol Empire lasted hardly three or four generations. While the Mongols were successful conquerors, they were poor administrators. Overspending led to inflation in different corners of the empire, and after the death of Kublai, leadership was weak and ineffectual. Rivalry among the successors of the great Khan further destabilized the empire, and the vast domain was divided among various generals. By 1350, most of the Mongols' huge territory had been reconquered by other armies.

IMPACT OF INTERACTION

West African Kingdoms

One area that was greatly affected by the increase in interaction throughout this period was the region of West Africa. The introduction of domesticated camel allowed for an increased flow of trade across the Sahara Desert, and as a result, Muslim and North African merchants began to establish commercial relations with West Africa.

Ghana (around 500 to 1200 CE)

Ghana was a regional state around the 400s or 500s CE, and an increase in **Trans-Saharan trade** led to its growth in power and influence. It became an important commercial site and a center for trade in gold from the south, which it controlled and taxed. In return, it provided ivory, slaves, horses, cloth, and salt.

As Ghana's wealth and power increased, it built a large army funded by the tax on trade, which kept order and trade safe. In the 900s CE, the kings converted to **Islam**, which led to improved relations with Muslim merchants. Islam was not forced on the people, however, and traditional animistic beliefs continued to be important. Those who did engage in the trade often converted to Islam.

After 1000 CE, Ghana found itself under assault from northern Berbers and other tribal groups nearby. It was eventually absorbed by the West African kingdom, Mali.

Mali (1235 to late 1400s CE)

During this period, the trans-Saharan trade in gold and salt continued to increase. Mali controlled and taxed all trade. The rulers honored Islam, and provided protection and lodging for merchants. Conversion to Islam was encouraged on a voluntary basis.

The most famous Mali emperor was **Mansa Musa**, who ruled from 1312 to 1337. A devout Muslim, Mansa Musa fulfilled one of the five pillars of faith, and went on a pilgrimage, or hajj, to Mecca, unlike most Muslims. He brought thousands of soliders, attendants, subjects, and slaves with him, as well as hundreds of camels carrying satchels of gold. He also built libraries, Islamic schools, and mosques throughout the kingdom.

Timbuktu was the political capital of Mali, and it was also a regional cultural center for all of West Africa. This was the peak of Malian power and wealth. After 1350 CE, provinces began to assert their independence and break away from the empire.

Christianity in North and East Africa (beginning in the 1st century CE)

Many Africans in the northern part of the continent converted to Islam after 700 CE, yet there remained a significant Christian tradition in **Egypt** and **Ethiopia**. It is believed that Saint Mark preached to the East Africans during the Roman period. Ethiopia evolved into a kingdom with strong Christian traditions. It also developed a unique style of art and architecture. There is a strong monastic strain in both Ethiopian and Egyptian (Coptic) Christianity. With the coming of Islam, Christians were allowed to worship freely, and a unique linguistic and artistic expression of Christianity emerged.

East African City–States (around 900 to 1500 CE)

As the Trans-Saharan trade was to West Africa, the **Indian Ocean trade** was to East Africa. Bantu people had settled on the coast, and Arabic merchants who traded along the East African coast interacted to create such East African city–states as **Mogadishu, Kilwa,** and **Sofala**. These states are often referred to as **Swahili city–states**, named so their language, which was a blend of Bantu language and Arabic.

In the 900s, Islamic merchants traded gold, slaves, and ivory for pottery, glass, and textiles from Persia, India, and China. As trade increased, so did the wealth of the city–states. Much like Ghana and Mali, these powerful city–states were governed by kings, who taxed and controlled the trade. They built stone mosques and public buildings, and the ruling elite dressed in silk from China.

In the 1200s, the kingdom of **Zimbabwe** created a magnificent stone complex known as Great Zimbabwe, which was a city of stone towers, palaces, and public buildings. The ruling elite and wealthy merchants of East Africa often converted to Islam, but did not completely give up their own religious and cultural traditions. For the rulers, Islam meant legitimacy and alliances.

Europe during the High Middle Ages (around 1000 to 1450 CE)

While the traditional feudal economy was based on agriculture in the countryside, a new pre-modern economy was evolving by the year 1100 CE. During the early medieval period, the old Roman towns shrank in size. Now, after centuries of decline, increased trade began to stimulate the growth of commercial cities in the heart of Europe. Most often located on riversides, these towns grew into marketplaces where goods could be sold. Some representative examples of these new urban centers include:

Bruges: Located in Flanders, Bruges was ideally located on a river system that connected the North Sea with Central Europe along the Rhine. Cross-channel trade brought raw wool from England, which was made into clothing to sell.

Hamburg: Part of a league of cities called the Hanseatic, Hamburg was a major port on the North Sea. The league regulated taxes and created rules for fair trade among the member cities.

Florence: This central Italian city controlled the flow of goods up and down the peninsula. Called the "Republic of Florence," this city-state became a center for banking and commerce by 1300 CE.

Service providers and craftspeople set up businesses in these towns, further stimulating growth. Among those providing services were barbers, blacksmiths, coopers (barrel makers), jewelers, leatherworkers (tanners), innkeepers, and wine/beer merchants. These cities began to plan their growth, regulate business, and collect taxes. Wealthy towns in Italy invested in new buildings and statuary for beautification.

Crusades (1095 to 1204 CE)

The Crusades were a series of Christian holy wars conducted against infidels. The most significant was a massive expedition led by the Roman Catholic Church to recapture Palestine (the land of Christian origins) from the Muslims. **Pope Urban II** launched the Crusades in 1095 when he called for Christian knights to take up arms and seize the Holy Land.

After the First Crusade, the Christians captured Edessa, Antioch, and Jerusalem, and carved up that territory into feudal states. But the disorganized Muslim forces reorganized, and retook Jerusalem in 1187. The Fourth Crusade went terribly wrong when crusaders conquered Constantinople and severely weakened the Byzantine Empire.

Though the quest for the Holy Land was a failure, it led to great economic developments in Europe; it encouraged **trade with Muslim merchants** and created an increase in European demand for Asian goods. As a result, Italian merchants from places like Venice and Genoa greatly profited, and Europe was reintroduced to the goods, technology, and culture of the outside world.

Long Distance Trade

The period 600 to 1450 witnessed a large increase in the volume of long distance trade. Overland trade included luxury goods of high value, such as silk and precious stones. The sea lanes were used for bulkier commodities such as steel, stone, coral, and building materials.

The **Silk Road** linked the Eurasian land mass through trade. **Trans-Saharan trade** connected West Africa to other parts of the Muslim world and beyond. The **Indian Ocean** linked China, Southeast Asia, India, Arabia, and East Africa through ocean trade. The **Mediterranean Sea** linked Europe with the goods from the Muslim world and Asia.

As a result of so much exchange, cities that srategically sat along the trade route grew substantially. Melaka, for instance, served as an important trade port city in the Indian Ocean. It maintained a safe environment for the markets, welcomed all merchants, and charged reasonable fees. As a result, it thrived, along with cities like Hangzhou, Samarkand, Baghdad, Kilwa, Venice, and Timbuktu in this interconnected world.

Missionary Campaigns

Buddhism

From the start, Buddhism was a missionary religion. **Theravada** Buddhism, the stricter form of the religion, spread to Southeast Asia, while **Mahayana** Buddhism spread to Central and East Asia. The latter form focused more on meditation and on rituals, and included the worship of holy people, known as bodhisattvas. Also, it had a greater tolerance for prior cultural traditions.

Along the Silk Road, Buddhism traveled to **Central Asia** and adapted to polytheism. In **Tibet**, Buddhism became popular as it combined shamanism and the importance of rituals. In East Asia, monks, merchants, and missionaries adapted Buddhism to the political ideas of Confucianism by including ancestor-worship and a focus on family. They also mixed in Daoist ideas.

Particularly during chaotic times, Buddhism appealed to people as an avenue toward **personal salvation**. Chinese Buddhism spread to **Korea,** where it received royal support, and to **Japan**. In Japan, it was initially resisted by Shinto leaders, but eventually, **syncretism** (the fusion of differering systems of beliefs) occurred after Buddhism blended in the worship of Shinto divinities.

Because Buddhism lacked an organized church, it was able to merge with the local ideas of the people. However, it did become vulnerable to more organized forces. In Central Asia, for instamce, Islam eventually replaced Buddhism as the dominant religion. In China, the Tang dynasty turned against it in the 9th century.

Christianity

Like Buddhism, Christianity became a missionary religion early on. When the Western Roman Empire was declining, Christian missionary efforts turned toward Northern Europe. The Western Church and the **Pope** sponsored missionary campaigns aimed at converting the Germanic people. The Eastern Orthodox Church also spread Christianity to Eastern Europe and Russia.

Like Buddhism, syncretism aided the spread of Christianity. Pagan heroes or holy figures (the saints) were seen as mediators between God and his people. Polytheistic holidays such as winter solstice were incorporated by placing Christmas on the same day. In Asia, **Nestorian Christianity** spread to Mesopotamia and Persia, where Islamic conquerors allowed them to practice their religion. Merchants spread Nestorian Christianity as far as India, Central Asia, and China, but they received little or no support from the established rulers. For the most part, Christianity seemed alien to most East Asians.

Islam

Islam spread through two main avenues: **military conquest**, and **trade and missionary activity**. Through military conquest and political influence, the religion spread because of its **tolerance** for other beliefs (people were rarely forced to convert) and a special tax levied against non-Muslims.

Through trade and missionary activity, the religion spread because of its simple message of what to do and what not to do. Plus, lower-class individuals welcomed their inclusion as spiritual equals as well as Islam's emphasis on charity.

Islam also legitimized the role of merchants. The **Sufis** were the most active missionaries after 900 CE, spreading Islam to Southern Europe, sub-Saharan Africa, Central Asia, India, and Southeast Asia. In sub-Saharan Africa, merchants introduced Islam to the ruling class through trade, where syncretism occurred. The kings still held a divine position, and women continued to have a prominent place in society, as was the local custom. In East Africa, Islam arrived via the Indian Ocean, where it mixed Arabic and African languages to create Swahili. In India, Turks brought Islam in the 11th century when they formed the Delhi Sultanate and used Hindu stories with Muslim characters, attracting both warriors and low-caste Hindus.

Agricultural and Technological Diffusion

The increase in global interaction through this time period led to the spread of agriculture and technology, and great changes throughout the world.

Originated	Spread to	Caused
Magnetic compass from China	Europe via the Indian Ocean trade	Increase in maritime trade and exploration
Sugarcane from Southwest Asia	European Crusaders	Italian Mediterranean island plantations and an increase in slave labor
Gunpowder from China	Persia, the Middle East, and eventually Europe by the Mongols	Increase in gunpowder weapon technology

Travelers: Ibn Battuta, Marco Polo, and Rabban Sauma

The tremendous amount of long-distance interaction in this time period can be illustrated through the travels of 3 individuals: a Muslim scholar, an Italian merchant, and a Nestorian Christian priest. Each recorded his observations while traveling.

	Ibn Battuta 1304–1369	Marco Polo 1253–1324	Rabban Sauma 1225–1294
Background	Muslim scholar from Morocco	Italian merchant form Venice	Nestorian Christian priest from Mongol empire in China.
Places traveled	Throughout Dar al-Islam: West Africa, India, Southeast Asia	Over the Silk Road to the Mongol Empire in China. Traveled throughout the empire.	Began pilgrimage to Jerusalem in Beijing, but diverted when sent by Mongol Ilkhan of Persia to meet with kings of France and England and Pope to negotiate alliances against Muslims.
Significance	Demonstrated the widespread influence of Islam. Found government positions as a qadi or judge throughout the lands he traveled.	Allowed by Kublai Khan to pursue mercantile and domestic missions throughout the empire. Influenced European interest in goods from the East.	Did not succeed to attracting the support of Christian Europe to the Mongol cause. Europeans never conquered the Middle East, but instead went around them to reach the Indian Ocean.

The Spread of Disease: Plague (1340s to late 1600s CE)

Along with the spread of religion, technology, and goods along the trade routes came disease. The **Black Plague** spread from the Yunnan region of southwest China. It spread by way of rodents: First, it infected the rodent, then the fleas living on the rodents spread the disease to humans. In the 1340s, Mongols, merchants, and travelers spread the disease even farther along the **trade routes** west of China. Oasis towns, trading cities of Central Asia, Black Sea ports, the Mediterranean Sea, and Western Europe were all affected.

Most victims of this devastating disease died in just a few days. As a result, population decreased sifnificantly, causing great **labor shortages**. In Western Europe, workers demanded higher wages and peasants rebelled, leading to a decrease in serfdom and a weakening of the feudal system. **Anti-Semitism** also increased, as Jews, used as scapegoats, were accused of poisoning the wells. Some Christians, questioned their faith amid all of the death and seemingly senseless destruction.

RECOVERY AND RENAISSANCE IN ASIA AND EUROPE (BEGINNING AROUND 1400 CE)

Chinese Political Development

The Ming dynasty might be viewed as China's comeback dynasty after the rule of the Mongols. In 1368, the Mongol Yuan dynasty collapsed, after which Emperor Hongwu started the Ming dynasty. His first order of business was to eliminate all evidence that the Mongols had ever ruled China. The Confucian education system and **civil service exam** were reinstated, and central authority was tightened.

The Ming relied on mandarins, a class of powerful officials, to implement their policies on the local level. Laborers were conscripted to rebuild irrigation systems, and as a result, agricultural production increased. Though the Ming did not actively promote trade, private merchants traded manufactured porcelain, silk, and cotton. The dynasty lasted until 1644.

European Political Development

By the 1400s, the regional states in Europe were developing into **strong, powerful monarchies**. They were now in a position to tax citizens directly and to maintain large standing armies. Italy, Milan, Venice, and Florence benefited greatly from the increase in trade, which led to an increase in tax collection. That, in turn, led to an increase in strength and authority.

Kings in France and England began to successfully assert their authority over their feudal lords. In Spain, Fernando of Aragon and Isabel of Castile married, and went on to unite Spain by reconquering the lands formerly controlled by Muslims. The **competition** seen among these states led to a refinement and improvement in weapons, ships, and technology, setting up these regional states for a more dominant position in the world.

Chinese Intellectual Developments

During the Ming dynasty, Chinese cultural traditions were strongly promoted, and **Neo-Confucian** schools were established and supported. Confucian values such as self-discipline, filial piety, and obedience to rulers were stressed. Projects were funded that emphasized Chinese cultural traditions, such as the **Yongle Encyclopedia**. Popular culture thrived with the increase in printing. Novels such as *The Dream of the Red Chamber* and *Journey to the West* were extremely popular.

Jesuit missionaries such as Matteo Ricci soon arrived, introducing European science and technology. The Jesuit goal of converting the Chinese population to Christianity proved to be unsuccessful, however.

European Intellectual Developments

The increase in interaction with and interest in the outside world sparked a major intellectual and artistic movement known as the **Renaissance**. Contact with the **Islamic world** reintroduced the ancient Greek and Roman texts that had been preserved and developed by Arabs. From the 1300s through the 1500s, painters, sculptors, and writers drew inspiration from the **Greek** and **Roman** classical past.

The humanists looked to the classical period to update medieval thought, and stressed the importance of human existence. In Italy, artists such as Leonardo da Vinci and Michelangelo used perspective to create realistic masterpieces. Famous noble families, such as the Medici family, had grown wealthy as merchants, since Italy was perfectly located for receiving goods from the Middle East and Asia. This lucrative trade with the Islamic and Byzantine cultures allowed wealthy Italians to become patrons of painters, sculptors, and scientists.

Chinese Exploration

After reestablishing authority over China, the Ming decided to refurbish the large Chinese navy and conduct a "comeback tour." From 1405 to 1433, seven massive naval expeditions were sponsored to re-establish Chinese presence in the Indian Ocean, impose imperial control over trade, and impress foreign people with Ming power.

The expeditions were led by the Muslim eunuch **Zheng He**. They involved over 300 ships with 28,000 troops, sailing to Southeast Asia, India, the Persian Gulf, Arabia, and East Africa, with Zheng dispensing and receiving gifts along the way. But in 1433, the voyages ended. Zheng's records were destroyed and the ships were allowed to rot. Pressure from Confucian officials convinced the emperor that the voyages were too expensive and offered nothing that China needed. Additionally, the age-old concern of a Mongol invasion from the North reappeared, and it was deemed more important to protect that northern border than explore the seas.

European Exploration

In the 1400s, the ideas of the Renaissance pushed some Europeans to look outward and explore. These explorations were not diplomatic, but instead focused on profits, the spread of Christianity, and the desire for adventure. The goods from the East—particularly spices—that Europeans desired were incredibly expensive because of the long overland journey they took to reach Europe.

But what if Europeans could find their own route to Asia by sea, and cut out the Muslim middleman's profits? The **Portuguese** were the early leaders in exploration, under the leadership of Prince Henry the Navigator. He set up schools in his native land and sponsored expeditions along the West African coast.

Competition heated up among European powers and a race to dominate the seas began. This competition continues well into our next time period, with the European involvement in the Indian Ocean trade and the encounter with the Americas.

AMERICAN CIVILIZATIONS

Maya (around 300 to 900 CE)

Borrowing from Olmec traditions, the Mayans developed a large domain and lived in scattered settlements on the Yukatan peninsula in southeastern Mexico. Archaeologists have discovered the following features of their regional culture:

- An agricultural economy
- Distinctive temple complexes and massive pyramids
- A ritualistic polytheism
- Urban areas with thousands of people
- Independent city–states, linked by trade
- A staple diet of maize (corn) and beans

Aztec (around 1400 to 1521 CE)

Also known as the Mexica people, the Aztecs were the last great Mesoamerican culture before the arrival of the Europeans. Taking advantage of the Toltecs' decline, the Aztecs used their fighting skills to take control of the Lake Texcoco region. The Aztec culture was characterized by:

- A militant warrior tradition
- Rule by severe despots
- A priestly class to oversee rituals, including human sacrifice
- A ritualistic polytheistic religion with an extensive pantheon
- A large urban capital with 150,000 inhabitants
- An agricultural economy with cacao beans sometimes used as currency
- A decentralized network of city-states that paid tribute

Inca (around 1400 to 1540 CE)

In the South American highlands, clans developed an Andean culture which led to the rise of an empire in the 1300s CE. These people—the Incas—conquered a large area and absorbed many tribes in central-western South America. In 90 years, the Incan empire grew into a stretch of land that covered over 3,000 miles from north to south. History remembers the Incas for:

- Centralized empire with its capital at Cuzco (present day Peru)
- An extensive, irrigated agricultural economy that adapted to the rugged terrain of the Andes
- Large urban centers
- A polytheistic religion centered around worship of the sun
- A patriarchal society with few rights for women
- A privileged class of nobles, headed by a king, in which royal ancestors were revered and worshipped
- No written language
- Impressive achievements in building with cut stone

IF YOU LEARNED ONLY SIX THINGS IN THIS CHAPTER . . . .

1. Like the Foundations period, this time period witnesses a tremendous growth in long distance trade due to the improvements in technology. Trade through the Silk Road, the Indian Ocean, the Trans-Saharan trade, and the Mediterranean Sea led to the spread of ideas, religions, and technology.

2. Major technological developments such as the compass, improved ship-building technology, and gunpowder shaped the development of the world.

3. The movement of people greatly altered our world. Nomadic groups such as the Turks, Mongols, and Vikings, for instance, interacted with settled people-often because of their technology-leading to further change and development.

4. Religions such as Islam, Christianity, and Buddhism preached the equality of all believers in the eyes of God. And though patriarchal values continued to dominate, the monastic life of Buddhism and Christianity offered an alternative path for women.

5. The spread of religion aided by the increase in trade often acted as a unifying force, though it sometimes caused conflict. Christianity and the Church served as the centralizing force in Western Europe, and throughout East Asia, the spread of Confucianism and Buddhism solidified a cultural identity. The new religion of Islam created a new cultural world known as dar-al Islam which transcended political boundaries.

6. The political structures of many areas adapted and changed to the new conditions of the world. Centralized empires like the Byzantine, Arab Caliphates, and the Tang and Song dynasties built of the successful models of the past, while decentralized areas (Western Europe and Japan) developed political organization that more effectively dealt with their unique issues. The movements of the Mongols altered much of Asia's political structure for a time, and the recovery from that Mongol period introduced political structures which defined many areas for centuries to follow.

REVIEW QUESTIONS

1. The fall of the Chinese dynasties was often aided by
   (A) Foreign interference
   (B) Japanese intrusions into China
   (C) Deflationary pressures on the economy
   (D) Peasant revolts
   (E) Military advancements

2. Most Mesoamerican rulers tended to be both
   (A) Benign and powerless
   (B) Warlike and irreligious
   (C) Scholarly and artistic
   (D) Despotic and severe
   (E) Liberal and generous

3. In what order did these three monotheistic religions come into being?
   (A) Judaism, Christianity, Islam
   (B) Christianity, Islam, Judaism
   (C) Judaism, Islam, Christianity
   (D) Islam, Shinto, Taoism
   (E) Christianity, Judaism, Islam

4. Rule by a small group of people is called a(n)
   (A) Empire
   (B) Oligarchy
   (C) Monarchy
   (D) Democracy
   (E) Theocracy

5. Written evidence of the life of Mohammed is largely found in the
   (A) Old Testament
   (B) Bible
   (C) Quran
   (D) Gospels
   (E) Hijra

6. The goal of the Christian Crusades was to
   (A) evangelize the Africans.
   (B) conquer Asia Minor.
   (C) increase papal territories.
   (D) retake the Holy Land from the Muslims.
   (E) share Jerusalem with the Turks.

7. The one unifying institution in medieval Europe was the
   (A) Monarchy
   (B) Roman Catholic Church
   (C) Artists' guilds
   (D) University of Paris
   (E) League of princes

8. Islam was brought into India over time by the
   (A) Umayyads
   (B) Ottomans
   (C) Delhi Sultanate
   (D) Sunni Caliphate
   (E) Afghan Wazir

9. The Mongolian empire declined because of:

    (A) religious differences with the native peoples.
    (B) administrative problems owing to the large territory involved.
    (C) feeble rulers after Genghis Khan.
    (D) Russia putting up a strong defense.
    (E) intertribal rivalry.

10. Two religions that encouraged the monastic life were

    (A) Islam and Confucianism
    (B) Taoism and Judaism
    (C) Buddhism and Christianity
    (D) Judaism and Islam
    (E) Animism and Christianity

11. Japan was indebted to China for all the following EXCEPT

    (A) Confucian values
    (B) A system of writing
    (C) The Bushido
    (D) Buddhist theology
    (E) A concept of a centralized government

12. The Black Death was

    (A) spread along Euro-Asian trade routes.
    (B) confined to China and South Asia.
    (C) primarily deadly in northern Europe.
    (D) purposely spread by the Mongols.
    (E) stopped before it reached Italy and Greece.

13. During the feudal period in Western Europe,

    (A) independent domains fought regularly with one another.
    (B) some women were allowed to rule fiefs.
    (C) priests were allowed to marry.
    (D) the birth rate declined.
    (E) scandals racked the Catholic Church.

14. Organizations of merchants and craftspeople in European cities were called

    (A) Granges
    (B) Guilds
    (C) Ecclesia
    (D) Fiefdoms
    (E) Bishoprics

15. Japanese feudalism resulted in part because of

    (A) the emperor's ability to rule effectively.
    (B) the failure of the Heian to govern efficiently.
    (C) the overthrow of the shogun after 1200 CE.
    (D) the decline of the samurai class.
    (E) widespread famine in Japan in 900 CE.

16. The strongest basis of the Mayan economy was

    (A) Crafts and manufacturing
    (B) Agriculture, which produced maize, beans, and cocoa
    (C) Trade with the Pueblos to the north
    (D) Fishing and hunting
    (E) The silver trade

17. Alliances between European feudal lords were often the result of

    (A) Trade relations between the domains
    (B) Papal decree
    (C) The need for a defense against the marauding Vikings
    (D) The Black Death
    (E) A rising birth rate

18. Which of the following statements is NOT true of the Tang dynasty?

    (A) The capital city was the largest in the world.
    (B) The empire expanded its territory to Tibet and Korea.
    (C) The government discouraged trade and foreign influence.
    (D) Buddhists were persecuted toward the end of the empire.
    (E) The Grand Canal was completed.

19. Which of the following statements is true of the Turks and the Mongols?

    (A) Both conquered and ruled Japan.
    (B) Both were skilled administrators and bureaucrats.
    (C) Both had written languages based on Arabic.
    (D) Both used the Confucian civil service examination system.
    (E) Both were pastoral nomads originally from the Central Asian steppes.

20. Which of the following happened after the fall of the Mongol empire?

    (A) The Byzantine Empire reunited the former Roman Empire.
    (B) Mohammed led his followers to Medina.
    (C) The Delhi Sultanate invaded and conquered India.
    (D) The Ming dynasty reunited China under Chinese rule.
    (E) Buddhism became popular in Southeast Asia.

21. Which of the following statements is true of the time period 600 to 1450?

    (A) The Tang dynasty stabilized China after Mongol rule.
    (B) The eastern hemisphere interacted little during this period.
    (C) Western Europe dominated global political affairs.
    (D) The Turks expanded as far as sub-Saharan Africa.
    (E) Long-distance trade flourished.

22. The term *chivalry* is most like

    (A) Salvation
    (B) Samsara
    (C) Bushido
    (D) Samurai
    (E) Reincarnation

23. Which of the following statements accurately compares West and East Africa during the time period 600 to 1450?

    (A) Trans-Saharan trade was for West Africa what Indian Ocean trade was for East Africa.
    (B) Christianity converted large parts of the population in both regions.
    (C) Both areas were ruled by centralizing governments controlled by an emperor.
    (D) The areas were relatively isolated throughout this time period.
    (E) Large percentages of the populations converted to Islam and eliminated native beliefs.

24. Melakka and Venice were important examples of

    (A) Silk Road oasis towns
    (B) Pilgrimage sites
    (C) Political capitals
    (D) Religious centers
    (E) Trading ports

25. Which of the following had the greatest navigational technology during the time period 600 to 1450?

    (A) West Africa
    (B) Japan
    (C) Western Europe
    (D) China
    (E) Byzantine Empire

Document-Based Question

Directions: The following question is based on the accompanying Documents 1 to 4. (The documents have been edited for the purpose of this exercise.)

This question is designed to test your ability to work with and understand historical documents. Write an essay that:
- Has a relevant thesis and supports that thesis with evidence from the documents.
- Use all of the documents.
- Analyzes the documents by grouping them in as many appropriate ways as possible. **Does not simply summarize the documents individually**.
- Takes into account the sources of the documents and analyzes the authors' points of view.
- Explains the need for at least one additional type of document.

You may refer to relevant historical information not mentioned in the documents.

> Based on the following documents, analyze and discuss the motivations for the Crusades. Explain what additional type of document(s) would help assess the motivations for the Crusades.

Document 1

Source: Pope Leo IV (847-855): Forgiveness of Sins for Those Who Dies in Battle with the Heathen

Given to the Frankish Army

Now we hope that none of you will be slain, but we wish you to know that the kingdom of heaven will be given as a reward to those who shall be killed in this war. For the Omnipotent knows that they lost their lives fighting for the truth of the faith, for the preservation of their country, aid the defense of Christians. And therefore God will give them, the reward which we have named.

Document 2

Source: Pope John VIII: Indulgence for Fighting the Heathen, 878

John VIII to the bishops in the realm of Louis II [the Stammerer].

You have modestly expressed a desire to know whether those who have recently died in war, fighting in defense of the church of God and for the preservation of the Christian religion and of the state, or those who may in 'he future fall in the same cause, may obtain indulgence for their sins. We confidently reply that those who, out of love to the Christian religion, shall die in battle fighting bravely against pagans or unbelievers, shall receive eternal life. For the Lord has said ' through his prophet: "In whatever hour a sinner shall be converted, I will remember his sins no longer." By the intercession of St. Peter, who has the power of binding and loosing in heaven and on the earth, we absolve, as far as is permissible, all such and commend them by our prayers to the Lord.

Document 3

Source: Pope Gregory VII: Call for a Crusade, 1074

Gregory, bishop, servant of the servants of God, to all who are willing to defend the Christian faith, greeting and apostolic benediction.

We hereby inform you that the bearer of this letter, on his recent return from across the sea [from Palestine], came to Rome to visit us. He repeated what we had heard from many others, that a pagan race had overcome the Christians and with horrible cruelty had devastated everything almost to the walls of Constantinople, and were now governing the conquered lands with tyrannical violence, and that they had slain many thousands of Christians as if they were but sheep. If we love God and wish to be recognized as Christians, we should be filled with grief at the misfortune of this great empire [the Greek] and the murder of so many Christians. But simply to grieve is not our whole duty. The example of our Redeemer and the bond of fraternal love demand that we should lay down our lives to liberate them. "Because he has laid down his life for us: and we ought to lay down our lives for the brethren," [1 John 3:16]. Know, therefore, that we are trusting in the mercy of God and in the power of his might and that we are striving in all possible ways and making preparations to render aid to the Christian empire [the Greek] as quickly as possible. Therefore we beseech you by the faith in which you are united through Christ in the adoption of the sons of God, and by the authority of St. Peter, prince of apostles, we admonish you that you be moved to proper compassion by the wounds and blood of your brethren and the danger of the aforesaid empire and that, for the sake of Christ, you undertake the difficult task of bearing aid to your brethren [the Greeks]. Send messengers to us at once to inform us of what God may inspire you to do in this matter.

Document 4

Source: Chronicle of Fulcher of Chartres, written between 1101 and 1128. Fulcher was present at Council of Clermont, where Pope Urban II issued his call for the First Crusade in 1095 and participated in the Crusades.

The Pope's Exhortation Concerning the Expedition to Jerusalem

3. "For, as most of you have been told, the Turks, a race of Persians, who have penetrated within the boundaries of Romania even to the Mediterranean to that point which they call the Arm of Saint George, in occupying more and more of the lands of the Christians, have overcome them, already victims of seven battles, and have killed and captured them, have overthrown churches, and have laid waste God's kingdom. If you permit this supinely for very long, God's faithful ones will be still further subjected.

4. Concerning this affair, I, with suppliant prayer – not I but the Lord, exhort you, heralds of Christ, to persuade all of whatever class, both knights and footman, both rich and poor, in numerous edicts, to strive to help expel that wicked race from our Christian lands before it is too late."

5. I speak to those present, I send word to those not here; moreover, Christ commands it. Remission of sins will be granted for those going thither, if they end a shackled life either on land or in crossing the sea, or in struggling against the heathen. I, being vested with that gift from God, grant this to those who go."

Change-Over-Time Question

Directions: You are to answer the following question: You should spend 5 minutes organizing or outlining your essay. Write an essay that:

- Has a relevant thesis and supports that thesis with appropriate historical evidence.
- Addresses all parts of the question.
- Uses world historical context to show change over time and/or continuities
- Analyzes the process of change over time and/or continuity

> Describe and analyze the impact of nomads on ONE of the following areas from 600 to 1450. Be sure to discuss continuities as well as changes.
>
> East Asia (China and/or Japan)
> Russia
> Middle East

Comparative Question

Directions: You are to answer the following question: You should spend 5 minutes organizing or outlining your essay. Write an essay that:

- Has a relevant thesis and supports that thesis with appropriate historical evidence.
- Addresses all parts of the question.
- Makes direct, relevant comparisons.
- Analyzes relevant reasons for similarities and differences.

> Major religions and philosophies have served as the foundation for many societies. Discuss the similarities and differences in the political and social influence that two of the following religions had on their respective societies from 600 to 1450.
>
> Christianity—Europe
> Islam—West Africa
> Buddhism—China

_____
_____
_____
_____
_____
_____
_____
_____
_____
_____
_____
_____
_____
_____
_____

ANSWERS AND EXPLANATIONS

1. D

When dynasties began to collapse over time in China, administrative control began to weaken. In times of famine or if taxes were too high, the peasants would rise up, sometimes leading to the overthrow of the dynastic government. Foreign powers sometimes aided declining dynasties as in the 1800s. The Japanese did not have the military might to intrude in China until after the 1920s and the end of Chinese imperial history.

2. D

Mesoamerican kings were very powerful and ruled with an iron hand. The punishments they meted out were often cruel and painful. Human sacrifice was common within the context of religious practices.

3. A

Judaism emerged first in the deserts of Mesopotamia around 2000 BCE. Christianity was a sect within Judaism that broke away in the 1st century CE. Islam came into being in the mid-600s CE in Arabia. Daoism is not a monotheistic faith.

4. B

Rule by a small elite is called an oligarchy. This can be a ruling council or a small subsection of society such as a landed class. A monarchy is rule by a single king or queen, and a democracy is when the people share power and rule together.

5. C

Historical evidence about the life of Mohammed is mostly found in the scriptures that he himself dictated. These make up the Holy Book of Islam called the *Quran* (Koran). Both the Old Testament and the Gospels were written long before Mohammed lived.

6. D

Pope Urban II urged Christian soldiers to liberate the Holy Land from the Muslims in 1095. He offered an indulgence, or pardoning of sins, for all who answered this call to arms. Urban urged solidarity with the Byzantine Empire and sought Christian control over the holy sites, such as Jerusalem.

7. B

With the fragmentation of political power after the collapse of the Roman empire, the Christian Church became the most important institution in Europe. It supported many of the universities where priests were often professors. Artists' guilds were local organizations in some urban areas.

8. C

The Muslims gradually conquered the subcontinent and established the Delhi Sultanate by 1200 CE. Also called the "slave" dynasty in its early period, this sultanate was a succession of Muslim rulers who ruled northern India from the 13th century. The Ottoman empire did not extend as far east as India. A wazir was an Islamic political post and does not pertain to the conquering of India in the 13th century.

9. B

The Mongolian empire was vast and did not long survive the death of Kublai Khan. Though they were able military conquerors, the Mongols were challenged as administrators of so large an empire. The Russians were conquered by the Mongols and were ruled by them for many years.

10. C

Both Buddhism and Christianity developed strong monastic traditions. Living a devotional life separate from the rest of the world has continued to have appeal for the faithful. Monasteries are not a feature of Judaic or Islamic traditions.

11. C

The Bushido, or "way of the warrior," is a uniquely Japanese tradition that defined samurai culture. This elite warrior caste developed over many centuries in feudal Japan. China was the origin of many other aspects of Japanese culture such as the ideographs used in writing and strong Confucian values within the family and society.

12. A

Believed to have originated in China in the 1330s, the plague, or "Black Death," came to Europe aboard trading ships. It is estimated to have killed 25 million people throughout Europe and was weaker in the northern climes where the fleas that spread it could not survive the cold.

13. A

Warfare was a constant feature of the feudal period in Europe. Local lords often fought with nearby rivals for territory. Although women were involved in political marriages where large land was transferred, they were not rulers. Priests were expected to be celibate and not to marry, according to the traditions of the Roman Catholic Church.

14. B

Guilds were early associations to which artisans and craftspeople could belong in medieval Europe. They existed partly to encourage public service, but also to act as a kind of fraternity for their members. Granges were farmer associations in 19th century-America and ecclesia has to do with the Church.

15. B

The collapse of Heian rule in Japan encouraged a descent into decentralized warfare after 1179 CE. The warrior class had evolved into many small armies, and feudal domains began to define the political order in Japan. The emperor continued to be marginalized in the imperial capital of Kyoto.

16. B

The growth of maize and beans was the mainstay of the Mayan economy, and these products were also the staples in their diet. Fish was not a common feature of their everyday diet. As a pre-industrial society, there was no manufacture of goods in great quantity in the Mayan empire.

17. C

Feudal lords that might otherwise have fought one another found common cause when Norsemen, or Vikings, attacked from the North. Lords in Scotland, England and France were very afraid of the quick and brutal Viking raids from 800 CE. The Black Death caused a net drop in the population and birth rate of Europe in the 14th century.

18. C

The Tang dynasty supported long-distance trade, and the Silk Road trade flourished during its reign. Foreigners were welcome, particularly in the capital city of Changan, which was known for its quarters of foreign merchants.

19. E

Although the Mongols attempted to conquer Japan, they were unsuccessful. Neither the Turks nor the Mongols were skilled administrators, and they often used local people to help them rule. They did not base their written languages on Arabic, nor did they use the civil service exams, but both were originally from the Central Asian steppes.

20. D

After the Mongols rule ended, the Ming dynasty established Chinese rule in China. The Byzantine empire never successfully reunited the Roman empire. Mohammed led followers to Medina, the Delhi Sultanate conquered India, and Buddhism became popular in Southeast Asia before the Mongol empire was established.

21. E

Due to trade routes such as the Silk Road, Indian Ocean, trans-Saharan, and Mediterranean Sea, long-distance trade flourished during this period. The Tang dynasty ruled before the Mongols. Western Europe was decentralized and did not dominate global political affairs. The Turks never made it as far as sub-Saharan Africa.

22. C

The Japanese term *bushido* refers to the samurai code of conduct. The European term *chivalry* refers to the code of conduct for knights.

23. A

Trans-Saharan trade and Indian Ocean trade were the life blood of West Africa and East Africa, respectively. Christianity influenced parts of the population in East Africa. West Africa was controlled by a centralizing emperor, but East Africa was organized into city–states. The areas were not isolated, but interacted extensively. Large parts of the population did convert to Islam, but native beliefs were incorporated into Islam, not eliminated.

24. E

Melakka was an important trading port in Southeast Asia in the Indian Ocean. Venice was an important trading port in Italy in the Mediterranean Sea.

25. D

The Chinese were the dominant force in navigational technology during this period, with inventions such as the compass and sternpost rudder, and later with the Ming fleet that sailed the Indian Ocean under the leadership of Zheng He.

Document-Based Question: Sample Response

From 600 to 1450, the Catholic Church held great power over the Western European world. Kings at the time were relatively weak and the Pope was the centralizing figure in the region. As the Islamic world grew stronger and more powerful, the Catholic Church took note. In an attempt to combat the Muslim threat, the Church called for a series of Crusades. The goal of these crusades was to push back the Muslims and protect fellow Christians. The motivations given to recruit willing participants in these efforts were primarily religious and political.

Since the Catholic Church held the power to decide who could receive salvation, a major religious motivation for participation in the Crusades was the promise of eternal life. Pope Leo IV, with the purpose of motivating the troops, gave a message to the Frankish army in the 9th century that promised heaven as the reward for anyone who was killed in the fighting. Since the Franks, according to the Pope, were fighting for the truth of the faith and aiding the defense of Christians, God would look out for them in the afterlife. Later in the 9th century, Pope John VIII gave a message to his bishops, again with the purpose of motivating and encouraging participation in the fight. It promised indulgence for the sins of those who fought for the Christian religion and state. It would be helpful to know if the bishops receiving the pope's letter were convinced of the validity of this mission and more important, if the soldiers who received the promise of salvation were truly motivated by this reason or other more economic reasons, such as the opportunity to obtain their own land. Lastly, Pope Urban II, as told by Fulcher of Chartres, told his audience at the Council of Clermont in 1095, that Christ commanded the Crusades, and that those who participated would have their sins forgiven. Pope Urban, also, with an intent to stir up hatred for the Muslim, told his audience that the Muslims had already killed and captured Christians, and had destroyed God's churches.

In addition to the religious motivation to fight in the Crusades, the Church used political incentives to draw in participants. In his letter, Pope John VIII explicitly linked Christianity and the state, giving the mission a political, as well as religious, purpose. By doing this, the Pope made the state an instrument of the Church. Almost 200 years later in 1074 CE, Pope Gregory VII called for his own Crusade. In his statement, he pointed out that "a pagan race had overcome Christians and with horrible cruelty had devastated everything almost to the walls of Constantinople, and were now governing the conquered lands with tyrannical violence..." His purpose was to equate the Muslims with an almost sub-human race that was threatening Christian civilization. His was trying to appeal to Western European Christians to defend their fellow Christians in the Byzantine Empire, thus creating a religious and political bond between the two. Since the call from Pope Urban II in 1095 initiated the Crusades to recapture the Holy land in Palestine, it would be helpful to know how Pope Gregory's message was received and why the mass movement did not begin after his call for a Crusade. Additionally, did the average Christian in Western Europe feel an allegiance to Byzantine Christians because of their common faith, or were there other motivations to get involved?

After Pope Urban's call for a Crusade in 1095, much of the next 200 years involved a movement by the Catholic Church and Christian kingdoms to re-conquer the Holy land. The Church used both religious motivation (the promise of salvation) and political motivation (the re-conquering of land) to stir up involvement. Additionally, the economic motive of potential wealth drove many crusaders into the movement.

Change-Over-Time Question: Sample Response

The interaction between nomadic and settled people has affected world history for thousands of years. Between the years 600 and 1450, China was greatly influenced by nomadic peoples. The invasion of the Mongols led to the creation of the world's largest empire and influenced China politically, economically, and socially. Throughout the rule of the Mongols and the recovery after, however, China was able to maintain its unique identity and culture.

During the rule of the Song dynasty, the Chinese had a tenuous relationship with their nomadic neighbors to the north. As long as the settled Chinese could supply the nomads with the goods they required, peace was usually secure. However, the Song dynasty had a much weaker military than their predecessors the Tang dynasty and had difficulty defending their northern border. They lost the northern half of the empire in 1126. This opened up the way for the eventual invasion of the Mongols in the 13th century.

When the Mongols conquered China under the rule of Genghis Khan's grandson, Kublai Khan, they had thoughts of turning much of the land into grazing land for their animals, but they thought better of it. Instead, Kublai Khan created a Chinese-style dynasty called the Yuan dynasty. However, in this dynasty, the Mongols-not Chinese-were superior. This affected China politically because only Mongols were allowed to serve in the highest government positions, and Confucian scholars lost much of their former position and status. Socially, Chinese and Mongols were forbidden from intermarrying. Economically, the Mongols greatly benefited the economy of China by reestablishing the Silk Road and encouraging trade and interaction throughout the region. The Mongols were able to keep the trade routes safe which encouraged the free flow of good and ideas.

When the Mongols were eventually defeated in the 14th century, China reestablished a "Chinese" dynasty with the Ming. The Ming worked to eliminate all evidence that the Mongols ever ruled China by bringing back the Confucian scholars and stabilizing the government. The Ming also worked to build much of the Great Wall to make sure the Mongols could never return again. The invasion of the Mongols had changed China politically and economically, but culturally the Chinese were able to hold on to their strong sense of tradition and identity through the establishment of the Ming dynasty.

Comparative Question: Sample Response

Both Christianity in Europe and Buddhism in China were used by political authorities to establish legitimacy from 600 to 1450, and they both offered universal salvation. In Europe, Christianity became the dominant religious force, while in China, Buddhism was important, though it did not replace other philosophies or religions as the dominant belief.

Politically, both Christianity and Buddhism thrived due to official patronage. In Europe, following the fall of the Western Roman Empire, the Christian Church became the only centralizing force in the region. The Pope grew to be the most powerful religious and political figure. Kings, who were relatively weak at this time, owed allegiance to the Pope as the supreme power. Christianity served as a vehicle for leaders to unit their people under a common belief. German kings, like Clovis, converted to Christianity and their subjects soon followed. The religion and its Pope were even powerful enough to compel kings and knights to fight on behalf of the faith against the perceived infidels the Muslims. Buddhism also benefited from political patronage, but its hold over all of China was not very powerful. It became more popular in China during the unstable times after the Han Empire fell. So similar to Christianity, Buddhism offered some solace in a time of disorder. During the Sui and later Tang dynasties, emperors used a connection with the religion to establish their own legitimacy. Empress Wu, in particular, favored Buddhism and had many schools and monasteries established. But toward the end of the Tang dynasty, Buddhism suffered persecution during anti-Buddhist campaigns. The "foreign" religion was blamed for many of China's problems and attacked for much of its wealth. Although Buddhism remained influential in China's culture, it did not take on the dominant all-consuming characteristic of Christianity in Europe.

Socially, Christianity and Buddhism had many similar effects. Both religions offered a form of universal salvation. Christianity promises all who believe a place in heaven after this life. This afterlife was not determined by gender, social, or economic status, but by faith. As a result, Christianity attracted large numbers of poor, as well as women. Similarly, Buddhism preached that all could (after many lives) achieve nirvana, or a release from reincarnation and suffering. This idea appealed to many women. Additionally, in both religions, life as a nun in a convent offered an alternative life to women who did not want to follow the traditional path.

Christianity and Buddhism both thrived and spread from 600 to 1450. Political patronage helped both the religions and the rulers who used them to help establish legitimacy. Socially, both religions opened up a chance for salvation or escape to those who always felt disenfranchised.

Chapter 5: 1450 to 1750

- The Big Picture
- Why This Periodization?
- Impact of Interaction—The Development of a Global Economy
- State-Building
- Systems of Forced Labor
- Cultural and Intellectual Changes

THE BIG PICTURE

1. Patterns and effects of interactions among major societies and regions: trade, war, diplomacy, and international organizations

   In other words: **What happens when people come in contact with each other?**

During this period, the world becomes truly global. For the first time, the Americas are included in the global trade network and the process of true globalization begins. Trade is extended throughout all parts of the world. The European nations gain access to Asian trade routes and attempt to control them. The Colombian Exchange of goods, disease, and cultures spreads throughout the world.

2. The dynamics of change and continuity across the world history periods covered in this course, and the causes and processes involved in major changes of these dynamics.

   In other words: **Why do some things change while other things stay the same?**

The most significant change in this period is the inclusion of the Americas. These encounters with the Americas set off a tremendous chain of events that were felt throughout the world.

3. The effects of technology, economics, and demography on people and the environment (population growth and decline, disease, labor systems, manufacturing, migrations, agriculture, weaponry)

   In other words: **How does the development of new technology and movement of people affect the world?**

Improvements in the spread of shipping technologies and gunpowder weapons allowed European countries to begin their dominance of the world. Native Americans people died by the millions due to their exposure to previously unknown European diseases, and in Africa, people were forcibly transported across the Atlantic Ocean to fill the need for labor on plantations.

4. Systems of social structure and gender structure (comparing major features within and among societies and assessing change)

   In other words: **How do societies organize themselves socially, and what roles do men and women play?**

In the Americas, a new social structure emerges based on race. Those with pure European blood are considered the highest socially and politically, and those with indigenous or African blood were considered the lowest. Women of the harem in the Ottoman Empire wielded considerable power behind the scenes.

5. Cultural, intellectual, and religious developments and interactions among and within societies

   In other words: **How do people identify themselves and expresses themselves culturally and intellectually?**

In Europe, the Renaissance and Reformation challenge, previously accepted beliefs and the power of the Roman Catholic Church. In others parts of the world, like China, reaffirmation of more traditional beliefs was viewed as the key to stability.

6. Changes in functions and structures of states and in attitudes toward states and political identities (political culture), including the emergence of the nation-state (types of political organization)

   In other words: **How do people govern themselves?**

The predominant form of political organization remained the empire. European empires, like those of Spain and Portugal, stretched their power overseas to conquer and control the newly encountered Americas. At the same time, dominant land-based empires such as the Ottoman, Mughal, and the Qing grew powerful.

WHY THIS PERIODIZATION?

The most significant change that occurs in this time period is the inclusion of the Americas in the global trade network. With this inclusion, a truly global economy develops. As Europeans are getting ready to reach out and explore the world around them, the previous world power, China, is more focused on internal stability. This shift allows Europe to rise as a dominant world power.

The empires of the day needed to decide the degree to which they should interact with the outside world. While Europe was embracing outside interaction and conquest, many other empires were more insular and focused on their own preservation and stability.

IMPACT OF INTERACTION—THE DEVELOPMENT OF A GLOBAL ECONOMY

European Exploration

As discussed in the last chapter, the Ming dynasty had extensively explored the Indian Ocean from 1405 to 1433, but under pressure from conservative forces, decided to halt the voyages and destroy their ships. The Indian Ocean continued to be a thriving trade route, however, with participants such as **Muslims, Indians, Malays,** and others. So when the European powers entered Indian Ocean trade, they were not so much creating this vibrant trade route as inserting themselves into an existing one. But by doing so, the world shifted from a primarily Asian-centered economy to a global economy.

As Europe emerged out of its more isolated and self-sufficient period, the desire to explore came with it. The major motivations for this exploration included the search for resources, new trade routes to Asian markets, and the desire to spread Christianity. The Asian goods that Europe received—**pepper, ginger, cloves,** and **nutmeg**—were very expensive, and so Europe wanted to gain direct access to these trade routes and cut out the middleman. The acquisition of technology from China and the Muslim world helped to achieve this goal with such things as the sternpost rudder, triangular lateen sail, magnetic compass, and astrolabe. The early leader in exploration was **Portugal**, which established sugar plantations on islands in the Atlantic off the coast of Africa, but many other expeditions would follow.

Columbus' First Voyage

Explorer	Year	Accomplishment
Bartolomeu Dias (Portugal)	1488	Rounded Cape of Good Hope at the tip of Africa and entered the Indian Ocean.
Christopher Columbus (Spain)	1492	Sailed west to reach Asia and instead reached the Bahamas. Sailed around Caribbean, but thought he had reached island just off the coast of Asia. Reached Calicut in India by rounding Africa.
Vasco de gama (Spain)	1497	Reached Calicut in India by rounding Africa.
Magellan (Spain)	1519–1522	Sailed around South America to the Philippine Islands (where he was killed). His men sailed back through the Indian Ocean and were the first to circumnavigate the globe.

Trading Post Empires

The initial goal of European powers in exploring the Indian Ocean was not to conquer, but rather to control the lucrative trade. They wanted to force merchant ships to trade in fortified trading sites and to pay duties for the privilege. By the mid-1500s, Portugal had 50 trading posts from West Africa to East Asia, but by the late 1500s, its power began to decline. The small country with its small population could not sustain the large seaborne empire.

The English and the Dutch quickly took Portugal's place as the dominant powers with their faster, cheaper, and more powerful ships. Additionally, they used **joint stock companies**, in which investors funded the expeditions rather than the crown.

Trading Posts

Colombian Exchange

The inclusion of the Americas in the global trade network set off the global diffusion of plants, food, crops, animals, humans, and diseases known as the Colombian Exchange. The most devastating effect of this diffusion was the spread of **smallpox** to the Americas, to which the native people had no immunity. The Aztec empire lost 95% of its population within a century, and in this weakened state, was controlled by its Spanish conquerors. Between 1500 and 1800, 100 million people died from the spread of disease to the Americas.

The **diffusion of food crops and animals** also revolutionized life around the world, leading to an increase in the nutritional value of diets and a population increase worldwide.

Europe to the Americas	Americas to Africa, Asia, and Europe
Wheat Sugarcane Cotton Horses Cattle Pigs Sheep Goats Chickens	Maize Potatoes Beans Tomatoes Pepper Peanuts Avocadoes Pineapples Tobacco

Role and Impact of Silver

Silver, the most abundant American precious metal, was responsible for stimulating a truly global trade network. The two areas rich in silver were Mexico and the Potosi mines in the Andes, which employed large numbers of indigenous labor. Driven by China's desire for silver, this mining industry powered the Spanish economy and stimulated the world economy. It was used to trade for silk and porcelain in Asia, and it financed Spain's powerful army and bureaucracy; in order for the Spanish to purchase Chinese goods at that time, they needed to use Mexican silver.

Role and Impact of Sugar

Another influential product of this time period was sugar. The cultivation and production of sugar was a complex production of land, labor, buildings, animals, capital, and technical skills. It required both heavy labor (for planting and harvesting the cane) and specialized skills (for the sugar-making process). Because small pox had wiped out so many native peoples in the Americas, imported Africans became the main labor force. These slaves often worked under very harsh conditions—mistreatment, extreme heat, and poor nutrition—leading to significant disease and death.

STATE-BUILDING

Ottoman Empire (early 1300s to 1923)

The Ottoman Empire got its start as a band of semi-nomadic Turks who migrated to northwest Anatolia in the 13th century, but through their military might, transformed into a major political power. As the Mongols' power declined in the Middle East, the Ottomans replaced them as the dominant influence.

Military might and gunpowder weapons drove the Ottomans to power. An elite fighting force of slave troops made of Christian boys (called **janissaries**) led the military powerhouse. In 1453, the Ottomans captured Constantinople and ended the long life of the Byzantine Empire. Under the leadership of sultans such as Mehmed and Suleyman, a tightly centralized absolute monarchy ruled the land. Additionally, Islamic religious scholars and legal experts served administrative functions. As the empire became more wealthy, though, the sultans grew more distant and removed themselves from the running of the government. The vizier headed the bureaucracy and often had more control and power than the sultan.

Political succession was also a serious problem; in the capital city Istanbul (formerly Constantinople), for instance, the cathedral Hagia Sophia was converted to a grand mosque. This thriving city also had aqueducts, a thriving marketplace, rest houses, religious schools, and hospitals. A large merchant and artisan class conducted business, but commercial exchanges and handicraft production were closely regulated by the government.

The sultan's harem, or private domain, was an influential element in Ottoman politics and society. His concubines and female relatives resided in the harem, and were accorded status when they had sons. Members of the harem—who were very close to the sultan and wielded a lot of political power—were often of slave origin and were non-Mulsim, as the enslavement of Muslims was forbidden. They were trained and educated in reading, the Koran, sewing, and music.

The sultan's mother was given the title *queen mother*, and she served as an advisor to the throne. She administered the imperial household and engaged in diplomatic relations.

The empire reached its peach in the mid-1600s but became too large to maintain. The effectiveness of the administration declined and was plagued by corruption. The successors to the throne often lived sheltered lives and were unequipped to rule. Finally, as European military and naval technology outpaced theirs, the Ottomans were ill-equipped to effectively compete.

Expansion of the Ottoman Empire

Mughal India (1523 to mid-1700s)

India's predominantly decentralized history of regional kingdoms was interrupted during this time by the conquest of Babur and the establishment of the Mughal Empire. Babur, a descendant of Turkic nomads, began his conquest of India in 1526, and his grandson **Akbar** continued in this vein for the rule of India.

Akbar, a strong military commander, was also interested in uniting his empire. He patronized the arts and was very interested in religious discussion. He initiated a policy of cooperation with Hindu rulers and the Hindu population by encouraging intermarriage; he **abolished the jizya** (non-Muslim tax); and he promoted Hindus to high-ranking government jobs. His descendants, Jahangir and Shah Jahan, were also **great patrons of the arts**. Painting workshops were expanded, leading to the creation of thousands of exquisite miniatures. Mughal architecture often blended Persian and Hindu traditions by using Islamic domes, arches, and minarets, along with Hindu ornamentation. The most famous example of Mughal architecture is the **Taj Mahal**, which Emperor Shah Jahan built as a tomb for his late wife.

Taj Mahal

Aurangzeb, Shah Jahan's son, seized the throne with a neglected and corrupt bureaucracy, and pushed to extend Muslim control to the whole of India. He also sought to rid India of all Hindu influences (bringing back the non-Muslim tax) and to purify India's Islam. His many wars drained the treasury, and peasant uprisings and revolts by both Muslim and Hindu princes weakened the empire.

Additionally, India had become a major overseas destination for European traders who demanded cotton. With a weakened empire, those traders were able to increase their influence.

Songhay (1464 to 1591)

In the 1400s, the West African state of Songhay emerged to take power over the weakened Mali empire. Its leader, Sunni Ali, consolidated his empire by appointing governors to oversee the provinces, building a hierarchically commanded army, and creating an imperial navy to patrol the Niger River. The lucrative **trans-Saharan trade** flowed through the city of Gao, which brought salt, textiles, and metal in exchange for gold and slaves.

All Songhay emperors were **Muslims** who supported mosques, schools, and the Islamic university at **Timbuktu**. Still, even though Islam served as the cultural foundation of the empire and a key element in establishing cooperation with Muslim merchants, traditional religious beliefs were not abandoned.

Just as the Europeans were making inroads into Africa, the Songhay empire began to lose control of its many subject peoples. The empire went into decline and was defeated by the Moroccans in 1591.

Kongo (around 1300s to 1600s)

In the 14th century, the Kongo emerged as a **centralized state** along the west coast of central Africa. In this organized state, a powerful king ruled and officials oversaw military, judicial, and financial affairs. In 1482, a small **Portuguese** fleet arrived and initiated **commercial relations**, and within a few years the Portuguese had developed a close political and diplomatic relationship with the king. They provided him military force, which supported both of their interests. The kings also converted to **Christianity** in an effort to improve commercial and diplomatic relations. King Affonso I was a devout Roman Catholic and attempted to convert all of his subjects to Christianity.

The relationship between Portugal and Kongo seemed like one in which the participants were equal. The interaction brought wealth and foreign recognition to Kongo, but it eventually led to its decline. The Portuguese brought textiles, weapons, and craftsmen there, and they wanted gold, silver, and ivory. They especially wanted slaves, though, and in exchange for weapons, they began **slave raids** with the cooperation of local leaders. These dealings undermined the king's authority, however, and Kongo was defeated in war with the Portuguese in 1665. Thereafter, the kingdom's power was not recovered.

Spanish and Portuguese Overseas Expansion/Empire (1500s to early 1800s)

Although Spanish conquistadors led the way in the conquest of the Americas, the Spanish crown was not far behind. The two major areas of the empire—New Spain (Mexico) and New Castile (Peru)—were each governed by a **viceroy**, who was responsible to the Spanish king. In 1494, the Treaty of Tordesillas divided the Americas in half: The Spanish controlled the west, and the Portuguese controlled the east.

The social result of the conquest of this new empire was a multicultural and ethnically mixed population. The majority of the early migrants were men. The **peninsulares**, the highest social class, came directly from the Iberian peninsula, and their descendants were the **creoles**. The mix of Europeans and Native Americans were the **mestizos**, and the mix of European and Africans were the **mulattoes**. At the bottom of the social order were the Native Americans, Africans, and the mixed class of **zambos.**

Economically, the empire thrived with silver mining, farming, stock raising, and craft production. The haciendas (large estates) were served initially by labor acquired through the **encomienda system**, which gave settlers the right to demand labor from native peoples. This system was later replaced with the **repartimiento system**, which compelled native communities to supply laborers but only for limited periods of time and for a fair wage. As the **plantation system** grew in the Americas, so did the use of African slave labor.

Right behind the conquistadors and settlers came the **missionaries**, who hoped to spread the Christian faith to the natives. Many did adopt **Christianity**, but chose to blend it with their own traditions.

Qing Dynasty (1644 to 1911)

By the 1640s, the Ming dynasty had declined and had been taken over by the pastoral nomadic Manchus from the north. This "foreign" dynasty, the Qing, would be China's last. It was important for the Manchus to preserve their own ethnic and cultural identity, but in many ways they ruled like a Chinese dynasty: They outlawed intermarriage of Manchu and Chinese, forbade Chinese from traveling to Manchuria and from learning the language, and forced Chinese men to wear their hair in a **queue** braid as a sign of submission.

Manchus were appointed to the highest political posts and administered a bureaucracy of Confucian scholars. **Civil-service exams** based on Confucian learning were still the way to career advancement, and Chinese traditional patriarchal views, along with the practice of footbinding, continued through this period.

China was an important part of the **global trade network**, and it experienced great prosperity as a result of the world's desire for such products as silk, porcelain, lacquerware, and tea. The Chinese, on the other hand, desired few imports, with the exception of silver. The trade was conducted under the watchful eye of tight government regulation, which became even tighter over time.

During this period, the government favored stability over innovation, and Chinese technological innovation slowed. Additionally, the growth in population allowed for increased production by way of an increased labor pool, and not by way of the advent of innovative technologies.

Russian Empire (1480 to 1917)

After hundreds of years under Mongol rule, Russia emerged as an empire of it own merit. Ivan III, a grand prince of Moscow, stopped paying tribute to the Mongols and in 1480, began building an empire for himself. He established a strong central government ruled by an absolute monarch, the **czar**, who was also the head of the **Russian Orthodox Church**. The czar also received his authority from God. After a reign of terror by Ivan the Terrible, the **Romanov family** came to power, and it ruled Russia for the next 300 years.

Peter the Great, who reigned from 1682 to 1725, was fascinated with **Western technology** and instituted a policy of forced and rapid modernization. He established industries based on the most advanced science and technology. He was not interested in representative government, though, and instead reformed the military with professional soldiers and began to construct a navy. His obsession with "everything western" is best symbolized by his insistence that all Russian men wear western clothes and shave their beards, and by his construction of the capital city, **St. Petersburg**, his window to the West.

Catherine the Great continued Peter's policies of westernization from 1762 to 1795, though she added her own ideas about the Enlightenment. She sought to improve the lives of her subjects as long as it didn't limit her own power. As the Russian empire expanded east, the institution of **serfdom** expanded with it. A law code written in 1649 placed serfs under tight control of their landlord.

Tokugawa Shogunate (1600 to 1867)

After a period of civil war and disorder, Tokugawa Ieyasu established the Tokugawa Shogunate in 1600. He wanted to stabilize the region and prevent civil war. He did this by increasing his control over the daimyos, insisting that they spend every other year at the **capital, Edo (now Tokyo)**, where he could keep an eye on them.

Relationships with the outside world were also **closely controlled**. Japanese were forbidden from going abroad and from constructing large ships. Europeans were expelled from Japan and foreign merchants were not allowed to trade in Japanese ports (the only exception was a small number of Chinese and Dutch ships). Despite all these restrictions, the Japanese **economy grew**, as agricultural production increased and the population grew. In these more peaceful times, the samurai became government administrators.

Christianity had made some important inroads in Japan by 1580, with 150,000 Japanese Christian converts, but the government ended these missions and went as far as torturing and executing the missionaries who did not leave. The **Dutch merchants** continued to be the principal source of information about Europe, keeping the Japanese up-to-date with important scientific and technological developments.

SYSTEMS OF FORCED LABOR

Atlantic Slave Trade

The forced migration of over 15 million Africans to the New World is one of the most significant outcomes of both the Age of Exploration and the Columbian Exchange that followed. Slavery existed in Africa since ancient times: Tribes would often take prisoners from neighboring tribes and enslave them. African law did not recognize private property, so land did not equal wealth. Control over human labor was what equaled wealth. The spread of Islam also established new trade routes across the northern part of the continent that took African slaves to the Middle East.

By the time Europeans ventured into sub-Saharan Africa, the slave traffic had been well-established for 500 years. The Portuguese explored the west coast of Africa in the 1500s, establishing trade relations with various tribes, and after they secured a piece of the New World in Brazil, brought slaves from Africa for their newly established **plantations.** The slave trade had become **trans-oceanic**, and profits from it encouraged other Europeans to enter the business.

By the mid-1600s, competing stations and fleets brought thousands of slaves monthly across the ocean. This ocean journey, known as the **Middle Passage**, consisted of a 4- to 6-week trip below-deck in cramped quarters. The death toll en route was considerable, and many slaves died upon arrival at the tropical fields of South America. For most African slaves, the end destinations were either Brazil or the sugar plantations in the Caribbean. The **triangular trade** that developed sent European manufactured goods (firearms, in particular) to Africa for slaves, slaves to the Caribean and American mainland, and American products back to Europe.

As more slaves were brought to the coast, African kingdoms reoriented their economies to trade with the Europeans. Some African societies benefited economically from the trade, but several experienced severe population loss. Also, many slaves were traded for guns, and the addition of firearms led to an increase in political conflict in Africa.

Plantation societies were located in the most tropical regions of the Americas, cultivating **cash crops** such as sugar, tobacco, cotton, or coffee. The goal and purpose of the plantation was to gain as much profit as possible from the export of these cash crops.

Though many of the transplanted Africans were Christianized by the Europeans, they retained parts of their language and culture. A unique cultural synthesis occurred, as African music, dress, and mannerisms mixed with Spanish and indigenous cultures in the Americas.

Encomienda System

The early Spanish settlers in the Caribbean needed to recruit a great deal of labor. In fact, the encomienda system gave them the **right to demand labor** in the mines and fields of native peoples. The laborers were worked hard and punished severely.

Cortez and Pizarro brought this system to the American mainland. On the **haciendas** (large estates), natives were often abused; as a result, Spanish officials replaced the encomienda system with the repartimiento system. This system compelled native communities **to supply labor** for Spanish mines and farms, but it limited their work time and it compensated them with wages. Many communities, however, were required to send groups of laborers to work on state projects. In Peru, for instance, the labor system called **mita** mobilized thousands of natives to work in the silver mines. They were paid wages, but there were also many abuses.

Russian Serfdom

After the Mongol rule of Russia, many free peasants fell into **great debt** and were forced to become serfs on large estates. The Russian government encouraged this process beginning in the 1500s because it was a way to satisfy the nobility and to **regulate the peasants** at the same time. As new territories were added to the empire, serfdom extended along with it.

In 1649, an act proclaimed that serfs were born into their status and could not escape it. Serfs could be bought and sold, gambled away, and punished by their masters. Whole villages could be sold to supply manufacturing labor, but serfs were not literally slaves. Serfs who were illiterate and poor had to pay high taxes and owed extensive labor service to their landlords in the form of agriculture, mining, or manufacturing.

CULTURAL AND INTELLECTUAL CHANGES

Renaissance (beginning in the 1400s)

Changes and tensions in the 15th century CE led to new ways of thinking about the nature of humanity and the world. The changes took place slowly, starting on the Italian peninsula. The Crusades had brought Southern Europe into contact with Arab culture, and this stimulated an interest in other cultures and trade. Scholars were uncovering long-forgotten **Roman and Greek** written works that fired the minds of intellectuals in southern Europe. This intellectual reorientation became known as the Renaissance, or "rebirth." The **rebirth** referred to the reappearance of ancient approaches to understanding the world.

The hallmarks of the Renaissance include the following:
- A new view of man as a creative and rational being
- A rediscovery of ancient Greco–Roman knowledge
- Unparalleled accomplishments in literature, music, and art
- A celebration of the human individual

Renaissance Italy was a patchwork of feudal domains—lands belonging to the Roman Catholic Church, kingdoms, and city-states. Famous noble families such as the Medicis had grown wealthy as merchants, since Italy was perfectly located for receiving goods from the Middle East and Asia. This lucrative trade with the **Islamic** and **Byzantine cultures** allowed wealthy Italians to become patrons of painters, sculptors, and scientists. The period was also a celebration of the Roman past; classical architecture and engineering were reexamined and relearned.

A new human ideal was created as the concept of a multifaceted **"Renaissance man"** emerged. Perhaps the best example of such a learned and talented individual was **Leonardo da Vinci**: As an artist, scientist, musician, architect, and engineer, he combined the talents of many men into one person.

Reformation (beginning in the 1500s)

Just as the Renaissance inspired an era of exploration, it also created an atmosphere that encouraged debate and criticism of the existing order. The most powerful institution of the day was the Catholic Church, headquartered in Rome. It had held great power over king and peasant alike for centuries, and had grown large, wealthy, and corrupt. Practices such as selling forgiveness and salvation began to offend even those in the priesthood.

A movement to reform the Church grew out of these concerns. In 1517 in the German domain of Wittenburg, an obscure priest named **Martin Luther** posted a list of issues that he believed the Church should address. The main issues raised by those that would reform the Church were:
- Divisions within the Papacy, in which more than one Pope claimed authority
- Religious traditions and rituals that were not derived from the Scriptures (such as purgatory, pilgrimages, and worship of the saints)

- Corrupt practices such as the sale of indulgences (forgiveness) and religious relics
- Church finances and income
- Lack of piety in the priesthood

Martin Luther's views unleashed a storm of controversy that eventually split the Catholic Church. It divided Europe between those loyal to the Pope in Rome and those who broke away to form other churches. Luther was **excommunicated** from the Church and forced to seek the protection of sympathetic German princes. The Northern European nobility had been under the power of the Pope, and was now able to gain more power by siding with the dissidents, who became known as **Protestants**. This movement of protest spread from central Europe to Holland, Switzerland, and Scandinavia. It eventually took root in England and Scotland as well.

Major outcomes of the Protestant movement included:
- A redrawing of the religious map of Europe, with the Protestants in the north and the Catholics in the south
- A decline in the power of the Roman Catholic Church
- Further power struggles between the citizenry and monarchs; in England, when Protestants took over the Parliament, civil war erupted and the king was arrested and later publicly beheaded
- A series of wars that would pit Catholics and Protestants against each other for the next 200 years

Enlightenment (beginning in the 1700s)

The Enlightenment is known for its outpouring of **intellectual** and **philosophical thought**. It was centered in France, as that kingdom was the cultural heart of Europe at the time. Intellectual revolutionaries in their own right, Enlightenment thinkers were reformists who put forth ideas such as the following:

John Locke (England)	Voltaire (France)	Montesquieu (France)
thought all men are born with natural rights and should be free	said freedom of speech should be permitted	urged tolerance and a government segmented into parts that shared power

This new emphasis on free thought led to the **questioning of traditional authority**. Both the Church and the monarchy were being challenged, and the political radicalism of the Enlightenment would cause great anxiety in the courts of Europe.

As a result of the Roman Catholic mission to China, Jesuits brought back **Chinese knowledge to Europe**. The Confucian civil-service exams influenced European rulers and the rational morality of Confucianism appealed to Enlightenment philosophers.

Scientific Revolution

During the 17th and 18th centuries, a transformation occured in Europe that we call the Scientific Revolution. This was a logical follow-up to the Renaissance, as more and more people wished to investigate the many mysteries of nature. The Scientific Revolution was primarily a period of **intense experimentation and discovery** in fields ranging from medicine to engineering.

Part of the revolutionary approach of scientists was the view that the world functions as a machine. Plants, for example, absorb light and release gas, while the human body processes food and turns it into energy. The Scientific Revolution took place over many decades, but it is usually associated with the famous discoveries of people such as Galileo, Francis Bacon, and Isaac Newton.

IF YOU LEARNED ONLY SIX THINGS IN THIS CHAPTER . . . .

1. As a result of the search for a faster way to the trade routes of the Indian Ocean, the Americas are included in the global trade network, and the process of true globalization begins. This encounter sets off the Colombian Exchange of goods, disease, and cultures which spreads throughout the world.

2. Improvements in and the spread of shipping technologies and gunpowder weapons allow European countries to begin to exercise a more prominent role in world affairs.

3. Native American people die by the millions due to their exposure to previously unknown European diseases. African people are forcibly transported across the Atlantic Ocean to fill the need for forced labor on plantations.

4. New social structures emerge like those in the Americas based on race. While few women exert power publicly, women of the harem in the Ottoman Empire wielded considerable power behind the scenes.

5. In Europe, the Renaissance and Reformation challenge previously accepted beliefs and the power of the Roman Catholic Church. In others parts of the world such as China, reaffirmation of more traditional beliefs is viewed as the key to stability.

6. European empires such as Spain and Portugal stretch their power overseas to conquer and control the newly encountered Americas. At the same time, dominant land-based empires such as the Ottoman, Mughal, and the Qing grow powerful.

REVIEW QUESTIONS

1. The Manchu Qing dynasty adopted many Chinese customs from the Ming dynasty such as

   (A) granting higher status to the merchant class.
   (B) the examination system for choosing government officials.
   (C) wearing elaborate hairpieces at festivals.
   (D) refusing to eat pork.
   (E) banning the Daoist religion.

2. An ideal Renaissance man is one who

   (A) is knowledgeable in many fields and proficient in the arts.
   (B) paints like Leonardo.
   (C) knows the arts of war.
   (D) is a patron of the guilds.
   (E) studies the Byzantine classics.

3. Central to the thinking of 17th century scientists in Europe was

   (A) a central focus on the Christian belief in original sin.
   (B) a mechanistic view of the human body and the world at large.
   (C) a defense of Ptolemy's geocentric theory.
   (D) a belief in the expanding universe.
   (E) a focus on women's rights.

4. The late Mughals created discontent among their people by

   (A) easing the tax burdens of the wealthy.
   (B) forfeiting territory to the Marathas.
   (C) making secret treaties with the Europeans.
   (D) allowing too much autonomy in the provinces.
   (E) discriminating against Hindus and promoting Islamic law.

5. Merchants were at the bottom of the Confucian social hierarchy because

   (A) they had too much power in the imperial court.
   (B) they did not produce anything.
   (C) artisans were jealous of their wealth.
   (D) the emperors were often indebted to them for loans.
   (E) they were always intriguing against the Mandarin class.

6. The Aztec and Incan civilizations were unable to defend themselves against the aggression and weaponry of the

   (A) Portuguese military
   (B) Spanish conquistadores
   (C) Dutch mariners
   (D) English diplomats
   (E) French couriers

7. After 1603, the Tokugawa Shogunate disallowed

   (A) merchant families from trading outside their home domain.
   (B) any Japanese from traveling outside the home islands.
   (C) the daimyo from collecting taxes.
   (D) the making of sake in the rural domains.
   (E) all trade with foreigners.

8. Renaissance interest in the Greek and Roman texts was due in large part to

   (A) the continued focus on these texts throughout Europe since the fall of Rome.
   (B) the reintroduction of these texts from the Muslim world.
   (C) the discovery of these texts during the voyages to the New World.
   (D) the rejection of outside influence and focus on values of the Middle Ages.
   (E) encouragement by the Roman Catholic authorities to reexamine the past.

9. The African slave trade delivered the majority of slaves to

   (A) New France
   (B) The Caribbean islands and Brazil
   (C) British America
   (D) Mexico
   (E) The Gold Coast

10. Renaissance paintings were characterized by all the following EXCEPT

    (A) Use of perspective
    (B) Large frescoes on walls
    (C) Realism
    (D) An emphasis on light striking the subject
    (E) Epic romantic scenes from nature

11. In the late Middle Ages one of the causes of the decline of papal authority was

    (A) a long famine in Central Europe.
    (B) the decline of the monastic orders.
    (C) Islamic conquering of Europe.
    (D) the massive mortality rate during the Black Death.
    (E) the ongoing war between England and Spain.

12. Enlightenment philosophy was a threat to European monarchies because it

    (A) supported the authority of the Pope.
    (B) supported state-run education.
    (C) suggested the idea of individual liberty and rights.
    (D) pushed for the overthrow of the capitalist system.
    (E) was so popular with the peasant class.

13. The Qing rulers of China segregated themselves from their subjects by doing all of the following EXCEPT

    (A) Forcing Chinese men to wear their hair in a long braid
    (B) Forbidding Chinese to travel to Manchuria
    (C) Disallowing marriage between Manchu and Chinese
    (D) Not using the traditional examination system to choose government officials
    (E) Not allowing Chinese to learn the Manchu language

14. Magellan's voyage around the world in 1519 resulted in

    (A) the further spreading of Protestantism.
    (B) Spanish claims in the Pacific.
    (C) a visit to the Forbidden City.
    (D) a knighthood for Magellan upon his return.
    (E) the decline of capitalism in the Mediterranean.

15. Which of the following was NOT a global impact of silver?

    (A) It strengthened and integrated the world economy.
    (B) It increased outside interest in the Americas.
    (C) It increased the power of the Spanish crown.
    (D) It bypassed the need for China in global trade.
    (E) It led to the exploitation of indigenous labor in the Americas.

16. Which of the following was NOT an important feature of Peter the Great's efforts to westernize Russia?

    (A) Modernizing the army and navy
    (B) Instituting a parliamentary style government
    (C) Encouraging western-style dress
    (D) Traveling abroad to study technology
    (E) Increasing trading relations with Western Europe

17. Which of the following rulers was the most religiously tolerant?

    (A) Louis XIV of France
    (B) Henry VIII of England
    (C) Akbar the Great of the Mughals
    (D) Aurangzeb of the Mughals
    (E) Philip II of Spain

18. A significant effect of the Colombian Exchange was that

    (A) European power slowly declined
    (B) American diseases spread to Europe
    (C) World population declined
    (D) The Atlantic slave trade declined
    (E) American foods were introduced to European diets

19. Which of the following statements accurately reflects a major difference between slavery in the Americas and Russian serfdom?

    (A) Russian serfs were the local peasant population, while slaves in the Americas came from Africa.
    (B) Slaves in the Americas performed primarily agricultural work, while serfs in Russia did not.
    (C) Serfdom was a permanent institution, while slavery in the Americas was always temporary.
    (D) Serfs were bound to their owner, while slaves were bound to the land.
    (E) Slaves in the Americas were subject to brutal working conditions, while serfs in Russia were not.

20. Sugar and tobacco are important examples of

    (A) African products
    (B) Cash crops
    (C) Crops requiring cooler climates
    (D) Products originating in Asia
    (E) European products

21. Which of the following is true of both Spanish and Portuguese colonies in the Americas from 1450 to 1750?

    (A) They both outlawed slave labor by 1750.
    (B) Little to no intermarriage occurred with the indigenous populations.
    (C) As the plantation system grew, so did the use of slave labor.
    (D) The Catholic Church was not successful in converting natives in the regions.
    (E) The colonies had gained their independence by the end of the time period.

22. After Columbus's encounter with the Americas,

    (A) the Ming dynasty stopped its voyages.
    (B) the Byzantine Empire was conquered by the Ottoman Empire.
    (C) slavery was introduced to Africa.
    (D) Native American population drastically declined.
    (E) the Crusaders began to conquer the Holy Land.

23. The statements below refer to which empire?

    - Originally were semi-nomadic Turks
    - Had an elite fighting force of slave troops made of Christian boys
    - Islamic religious scholars served administrative functions

    (A) Mughal Empire
    (B) Ottoman Empire
    (C) Songhai Empire
    (D) Qing Empire
    (E) Safavid Empire

24. What distinguishes the time period 1450 to 1750 from earlier time periods?

    (A) Inclusion of the Americas in global trade
    (B) The introduction of the institution of slavery
    (C) The first use of ships in Indian Ocean trade
    (D) The removal of China from any involvement in world trade
    (E) The end of the Ottoman empire

25. The Manchus and the Mongols were both

    (A) defeated by the Ottomans.
    (B) involved in the Atlantic Ocean trade.
    (C) rulers of Japan.
    (D) uninterested in empire building.
    (E) nomadic people who conquered China.

Document-Based Question

Directions: The following question is based on the accompanying Documents 1 to 4. (The documents have been edited for the purpose of this exercise.)

This question is designed to test your ability to work with and understand historical documents. Write an essay that:
- Has a relevant thesis and supports that thesis with evidence from the documents.
- Uses all or all but one of the documents.
- Analyzes the documents by grouping them in as many appropriate ways as possible. Does not simply summarize the documents individually.
- Takes into account the sources of the documents and analyzes the authors' points of view.
- Explains the need for at least one additional type of document.

You may refer to relevant historical information not mentioned in the documents.

> Based on the following documents, analyze and discuss the impact of Mughal rule on India.
>
> <u>Historical Background</u>
> India's predominantly decentralized history of regional kingdoms was interrupted by the conquest of Babur and the establishment of the Mughal Empire, a Muslim–Turkish dynasty, which ruled from 1523 to the mid-1700s.

Document 1

Mughal Empire

Document 2

Source: The Great Moghul Jahangir: Letter to James I, King of England, 1617 AD

When your Majesty shall open this letter let your royal heart be as fresh as a sweet garden. Let all people make reverence at your gate; let your throne be advanced higher; amongst the greatness of the kings of the prophet Jesus, let your Majesty be the greatest, and all monarchies derive their counsel and wisdom from your breast as from a fountain, that the law of the majesty of Jesus may revive and flourish under your protection.

The letter of love and friendship which you sent and the presents, tokens of your good affections toward me, I have received by the hands of your ambassador, Sir Thomas Roe (who well deserves to be your trusted servant), delivered to me in an acceptable and happy hour; upon which mine eyes were so fixed that I could not easily remove them to any other object, and have accepted them with great joy and delight.

Upon which assurance of your royal love I have given my general command to all the kingdoms and ports of my dominions to receive all the merchants of the English nation as the subjects of my friend; that in what place so ever they choose to live, they may have free liberty without any restraint; and at what port so ever they shall arrive, that neither Portugal nor any other shall dare to molest their quiet; and in what city so ever they shall have residence, I have commanded all my governors and captains to give them freedom answerable to their own desires; to sell, buy, and to transport into their country at their pleasure.

For confirmation of our love and friendship, I desire your Majesty to command your merchants to bring in their ships of all sorts of rarities and rich goods fit for my palace; and that you be pleased to send me your royal letters by every opportunity, that I may rejoice in your health and prosperous affairs; that our friendship may be interchanged and eternal.

Your Majesty is learned and quick-sighted as a prophet, and can conceive so much by few words that I need write no more.

The God of heaven give you and us increase of honor.

Document 3

Source: Francois Bernier, a French physician who visited India and Bengal between 1656 and 1668

An Account of India and the Great Moghul, 1655

He who reigned there was called Chah-Jehan [i.e., Shah Jahan],... who have left and communicated their name to the strangers that now govern Indostan, the country of the Indians; though those that are employed in public charges and offices, and even those that are listed in the militia, be not all of the race of the Moguls, but strangers and nations gathered out of all countries, most of them Persians, some Arabians, and some Turks. For, to be esteemed a Mogul it is enough to be a stranger, white of face, and a Mohammedan; in distinction as well to the Indians, who are brown and pagans, as to the Christians of Europe, who are called Franguis [i.e., "Ferengis" or "Franks"]....

My lord, you may have seen before this, by the maps of Asia, how great every way is the extent of the empire of the Great Mogul, which is commonly called India or Indostan

In this same extent of country there are sundry nations which the Mogul is not full master of, most of them still retaining their particular sovereigns and lords that neither obey him nor pay him tribute but from constraint; many that do little, some that do nothing at all, and some also that receive tribute from him...

Of the like sort are more than a hundred rajahs, or considerable heathen sovereigns, dispersed through the whole empire, some near to, others remote from, Agra and Delhi; amongst whom there are about fifteen or sixteen that are very rich and puissant; such are Rana (who formerly was, as it were, emperor of the rajahs, and who is said to be of the progeny of King Porus [who fought Alexander the Great at the Battle of the Hydaspes]), Jesseigne, and Jessomseigne, who are so great and powerful that if they three alone should combine they would hold him [i.e., the Great Moghul] back; each of them being able in a very short time to raise and bring into the field twenty-five thousand horse, better troops than the Mogul's...

Continued →

The Mogul is obliged to keep these rajahs in his service for sundry reasons: the first, because the militia of the rajahs is very good (as was said above) and because there are rajahs (as was intimated also) any one of whom can bring into the field above twenty-five thousand men; the second, the better to bridle the other rajahs and to reduce them to reason, when they cantonize, or when they refuse to pay tribute, or when, out of fear or other cause, they will not leave their country to serve in the army when the Mogul requires it; the third, the better to nourish
jealousies and keenness among them, by favoring and caressing one more than the other, which is done to that degree that they proceed to fight with one another very frequently.

Document 4

Source: Baktha'war Khan, early 1680s, an advisor to Aurangzeb [Mughal emperor 1658–1707], excerpts from his history of the world

In consideration of their rank and merit, he (Aurangzeb) shows much honor and respect to the saints and learned men, and through his cordial and liberal exertions, the sublime doctrines of our pure religion have obtained such prevalence throughout the wide territories of Hindustan as they never had in the reign of any former king.

Hindu writers have been entirely excluded from holding public offices, and all
the worshipping places of the infidels (Hindus) and the great temples of these infamous people have been thrown down and destroyed in a manner which excites astonishment at the successful completion of so difficult a task . . .

Part Three: AP World History Review
Chapter 5

Change-Over-Time Question

Directions: Answer the following question: You should spend 5 minutes organizing or outlining your essay. Write an essay that:
- Has a relevant thesis and supports that thesis with appropriate historical evidence.
- Addresses all parts of the question.
- Uses world historical context to show change over time and/or continuities
- Analyzes the process of change over time and/or continuity.

> Choose ONE of the regions below and analyze the changes and continuities in their involvement and roles in trade from 600 to 1750.
>
> China
> Sub-Saharan Africa
> South Asia
> Middle East

Comparative Question

Directions: Answer the following question. You should spend 5 minutes organizing or outlining your essay. Write an essay that:
- Has a relevant thesis and supports that thesis with appropriate historical evidence.
- Addresses all parts of the question.
- Makes direct, relevant comparisons.
- Analyzes relevant reasons for similarities and differences.

As Western power and influence increased during the period 1450 to 1750, so did Western interaction with the outside world. Discuss the similarities and differences in the interaction with the West of TWO of the following during the era 1450 to 1750:

Russia
Ottoman Empire
Tokugawa Japan
Latin America

ANSWERS AND EXPLANATIONS

1. B

The Qings adopted many Neo-Confucian customs, such as the civil service system of choosing able men for government service. Merchants were looked down upon in the Confucian social hierarchy. During the Qing dynasty, ethnic Chinese were forbidden to wear Manchu clothes or speak the Manchu language. Chinese men had to wear a distinctive braid of hair down their backs. Pork is a standard part of the Chinese diet. Daoism was in no way forbidden during the Qing period.

2. A

In celebrating the individual, Renaissance ideals suggested that an educated person should be versed in many disciplines. Men were taught how to be literate, socially adept, and well-spoken. They were expected to be knowledgeable in music, science, and military affairs. Though the guilds existed during this time period, patronizing them was not a mark of learning or accomplishment. The focus during the Renaissance was on the study of ancient texts from Greece, not on those written during the post-ancient Byzantine period.

3. B

Part of the post-Renaissance view of the world involved looking into systems that one could observe; if the human heart is a pump, then the body is a kind of machine. Our earth was part of a "system" of other planets. The geocentric theory was already discredited by this time, and while some women made names for themselves during the Renaissance, feminism is a more recent consciousness. The church had great influence in the 17th century, but scientists were not limited by orthodox beliefs such as original sin.

4. E

The later Mughal rulers became increasingly orthodox in their Muslim faith and discriminated against the Hindu majority. This helped bring about their downfall, as rival Hindu kingdoms ate away at their territories. The Mughals overlapped with the arrival of the Europeans, but they did not make treaties with them. Taxation upon the wealthy was not a cause of instability as the Mughal reign declined.

5. B

Merchants were not part of the scholar elite in traditional China and they were not valued. They were seen as nonproductive members of society. They had no influence in the imperial court and they did not interact with the Mandarin elite. Artisans had a higher status because they made things of value for the population, unlike the merchants who bought and sold goods.

6. B

After initial successes by Spanish explorers, the crown sent out military adventurers in search of riches. These conquistadores were the first white men to encounter the Aztec and Inca peoples. Accompanying them were missionary priests, not diplomats. The French explored further to the north. Likewise, the Dutch explored the eastern coast of North America and South Africa. The Portuguese were given dominion over Brazil in eastern South America, so they did not have contact with the Aztecs or Incas, who were located in other regions of the Americas.

7. B

After 1603, Tokugawa Ieyasu disallowed any Japanese from traveling beyond the home islands. This edict held sway for over two centuries, though there were some who defied the law and sailed to other lands. Very limited trade was allowed with the Dutch, and the daimyo certainly needed to continue collecting taxes from the peasantry. Merchants tended to work in their own provinces, but as the Tokugawa era progressed more widespread commerce developed. Sake was never prohibited in Japanese history.

8. B

The Islamic world had preserved, developed, and studied the ancient texts of the Greek and the Romans. The increase in trade in Europe after the Crusades led to the reintroduction of these texts after they had been translated into Arabic.

9. B

As the New World economy evolved, the slave trade expanded to meet its demands. The Spanish and Portuguese set up large plantations in Central and South America to grow sugar and other products. Most of these plantations were in Brazil and the islands of the Caribbean. The slaves came primarily from the Gold Coast of Africa, and relatively few were sent to British America to work the farms there. Very few slaves were transported to New France on the St. Lawrence seaway, as the commerce there focused on the fur business. The Spanish were involved in the slave trade, but only a small percentage of slaves were used in Mexico, since large plantations were not common.

10. E

Epic scenes of nature were common during the Romantic period in the 19th century—not during the Renaissance. Painters during the Renaissance pioneered the use of perspective and light when creating their works. Raphael's wall frescoes are some of the most famous works of Renaissance art. A new lifelike realism was also a hallmark of the period's art.

11. D

The huge mortality rate of the Black Death in medieval times had a great impact on Europe. One effect was a spiritual malaise that caused disenchantment with the Church and its leaders. The prayers to save loved ones from the scourge often went unanswered, and this produced a crisis of faith. There was no famine in Europe of any significance and the monastic orders were a tiny part of the greater population. The Popes used the Crusades against Islam as a means to rally support for the Church. Wars between various kingdoms were not the direct provenance of the Church in the Middle Ages.

12. C

Enlightenment philosophy produced work that both supported and challenged the kings and dynasties of the day. Voltaire and Rousseau suggested that humans have innate dignity and should enjoy the right to freedom and happiness. These thoughts framed the political revolutions in America, France, and many other locales later on. Philosophers of the time period were anti-clerical, and by extension critical of the Church and its influence. The Church-run schools were also criticized by the philosophers as they advocated a national system of education that would not be influenced by the Catholics. Enlightenment emphasis on rights would later influence the abolition movement, but this was not connected to monarchy. At this time, most of the peasants were illiterate so they did not have access to the intellectual influences of Voltaire and others.

13. D

The Qing separated themselves from the Chinese in terms of dress and mandating hairstyles, and limiting travel within the empire. However, they did borrow the Confucian tradition of using the classic examinations to select promising young scholars for civil service. Manchu and Chinese were not allowed to marry each other. Likewise, the use of the Manchu language was forbidden for the Chinese.

14. B

Sailing west for the Spanish, Magellan beat the other European nations to the Pacific. On that voyage, he was able to claim Guam and the Philippines before he was killed by the natives. One boat survived, however, and returned to Spain to record the new claims. Guam and Manila became new outposts for Spain until the 19th century. This furthered the spread of Catholicism as the empires of Europe grew around the world. Magellan was killed in the Philippines and did not land in northern China. Del Cano was the one to continue the voyage after Magellan's death, and it was he who was honored back in Spain. The voyages of both Columbus and Magellan established Spain as the new maritime power in western Europe. As the riches flowed in from the New World in the form of gold and silver, Spain became a major consumer of goods from the rest of Europe.

15. D

China was the integral player in the silver trade, since it was the demand for silver in China and the demand for Chinese goods that drove the trade. As a result of the silver trade, the world economy strengthened, interest in America's silver mines increased, Spain gained wealth and power, and Native American labor was exploited in silver mines such as Potosi.

16. B

Peter the Great was interested in westernizing and modernizing Russia, but he was not interested in liberalizing the government. He wanted to the modernize the army, navy, dress, technology and trade, but he also wanted to maintain absolute power.

17. C

Akbar the Great, the Mughal emperor, was a Muslim but was religiously tolerant of Hindus in his empire that ruled India. He abolished the non-Muslim tax and gave Hindus positions in the government. Aurangzeb ruled the Mughals toward the end of the empire, reinstated the non-Muslim tax, and persecuted Hindus. The other three rulers listed were Europeans known for being religiously intolerant: Louis XIV (France), Henry VIII (England), and Philip II (Spain).

18. E

American foods such as potato, corn, and tomatoes were introduced to European diets and influenced the cultural traditions of that area. European power increased not declined during this period. European diseases such as smallpox spread to the Americas, not the other way around. World population increased overall, not declined, because of the healthier diets. And the Atlantic slave-trade increased because of the increased demand for slave labor on American plantations.

19. A

Serfdom in Russia developed as a way to control the peasant population and satisfy the noble class. Slaves in the Americas were imported from Africa through the Atlantic slave trade. Both serfs and slaves performed agricultural work, such as working on plantations. Both institutions were permanent: serfs were bound to the land, while slaves were bound to their owner. Both systems of forced labor could be brutal.

20. B

Both sugar and tobacco were cash crops that were grown in the Americas and Caribbean on large plantations. The growth of products like these led to an increase in demand for African slave labor, and in turn, the slave trade.

21. **C**

In both colonies, the plantation system grew throughout the period, and with that came the demand for slave labor. Slave labor was not outlawed until the next period. Intermarriage with indigenous people did occur and created a class of mestizos. The Catholic Church was powerful and influential in both areas. The colonies did not gain their independence until the early 19th century.

22. **D**

Due to the introduction of diseases such as smallpox, the Native American populations drastically declined. Their lack of immunity to these diseases led to devastating consequences. The Ming voyages were halted 60 years before Columbus set sail. The Byzantine Empire was conquered by the Ottomans in 1453. Slavery had been an institution in Africa. The Crusades attempted to conquer the Holy Land in the 11th and 12th centuries.

23. **B**

The Ottoman Empire was founded by a group that was originally semi-nomadic Turks who settled in Anatolia, the elite force of slave troops was known as janissaries, and the Islamic scholars served as administrators in the empire.

24. **A**

The encounter with the Americas in 1492 set the stage for truly global trade. Slavery had been an institution throughout history. Ships had been used in Indian Ocean trade for centuries. China remained involved in world trade, in particular the silver trade. The Ottoman Empire lasted until 1918.

25. **E**

Both the Manchus, who established the Qing dynasty, and the Mongols, who established the Yuan dynasty, were nomads who conquered and ruled China.

Document-Based Question: Sample Response

During the time period 1450 to 1750, the subcontinent of India was ruled by the Mughal dynasty. While the Mughals conquered almost the entire subcontinent, they ruled with the cooperation of the local princes. This cooperation was later extended to the European merchants who came to trade along the Indian Ocean. However, unlike the control and cooperation established with the local Indian princes over whom the Mughal always had the upper hand, they allowed the European traders too much independence, which eventually led to their ability to control the area. Additionally, the exclusion and persecution of the majority population of Hindus led to the decline in the empire.

As seen in the map, the Mughals, who were Turkish nomads, successfully came from Central Asia to conquer and dominate most of the Indian subcontinent. The domination of the Indian subcontinent by a centralizing power had only happened a few times in history before. However, this domination would not have been possible without the help and cooperation of the local Indian princes, or rajahs. According to the account written by Francois Bernier, a French physician writing during his travels to India, the Mughals had conquered a large and wealthy empire but they allowed some local rulers to remain in power. This outsider view expresses the idea that wealthy rajahs thrived in this period and that the Mughals kept them in power for particular reasons, such as the fact that they could use their own strong militias to defend the empire. Also, the relationship of the rajahs with the empire often prevented them from allying together against the Mughals; instead it often pitted one against another. It would be helpful to have evidence from the perspective of both the rajahs themselves, as well as the Mughal emperors to determine if their interpretation of the relationship would concur with that of Francois Bernier.

It appears that the Mughals tried to establish a similar relationship with the European traders who entered Indian ports in hopes of profiting from the lucrative Indian Ocean trade. The emperor Jahangir wrote a letter to King James I of England in 1617 expressing his wishes to fully cooperate with the English. The tone of this letter seems almost overly accommodating, especially coming from the emperor of the Mughals. The emperor, in his letter, promises to receive the English as friends and give them full liberty in their port of choice. The purpose seems to be to encourage trade with the English, which could economically benefit the Mughals. However, the tone of this letter seems to give the English the upper hand in the relationship, rather than the Mughals. It would be helpful to have evidence of King James's response to Jahangir's letter, to see if the English king respected Mughal authority or disregarded it. Later, in the Mughal empire under the rule of Aurangzeb, the impact was also negative. In an effort to praise the efforts of his ruler, Baktha'war Khan, an advisor to the emperor, describes the emperor's efforts to eliminate the Hindu influence in the kingdom. Aurangzeb ordered the Hindu temples destroyed in order to promote what he believed to be the one true religion, Islam. This persecution led to discontent in a majority Hindu empire and weakened the Mughal ruler. It would helpful to get a first-hand account from a Hindu who lived during the rule of Aurangzeb to elevate the degree to which Hindus felt persecuted.

As the Mughal Empire declined, European influence increased in the area and religious division returned. The empire that had conquered almost the entire subcontinent of India and had succeeded in dealing with the decentralized nature of India (through cooperation yet control of the local rajahs), seemed to weaken under the influence of the European traders. It lost control of its economic affairs and divided itself along religious lines.

Change-Over-Time Question: Sample Response

Between 600 and 1750, China was continuously an integral player in the expanding global trade network. However, it simultaneously regressed from being the enthusiastic leader in an expansive world economy to playing more of a supporting role. This transition was partly self-imposed as its self views and worldview shifted, though the incorporation of the Americas by Europe into the global economy also caused a decline in China's centrality (even geographic) and dominance. However, while China may have grown more detached from the trade network, it was too strong and influential to ever disassociate completely.

The beginning of these thousand years in history was strong for China. The Tang dynasty was established around the year 600 and it prospered agriculturally (3 field system), politically (civil service examinations), and technologically. These factors combined created a strong, stable China based on a Confucian traditional foundation, allowing for a strong economy to arise. Between 600 to 1450, China was truly the world leader in trade. It increased its presence in and then came to dominate the Indian Ocean and the South China Sea, building connections with the Middle East and Southeast Asia, respectively. This maritime advancement was made possible by new naval technologies developed under the Tang and Song dynasties, such as the magnetic compass and improved ships. Gunpowder, another technological improvement, would make its way through the trade network to the Middle East and aid the later establishment of Islamic Empires, and to Europeans who used firearms to help conquer the Americas. Another change which took place during this earlier period was industrialization increase. Especially under Song rule, new port cities were built where Arab and Persian merchants became somewhat assimilated into Chinese society. Larger cities and more expansive trade cycles necessitated the development of new economic systems in China, and paper money, banking, and a "flying cash" system all were established. Also, trade increase leads inevitably to interaction increase, and new religions, such as Buddhism, integrated themselves into Chinese culture. Buddhism blended with the consistently prominent Confucianism to create a new special type of Confucianism known as Neo-Confucianism, which had profound political consequences. Throughout this period China continued using the Silk Roads as a means of relations with the Mediterranean world and Chinese luxury items such as porcelain and silk were in high demand. Closer to the end of this period, the Yuan dynasty (Mongol rule) was replaced by the Chinese Ming's, who radically altered China's position as the most dominant global trader.

From around 1450 to 1750, China separated itself from the global market significantly. The beginning of this movement was marked by the closing of many ports and the destruction of ships and travel records by the Ming (through the following Qing dynasty similarly regulated trade.) These actions were very consequential, for China lost its dominance in Indian Ocean and Pacific trade, allowing Arabs, Persians, and Europeans to grow politically and economically stronger. China self-imposed this isolation because it feared foreign influence after being under Mongol control, and also because it was ethnocentric and found little value in foreign goods. This attitude, along with the decrease in technological development (Chinese Confucianism, still prominent, favored government stability over technological innovation) greatly reduced China's previous enthusiastic trade participation and allowed a rising Europe to dominate the world with their age of colonization. Still, China remained consistently important to global trade, greatly due to the desire for Chinese luxury goods. Europeans extracted silver (the new global commodity) from the Americas and used it to pay for Chinese products. Japan paid China with silver as well. While the Chinese were exporting porcelain, silk, and spices as before, they did not import many products, but rather used silver as their currency. The Chinese consumption of silver (which eventually led to severe dependency based economic problems) kept them an active member of global trade, for they were too great and influential a country to ever completely detach. However, China lost its desire to steer the world economy, and in doing so handed the reins over to Europe.

China was always important to global trade during the years 600 to 1750, though its dominance and desire to incorporate foreign ideas and products decreased. These years in history are best defined by the establishment of a truly global economy, especially with the inclusion of the Americas. China's regression in trade impacted not only their society, but also European society. China closed the door to the Western world (through remained connected), and allowed Europe to rise to become the most influential and powerful area in the global economy and the world.

—Written by Gabi Tortorello, Fox Lane High School, Bedford, New York

Comparative Question: Sample Response

From 1450 to 1750, Western interaction with the outside world reached new heights. Due to improvements in navigational technology, Western European countries began to explore the outside world. While Russian leaders embraced Western ideas and technology in hopes of strengthening their own empire, Japanese leaders rejected Western influence because they viewed it as a threat to stability. However, despite their radically different approaches in interacting with the West, both countries improved economically during this time period.

Economically, while Russia encouraged trade and interaction with the West, Japan rejected it. Czars like Peter the Great believed that Russia had fallen drastically behind the advancements of the West and was determined to have Russia catch up. After traveling to Western Europe, Peter brought back advisors to help him remold Russia in a more Western image. He encouraged use of Western shipping technology to modernize his navy and increased trading relationships with Western Europe. However, as serfdom was declining in Western Europe, it was extended in Russia in an effort to control the peasant population and satisfy the noble class. On the other hand, in Japan, after some initial dealings with European traders, the Tokugawa Shogunate closed its ports. Trade was not permitted with Europe, n or was outside travel. The Shogun viewed Western influence as a destabilizing force that could damage Japanese society. The one exception was the trade that was established with Dutch traders. This selective trade allowed the Japanese to stay abreast of developments in Europe while controlling outside interaction. Despite this external trade cut-off, internal trade flourished throughout Japan in this period and the Japanese economy improved.

Culturally, Russian leadership wanted to imitate Western culture and style. Peter the Great insisted that nobles no longer wear traditional Russian robes, but instead wear Western European-style clothes. Peter even insisted that Russian men shave their beards. For those who resisted, Peter was known to rip off the beard himself. Also, the seclusion of women was ended, and men and women were encouraged to socialize openly in public. In Japan, Christian missionaries had, at first, converted some native people. The Tokugawa Shogunate, however, expelled the missionaries and executed those who would not leave. Again, this Western influence was seen as a destabilize force and something that would weaken Japan.

During this age of interaction, Japan and Russia took radically different paths. Russia, with some success, tried to actively copy Western economic and cultural developments, while Japan rejected them. Both countries had the goal of strengthening their homelands, but used different methods to achieve that aim.

Part Three: AP World History Review | 173

Chapter 6: 1750 to 1914

- The Big Picture
- Why This Periodization?
- Revolutions and Independence Movements
- Nationalism and the Nation-State
- Industrialization
- Reform and Reaction
- Imperialism and Its Impact
- Emancipation
- Cultural Influences

THE BIG PICTURE

1. Patterns and effects of interactions among major societies: trade, war, diplomacy, and international organizations

    In other words: **What happens when people come in contact with each other?**

With the development of industrialization, the world became truly interdependent. The industrialized nations in search of raw materials and new markets often imperialized areas to protect economic interests.

2. The dynamics of change and continuity across the world history periods covered in this course, the causes and processes involved in major changes of these dynamics

    In other words: **Why do some things change while other things stay the same?**

Industrialization changed almost everything. The way people worked, lived, traveled, related to their families, communicated, and identified themselves changed for many people. At the same time, many traditional forces resisted change. Religious influence and patriarchal gender structures remained in many parts of the world.

3. The effects of technology, economics, and demography on people and the environment (population growth and decline, disease, labor systems, manufacturing, migrations, agriculture, weaponry)

   In other words: **How does the development of new technology and movement of people affect the world?**

New technologies quickened the pace of life. As population grew, many migrated to the cities in search of opportunities in the factories. Free wage laborers were more desirable in this new market-driven economy than forced labor and as a result slaves and serfs were emancipated.

4. Systems of social structure and gender structure (comparing major features within and among societies and assessing change)

   In other words: **How do societies organize themselves socially and what roles do men and women play?**

The middle class emerged as a new force both economically and politically. It often led the political revolutions of the period, and benefited in the new industrial age. Women gained some economic opportunities in factories, but they were paid considerably less than their male counterparts. These new economic opportunities and Enlightenment ideals pushed women to fight for political rights. The working class also emerged as a force for change: Through organization into unions, it was able to advocate for change in working conditions.

5. Cultural, intellectual, and religious developments and interactions among and within societies

   In other words: **How do people identify themselves and express themselves culturally and intellectually?**

As the world interacted more than ever, so did the cultures of the world. Western culture strongly influenced many Asian and African areas through colonization, and Asian and African culture and art were extremely influential on European intellectuals and artists. Enlightenment ideals such as equality, freedom of speech, and freedom of religion became very influential in many parts of the world. At the same time, traditional religious organizations maintained power and influence in other parts of the world.

6. Changes in functions and structures of states and in attitudes toward states and political identities (political culture), including the emergence of the nation–state (types of political organization)

   In other words: **How do people govern themselves?**

The ideas of the Enlightenment said that the government was responsible to its people. This idea inspired revolutions and independence movements throughout the period. Governments experimented with democratic values, but this democracy was extended to a limited class of people. Older land-based empires struggled with change and the adaptation to the new age. The nation became the new concept of identity in the 19th century and would soon spread worldwide.

WHY THIS PERIODIZATION?

This time period can be summarized into five key words: revolution, nationalism, industrialization, imperialism, and emancipation. The revolutions and independence movements inspired by the Enlightenment had worldwide effects, redefining the relationship between the government and the governed. The concept of the nation shaped how people defined their identity and it became the dominant political force.

Industrialization changed the way people worked and lived. More powerful, industrialized nations reached out to dominate Asian and African areas economically and politically to protect their own interests. Slaves and serfs were emancipated in this new wage- and market-driven world, and women fought for their own emancipation.

REVOLUTIONS AND INDEPENDENCE MOVEMENTS

North America

Britain's empire in America seemed secure after its victory over France in 1763, but the cost of the war had been high. Dealing with this debt started a chain of events that led to deteriorating relations between the crown in London and its subjects in North America.

The American colonists argued that they could govern their own affairs with the famous quote, "no taxation without representation." In 1774, the Continental Congress organized and coordinated colonial resistance, and in 1775, British troops and American militia clashed at Lexington, Massachusetts. On July 4, 1776, the **Declaration of Independence**—inspired by Enlightenment ideas—justified independence. It listed a long list of abuses by the British king amid a declaration that **all men were created equal**. Though the British enjoyed many advantages such as the strong government, navy, army, and loyalists, the war was fought from a great distance, and the colonists had the support of other European states.

By 1781, the British surrendered to George Washington, and in 1783, the Peace of Paris formally recognized American independence. The colonies created a federal republic with 13 states and a written constitution that guaranteed freedom of speech and religion.

In reality, however, there was no legal and political equality. Only men of property enjoyed full rights and the landless men, women, slaves, and indigenous people did not have access to this new freedom. Yet this was an important step in the development of a government responsible to its people.

France

Unlike the Americans who wanted the right to self-govern, the French revolutionaries in France wanted to replace the "old order" with completely new political, social, and cultural structures. The causes of this discontent included large war debts, a large tax burden on the peasants, and the increasing gap between the rich and poor. The king was forced to call the Estates General in hopes of addressing the war debts by increasing tax on the nobility.

The three estates consisted of:

1st estate:	100,000 clergy
2nd estate:	400,000 nobles
3rd estate:	24 million serfs, free peasants, and bourgeoisie

Each of these estates had one vote. When the 3rd estate demanded political and social reform, the 1st and 2nd estates mostly resisted. This led the 3rd estate to secede from the Estates General and from the National Assembly. Further tensions led to a disintegration of royal authority in Paris. Some military joined the masses, and a royal fortress, the Bastille, was stormed in July 1789. **The Declaration of Rights of Man and Citizen** declared the equality of all men, the sovereignty of the people, and the rights to liberty, property, and security. The new constitution created a constitutional monarchy.

The masses rose up and radicals within the revolution took control. As in England a century earlier, the king was executed in public. Later, the queen and many other aristocrats were beheaded as the revolution sought to stamp out the old elite.

The Committee for Public Safety, led by Maximilien Robespierre, now governed France and instigated a "Reign of Terror," executing many aristocrats. Eventually, the revolution turned on the very radicals that started it, and it thrust France into war with the powers of Europe. The kingdoms of Austria, Britain, and Russia combined in a coalition that was meant to defeat France and undo the revolution.

The creation of a large revolutionary army to defend France helped catapult **Napoleon Bonaparte** to power. He named himself First Consul, then Consul for Life, and finally Emperor. In 1804, Napoleon issued his moderate Civil Code, which affirmed the political and legal equality of all adult men, established a merit-based society, and protected private property. However, it also limited free speech and allowed censorship of the newspapers.

Napoleon and his army defeated many of the powers of Europe and took control of much of the continent. The Napoleonic era lasted from 1803 to 1814, as warfare ranged from Europe to North Africa and the Middle East. At times, France found itself faced with multiple enemies. Taking on Russia in 1812 proved fatal, however, as the army did not survive the winter campaign. The victors met at the **Congress of Vienna** in 1815 to restore the French monarchy and protect the old regimes. Attempted revolutions (most notably in 1830 and 1848) continued to shake the old monarchies throughout the 1800s. Meanwhile, the experiment in democracy in North America continued as the United States survived a bloody civil war and industrialized rapidly in the late 1800s.

Haiti

The island of Hispaniola in the Caribbean was the major center of **sugar production**. The Spanish controlled the east (Santo Domingo) and the French controlled the west (Saint Domingue), one of the richest of all the European colonies. Saint Domingue's population consisted of 40,000 white French settlers, 30,000 gens de couleur (free people of color), and 500,000 black slaves, most born in Africa. These slaves worked under brutal conditions and the mortality rate was very high. There was also a large community of escaped slaves, known as maroons.

The French colonial government had sent 800 gens de couleur to fight in the American Revolution and they returned with ideas of reforming their own society. When the French Revolution broke out in 1789, the white settlers sought the right to govern themselves, but opposed extending political and legal equality to the gens de couleur. This led to civil war between these two groups.

While these two groups were in conflict, a **slave revolt** occurred in August of 1791. As a result, the whites, gens de couleurs, and slaves battled each other. French troops—and later, British and Spanish troops—invaded the island in hopes of gaining control. The slaves, however, were led by Toussaint Louverture, who built a strong and disciplined army, and by 1797 controlled most of Saint Domingue.

In 1801, a constitution was written that granted equality and citizenship to all, and in 1803, independence was declared. By 1804, Haiti was the **second independent republic in the western hemisphere**, and the first republic that abolished slavery. Great economic difficulty followed independence, however. Many nations such as the United States refused to recognize or conduct trade with Haiti because of slave emancipation, and a new nation of small farmers was not as productive as the former large-scale plantation economy.

Latin America

In Latin America, the colonies controlled by the Spanish and Portuguese were comprised of a governing class of 30,000 peninsulares, 3.5 million Creoles, and 10 million less-privileged classes including black slaves, indigenous people, and those of mixed racial backgrounds. The Creoles were a wealthy class from the plantation economy and trade, but they had grievances about the administrative control and economic regulations of the colonies. They did not seek social reform, but rather sought to displace the powerful peninsulares.

Napoleon's invasion of Spain and Portugal in 1807 weakened the authority of those countries in the colonies, and by 1810, revolts were occurring in Argentina, Venezuela, and Mexico. In Mexico, a peasant rebellion was led by Father Miguel de Hildalgo, but conservative creole forces gained control of the movement. Simon Bolivar led the revolts in South America and by 1824 deposed the Spanish armies. His goal was to achieve a United States of Latin America, but it did not last. In Brazil, the Portuguese royal family had fled to Brazil when Napoleon invaded in 1807. When the king returned in 1821 he left his son, Pedro, to rule as regent. Pedro agreed to the demands of Creoles and declared Brazil independent.

As a result of these independence movements, the creoles became the dominant class and the peninsulares returned to Europe. The society remained quite stratified and slavery continued. The wealth and power of the Roman Catholic Church remained and the lower classes continued to be repressed.

NATIONALISM AND THE NATION–STATE

Europe was also seeing major shifts in political power at this time. Britain had made itself the model of an imperial power with a strong military and commercial base. Older powers—such as Russia and Austria—showed their age as their autocratic traditions created increasing tension within their large empires.

During the 19th century, people came to identify themselves as part of a community called a **nation**. The forces that drew these people together were that they had a common language, customs, cultural traditions, values, historical experiences and sometimes, religion.

Unification of Italy and Germany

The spirit of nationalism was rising in two regions where small domains left over from the Middle Ages were still in place. On the Italian peninsula, the Roman Catholic Church still had great influence and discouraged the growth of Italian nationalism. The pope himself personally held large estates in central Italy. Under the leadership of Garibaldi in the south, young men pushed for an Italian nation, fighting a military campaign to unite the people behind this idea. In the north, **Count Camillo di Cavour**, the prime minister to King Emmanuell II of Sardina, aligned with France and expelled Austria from northern Italy. In 1870, the nation of Italy was proclaimed, and the king of Sardinia was chosen as its sovereign.

Farther north, the kingdom of Prussia was becoming more powerful after the defeat of Napoleon. The chancellor of Prussia, **Otto von Bismarck**, had a vision of a united Germany and so engineered a series of wars with Denmark and Austria to consolidate the territory needed for a nation. The final stroke was to maneuver France to declare war on Prussia, and to use that as a pretext for gathering all the German domains together to fight as one. The war was a resounding victory for Prussia, and Bismarck proclaimed the birth of the German nation. He did this in the French palace at Versailles, humiliating France by taking territory on the French–German border.

The birth of a unified Germany would cause a noticeable shift in the balance of power in Europe. France was in decline, and Germany would now begin to rival Great Britain as an industrial producer and leader in technology. Prussia was proud of its army, and German tactics were becoming well-known around the world. The military traditions of old Prussia would now flex their muscles, as Germany looked to be a new power that the world would have to respect.

Zionism

One problem with the formation of nations was the issue of the **minority.** Often, a minority living within a nation did not fit the nation's identity. One such group was the Jews. The Jews did not have their own territory, but rather lived as a minority in other nations. As **anti-Semitism** rose in the 19th century, so did the Zionist movement. This movement fought to establish a Jewish state in Palestine. A Jewish reporter, Theodor Herzl, launched the Zionist movement in 1897.

Latin America

By the 1830s, most of Latin America was made up of independent nations. The leaders of these independence movements had hoped to create representative governments with freedom of commerce and protection of private property. They often feared, however, that the mass population was unprepared for self-rule. **Early constitutions** were written to create order and representation, but voting restrictions regarding property and literacy were instituted. Some early leaders, like Simon Bolivar, dreamed of a unified nation, but regional rivalries and economic competition prevented that from occurring.

These new nations faced many problems, such as economies that had been disrupted by many years of warfare and by large armies loyal to regional commanders (**caudillos**) instead of the new national government. Most leaders agreed that the governments should be a republic, but disagreed on what kind. That is, should it be a strong central government or a regional state-based government?

Additionally, the role of the **Catholic Church** remained strong. Few questioned its doctrine, but many wanted to limit its role in civil life. In Mexico, for example, politics was a struggle between conservatives and liberals, and instability and financial difficulty made it a target for **foreign intervention** by the United States and Europe.

INDUSTRIALIZATION

The rise of modern industry was a direct outcome of the scientific activity and invention of the 1600s. Water power was being harnessed to create mechanical energy, which would run more efficient mills. A machine that pumped water out of mines was patented in 1769. It ran on coal that heated water, and the steam pressure was used to push a piston. The "steam" engine would be the foundation of a new mechanical age in which cars, trains, boats, and factories would all be piston-driven.

The consequences of this revolution would impact human labor, consumption, family structure, and much more. Major economic and social changes that occurred in industrialized nations were:

Before Industrialization	After Industrialization
Agricultural–rural economy	Capitalist–urban economy
Family-farm economy	Wage-earning economy
Asian-based manufacturing	Factory-based manufacturing
Rural-based population	Urban population

Preconditions for Industrialization

Why was England the first to make the technological leap into a modern economy? Several factors encouraged industrialization, and England possessed all of them in the early 1700s. They included the following:

- Technical knowledge and invention
- A large population to serve as a workforce
- Possession of natural resources to be turned into manufactured goods
- Investment capital (money) to build factories
- A stable and capitalist-minded government

Poorer nations often have plenty of people, but they struggle to come up with investment capital and a stable government to help along industrialization. France and the United States were close behind Great Britain in developing industrial capability. The United States and Germany both surpassed Britain in terms of steel production by 1900, while other nations such as Russia lagged behind.

Technology

Major developments took place in the area of technological advancement prior to 1914. Higher-grade steel was adapted for use in transportation and weaponry. Naval warships transitioned from wind-powered wooden frigates to engine-driven steel ships weighing many tons. Trains revolutionized transportation for industrialized nations, and were transplanted to their Asian and African colonies.

Impact on Gender, Family, and Social Structures

Industrialization greatly impacted gender roles and families. It also radically altered the traditional social structures of the day. Slavery declined, because slaves could not consume industrial products as did free-wage laborers. The family, which had been an economic unit, moved that economic production outside the home.

A sharp distinction was now being made between family life and work life. Men's status increased because industrial work and the wage were considered more important than domestic work. Middle-class values became distinct from those of the working class. Middle-class women generally did not work outside the home, but instead were pressured to conform to the new models of behavior often referred to as the **"cult of domesticity."**

Global Effects of Industrialization

As a result of industrialization, a new **global division of labor** emerged. Industrial societies needed raw materials from distant lands and a large demand for materials such as raw cotton from India and Egypt, and rubber from Brazil and the Congo. Latin America, Sub-Saharan Africa, South Asia, and Southeast Asia became dependent on exporting cash crop products to the industrialized nations, but established little or no industrialization themselves. Most of the profits from these cash crops went abroad, and wealth was concentrated in the hands of the few.

The **dependency theory** attempts to explain the uneven result of development. Instead of underdevelopment being a result of failed modernization, it claims that underdevelopment and development are part of the same process because the development of some areas is achieved at the expense of others.

Reactions to Industrialization

Socialism

As the 19th century progressed, the ideas of tolerance and egalitarianism from the Enlightenment inspired many political movements. Some were revolutionary, while others were liberal or reformist. As the Industrial Revolution redefined both society and the economy, other tensions arose.

The appalling conditions that workers experienced in the 1800s inspired **anti-capitalist reform** and revolutionary movements. Under the broad title of *socialism*, these movements critiqued the money economy and suggested instead a utopian alternative—an economy that was run by the workers. One of the most prominent socialist thinkers was **Karl Marx**, who advocated the **overthrow of the moneyed classes**, to be followed by a "workers' state." Socialist movements ranged from revolutionary to liberal.

Unionism

Less radical was the "union" movement, which advocated the organization of workers so that they could negotiate with their employers for **better wages** and **working conditions**. This led to extreme tensions and considerable bloodshed: Factories fought to stop workers from banding together, and workers fought to remain unified. As a left-wing movement, unionism was often accused of being socialistic. The lines became blurred, as some workers became radicalized and adopted violence as a tactic.

REFORM AND REACTION

The traditional empires of the Ottomans, Russia, China, and Japan all had to deal with similar issues during this period. They had to decide **how much they wanted to reform** in the new industrial world. How much should they change their societies? They all tried to change with the times, but with varying degrees of success. In each case, conservative forces came to resist the attempts at reforms.

Ottoman Empire

By the 1700s, the armies of the Ottoman Empire had fallen behind those of Europe, in both strength and technology. And as the empire's military weakened, its vulnerability increased. The central government was becoming less effective, while the provinces were becoming increasingly independent—often controlling their own private armies.

The center of the empire in Anatolia and Iraq was Muhammad Ali, who seized power after Napoleon's departure. He built a powerful army and sponsored industrialization with cotton textiles and armaments. Egypt remained nominally subordinate to the sultan, but by 1820, Ali was the effective ruler of Egypt. His son went on to commission a French firm to build the **Suez Canal**, which opened in 1869. This transformed Egypt into a crucially strategic location, creating a link between Europe and its empires in Asia and East Africa.

In addition to losing territory, the Ottomans also experienced a decrease in trade. They were circumvented as Europe began to trade directly with India and China. Also, much trade shifted to the Atlantic Ocean, in which the Ottomans had no involvement. European products flowed into the empire and it began to depend heavily on foreign loans. Europeans were even given **capitulations** (special rights and privileges), such as being subject to only their own laws, not those of the Ottomans. All of this was a great blow to the empire's ego.

The empire did attempt to reform itself beginning with the rule of Mahmud II. Mahmud organized a more effective army and a system of secondary education, and built new roads, telegraph lines, and a postal service. These reforms continued into the **Tanzimat era** (1839–1879), when the government used the French legal system as a guide to reform its own laws. Additionally, public trials and equality were instituted before the laws for Muslims and those from other religious groups.

These reforms were met with much opposition, particularly from religious conservatives and the Ottoman bureaucracy. The **Young Turks**, a group of exiled Ottoman subjects, pushed for universal suffrage, equality before the law, and emancipation of women. In 1908, they led a coup that overthrew the sultan and set up a "puppet" sultan that they controlled. Though the Ottoman Empire had attempted to reform and change with the changing times, it was left weak and vulnerable by the end of the 19th century.

Russia

Much like the Ottoman Empire, the Russian empire was autocratic, multiethnic, multilingual, and multicultural. The ruling czars were supported by both the Russian Orthodox Church and the noble class, which owned most of the land. The peasants were the majority of the population, and the institution of serfdom served as a guarantee of social stability. But unlike the Ottomans who were losing territory, the Russia empire had **vastly expanded**—east to Manchuria, south into the Caucasus and Central Asia, and southwest to the Mediterranean. Its military power and strength was not up-to-par with that of Europe, however, as demonstrated in its defeat in the **Crimean War.**

The military defeat of the Crimean War highlighted the weakness of Russia's military and economy as compared to Europe's, pushing the government to modernize. A first step was the **emancipation of the serfs** by Czar Alexander II in 1861. He also created district assemblies (**zemstvos**) in 1864, where all classes had elected representatives, but were subordinate to czarist authority.

The government also encouraged industrialization. Policies designed to stimulate economic development were issued, such as the construction of the **Tran-Siberian railroad** and the remodeling of the state bank. This relatively fast-paced, government-sponsored industrialization led to many peasant rebellions and industrial worker strikes. The government limited the maximum workday to 11.5 hours in 1897 as a response, though it also prohibited trade unions and outlawed strikes.

The anti-government protest increased through the involvement of the university students and intellectuals known as the **intelligentsia**. The more these groups were repressed by the government, the more radical they became. The Land and Freedom Party assassinated Czar Alexander II in 1881, bringing an end to government reform. The new czars used repression—not reform—to control the people. Czar Nicholas II, in an attempt to deflect attention from the growing opposition, focused on expansion through the **Russo–Japanese War** in 1904, but the Russians suffered an embarrassing defeat.

In January 1905, a group of workers marched to the czar's Winter Palace to petition, and were killed by government troops. The **Bloody Sunday** massacre set off anger and rebellion across the empire, which as a whole was known as the Revolution of 1905. The government made concessions by creating a legislative body called the Duma, but in reality, not much changed in Russia.

China

The Chinese, like the Ottomans and Russians, had to deal with their own issues of reform and reaction in the 19th century. The Qing had grown more and more ineffective as rulers of China. New food crops brought about a rapid population increase. During the Qing dynasty, it is estimated that the Chinese population quadrupled to 420,000,000. This increase created great strains on the nation, and famines were increasingly common. A series of wars and rebellions further weakened the dynasty in the 1800s.

Aggressive British traders began to import opium from India into China and a customs dispute in Guangzhou led to the first **Opium War** in 1839. This resulted in two humiliating defeats for China and a series of **unequal treaties** that gave Britain and other European nations commercial entry into China.

Rebellions such as the **Taiping Rebellion** placed further stress on China. An obscure scholar named **Hong Xiuquan**, who believed he was the brother of Jesus Christ, founded an offshoot of Christianity. A social reform movement grew from this in the 1850s, which the government began to suppress. Hong established the Taiping Tianguo (Heavenly Kingdom), and his followers created an army that, within two years of fighting, controlled a large territory in central China.

Internal disputes within the Taipings finally helped the Qing dynasty defeat them, but it was a desperate 10-year struggle that exhausted the imperial treasury. The death toll is estimated in the millions, making it the bloodiest civil war in human history.

The government did attempt reforms so it could change with the times. With government-sponsored grants in the 1860s and 1870s, local leaders promoted military and economic reform in China using the slogan, "Chinese learning at the base, Western learning for use." These leaders built modern shipyards, railroads, and weapon industries, and they founded academies for the study of science. It was a great foundation and beginning, but the **Self-Strengthening Movement** only brought change to the surface. It also experienced resistance from the imperial government.

The last major reform effort was known as the **Hundred Days of Reform**. This ambitious movement reinterpreted Confucian thought to justify radical changes to the system, with the intent to remake China into a powerful modern industrial society. The Emperor Guangzu instituted a program to change China into a constitutional monarchy, guarantee civil liberties, and encourage foreign influence. These proposed radical changes were strongly resisted by the imperial household. Particularly upset was the Empress Dowager Cixi, who cancelled the reforms and imprisoned the emperor. With that, China's chance for a reformed society ended.

Another rebellion further complicated issues in China. In 1900, the anti-foreign **Boxer Rebellion** sought to rid China of foreigners and foreign influence. Empress Cixi threw her support behind the movement, hoping to end all foreign influence. A multinational force from countries such as the United States, Russia, and Japan, however, handily defeated the Boxers and forced China to pay an indemnity for the damages.

Amidst all of these rebellions and attempts at reform, a revolutionary movement was slowly emerging in China. It was composed of young men and women who had traveled outside Asia—who had seen the new liberalism and modernization of the West, and hoped to import it to China. Cells were organized in Guangzhou and overseas in Tokyo and Honolulu, where plots to overthrow the Qing were made.

Under the leadership of **Sun Yixian** (Sun Yat Sen), the revolutionaries attempted many unsuccessful uprisings, but it wasn't until 1911 that the Qing were forced to abdicate. With the dynasty in considerable chaos, the **modern Republic of China** was proclaimed. Sun dreamed of a progressive and democratic China based on his **Three Principles of the People**, but China's huge population was largely undereducated and unable to feed itself.

Sun Yixian's Three Principles of the People:

1. Nationalism: Self-determination of the Chinese people; freedom from foreign influence (pertaining to both Manchu rule and European encroachment)
2. Democracy: Self-rule with a constitutional government
3. Socialism: "The People's Livelihood," which combined a desire to modernize and a desire to institute land reform in China

Japan—The Meiji Restoration

Japan made the most radical reforms and changes in its response to the challenges of reform and reaction, and emerged from this period as a world power. Even as it continued to selectively isolate itself from the rest of world, it was changing from a feudal to a commercial economy.

The Japanese knew of China's humiliation at the hands of the British in the mid 1800s. After the California Gold Rush of 1849, the United States became more interested in Pacific commerce, sending a mission to conclude a trade agreement with Japan. It arrived in Edo (Tokyo) Bay in 1853 with a modern fleet of armed steamships. For the Japanese, who had restricted its trade from much of the world for over two centuries, this was an awe-inspiring sight. They told the Americans to leave, but this caused tense debate within the shogunate and the samurai class.

Two clans in the south—Satsuma and Choshu—supported a new policy to **"revere the emperor and repel the barbarians."** This was a veiled critique of the Shogun in Edo, as they perceived his inability to ward off the Western "barbarians" as embarrassing. This was their chance to restore the emperor in Kyoto to prominence.

A younger generation of reform-minded samurai from domains distant from Edo made bold plans to undermine the bakufu. These "men of spirit" banded together to overthrow the Shogun and to advance the idea that Japan needed to modernize. They armed themselves with guns from the West and a civil war broke out in 1866. When the antigovernment forces showed their superiority of outside technology, the momentum began to shift in favor of the rebels.

The overthrow of the Tokugawa regime was complete in 1868, when the victorious reformers pronounced that they had restored the emperor to his throne. They named him **"Meiji," or "Enlightened One."** The nation rallied around the 16-year-old emperor, and plans were made to move the imperial "presence" to the renamed capital of Tokyo (Eastern Capital). This great transition in Japanese history has been called both a **revolution** and a **restoration**. Historians debate about which term to use because the Japanese did not overthrow the old order and replace it with something new. Rather, they reached into their past and used an older model to transform their nation.

The rapidity of the industrialization and modernization of Japan became a marvel to the observing world. Within the first generation of the Meiji period, Japan had built a **modern infrastructure** and **military**, had defeated the Chinese and Russians in war, and had begun building an empire in the Pacific that European powers had to take note of. This was a clear sign that the industrial revolution was achievable by non-Europeans and that new power shifts were in the wind.

Comparative Close-up: Reform and Reaction in the 19th Century

	Political	Economic	Social
Ottoman Empire	Instituted French legal system (equality before the law, public trials) but that met with considerable opposition. Empire collapses after World War I.	As trade shifted to the Atlantic Ocean, becomes heavily reliant on European loans.	Young Turks pushed for universal suffrage and emancipation of women.
Russia	Zemstvos (local assemblies) were created. Duma established after Revolution of 1905, but was subject to whim of czar. Czar overthrown in 1917.	Government sponsors industrialization projects such as the Trans-Siberian Railroad.	Emancipated the serfs in 1861. Students and intelligentsia spread ideas of change in the countryside.
China	Hundred Days of Reform attempts to create constitutional monarchy, but halted by Empress Cixi. Rebellions like the Taiping and Boxer weaken the empire. Dynasty overthrown in 1911.	After loss in Opium War, European powers gain economic concessions under the Unequal Treaties and divide China into spheres of influence.	Peasant-led Taiping Rebellion attempts to create a more egalitarian society, but was eventually defeated.
Japan	Tokugawa Shogunate is overthrown and the emperor is restored to power. A legislative body, the Diet, is formed.	Government sponsors massive industrialization and trade. Japan rises to economic prominence.	The old feudal order is disrupted. Samurai class loses power, but some transition to roles in industrial leadership. New industrial working class develops.

IMPERIALISM AND ITS IMPACT

The European (and later U.S. and Japanese) drive to imperialize had three major motives: economic, political, and cultural. Economically, the overseas colonies served as **sources of raw materials and markets for manufactured goods**. Politically, these colonies were strategic sites with harbors and supply stations for commercial ventures and naval ships. The key was to gain the advantage before one's rival did. It also focused public attention on the quest of imperialist ventures and stirred up feelings of nationalism at home.

Culturally, **missionaries** hoped to convert the Asian and African people to Christianity. While many missionaries served as protectors of native peoples, some saw their mission as one of bringing civilization to the uncivilized

European Imperialism

India

England's involvement in India began strictly as a business venture. The **British East India Company** enjoyed a monopoly on English trade with India, and it soon took advantage of the Mughal empire's weakness. Expanding its trading posts, it began a campaign to the British government to outright conquer and protect its interests. It enforced its rule with a small British army and Indian troops, known as **sepoys**. In 1857, the sepoys **mutinied** after they received rifles with cartridges greased in animal fat (cow fat was offensive to Hindus and pig fat was offensive to Muslims). The sepoys killed British officers, escalating the conflict into a large-scale rebellion.

By May 1858, the British government had crushed the rebellion and restored authority. It went on to impose direct imperial rule on India with a viceroy who served as the representative of British authority.

Under British rule, forests were cleared; tea, coffee, and opium began to be cultivated; and railroads, telegraphs, canals, harbors, and irrigation systems were built. English-style schools were set up for Indian elites and Indian customs such as sati were suppressed.

British rule in India helped to create a sense of Indian identity. The elites who had been educated in British universities were inspired by Enlightenment values and began to criticize the British colonial regime. They called for political and social reform. As such, with British approval, the **Indian National Congress** was founded (1885) as a forum for educated Indians to communicate their views on public affairs to colonial officials. By the end of the 19th century, the Congress sought self-rule and joined forces with the **All-Indian Muslim League**. In 1909, wealthy Indians were given the right to vote, but by that time, the push for reform had become a mass movement.

Africa

With the exception of coastal colonies and trading posts, Europeans had little presence in Africa during this time period, but the scramble for Africa would change all that. From 1875 to 1900, almost the entire continent was carved up by European nations spurred on by the quest to exploit African resources and outmaneuver their rivals.

In 1885, **King Leopold II of Belgium** established the Congo Free State. He called it a free-trade zone, but in reality it was his personal colony with rubber plantations supported by forced labor. The labor conditions were harsh—so harsh, that they drew the attention of humanitarians who fought to end the treatment. The British gained influence in Egypt in 1882, when they occupied the area to protect their financial interests and the **Suez Canal**.

As European competition heated up, the potential for conflict seemed imminent. In response to this rising tension, German Chancellor Otto von Bismarck called the **Berlin Conference.** Delegates (none of which were African) were invited to establish the ground rules for the colonization of Africa. It was decided that any European state could establish an African colony after notifying the others.

Japan

Because Japan was so greatly strengthened by the government-sponsored industrialization, it too, was able to enter the imperialism game. In 1876, the Japanese bought modern warships from the British and went on to defeat Korea easily. In fact, it forced Korea to sign unequal treaties, much like those to which Japan itself had been subjected earlier.

The **Sino-Japanese War** (1894) was sparked by a rebellion in Korea. Japan quickly defeated the Chinese fleet and Korea became a dependency of Japan. China also ceded Taiwan, the Pescadores Islands, and the Liaodong peninsula, and was forced to sign unequal treaties. Japan also defeated Russia in the **Russo-Japanese War** (1904) over territory in Manchuria and Korea, solidifying itself as a world player.

Legacies of Imperialism

Many economic and social changes occurred throughout the world as a result of imperialism. For one, manufacturers were transformed into suppliers of raw materials and consumers of imported goods. In India, for instance, the cultivation of cotton became solely used for export to England, and inexpensive English textiles were then imported. India, once the world's leading manufacturer of cotton, became a consumer of British textiles.

Migration increased as well. Europeans migrated to the United States, Canada, Argentina, Australia, and South Africa in search of cheap land and better economic opportunities. These Europeans often served as a new labor force in industrializing areas. Most traveled as free agents, though some were indentured servants.

Migrants from Asia and Africa, on the other hand, were most often **indentured servants**, and went to tropical lands in the Americas, the Caribbean, Africa, and Oceania. With the decrease in slavery, planters still needed laborers to work on their plantations. Indentured servants were offered free passage, food, shelter, clothing, and some compensation, in return for 5 to 7 years of work. As a result, large communities from around the world migrated to new lands, bringing their culture and traditions.

The theory of **scientific racism** developed during this period of imperialism to explain differences in race. These theorists assumed that humans consisted of several distinct racial groups, and that the European racial groups were intellectually and morally superior. These ideas were often used as justification for the treatment of colonial peoples. In addition, **Social Darwinists** adapted Darwin's evolutionary idea of "survival of the fittest" to explain the development of human societies. These ideas were used to justify European domination over their subject people.

EMANCIPATION

Slavery

Many 19th-century liberals in Europe and North America supported the abolition of slavery, as the Enlightenment ideas of liberty and equality seemed to openly conflict with that institution. Additionally, frequent slave revolts in the 1700s and 1800s were making slavery an expensive and dangerous business. Economically, it became **less profitable**, as protection from the revolts required an expensive military force. Also, even in more peaceful times, slaves generally worked unenthusiastically.

As the price of sugar decreased, the profitability of sugar decreased, but the price for slaves increased. Many plantation owners shifted their investments to manufacturing, where wage labor was cheaper. In turn, those laborers would buy the manufactured goods. Though a secret slave trade continued through much of the century, the slave trade ended first in Great Britain in 1807, and then in the United States in 1808. (Here, however, the importation of slaves ended, though not the trade itself.) The emancipation of the slaves came later, though that took much longer: British colonies in 1833, French colonies in 1848, the United States in 1865, and Brazil in 1888.

Freedom, however, did not bring equality. In many areas, property requirements, literacy tests, and poll taxes were required to prevent freed slaves from voting, and many individuals were forced to continue with low-paying jobs.

Serfdom

The key to social change and reform in Russia was the emancipation of the serfs. Opposition to serfdom had been growing since the 1700s. While some opposed it on moral grounds, most saw it as an **obstacle to the economic development** in Russia, as well as a source of instability and potential peasant revolt.

In 1861, Czar Alexander II abolished serfdom, and the government compensated landowners for the loss of land and serfs. The serfs gained their freedom and their labor obligations were gradually cancelled. They won very few political rights and had to pay a redemption tax for most of the land they received.

Few serfs prospered and most were desperately poor. Their emancipation led to very little increase in agricultural production, since peasants continued to use traditional methods of farming. It did, however, create a large urban labor force for the newly industrialized empire.

Changing Roles of Women

Generally speaking, Enlightenment thinkers were fairly conservative in their view of women's roles in society. In an effort to challenge these accepted beliefs, Mary Wollstonecraft wrote ***A Vindication of the Rights of Women***, which argued that women should possess the same rights granted to men (education, for one).

In Britain, Canada, and the United States, a reform and pro-democratic women's movement became active in the 19th century. Women began to push for the right to vote in democratic elections. These powerful feminist movements sought legal and economic gains for women, along with access to professions, education, and the right to vote. In 1848, an assembly of 300 women met in **Seneca Falls, New York**, demanding political rights, equality in marriage, and employment.

Some feminists, however, were wary of granting women the right to vote, fearing they were too conservative and religious and would thus vote accordingly. The movement continued, however, and Norway became the first country to grant women the right to vote (1910). Several others followed after World War I, including Great Britain (1918) and the United States (1920).

CULTURAL INFLUENCES

African and Asian Influences on European Art

During this time of seemingly Western cultural dominance, European artists took note of the artistic styles of both Africa and Asia. They admired the dramatic, spare style of traditional West African sculpture, wood, and metalwork, as well as the use of color and stylized forms of design in Japan. Based on those Japanese influences, the Impressionists focused on simple themes in nature, feeling that this type of art liberated them from the rules of classical painting. A new movement of modern art was soon launched, free of traditional constraints.

Cultural Policies of Meiji Japan

As Japan was opening up to the industrialization of the west, it was also heavily influenced by the culture of the West. Japanese literature was affected by European models, and writers experimented with Western verse. Architects and artists created large buildings of steel, with Greek columns like those seen in the West.

Many Japanese also copied Western fashion and hairstyles. Amidst all of these influences, however, Japan also continued to preserve its own values.

Leisure and Consumption

The industrial age brought higher wages and fewer work hours. These changes gave people new opportunities. The middle class increased, leading to a new focus on the concept of leisure. The field of advertising communicated to the people the sense of 'needing things.' The bicycle, for instance, became the "must-have item" of the 1880s. Popular newspapers, theaters, and professional sports all became popular in this new era of leisure and consumption.

IF YOU LEARNED ONLY SIX THINGS IN THIS CHAPTER . . . .

1. Industrialization led the world to become truly interdependent. Industrialized nations in search of raw materials and new markets often imperialized areas to protect their economic interests.

2. Populations grew and many people migrated to cities in search of work in factories. Free-wage laborers were more desirable in this new market-driven economy than force labor. As a result, slaves and serfs were emancipated.

3. Women gained some economic opportunities in the factories but were paid considerably less than their male counterparts. These new economic opportunities and Enlightenment ideals pushed women to fight for political rights, as well.

4. The working-class emerged as a force for change. Through organization into unions, these workers were able to advocate for improved working conditions.

5. Western culture strongly influenced many Asian and African areas through colonization. At the same time, Asian and African culture and art strongly influenced European intellectuals and artists. Enlightenment ideals such as equality, freedom of speech, and freedom of religion became very influential in many parts of the world, yet in other parts, traditional religious organization maintained power and influence.

6. The ideas of the Enlightenment said that the government was responsible to its people, inspiring revolutions and independence movements and pushing some governments to experiment with democratic values. This democracy, however, proved to extend to a limited class of people. "The nation" and nationalism became the new concepts of identity in the 19th century, and would soon spread to many parts of the world.

REVIEW QUESTIONS

1. A major factor in world industrialization was the development of

   (A) Socialism
   (B) Feudalism
   (C) Land grants
   (D) Railroads
   (E) Disability insurance

2. In the 18th century, France and England fought over territory in

   (A) Asia and Central America
   (B) Africa and the Balkans
   (C) Asia and the Caribbean
   (D) North America and Asia
   (E) South America and the Pacific

3. The Berlin conference of 1885 was able to

   (A) partition China so that Germany benefited.
   (B) deal with economic problems in Asia.
   (C) resolve issues of European rivalry in Africa.
   (D) bring all of Africa under European control.
   (E) divide Africa along tribal lines.

4. Industrialization is stimulated by all the following EXCEPT

   (A) Technical know-how
   (B) An ample population to serve as a work force
   (C) Investment capital
   (D) Access to natural resources
   (E) An organized union movement

5. The American and French Revolutions were both caused in part by

   (A) Food shortages owing to poor harvests
   (B) Problems of royal succession
   (C) High taxation that bred discontent
   (D) Lack of social mobility in the peasant class
   (E) Church interference

6. Which of the following statements is true regarding the growth of nationalism in the 19th century?

   (A) War and conflict were often used as vehicles to unite the people.
   (B) The transition to nationhood was usually smooth with little internal conflict.
   (C) Only European nations experienced a growth in nationalism.
   (D) Minorities were usually viewed as equal members of society in the new nations.
   (E) European imperialism prevented the rise of nationalism in Asia.

7. The American desire for a trade relationship with Japan in 1853 led to

   (A) the overthrow of the shogun and the modernization of the country.
   (B) increased tensions between China and Korea.
   (C) greater Russian influence in Manchuria.
   (D) the colonization of Taiwan.
   (E) American political and economic dominance in Japan.

8. All the following are helpful catalysts leading to political revolution EXCEPT

   (A) Excessive taxation
   (B) A large gap between rich and poor
   (C) A powerful feminist movement
   (D) A large underclass
   (E) A corrupt and uncaring regime

9. In the 18th century, MOST revolutionary leaders tended to be members of the

   (A) Slave class
   (B) Working class
   (C) Catholic clergy
   (D) Educated middle class
   (E) Nobility

10. The 17th- and 18th-century slave trade had the greatest impact on which part of Africa?

    (A) The Sinai
    (B) West Africa
    (C) Sub-Saharan Africa
    (D) South Africa
    (E) East Africa

11. Which of the following statements best describes the significance of Social Darwinism?

    (A) It was a significant breakthrough in revolutionary theory.
    (B) It led to an increase in urbanization throughout much of Europe.
    (C) It influenced the development of the factory model of production.
    (D) It was used as a justification was the inferior treatment of colonial people.
    (E) The Atlantic slave trade declined as a result.

12. The first republic to grant equality to all its citizens in the western hemisphere was

    (A) The United States
    (B) Bolivia
    (C) Haiti
    (D) Jamaica
    (E) Mexico

13. The early leaders in Indian nationalism came primarily from which class?

    (A) Urban elites educated in the West
    (B) Labor leaders
    (C) Landed peasants
    (D) The aristocracy
    (E) Tribal leaders

14. All of the following were effects of the Haitian Revolution EXCEPT

    (A) The plantation economy continued to flourish
    (B) Slaves were freed
    (C) The United States refused to recognize Haiti's independence
    (D) Other independence movements followed
    (E) The economic growth of the island was slowed

15. Japan's industrialization was greatly helped by

    (A) Large mineral deposits in Hokkaido
    (B) A growing support for democracy
    (C) A centralized pro-business government
    (D) The partnership with China
    (E) Foreign control of the economy

16. Global maritime trade in the late 19th century was stimulated by

    (A) War in Turkey
    (B) The Crash of 1892
    (C) Political revolutions in the Americas
    (D) The opium trade in Asia
    (E) Canals that created short cuts to Asia

17. Which of the following African regions was able to defeat European powers in the 19th century?

    (A) Liberia
    (B) Ethiopia
    (C) Egypt
    (D) Syria
    (E) Morocco

18. Natives challenged British power in the _____ Rebellion in India in the mid-1800s.

    (A) Zulu
    (B) Taiping
    (C) Boxer
    (D) Hottentot
    (E) Sepoy

19. Capitalism is usually characterized by all the following EXCEPT

    (A) Private ownership of property
    (B) Upward social mobility
    (C) The dynamics of supply and demand
    (D) Government ownership of industry
    (E) Private investment in small and large businesses

20. Independence movements in South America in the early 19th century took advantage of the

    (A) Inflationary policies instituted by Spain
    (B) Spain's involvement in the Napoleonic Wars
    (C) American victory over Spain in Cuba
    (D) Silver trade in Asia
    (E) Rise of Japan as an imperial power

21. The statements below refer to
    - Abolished serfdom in 1861
    - Witte, finance minister, pushed for modernization
    - Humiliating loss in Crimean War

    (A) China
    (B) England
    (C) Russia
    (D) Ottoman Empire
    (E) Spain

22. Revolutionary activists seeking to overthrow the Qing dynasty in the 19th century tended to be

    (A) Disaffected Mandarins
    (B) Court eunuchs
    (C) Disgruntled peasants
    (D) Young, educated men who had traveled abroad
    (E) Impoverished soldiers

23. Mercantilism promoted the idea that national wealth was based on

    (A) A favorable balance of exports over imports
    (B) Imperial taxation
    (C) Foreign investment in infrastructure
    (D) An isolationist military policy
    (E) Land redistribution

24. China was able to avoid imperial control in the early 20th century because

    (A) Britain and the United States were opposed to outright colonization.
    (B) Europe was more concerned with the rise of Japan.
    (C) China was too far away from Europe.
    (D) Russia agreed to stay out of Asia.
    (E) many Westerners were sympathetic to the aims of Sun Yixian.

25. The statements below refer to
    - Unequal trading agreements with western Europeans
    - Anti-Western uprising in 1900
    - Self-strengthening movement was met with imperial opposition

    (A) Japan
    (B) India
    (C) China
    (D) Ottoman Empire
    (E) Korea

Document-Based Question

Directions: The following question is based on the accompanying Documents 1 to 4. (The documents have been edited for the purpose of this exercise.)

This question is designed to test your ability to work with and understand historical documents. Write an essay that:

- Has a relevant thesis and supports that thesis with evidence from the documents.
- Uses all or all but one of the documents.
- Analyzes the documents by grouping them in as many appropriate ways as possible. **Does not simply summarize the documents individually.**
- Takes into account the sources of the documents and analyzes the authors' points of view.
- Explains the need for at least one additional type of document.

You may refer to relevant historical information not mentioned in the documents.

> Based on the following documents, analyze and discuss the unique issues Latin American nations had to deal with in achieving independence and building a new nation. Explain what additional kind of document(s) would help assess the unique issues Latin American nations were dealing with.

Document 1

> Source: Simón de Bolívar, leader of independence movements in South America: Message to the Congress of Angostura, Venezuela, 1819
>
> We are not Europeans; we are not Indians; we are but a mixed species of aborigines and Spaniards. Americans by birth and Europeans by law, we find ourselves engaged in a dual conflict: we are disputing with the natives for titles of ownership, and at the same time we are struggling to maintain ourselves in the country that gave us birth against the opposition of the invaders.
>
> ...Nothing in our fundamental laws would have to be altered were we to adopt a legislative power similar to that held by the British Parliament. Like the North Americans, we have divided national representation into two chambers: that of Representatives and the Senate. If the Senate were hereditary rather than elective, it would, in my opinion, be the basis, the tie, the very soul of our republic. In political storms this body would arrest the thunderbolts of the government and would repel any violent popular reaction. Devoted to the government because of a natural interest in its own preservation, a hereditary senate would always oppose any attempt on the part of the people to infringe upon the jurisdiction and authority of their magistrates...The creation of a hereditary senate would in no way be a violation of political equality. I do not solicit the establishment of a nobility, for as a celebrated republican has said, that would simultaneously destroy equality and liberty. What I propose is an office for which the candidates must prepare themselves, an office that demands great knowledge and the ability to acquire such knowledge. All should not be left to chance and the outcome of elections. The hereditary senate will also serve as a counterweight to both government and people; and as a neutral power it will weaken the mutual attacks of these two eternally rival powers.
>
> ..Precisely because no form of government is so weak as the democratic, its framework must be firmer, and its institutions must be studied to determine their degree of stability...unless this is done, we will have to reckon with an ungovernable, tumultuous, and anarchic society, not with a social order where happiness, peace, and justice prevail.

Document 2

Source: *Plan of Iguala* issued on the eve of declaring independence from Spain. Mexican elites intended it to act as a compromise between Mexico's divided classes on February 24, 1821.

ART. 1. The Mexican nation is independent of the Spanish nation, and of every other, even on its own Continent.

ART. 2. Its religion shall be Catholic, which all its inhabitants profess.

ART. 3. They shall be all united, without any distinction between Americans and Europeans.

ART. 4. The government shall be a constitutional monarchy.

ART. 11. The distinction of castes is abolished, which was made by the Spanish law, excluding them from the rights of citizenship. All the inhabitants of the country are citizens, and equal, and the door of advancement is open to virtue and merit.

Document 3

Source: Memoirs of Peru's Jose Rufino Echenique, a successful caudillo (military leader), 1840s

I had left my hacienda and come to Lima to buy some mules that I had heard were on sale near the port. Passing the street which runs in front of the Palace of Government, I met my friend Colonel Ros, who told me of Hercelles's defeat. He also said that Hercelles himself had been captured and was presently being brought as prisoner to Lima, but that an order had been issued to execute him before arriving.....

As soon as I got home, steadfast in my purpose, I sent for a well-known war-captain named Contreras who was extremely loyal to me. I told him to gather 25 men of absolute trustworthiness, to arm them, to lead them out the road to Chancay, to ambush the party that was bringing Hercelles prisoner, and to rescue him. He agreed but, as he gathered the men and arms, the news arrived that Hercelles had been executed immediately upon receipt of the order to that effect. Not only that, his head had been cut off and sent to the place where he began the revolution, to be displayed as an example and a warning. Lazo, the Minister of Government, gave that order, and it was the last straw for me. I determined to move against the government at the first opportunity.

Document 4

Source: Francisco Bilbao (1823–1865), a Chilean liberal, critical of the government, from *America in Danger*, 1862

The conquest of power is the supreme goal. This leads to the immoral doctrine that "the end justifies the means..." But since there are constitutional provisions that guarantee everyone his rights, and I cannot violate them, I invoke the system of "preserving the form." If the constitution declares: "Thought is free," I add: "within the limits established by law"—and since the law referred to is not the constitutional provision but one that was issued afterwards...The election is free, it is said: but what if I control the election returns? What if I, the established power, name the inspector of the election returns, if the law permits one to vote 20 times a day in the same election? What if I dominate the elections and frighten my opponents away with impunity? What happens then? Why, the government party is perpetuated in office, and the popular will is flouted and swindled. But "the form has been preserved," and long live free elections!... "The death penalty in political cases is abolished," but I shoot prisoners because I consider that these are not "political cases"; and since I am the infallible authority I declare that these political prisoners are bandits, and "the form has been preserved."

"The guarantees established by this constitution cannot be suspended." But if I have the power to declare a province or the Republic in a state of siege...what security can a citizen have?...There is discussion, the press is free; citizens come together, for they have the right of assembly; an enlightened public opinion almost unanimously clamors for reforms; preparations are made for elections that will bring to power representatives of the reform movement; and then the Executive Power declares the province or the Republic in a state of siege, and the suspended guarantees soar over the abyss of "legal" dictatorship and constitutional despotism! And then? Either resignation or despair, or civil war, etc., etc.

Continued →

> Then revolution raises its terrible banner, and blood flows in battles and on scaffolds. Respect for law and authority is lost, and only force holds sway, proclaiming its triumph to be that of liberty and justice...And if it governs with *coups d'etat*, states of siege, or permanent or transitory dictatorships, while the constitutional guarantees are flouted, mocked, or suppressed, the party in power will tell you: civilization has triumphed over barbarism, authority over anarchy, virtue over crime, truth over lie...We have behind us a half-century of independence from Spain. How many years of true liberty have any of the new nations enjoyed? That is difficult to say; it is easier to reckon the years of anarchy and despotism that they have endured.

Change-Over-Time Question

Directions: You are to answer the following question: You should spend 5 minutes organizing or outlining your essay. Write an essay that:

- Has a relevant thesis and supports that thesis with appropriate historical evidence.
- Addresses all parts of the question.
- Uses world historical context to show change over time and/or continuities
- Analyzes the process of change over time and/or continuity.

> Describe and analyze the impact of industrialization from 1750 to 1914 on ONE of the following countries. Be sure to discuss continuities as well as changes.
>
> China
> Japan
> Russia
> Ottoman Empire

Comparative Question

Directions: You are to answer the following question: You should spend 5 minutes organizing or outlining your essay. Write an essay that:

- Has a relevant thesis and supports that thesis with appropriate historical evidence.
- Addresses all parts of the question.
- Makes direct, relevant comparisons.
- Analyzes relevant reasons for similarities and differences.

Analyze and compare the approaches and resistance to political and economic reform in the 19th century of TWO of the following:

China

Japan

Ottoman Empire

Russia

ANSWERS AND EXPLANATIONS

1. D

The introduction of the railroad allowed industrialization to become a world event. The movement of goods and people became a standard feature of an industrialized nation, and the use of railroads increased a nation's ability to industrialize. The development of socialism and later disability insurance were results of industrialization. Feudalism predates industrialization. Land grants may have aided some factory owners, but did not contribute to industrialization becoming a more global event.

2. D

The Seven Years War was the first truly global conflict, pitting various European powers against each other. The two major rivals—France and Britain—fought over territories in Asia and the Americas. Britain won, and India and Canada were securely in the British empire. Britain and France were also claiming parts of the Pacific but did not contest these at that time. They had no imperial interest in the Balkans.

3. C

The 1880s were a time of aggressive empire-building by rival European nations. Germany invited other nations to Berlin so that territorial issues in Africa could be resolved. Except for Ethiopia and Liberia, all of Africa was colonized by the Europeans. China was able to play the powers off of one another, avoiding partition and colonization.

4. E

The four main stimulants of industrialization are all listed in answer choices (A) through (D). Nations need a large (preferably low wage-earning) work force, technical knowledge, money for investment, and natural resources. In the 1800s, England had all of these in the form of surplus farm workers, coal, and the best banking system extant. A labor movement can inhibit business growth if a nation is crippled with strikes or slowdowns.

5. C

The merchants in Boston and the peasants in Lille were both opposed to the taxes they paid in the 18th century. The Boston Tea Party and the storming of the Bastille both came about in part because of tax revolts. There were no peasants in America at this time. The French Revolution was in part a reaction to church power in Paris, but it was primarily a secular economic response that led people to revolt.

6. A

Nationalist leaders often used war and conflict to unite their people. Bismarck in Germany and Cavour in Italy engaged in war with neighboring areas. Internal conflict was quite prevalent on the path to the nation-state. The growth of nationalism was felt beyond the borders of Europe, such as in Latin America. Minorities were often excluded from equal membership in the new nations, and this often led to their own movements (Zionism, for one). In some ways, European imperialism contributed to the rise of nationalism in Asia, as in the case of Indian nationalism stemming from the British rule.

7. A

The Tokugawa Shogunate was coming under increasing attack from critical daimyo when the Americans arrived in 1853. The insistence of the United States in making a trade agreement led to the movement to oust the bakufu and restore the emperor. Taiwan was still a part of the Qing empire at this point. America was not able to dominate Japan as a result of the interest in trade.

8. C

Many revolutions, from France to China to Cuba, took place because a largely poor majority was being oppressed by a wealthy elite. Feminism, which has to do with equality between the sexes, is not a factor in political revolution, although it is a dynamic in social revolution.

9. D

Education seems to be the common background of revolutionaries, whether from the 18th century or after. Men such as John Adams and Danton were well-schooled, and most belonged to the middle class. While the working class was often oppressed, it did not have the skills to organize and express revolutionary thinking. The nobility usually resisted reform or radical change in the government.

10. B

The slave trade evolved partly from the profits to be had and the supply of human beings available. The Portuguese were some of the first to establish relationships with West African tribes that delivered captured peoples for transport to the New World. The Sinai is a remote desert region of Egypt and is sparsely populated. Sub-Saharan Africa encompasses the continent south of the Sahara desert. There was slave trading in this region, but not as much as in the north and west. East Africa was the farthest from the Atlantic, so few slaves were shipped from there across the continent.

11. D

Social Darwinists used Charles Darwin's theory of evolution and survival of the fittest to justify the inferior treatment of colonial people. According to the theory, the non-Europeans were "less-evolved" or "less fit" to rule themselves and needed the guidance of the "more fit" Europeans.

12. C

The only republic to outlaw slavery and grant freedom to all of its citizens was the former French colony of Saint Domingue, which was renamed Haiti.

13. A

Asian leaders in the various independence movements were all educated professionals, for example, members of the Indian National Congress. Most had received their educations in Europe. Studying law in England could expose them to western liberalism. They also met whites who were sympathetic to their cause.

14. A

The plantation economy was hurt by the revolution in Haiti because the newly freed slaves wanted their own smaller plots of land and did not want to work on plantations like when they were slaves. Haiti's economy had been flourishing because of sugar plantations, but without slave labor, it steadily declined.

15. C

A newly constituted government after 1867 was involved in many aspects of the modernization of Japan. Loans were given to help new companies get started, and close ties were forged between big business and the government. This new government was a very limited form of democracy, and there were no natural resources to speak of under Japan's control.

16. E

Both the Suez and the Panama canals created shorter voyages between the oceans for commercial ships by 1914. War does not usually stimulate ocean-going trade; it tends to discourage it. To illustrate, think of the American Civil War and the Crimean War in the 1800s.

17. B

Ethiopia defeated the Italians in the battle of Dugali in 1887. This thwarted Italian designs on Ethiopia as the Europeans sought to gain colonies in Africa. Liberia was an American-sponsored haven for slaves who wanted to return to Africa. Egypt was dominated at different times by France and Britain. Syria was part of the Ottoman empire and did not have an opportunity to fight Western armies. Parts of Morocco were absorbed into the Spanish and French empires.

18. E

The Sepoy uprising was a rebellion against British rule in northern India. The sepoys were Indians serving in the British army. After it was put down, the British were more vigilant about their colonial subjects serving in their military. The Zulus had attacked the British in rural South Africa. The Boxer Rebellion was against all foreigners in China in 1900.

19. D

Government ownership of property or industry is usually a feature of socialism. Today, most governments combine elements of both capitalism and socialism, as private property is allowed. Capitalism has safeguarded the ownership of private property. Property, whether in the form of money, valuable commodities, or other equity, is what defines wealth in the modern capitalistic world. The opportunity for advancement or upward mobility has been the motivation for many who want to better their socio-economic status in a monetary-based system. In a capitalistic, market based economy; the prices of goods are often determined by the laws of supply and demand. The more scarce and desirable the product, the higher its cost. Likewise, overproduction leads to falling prices. Businesses often rely on available money or investment so they can grow and expand. This risk capital is given to businesses in return for a share of the potential profits.

20. B

When Napoleon took control of Spain in the early 1800s, advocates of independence in South America were encouraged to push for their freedom. The Spanish were defeated by the United States in the Spanish American War in the late 19th century (1898). The silver trade in Asia and the rise of Japan as an imperial power did not directly contribute to the independence movements in South America.

21. C

The statement above refers to Russia which abolished serfdom in 1861, and was involved in government sponsored industrialization, but whose military inferiority was highlighted during its loss to superior European powers during the Crimean War.

22. D

Revolutionary activists in China tended to be educated and had some foreign contacts. Sun Yixian traveled widely, studied Western government, and dreamed of transforming China into a modern nation. Mandarins had the most to lose in a reformed China and did support the revolutionaries. Court eunuchs had only their influence in court as a power base, and would not tend to join a liberal movement. Peasants were mostly illiterate and did not have access to revolutionary propaganda. This was especially true in the countryside, which was quite isolated from urban political unrest. Guangzhou, in the south, was the focus of much revolutionary activity from the 1890s forward. Qing soldiers did not join the rebels as the dynasty was declining after the turn of the 20th century.

23. A

Mercantilism promoted the idea that an imperial autarky would create a favorable flow of wealth into the country. Raw materials would be derived from the nation's colonies and turned into goods to sell to other nations. Money would thus flow in as goods were transported out.

24. A

There was considerable competition for Chinese commercial advantages by foreign nations from the mid-19th century. This led to much tension amongst the great powers of the day. By 1900, the U.S. and Britain sponsored the idea of the Open Door, whereby all nations would be able to trade with China equally. This was done in the hope of easing international problems in Asia, and also to limit Russian and German aspirations in China. Japan was a rising power, but also an imperialistic party in China. As an ally of Britain and a new military power, it tended to take a reactive stance in China. During the Boxer Rebellion, Japan joined with the other European powers in relieving the legations in Beijing. China was very accessible by sea and also overland via Russia. Russia was very involved in establishing a sphere of interest in Manchuria in northeast China.

25. C

The three statements refer to China during the Qing dynasty. After their defeat in the Opium Wars, China was forced to sign unequal treaties with Britain and other European powers that gave them exclusive trading in sections of China. The anti-Western uprising, known as the Boxer Rebellion, was aimed at ridding China of foreign devils, but was ultimately unsuccessful and put down by European powers. Chinese intellectuals pursued a self-strengthening movement to improve China intellectually and technologically, but imperial forces, in particular the Empress Dowager, opposed the movement and suppressed it.

Document-Based Question: Sample Response

The Spanish colonies of Latin America struggled for their independence from the crown in the early 19th century. The Creoles often led these movements, seeking more economic and political freedom. The unique features of the independence movements and nation-building in Latin America included their mix of Spanish and indigenous heritages and their struggles to uphold the constitution guidelines they set for themselves while keeping the nation united.

Latin American nations struggled to create a national identity and unite the diverse social and cultural groups in their lands. Simon Bolivar, a leader of the independence movements, wrote in his message to the Congress of Angostura in 1819 that the Latin Americans are a unique group. They are not solely Europeans and they are not solely Indians, but rather, a mix of the two. This mix is something unique upon which a national identify could be built. Bolivar's point of view was that of an independence leader and a Creole attempted to inspire and motivate the congress he addressed. The *Plan de Iguala*, written by Mexican elites on the eve of declaring independence, attempts to address to racial divide. The provision calls for "all united, without any distinction between Americans and Europeans" and any distinction of castes was to be abolished. The inclusion of these provisions points out the problem that existed between the European, mixed, and native populations. This document attempted to bring the groups together by creating a united front against Spain. It would be helpful to find out if these provisions were also included in the constitution and if they were carried out. Politically, Latin American nations struggled to create a stable government that united and had the allegiance of its people. Bolivar states that Latin America should not build its republic like North America, but rather like the English parliamentary system. Unlike North America, he advocated the creation of a hereditary senate to watch over the people.

Fifty years later, Chilean liberal Francisco Bilbao commented on what became Bolivar's vision for a republican Latin America. Bilbao criticizes that although the constitution guarantees freedom and rights, in practice, these things are ignored. Instead, freedom is limited by the law; elections may be free, but they are extremely corrupt, and a hypocritical system has developed. Instead of upholding the ideals of a free constitutional republic, in many ways, Latin American independent countries replicated the colonial system they sought to oppose. Bilbao states that instead of 50 years of liberty since independence, Latin American countries, in particular Chile, have endured 50 years of anarchy and despotism. These two points of view come from educated members of society heavily involved in governmental affairs. It would help to have evidence from the lower class to confirm that this mistreatment is occurring. Also, a document of the actual constitutions of these new nations would be helpful to analyze what rights are supposed to be upheld. To further complicate matters, the memoir of Peru's Jose Rufino Echenique points out the role of the caudillos. These regional military leaders often commanded more allegiance than the federal governments. In his memoir Echenique describes how he was able to gather a force quickly to defend a friend against the government and when this friend was executed, Echenique was ready to move against the government. As a personal memoir, this account may exaggerate Echenique's willingness to risk life and limb for his friend, but it does demonstrate the extreme loyalty the caudillos were able to garner from the people.

The Latin American independence movements were often fought in the name of freedom and new opportunities, but unfortunately, these freedoms were often violated. The Creole class who led the movement often replaced the peninsular class it overthrew, and retained the same privileges as their former oppressors. Socially, mistreatment of non-Europeans continued to be an issue, and politically, forming a stable government with a strong allegiance from the people remained a challenge.

Change-Over-Time Question: Sample Response

The process known as industrialization revolutionized the world starting in the 18th century. Beginning in England, industrialization spread throughout the world, although not necessarily evenly, and left no area untouched. Japan was revolutionized by industrialization. At the beginning of that time period, Japan was a relatively isolated country with little involvement in world trade. The opening of Japan, followed by the Meiji Restoration, radically altered the country as it became both an industrial and imperialist power. Yet through all the change, Japan still held on to important elements of its unique culture.

As the time period begins in 1750, Japan was ruled by the Tokugawa Shogunate, a feudal government that closely controlled the country's interaction with the outside world. However, Commodore Matthew Perry from the United States entered Japan's ports with gunpowder weapons and insisted that they change their trade policy in 1853. This encounter resulted in Japan being forced to sign a series of unequal treaties. This interaction led to the overthrow of the Shogun and the return of the emperor to power, known as the Meiji Restoration.

With the government under the centralized control of the emperor, major changes occurred. Japan initiated a government-sponsored industrialization, which included the building of railroads and factories. Unlike China, which had European-built and owned factories and railroads, these were Japanese-owned and controlled. Japan also industrialized its military with the latest weapons and fighting techniques. With the backing of industrial strength, Japan began to reach out and dominate its neighbors. Japan's newly industrialized military was able to defeat Korea, China, and Russia in the early 20th century. These defeats served as a wake-up call to the outside world of all the changes that were occurring in Japan. Culturally, Japan was also adopting some Western traditions such as fashion, art, and writing styles. Through all of these changes, Japan was able to hold on to its unique cultural identity and values.

Industrialization brought radical changes to Japan from 1750 to 1914. A feudal, isolated kingdom in 1750, Japan became a burgeoning world power by 1914. Government-sponsored industrialization followed by imperial conquests helped Japan become a defeater of Western powers, instead of being defeated by Western powers.

Comparative Question: Sample Response

During the 19th century, many nations were faced with the need to react to changes in the industrializing world and make necessary reforms to deal with these changes. Russia and China both attempted to reform their countries, and both faced internal resistance to a complete modern change. Russia's government pushed for economic change in the form of government-sponsored industrialization, but resisted most political changes and instead retained an absolute monarchy. China had some successful attempts at reform and change, but internal rebellions and imperial resistance to change prevented real reform from taking place. As a result, by the end of the 19th century, both dynasties were on the verge of revolution.

Economically, Russia was more successful at reform than China. The Russian serfs were emancipated in 1861 in the hopes of creating an urban working-class to work the developing industrial factories. Under the leadership of finance minister Serge Witte, the government pushed hard to industrial Russia by sponsoring such projects as the Trans-Siberian railroad. Unfortunately, Russia was very far behind the West and much of the government pushing led to civil unrest. In China, the defeat to the British in the Opium Wars forced the Qing dynasty to sign a series of unequal treaties with European powers, allowing them to establish exclusive trading rights in China. As a result, the factories and railroads built in China were built and controlled by foreigners.

Politically, both Russia and China were resistant to long-lasting change. In Russia, the czar did free the serfs and allowed for the creation of zemstvos, or local assemblies, but any real attempt at curtailing his own power was avoided. After Czar Alexander II was assassinated, the czars who followed were more oppressive and more resistant to political change. This came to a head during Bloody Sunday in 1905 when a group visited the czar's winter palace to present a petition, but was met with gunfire. The Revolution of 1905 followed, after the czar permitted the creation of a duma, or parliament, but the czar would dismiss this body if he did not approve of its decisions. China also struggled with political change because of imperial resistance. Additionally, internal rebellions such as the Taiping Rebellion disrupted the country and highlighted the growing dissatisfaction with the Qing dynasty. The government attempted reforms during the Self-Strengthening movement, but much of these reforms were not carried out. During the 100 Days of Reform, the emperor suggested the creation of a constitutional monarchy, but he was soon deposed by the Empress Dowager and his dreams of reform were never fulfilled. In 1900, a group called the Boxers rebelled against the foreign control in China. The Empress Dowager gave the group her support, hoping they could remove the foreign influence, but the Qing dynasty was proven politically bankrupt when foreign powers had to put down the rebellion. By 1911, the last Chinese dynasty was overthrown.

The 19th century presented the world with many new economic and political changes. Those countries that successfully reformed and reacted, both politically and economically, survived and became powerful in the 20th century. Those who could not reform and react, like Russia and China, lost control of their empires politically and economically, and were overthrown.

Chapter 7: **1914 to Present**

- The Big Picture
- Why This Periodization?
- Global Conflict
- Independence and Nationalist Movements
- Revolutions
- Political Reform and Economic Changes
- Demographic and Environmental Issues
- Societal Changes

THE BIG PICTURE

1. Patterns and effects of interaction among major societies and regions: trade, war, diplomacy, and international organizations.

    In other words: **What happens when people come in contact with each other?**

The pace and rate of interaction grows rapidly during this time period. From the world wars to the United Nations to the World Trade Organization, the world becomes closely connected, and not always with positive results.

2. The dynamics of change and continuity across the world history periods covered in this course, and the causes and processes involved in major changes of these dynamics.

    In other words: **Why do some things change while other things stay the same?**

It can be said that much of the change that occurs in this century had its beginning in the 19th century. The industrialization, democratic movements, rise of nationalism, and increase in communication that began in the 19th century continued to grow and spread at a tremendous rate in the 20th century. Women made tremendous strides politically and economically, but in many societies, they still continue to hold traditional roles. Also, unrepresentative government continues to be more of the norm than the exception throughout the world.

3. The effects of technology, economics, and demography on people and the environment (population growth and decline, disease, labor systems, manufacturing, migrations, agriculture, weaponry)

   In other words: **How does the development of new technology and movement of people affect the world?**

One of the most significant changes in the 20th century was the growth from one billion people worldwide in 1900 to over 6 billion. The increase in technology and health care has led to longer lives and a higher rate of infant survival throughout the world. Movement of people has also increased throughout the world, with many individuals seeking better economic opportunities in new areas. Additionally, some refugees are forced to leave their homelands.

Though health care has improved tremendously, epidemic diseases such as AIDS have continued to plague the world, particularly in developing countries with the least access to new medicines. The development of nuclear weapons changed the nature of war. During the Cold War, the major goal was to stop the other side from dominating. Now that more nations have access to weapons of mass destruction, diplomatic issues are more tenuous than ever.

4. Systems of social structure and gender structure (comparing major features within and among societies and assessing change).

   In other words: **How do societies organize themselves socially, and what roles do men and women play?**

The introduction of communist governments in various parts of the world challenged traditional social structure models, attempting to empower the working and peasant classes. Unfortunately, new elite party classes often emerged, which went on to replace the older ruling class. Women gained both the right to vote in many parts of the world as well as access to new economic opportunities and education. The development of the birth control pill empowered women by allowing them to control their own reproductive systems.

5. Cultural, intellectual, and religious developments, including interactions among and within societies.

   In other words: **How do people identify themselves and express themselves culturally and intellectually?**

Has our world developed a global culture? As the world becomes more and more integrated through technology, cultures blend and some come to dominate. Religious fundamentalism has developed in some parts of the world, partially to combat this Western-dominated global culture. Intellectually, the developments of the 20th century boggle the mind. From the airplane to the atom bomb, the discoveries in math, science, and technology have revolutionized how we live and communicate.

6. Changes in functions and structures of states, and in attitudes toward states and political identities (political culture), including the emergence of the nation-state (types of political organization)

   In other words: **How do people govern themselves?**

If in the 19th century the nation–state had its start, in the 21st century the nation–state seems to have taken over the world. There seems to be no area that is not a nation–state. This rise in the nation–state and nationalism has led to the use of a variety of political systems from totalitarianism to democracy. At the same time, the rise of a more globally connected world may blur the lines of the nation–state. As the European Union develops and becomes more interconnected and religious fundamentalism grows, are nation–states losing their political hold?

WHY THIS PERIODIZATION?

The year 1914 marks the beginning of World War I, which in many ways was caused by the tremendous changes of the long 19th century. This war marked a change in warfare, diplomacy, technology, communication, and global hegemony. At its conclusion, Europe was significantly weakened and had difficulty maintaining its global hegemony over the rest of the world. As a result, Europe's colonies developed their own sense of identity and nationalism, and rebelled against their rulers.

Political revolutions swept the world, as outdated and unresponsive governments were overthrown. The world became closer and more connected than ever with developments in technology and communication.

GLOBAL CONFLICT

World War I

Many historians cite the following list of **longer-term causes** to World War I:

- **Alliances**: The alliance system had led to many open and secret agreements between nations. Most of these were defensive plans that would protect a nation in the event it was attacked. Germany, Austria, and Italy all had agreements to this effect. Likewise, France and Russia were allied if Germany were to attack either one.
- **Imperialism**: Tensions stemmed from imperialism and the competition for foreign colonies, as in Africa.
- **Militarism**: The arms race between the major powers—especially Germany and Britain—that were maintaining increasingly large fleets also led to a hope that these new tools of war would be used in the future. Military leaders were anxious to fight sooner than later.
- **Nationalism**: After the successful creation of Italy and Germany by 1870, other ethnic groups hoped for nations of their own. This rising tide of nationalism was growing stronger among such peoples as the Poles, Bosnians, Czechs, and Yugoslavs. Pan-Germanism came into direct conflict with Pan-Slavism. An eagerness to redraw the map of Europe was mounting, and this was usually done through conquest and war.

The war actually began in the following way: During a tour of the southern Balkan provinces, the heir to the Austrian throne and his wife were assassinated in their car. The assassin was a Serbian Slav nationalist. Austria accused Serbia of supporting Yugoslav (southern Slavic) nationalism and it declared war. Russia sided with Serbia, while Germany pledged support for Austria. When Germany declared war on Russia, France joined Russia. Great Britain was the last major European power to join, when Germany violated Belgium's neutrality on its way to attack France.

World War I was a new kind of war, particularly because of recent improvements in military weaponry. The use of machine guns and gas led to a significant increase in casualties. The war became defensive as **trenches** were built and defended. The heroic notion of war was gone.

Civilians, too, were involved in the war effort, as women entered the workforce. This **"total war"** involved the entire nation. Governments controlled industry, and they used propaganda to reinforce the evilness of the enemy.

The Treaty of Versailles: The leading Allied powers—Italy, Great Britain, France, and the United States—were labeled the "Big Four." They called a conference near Paris at the palace of Versailles to settle the issues stemming from the war. In the end, France would not allow the generous peace that Wilson had envisioned. Instead, the treaty laid down harsh terms to which Germany had to agree. The map of Europe was redrawn, but nations such as Italy were still not satisfied with the results. Other nations such as Poland, Czechoslovakia, Hungary, and Yugoslavia were all created in 1919 by the peace settlement.

President Woodrow Wilson entered the Versailles meetings with his plan, called the **Fourteen Points.** In it, he called for self-determination of nationalities, peace without victory, disarmament, fair treatment of colonial peoples, and the establishment of the **League of Nations**. Most of his ideas were rejected at the meeting, though the League of Nations was created. Ironically, when Wilson brought the treaty back to the United States, Congress opposed it and the United States did not join the new League. The League of Nations was established in Geneva, Switzerland in 1921, but it struggled to keep the peace and control its members when tensions arose.

The **outcomes of the war** were numerous:

- Though victorious, **Britain** was profoundly affected by the Great War. It had lost a significant percentage of its youth, and its economy was strained. After the war, debts were considerable and the once-proud empire took on a tired look. Britain's great empire became more and more of a burden, and native movements for independence in Africa and Asia were underway.
- **France** was devastated by the war. Whole sections of the nation were destroyed, and the nation had also suffered many casualties. War widows and amputees were in evidence in every city.
- **Japan** had fought on the Allied side during the war, and hoped to add to its empire. It did not get what it wanted at Versailles, and a postwar economic downturn led to hard times for this country.
- **Italy** was one of the Allied leadership nations and had been promised large pieces of the Austrian empire when the Allies won. It received some, but not all it had hoped for. Post-war politicians were able to capitalize on this situation, and Italy continued to press for more territory along the Adriatic coast.

- The **United States** was elevated to true world-power status by the war but was not really interested in playing that role. Conservatives won the White House in 1920, and the United States largely retreated from European affairs.
- **China** entered the war late, and hoped for support as a large nation aspiring to democracy. When Japan gained some concessions in China through the treaty, there were riots in Beijing to protest. This led to a surge of nationalism in China and to a cultural and intellectual period known as the **May Fourth Movement**. During this period, Chinese reformers criticized Confucian traditions and looked to Western ideas.
- **Russia** was in shambles as the revolution gave way to civil war after 1918. Russia was not a party to the Versailles treaty because it withdrew from the war and signed a treaty with Germany in 1917. For two years, the forces of the left—led by the Bolsheviks (Reds), and the supporters of the czar (Whites)—fought to control Russia. It took two years of bitter fighting and the deaths of perhaps a million Russians for the Reds to claim victory and declare the birth of the Union of Soviet Socialist Republics. The Bolsheviks shot the Czar and his family to ensure the monarchy would be finished in Russia.
- **Germany** was economically, politically, and socially wrecked. It had lost millions of men in the fighting, and now, by the terms of the Versailles treaty, was forced to pay huge amounts of reparations to the Allies. In addition, it lost all of its overseas empire, along with provinces on both eastern and western borders. The Kaiser abdicated and fled Germany, leaving a political vacuum. With the monarchy gone, a new government was assembled in Weimar in 1919. A weak democratic Germany with a president and chancellor was created.
- The **Middle East**: The Ottoman Empire collapsed in 1918. Turkey declared itself a republic and under the leadership of Ataturk, followed a program of modernization and westernization. Arab nationalism rose, in part inspired by Wilson's self-determination, and disappointment in the terms of the peace treaty. In exchange for their help against the Central Powers, Arabs had been promised independence. Instead, their land was carved into French and British mandates. A center of tension was the British mandate of Palestine where Arab nationalists competed with Zionists for control of the land, land they had both been vaguely promised by the Allies.
- **India** fought on the side of the British in World War I and had been promised great self-government after the war. When the fighting ended, little change occurred. This led to a surge in Indian nationalism and under the leadership of Mohandas Gandhi, the eventual independence of India in 1947.

Global Depression

The economy of the United States was crucial to the health of world markets. Europe had already seen an outflow of capital as the bull market in American stocks drew money to itself. When the market collapsed in October 1929, the reaction was felt around the world. American and foreign investors lost billions of dollars in the first week.

The impact was especially severe in Europe, which had depended on American loans to recover from World War I. The wave of bank failures in the United States had a ripple effect in London, Berlin, Tokyo, and other financial capitals. The bond market also shrank, and many investors were caught off-guard as they tried to cover huge losses. This resulted in dramatic increases in bank failures and personal bankruptcies. Global unemployment rose to double-digit levels. In addition, the United States passed the highest tariff in its history, further blocking international trade.

The causes of the global depression most often cited are:
- Overdependence on American loans and buying
- Increase in tariffs and protectionism
- Industrial and farming surpluses leading to deflation
- Poor banking management

The great hardships of the Depression led to political instability and a rise in political extremism in many nations. Communists on the left criticized the obvious failings of capitalism, while fascists on the right sought to protect private enterprise and promote their nations. Japan, Italy, and Germany looked to dictatorial rule in an effort to pull themselves out of their economic hardships.

In the 1930s in Japan, the military replaced civilian politicians in the highest posts of government. Lacking natural resources, Japan needed an empire to provide crucial minerals for its own industrial needs. It had already gained Taiwan and Korea, but it now fixed its eye on Northeast China. **Japan's invasion of Manchuria** in 1931 led to diplomatic protests in the League of Nations, but the Japanese kept their new territory and soon walked out of the League. Similarly, **Italy invaded Ethiopia** in 1935.

Rise of Fascist and Totalitarian States

Italy

The triumph of Marxist revolution in Russia after 1921 had great impact on world political thinking in the 1920s. Fear about a spread of communism to other nations that had been destabilized by the war led to new political movements in Europe. Groups of reactionary men started to organize in various European nations, but it was in Italy that the first expression of anticommunism emerged. A small group of men led by **Benito Mussolini** marched on Rome in 1922, demanding that they be allowed to form a government. The king gave in to this demand and Italy was soon dominated by Mussolini and his fascists. Mussolini became the prototypical modern dictator as he accumulated more and more power.

Fascism as an ideology was defined by the following:
- Opposition to communism as a threat to tradition and private property
- Ultra-nationalism and glorification of the state
- Militarism and glorification of war as the ultimate expression of power
- Alliances with big business and destruction of the labor unions
- Rejection of liberalism and democracy, which was seen as weak and ineffective

Soviet Union

At the same time that Mussolini was consolidating his power in Italy, there was a transfer of power in Moscow. Lenin, the architect of the Russian Revolution, died of a stroke 7 years after the revolution. The power struggle within the Bolshevik party led to the rise of **Josef Stalin**, who took control in 1927.

Stalin's ruthless elimination of all his rivals allowed him to take complete power in Russia by the 1930s. His leadership became associated with Soviet communism, but it is also referred to as Stalinism. As practiced, Stalinism was defined by the following:
- Centralized control of the economy
- World leadership of the international communist movement
- Forced collectivization of all farming
- Promotion of atheism and control of organized religion

Germany

The establishment of the Soviet state in Russia led to political backlashes in many other countries. After the war, Germany rebuilt its government as a parliamentary democracy. Burdened with war debts and rampant inflation, the new government tried to reestablish Germany's place in the international community. With the coming of the Depression, many feared that Germany would experience its own revolution and become the next communist state.

One of the political parties was the National Socialist German Workers' Party (the Nazi Party). Its charismatic leader **Adolf Hitler** spoke out against communism, and used the anti-Semitic racism of his day to suggest that communism was really a global conspiracy organized by Jewish people. Hitler also preached ultra-nationalism and the promise of a greater Germany, much as Mussolini had done in Italy. In 1933, he was appointed chancellor through aggressive anti-communist propaganda. He became dictator, or führer, within a few years by eliminating most of his political opponents. He reorganized the government by insinuating the Nazi party into many areas of national life.

Stalin, Hitler, and Mussolini represented a new form of political leadership in the modern context. These 20th-century dictatorships defined the modern totalitarian regime. Whether in Berlin or Moscow, the following features were apparent:
- A single leader with almost unquestioned authority
- A single party in charge of all government
- Creation of a police state to terrorize and control the populace
- Aggressive elimination of all opposition groups

World War II

Many of the unresolved issues at the end of the Great War were instrumental in causing the Second—and far more devastating—World War. Tensions in both Europe and Asia were building throughout the 1930s, and both continents saw extensive fighting. As in the years before 1914, there were tense match-ups between nations, which would eventually lead to war breaking out.

Historians debate when the Second World War began. While many point to the **German invasion of Poland in 1939**, the war in Asia had been going on since the Japanese **invasion of China in 1937**. Events in Europe affected the Asian conflict, especially when Germany overran France in 1940. This allowed Japan to take French Indochina, which had rubber and tin that the Japanese needed for their military machine.

From 1938 to 1942, the expansionism of both Japan and Germany was impressive. The Germans first succeeded in taking control of most of Eastern and Northern Europe with few casualties. After the fall of France, only Britain was left to fight the German army and air force, which bombed England aggressively in anticipation of an invasion. But the Royal Air Force managed to defend the skies over England, and Hitler turned his attention to his proclaimed enemy, the Soviet Union. 1941 was a key year, as Germany launched a surprise invasion against the USSR, and Japan attacked the U.S. Navy in Hawaii. Both attacks were very well-planned, catching the Russians and Americans completely off-guard.

By mid-1942, Japan controlled most of the western Pacific Ocean from New Guinea to the Aleutians, and Germany controlled most of Europe and parts of North Africa. But the Germans were turned back at Stalingrad, and the Japanese lost a large naval battle near Midway Island in June of 1942. From that point on, the industrial capacities of the United States and the USSR were able to out-produce both of their enemies, and the Axis powers were put on the defensive.

The occupation of nations by Germany and Japan was a brutal exercise in militarist oppression and even extermination. Millions were killed in both Asia and Europe, as camps were set up to detain, and even murder, political enemies. China and Poland were the scenes of wholesale slaughter. The death toll in Europe alone is estimated at 20 million, as communists, labor leaders, Jews, homosexuals, the mentally disabled, and Gypsies were shot or gassed to death in specially designed chambers. In particular, Hitler targeted the Jews, blaming them for all of Germany's problems. Six million of Europe's 9.5 million Jews were killed in the Nazis' **Holocaust.** Millions of Chinese were also killed before the war ended, as the Japanese pushed across the continent.

New technologies were born during the war as both sides sought to outdo each other. The Germans and British developed radar to detect each other's planes. Sonar was invented to locate unseen submarines. Rockets were used in war for the first time—most notably by the Germans—as they delivered high explosives to Britain. But the most awesome weapon of all was the **nuclear bomb** that America developed and used to finish the war against the Japanese. Two bombs dropped, on Hiroshima and Nagasaki, killing over 150,000 people and forcing the final capitulation of Japan in August 1945.

Origins of the Cold War: There was no peace conference at the end of World War II. The Allies demanded unconditional surrender, and the Axis nations were in ruins from bombing raids. Their defeat had been total, and both Japan and Germany were occupied by the Allied armies. Within the framework of the occupation, the Allies held war trials to hold the Japanese and Germans accountable for the worst war in human history. Top generals and government officials were charged and convicted, and some were executed for crimes against humanity. This set a new precedent in **international law**, as making war would now be punishable in international courts.

The toll of the war was staggering. Some estimates of the dead exceed 60 million, and millions more were brutalized and wounded in the greatest example of total war in human history. The fighting ranged from Africa to Asia to Europe to Australia.

United Nations: Much of the responsibility for settling postwar problems fell on the United Nations (UN), headquartered in New York City. Led by the five Allied victors of the war (United States, USSR, Great Britain, France, and the Republic of China), the UN established relief agencies and peacekeeping mechanisms. The task of postwar recovery—especially in war-torn Asia and Europe—was immense. As the leading superpower and wealthiest nation, the United States took on many of the costs for postwar rehabilitation.

The UN is a confederation that nations join voluntarily. The **General Assembly** is a forum for discussing world problems and their solutions. It cannot pass laws but it can raise issues and suggest resolutions. Shortly after its founding, the UN was busy settling disputes in the Middle East and helping the many refugees left by World War II. To keep the peace, the UN has three responses to military aggression:

- Diplomatic protest and pressure brought to bear on the belligerent nation
- Economic sanctions used to pressure the aggressor nation
- Collective military action by member states to defend the nation(s) being attacked

The outcomes of World War II can be summed up as a **United States–Soviet ascendancy**:

- World War II only had two "winners" in that many of the victorious Allied powers were devastated in the fighting (especially **France** and **China**). **Britain** was crippled economically and was already losing control of parts of its once-great empire. The greatest postwar status fell to the **United States**, who had entered the war late but had built up a gigantic military and industrial response to the Axis. Possession of the A-bomb meant that the United States was now alone at the pinnacle of power. It had suffered smaller losses in terms of men killed and, except for the attack on Hawaii in 1941, none of its territory was damaged.
- On the other side of the world, the **Soviet Union** had faced annihilation and survived to emerge as a great military power. Its losses had been almost 27 million, which was immensely traumatizing. Whole tracts of land had been decimated. Once victorious, the USSR participated in the founding of the United Nations, participated in the War Crimes Tribunal, and established its hegemony in Eastern Europe.

The Cold War (1945–1989)

Within a year of the end of the war, there were already tensions between the former allies. Working together to occupy Germany and to help found the United Nations, the United States and the USSR found more and more points of contention. The Soviet Union sought to control the nations on its western frontier, partly as a promoter of communism, but also to create a buffer to protect itself from future invasions. The United States protested, as this was in violation of wartime agreements.

Eventually, a de facto division took place, which divided Europe into a **capitalist West** and a **communist East**. In the middle of it all stood the divided former capital of Germany. Berlin had British, Russian, French, and American troops stationed in close proximity to one another. War almost erupted in 1948 when the Russians sealed off the city, denying the others access, but they finally relented.

The following year, the USSR exploded its own nuclear device, and the rivalry with the United States turned to outright animosity and competition. This rivalry continued for four decades, as the United States and the USSR competed for political influence throughout the world. It all came to an end when the Soviet Union collapsed in 1991.

Major features of the competition between the two nations were:
- **Technological**: The race to build bigger and more destructive weaponry intensified after the USSR tested its first nuclear bomb in 1949. The thermonuclear bomb (H-bomb) followed in the 1950s. Space technology created new competition when the USSR launched the first satellite in 1957. After this, there was a "space race," and then a "moon race," with both nations hoping to be the first to launch people into space. Landing on the moon by the United States in 1969 and Soviet space stations of the 1970s were some of the byproducts of this competition.
- **Geopolitical**: Both superpowers vied for influence across the globe, especially in the developing nations of Asia and Africa. Wars in Korea, Vietnam, India, Afghanistan, and Angola were fought with weapons provided by the Americans and Soviets.
- **Ideological**: Capitalism and communism were presented to the world as the two choices available for political organization. At least four nations were divided by this Cold War dichotomy in the 1950s.

By the mid-1950s, relations between the Soviet Union and the People's Republic of China began to deteriorate as they differed in their interpretation of Marxism. China encouraged a movement of **nonaligned nations** made up of developing countries. India and Indonesia were two prominent nations in this group. A famous meeting in Indonesia in 1955 gathered these nations together and China cultivated the many national leaders present. China hoped to connect with the developing world and use this to counteract Soviet Russian diplomacy. Chinese aid flowed to African and Asian nations as a part of this ideological outreach.

The United States took advantage of the Sino–Soviet split and normalized relations with China in the 1970s. The Cold War took on more of a tri-polar feel, as China had its own nuclear weapons and space program by the 1970s.

INDEPENDENCE AND NATIONALIST MOVEMENTS

Throughout the 20th century, independence movements and nationalism rose in many parts of the world. They were often set off as an opposing response to a colonial power or a competitive nationalist group.

India

India's nationalist movement was led by the British-educated members of **the Indian National Congress**. The Government of India Act of 1919 transferred power over some domestic issues over to the Congress, but as political independence seemed to be on the rise, British repression rose alongside it. In 1919, the government cracked down on freedom of the press and assembly, and at Amritsar, a British general ordered troops to fire on a protest rally. In the eyes of India, British colonial rule had lost its legitimacy.

Under the leadership of **Mohandas Gandhi**, the Indian nationalist movement grew. Gandhi focused on the peasant roots and spiritual traditions of India and created a mass movement. His methods of **ahimsa,** nonviolence in the face of an attack, and **civil disobedience** against unjust laws effectively challenged British authority. Gandhi was unsuccessful, however, in allying with Muslim leadership, and a movement to create a separate Muslim state gained strength.

The British suspended the movement toward home rule during World War II, but after the war, it was difficult for them to maintain their empire. On August 15, 1947, independence was granted to India and Pakistan (the Muslim-dominated area led by Muhammad Ali Jinnah). This division led to a mass migration of Muslim and Hindu refugees and terrible violence. Gandhi was devastated by the division of India and was later assassinated by a Hindu extremist.

Sub-Saharan Africa

By 1914, almost all of Africa had been carved up by European powers. Economically, it had been transformed into a **monoculture** of cash crops and mines of precious metals such as gold and diamonds, but the ownership of these plantations and mines was exclusively in the hands of Europeans. As in India, the independence movements in Africa were often led by a small minority of Africans who had received a European education. Labor organizations, social clubs, literary circles, and youth movements all became vehicles for protest.

The process of independence itself varied widely across Africa. The Gold Coast, later **Ghana**, was the first to achieve its independence in 1957. Led by the U.S.-educated **Kwame Nkrumah**, strikes and protests were used to remove the British from power. **Kenya**, on the other hand, had a sizable European population that blocked independence. This led to an armed revolt and eventually independence, in 1963.

The independence of the Belgian Congo was not planned at all. The Belgian government departed the **Congo** suddenly in 1959, leaving behind a country of chaos and civil war.

The **political borders** created by the European colonial powers led to nations that were comprised of unrelated ethnic groups who often became rivals competing for power. This led to ethnic tension in many areas of Africa, including **Rwanda**, where conflict between the majority Hutus and minority Tutsis (formally favored by colonial powers) led to a 100-day genocide, resulting the deaths of almost one million Tutsis in 1994.

In **South Africa**, the path was very different. The Union of South Africa was formed in 1910 from former British colonies, but the majority black population was granted no rights. Instead, a series of restrictive laws was enacted with the goal of controlling the black population and maintaining the separate societies of black and white. This system was known as **apartheid.**

Under apartheid, 87% of the territory was designated for white citizens and the remaining area was for black citizens. But, under the leadership of the African National Congress (ANC), an organized resistance was formed. The government combated this resistance with repressive measures such as extensive jail times for opponents. International opposition against South Africa, like the United Nations economic sanctions and international boycotts, brought global attention to the problem.

Finally, in 1989, the National Party began to take apart the apartheid system. **Nelson Mandela** was released from jail after 26 years and the ANC was legalized. In 1994, elections for all people were held, and Mandela became the first freely elected president of South Africa.

Zionism and Palestinian Nationalism

Following World War I, the British held a **mandate** (a system in which a nation administers a territory on behalf of the League of Nations) in Palestine, but made conflicting promises to the Palestinian Arabs and the Jews. In the **Balfour Declaration of 1917**, the British government committed to support the creation of a homeland for Jews in Palestine, and allowed Jews to migrate to Palestine during the mandate period. The Arab Palestinians saw the British rule and Jewish settlement as forms of imperial control, however.

Jewish migration increased to Palestine as Nazi persecution increased during World War II. By the end of the war, the Pan-Arabism movement opposed the creation of a Jewish state, and the Holocaust increased the Jewish commitment to the creation of a homeland. By 1947, the British gave up the mandate and turned the land over the United Nations, which had plans to divide the area into two states. A civil war ensued and Jewish victories led to the creation of the Jewish state of **Israel** on May 1948.

Continued fighting has plagued this region, including the Six Day War in 1967. The **Palestinian Liberation Organization (PLO)** was created and is dedicated to reclaiming the land and establishing a Palestinian state.

Vietnam

The French colonial rule of Southeast Asia also had to deal with rising nationalism. Both France and her colonies were occupied by the Axis powers during the war. A group of Vietnamese nationalists under the leadership of **Ho Chi Minh** first fought the Japanese during the war, and then began a guerrilla campaign against the returning French. Ho was a Marxist who also admired the American revolutionary Thomas Jefferson. He hoped that the United States would support his movement, but the growing tensions between the United States and the USSR worked against him.

The French-Indochina war lasted a gruesome 9 years before the defeat at Dien Bien Phu forced France to admit it could not keep hold of its Asian possessions. A conference in Geneva in 1954 created four zones out of the former French Indochina: North and South Vietnam, Laos, and Cambodia.

After the French departure, Vietnam became a **Cold War** sideshow: The United States gave aid to the south, while Beijing and Moscow supported the communists in the north. This evolved into a large-scale American war after 1965, as the United States tried to protect South Vietnam from communist encroachment. The costly effort failed, ending in a negotiated peace and communist victory in 1975.

REVOLUTIONS

Russia

By 1914, Russia was far behind Western Europe economically and technologically. It lacked the capital to sufficiently build its own industry; was in debt to foreign investors; and was agriculturally unproductive. Losses in the Russo–Japanese War pointed out Russia's technological backwardness. After the Revolution of 1905, the czar conceded and allowed a legislative body (the **Duma**) to be assembled, but it was often dismissed if not in agreement with the czar. During World War I, Russian casualties numbered over 2 million, and that led to more tension throughout the country. Among other things, worker strikes began.

The disorder and chaos during **March of 1917** allowed the Duma to force the czar to abdicate the throne and put the provisional government in power. The government decided to stay in the war, and the food shortages, revolts, and continued strikes led to more disorder. **Vladimir Lenin**, the leader of the Bolsheviks, promised the people **"Peace, Land, Bread"**—exactly what they wanted and needed.

In November of 1917, Lenin's party seized power; in March of 1918, it signed the Treaty of Brest-Litovok with Germany, ending Russia's part in the war. For the next few years, a civil war raged throughout Russia between the Reds (Communists) and the Whites (Loyalists).

The **Bolshevik government** took control of the land, banks, and industries and used the Cheka, the secret police, to keep an eye on its people. However, the aftermath of World War I and civil war had caused drought and famine throughout, and so Lenin decided to take a more moderate course of action.

The **New Economic Policy**, NEP, in 1921 allowed peasants to sell their products, but the government controlled banking, trade, and heavy industry. Lenin died in 1924, and after a power struggle, **Joseph Stalin** came to power. Stalin instituted his **Five-Year Plans** with the goals of increasing industrial and agricultural productivity. Individual farms became collectivized (those who refused collectivization were killed, numbering over 14.5 million), and agricultural productivity declined, leading to great peasant hardship. Industrial productivity increased a few years later, however, when Western Europe and the United States were hurting from the Great Depression. The Russian people experienced tremendous oppression during Stalin's **Great Purges** of the 1930s. Thousands were tried and executed and millions were imprisoned.

China

China was on the winning side of both world wars, but few nations suffered more from World War II. Technically, the Nationalist (Guomindang) government had been ruling China since the **Revolution of 1911**, but in reality, the country was fragmented into a series of warlord-dominated zones. **Sun Yixian** (Sun Yat-sen), the father of modern China, died in 1924 and a young army officer named **Jiang Jieshi** (Chiang Kai Shek) inherited leadership of the struggling Republic of China.

After 1921, a new dynamic in the nation was exhibited by the stirrings of a **Chinese Communist Party** (CCP). Jiang tried to work with the communists until he turned on them in 1927, driving them underground. The CCP was tracked down throughout the 1930s until they retreated to the north and reorganized. The Japanese attacks in 1931 and 1937 rallied all of China to the defense of the nation. When Japan invaded, Chinese nationalists and communists alike tried to cooperate in their fight against the Japanese, but there was little trust.

After Japan surrendered in 1945, the United States tried to encourage a coalition government, but negotiations broke down and civil war resumed. For three years, the Chinese Communist Party (CCP) and the Nationalist Guomindang (GMD) fought each other. The communists prevailed in 1949, and their leader **Mao Zedong** proclaimed the birth of the People's Republic of China (PRC) from Beijing as the nationalists fled to Taiwan to regroup.

Mao's Initial Changes to China

Economic	• All businesses were nationalized • Land was distributed to peasants • Peasants were urged to pool their land and work more efficiently on cooperative farms
Political	• A one-party totalitarian state was established • Communist party became supreme • Government attacked crime and corruption
Social	• Peasants were encouraged to s peak bitterness" against landlords (10,000 landlords were killed as a result) • Communist ideology replaced Confucian beliefs • Schools were opened with emphasis on political education • Health care workers were sent to remote areas • Women won equality (but little opportunity in government and were paid less than men) • The extended family was weakened

In order to increase agricultural and industrial production, Mao came up with and instituted a personalized plan (as Stalin had done) in the late 1950s. In the **Great Leap Forward**, all life was to be collective—family houses were torn down, and commune life replaced family life. Backyard steel furnaces were set up, which used scrap metal to make iron and steel.

The Great Leap Forward proved to be a great failure. Initial production statistics had been grossly inflated, and the backyard furnaces did not turn out iron of acceptable quality. The bad weather of the 1950s and 1960s led to the deaths of at least 16 million Chinese.

As a result, some modifications were made to the system. Mao's second major initiative was the **Cultural Revolution** of the 1960s. In an effort to re-revolutionize China, a group of teenagers known as the Red Guards rampaged cities, ordered the destruction of temples, and closed schools. The military was eventually needed to suppress the anarchy created by the Red Guards. As a result, it cost the country the loss of an entire generation of educated people.

Comparative Close-up:
The Role of Women during the Russian and Chinese Revolutions

Russia	China
• Women served in the Red Army • 65% of factory workers were women • Government ordered equal pay (though it was not enforced) • Maternity leave with full pay was established • Women entered professions	• New marriage law forbade arranged marriage (was met with resistance) • Women worked alongside men in factories • State-run nurseries were set up to care for children • Party leadership remained male • Efforts were made to end foot binding

Mexico

In the late 19th and beginning of the 20th centuries, Mexico was ruled by the dictatorship of **Portfino Diaz**. Under this rule, 95% of the people owned no land, and foreign investors owned 20–25% of the land.

Very little changed after the independence movement of the 1830s. In 1910, the people rose up against Diaz and a civil war ensued. Many of the leaders, who were mestizos, wanted to break the control of the creole elite. Leaders such as Pancho Villa and Emiliano Zapata advocated land reform. Power changed hands continually throughout the civil war, as leaders were assassinated or overthrown. Eventually, conservative forces won out and Venustiano Carranza become president in 1916. He convened an assembly to write the **Constitution of 1917**.

The Constitution promised land reform, imposed restrictions on foreign economic control, set minimum salaries and maximum hours for workers, granted the right to unionize and strike, and placed restrictions on Church-ownership of property and control over education. In 1928, the National Revolutionary Party (later named the **Party of Institutionalized Revolution (PRI)**) was institutionalized as a more comprehensive party. Th PRI dominated politics for the remainder of the century, instituting land redistribution and standing up to foreign companies.

Iran

The **Shah Reza**, who ruled Iran from 1953 to 1979, was heavily influenced by the West and pushed to modernize his country. He was oppressive, using secret police to monitor his people. Opposition to the shah's rule came from three camps: **the religious ulama**, who felt that traditional religion was being suppressed; **students and intellectuals**, who felt deprived of freedom; and **farmers and urban workers**, who were hurt by inflation and unemployment.

In 1979, demonstrations led by the religious leader **Ayatollah Khomeini** forced the Shah into exile. Under Khomeini's rule, the sharia (Islamic law) became the law of the land. Women, for instance, were required to return to traditional Islamic clothing and were also placed under legal restrictions. Some women saw this return to tradition as a stand against Western culture and imperialism. After Khomeini's death in 1989, more moderate leaders have come to power.

Cuba

From 1939 to 1959, Cuba was ruled by the dictatorship of **Batista**, under which a small percentage of people were very wealthy and the masses of peasants were quite poor. **Fidel Castro** organized a guerrilla movement which initially failed, but eventually captured power in 1959. Though he had promised to hold elections, Castro did not do so, and at first, even denied that he was a communist. When he established close ties with the USSR, the United States viewed him as a threat.

In 1961, Castro announced his communist plans for Cuba: collectivized farms, centralized control of the economy, and free education and medical services. Tensions with the United States continued when a group of Cuban exiles in 1961, supported by the United States, attempted a failed invasion, known as the **Bay of Pigs**.

In 1962, a standoff known as the **Cuban Missile Crisis** occurred when Soviet missiles were discovered in Cuba. The United States and the Soviet Union compromised, and a third world war was avoided.

POLITICAL REFORM AND ECONOMIC CHANGES

Toward the second half of the 20th century, many countries experienced economic and political changes. These changes would set them on their future courses.

China

After Mao died in 1976, **Deng Xiaoping** came to power and instituted a new program of economic modernization. The **Four Modernizations** included the following: industry, agriculture, technology, and national defense. Foreign investment was encouraged, and thousands of students were sent abroad to study.

As a result of these capitalist reforms, the economy boomed. Deng, however, was criticized for leaving out any democratic reforms. Criticism of the past was acceptable, as long as it didn't directly involve criticism of Marxist ideology. In May of 1989, massive student demonstrations occurred in **Tiananmen Square**. Students called for democratic reforms, but instead were met with troops and tanks sent to crush the rebellion. The Chinese government reinforced the ideas that party leadership and political stability were the keys to China's success.

India

After independence from the British, India adopted under the leadership of Nehru a parliamentary political system based on that of Britain. The state took ownership of major industries, resources, transportation, and utilities, but local and retail businesses and farmland remained private.

Unlike Gandhi, Nehru advocated industrialization. India's foreign policy was one of **nonalignment** during the polarized Cold War. Tension continued with Muslim Pakistan when war broke out over the disputed land of **Kashmir.** Nehru's daughter, **Indira Gandhi** later became prime minister, and was extremely concerned about the growing population problem. As a result, she adopted a policy of forced sterilization that was extremely unpopular. Also, militant Sikhs in the Punjab demanded autonomy, and Gandhi ordered the rebels attacked. She was later assassinated by her Sikh bodyguard in 1984.

Soviet Union/Russia

After the death of Stalin, **Khrushchev** came to power in 1953 and initiated a de-Stalinization movement which criticized Stalin's faults and encouraged more freedom of expression. From 1964 to 1982, **Brezhnev** maintained power and retreated from de-Stalinization. He instead took a restrictive policy toward dissidents and free expression. During this period, industrial growth declined; the primary problem was the absence of incentives and a system of quotas.

When **Gorbachev** came to power in 1985, he introduced his policy of **perestroika** (restructuring), which marked the beginning of a market economy with limited free-enterprise and some private property. His policy of **glasnost** (openness) encouraged a discussion of the strengths and weaknesses of the Soviet system. The formation of other parties and two candidate elections were also introduced.

The Soviet Union, however, had major problems with its multiethnic population, and tensions rose along with the development of nationalist movements. The republics soon opted for independence, and the USSR came to an end, as did the Cold War.

In December of 1991, Gorbachev resigned and Boris Yeltsin came to power. As the new ruler of Russia, Yeltsin pushed for economic reform, fighting economic inequality and corruption. Russia continues to struggle with major problems of corruption and an unstable economy. Perhaps the changes were too great and too fast.

Eastern Europe

The Soviet Union heavily influenced their satellite states in Eastern Europe following World War II, installing communist leaders and closely monitoring their progress. However, the economic hardships there and lack of political liberties led to growing discontent.

In 1956, a student-led protest in Hungary expressed this discontent, but the powerful Soviet army was sent in to crush the movement. In the late 1960s in Czechoslovakia, a movement (known as the **Prague Spring**) began in the hopes of creating a form of socialism with more freedom of speech and economic freedom. This movement was short-lived, however, after Soviet troops invaded with the intention of crushing it.

Throughout the communist-controlled period, Eastern European nations did experience a rise in education and an increase in the urban-working class. The former 'privileged class' was removed and replaced by a new privileged class—members of the Communist Party.

As the USSR was declining in the 1980s, liberation movements spread throughout the area. An independent labor movement, *Solidarity*, led by **Lech Walesa** fought for change in Poland. Czechoslovakia split into the Czech Republic and Slovakia in 1994. In East Germany, mass demonstrations in the summer and fall of 1989 led to the opening of the border with West Germany; the tearing down of the **Berlin Wall**; and the eventual reunification of Germany.

Now that Soviet domination was removed, Eastern European countries moved to join **NATO** (North Atlantic Treaty Organization) and the **EU** (European Union). Beginning in 1990, ethnic conflict developed in Yugoslavia, and under the Serbian leadership of Slobodan Milosevic, a policy of ethnic cleansing in Bosnia and Kosovo was instituted. In 2000, Milosevic was ousted from power and is now being tried for war crimes at the **International War Crimes Tribunal**.

Japan

For the five years following World War II, Japan was governed by an Allied administration which instituted a constitution, land reforms, and an education system. The goal was to make Japan **economically strong** so it could serve as a defense against communism in East Asia. The Japanese and United States formed a defensive alliance which allowed Japan to spend almost no money on its own defense—less than 1% of its gross domestic product.

Without having to pay for its own defense, Japan was able to focus on its economy. It soon experienced tremendous growth through the development of an **export economy**, with a large focus on technology. In recent years, however, Japan has suffered economic difficulties, with long-lasting economic stagnation that began in the 1990s and still continues today. Culturally, it has become a more individualistic society, but it retains an emphasis on the importance of a strong work ethic.

DEMOGRAPHIC AND ENVIRONMENTAL ISSUES

The population of the world has grown tremendously in the past few centuries, topping **over 6 billion people**. The use of vaccines and antibiotics, and a decline in the death rates contributed to this rise. Additionally, high levels of fertility in Asia and Africa have led to large population increases.

The huge growth in population has contributed to **environmental problems**, including the loss of animal species and the overuse of natural resources. Though **migration** has been a theme throughout world history, it has increased throughout this century, both internally (when people move from rural to urban areas) and externally (when people migrate long distances and across borders). These migrations are caused by a lack of resources, religious or ethnic persecution, and population pressures. One result has been rapid **urbanization** in many parts of the world, which brings a whole new set of challenges: slums, unemployment, and underemployment for some recent migrants.

SOCIETAL CHANGES

Changing Gender Roles

In 1914, there were few opportunities for women in most professions. The 19th century had seen a few pioneering women become doctors, but most females were relegated to child-rearing, nursing, or teaching. The fight for female suffrage in the West saw its first successes in New Zealand, Australia, and Finland. Militant activists in Great Britain and the United States won the right to vote after 1920. Fashion and popular culture helped create a new image of the modern woman—free from some of the constraints of traditional gender roles.

Social and economic parity was a much longer fight. Both world wars gave women more and more power in terms of wage-earning, but the demands of the workplace and the home continued to be a challenge for the modern woman. The postwar **feminist movement** publicized the issues of child care and equal pay for equal work in the 1970s. Politics, law, and medicine have become more open to women in the last half of the 20th century. Successful female heads of government in Israel, Great Britain, and the Philippines demonstrated that politics was no longer an all-male domain.

The sexual revolution of the sixties and seventies further defined male and female roles. Key issues such as access to **birth control** were advanced, giving women more control over their own lives. Greater earning power in the workplace also meant more independence. The institution of marriage was challenged, and some women opted to remain unattached or even to have children by themselves. Given the magnitude of these recent social changes, the impacts are still being felt and processed.

In parts of the developing world, changes to gender roles have varied. Some socialist and communist societies instituted important legal reforms for women, such as the 1950 marriage law in China which grants free choice of partners. In reality, many traditional beliefs still exist in China and other areas. The large population problem in China led to the establishment of the **one-child policy**, and as a result half a million female births go unrecorded each year, demonstrating the continual preference for a male child. Despite having powerful female heads of state such as Indira Gandhi in India and Benazir Bhuto in Pakistan, **literacy rates** for women in South Asia are still far below those of men. In the 1980s, only 25% of the female population of India was literate.

Globalization

Regional and International Organizations

The 20th century brought about new patterns of economic and political organization that transcended national borders. **OPEC**, the Organization of Petroleum Exporting Countries, organized in 1960 in an effort to raise the price of oil through cooperation. The World Trade Organization (**WTO**) formed from the General Agreement of Tariffs and Trade (**GATT**) in 1995 to promote unrestricted global trade.

Regional organizations have also formed to protect more local interests. **ASEAN,** the Association of Southeast Asian Nations, formed in 1967 to accelerate economic progress and promote political stability. The **EU**, European Union, formed from the European Community in 1993 in an effort to strengthen European economic trade relations and distance itself from the influence of the United States. **NAFTA**, North American Free Trade Agreement, involves the United States, Canada and Mexico, working to remove trade barriers between these countries. Finally, non-governmental organizations (**NGOs**) such as the Red Cross and Greenpeace work to tackle problems that reach beyond national boundaries and governments.

Internationalization of Culture

As the world becomes more and more connected, cultural lines seemed to have become blurred. Some refer to this as **cultural imperialism**. As Western companies and entertainment spread worldwide, Western cultural ideas spread along with them. American companies like McDonalds, Coca-Cola, and Kentucky Fried Chicken can be found in most parts of the world today. With the spread of these products and ideas, some believe a consumer culture has developed, focusing on materialism and the promotion of **cultural conformity**.

The rise of the use of the English language is also an indication of a developing global culture. Transmitted through the Internet, movies, and music, the use of the English language has spread worldwide. Yet even with the prevalence of a Western-oriented consumer culture, traditional forces remain strong in many parts of the world. Islamic fundamentalism, for instance, is a traditional force that very much reacts against Western culture, and the two ideals often clash.

Since World War II and throughout the Cold War, the world saw certain mega-trends. Some of these have included:

- Rapid population growth: (world population in 1945: 2,350,000,000; in 2000: 6,100,000,000)
- Globalization in the form of multinational businesses such as Phillips, Bechtel, Microsoft, Ford Motors, and Sony
- Access to information through electronic/satellite transfer by phone, fax, and email
- Nationalism and the proliferation of nation–states
- Religious fundamentalism in many different varieties
- The rise of export economies

IF YOU LEARNED ONLY SIX THINGS IN THIS CHAPTER . . . .

1. Due to improvements in health care and the decrease of the death rate, the world population went from 1 billion people in 1900 to over 6 billion. The movement of people has also increased throughout the world, with many in search of better economic opportunities. Some refugees, too, are being forced to leave their homelands.

2. Traditional social structures have been challenged as a result of movements which have attempted to empower the working and peasant classes, such as the introduction of communist governments in various parts of the world.

3. Women gained the right to vote in many parts of the world and access to new economic opportunities and education. The development of the birth control pill empowered women by allowing them to control their own reproductive systems.

4. The world became more and more integrated through technology, cultures blended, and some came to dominate. At the same time, religious fundamentalism has developed in some regions, possibly to combat this Western-dominated global culture.

5. This rise in the nation-state and nationalism has led to the adoption of political systems from totalitarianism to democracy. At the same time, the rise of a more globally connected world may blur the lines of the nation-state.

6. The world wars demonstrated the influence of technology on warfare, but also indicated the decline of Europe as the global power. Colonial areas asserted themselves and fought for independence, but were later faced with a new global conflict called the Cold War. Since the end of the Cold War, nations have made attempts at both economic and political reforms, and international and multinational organizations have made attempts to find a new world order.

REVIEW QUESTIONS

1. All of the following have been given as long-term causes of World War I EXCEPT
   (A) The rise of nationalism
   (B) Imperialism and competition for foreign colonies
   (C) Arms competition
   (D) Economic recession prior to 1912
   (E) The diplomatic alliance system

2. All the following are features of fascism EXCEPT
   (A) Stamping out the labor movement
   (B) Ultra-nationalistic propaganda
   (C) Expansion and glorification of the military
   (D) Emphasis on sacrifice for the nation–state
   (E) Collectivization of farms

3. American President Woodrow Wilson's post-war aims in World War I were summed up in the
   (A) Potsdam declaration
   (B) Treaty of Versailles
   (C) Treaty of Brest-Litovsk
   (D) Fourteen Points
   (E) Four Freedoms

4. The failure of the League of Nations to keep the peace was largely due to
   (A) the aggressive leadership of the United States.
   (B) the fear of communism after 1917.
   (C) the hedonism of the 1920s.
   (D) vacillating leadership and lack of multilateral military resolve.
   (E) alliances made between the major powers after 1919.

5. Free-trade associations created after World War II were
   (A) OPEC and NATO
   (B) The EU and NAFTA
   (C) APEC and the Warsaw Pact
   (D) G-7 and UNESCO
   (E) The OAS and Mercur

6. One of the major causes of the Global Depression in 1930 was
   (A) War-debt restructuring in the 1920s
   (B) The rising stock market in the United States
   (C) Underproduction of agricultural goods
   (D) The rise of totalitarian regimes in Europe
   (E) Trade tensions that resulted in high protective tariffs

7. The purpose of the United Nations is to insure world peace based on
   (A) The European alliance
   (B) Détente between the superpowers
   (C) Political ideology
   (D) Military alliances
   (E) Collective security

8. Nations most affected by the Great Depression were those that
   (A) Lowered their taxes
   (B) Were dependent on global trade
   (C) Had centralized banking systems
   (D) Had the smallest territory
   (E) Were dependent on agriculture

9. India was partitioned as it gained independence in 1947 because

   (A) the British could not agree on the political boundaries.
   (B) Muslims had their own desire for a state in South Asia.
   (C) Gandhi supported the idea.
   (D) Jinnah was assassinated shortly afterward.
   (E) Sikhs in the Punjab demanded it.

10. The function of the World Trade Organization (WTO) is to

    (A) Negotiate free trade agreements
    (B) Buy and sell commodities
    (C) Oversee and manage world trade
    (D) Report to the United Nations about labor issues worldwide
    (E) Encourage protectionism

11. Internal migration is defined as the

    (A) importation of cheaper labor by industrialized nations.
    (B) creation of shanty towns in rural areas.
    (C) movement of people from rural to urban areas.
    (D) flight of refugees for political reasons.
    (E) the upward mobility of the middle class.

12. Nations in the Balkans and Africa have both suffered because

    (A) nationalism did not take root.
    (B) political boundaries were drawn without regard for ethnic or tribal groups.
    (C) of pan-Slavic solidarity.
    (D) of the indifference of the United Nations.
    (E) there was too much investment capital available.

13. Black South Africans struggled against white minority rule prior to 1990 by supporting the

    (A) UN efforts to raise living standards.
    (B) African National Congress (ANC).
    (C) local township councils.
    (D) movement to desegregate the universities.
    (E) black government in exile.

14. The main reason the United States increased its military support for South Vietnam in the 1960s was because

    (A) the USSR was threatening Berlin.
    (B) the French told it to do so.
    (C) it had been an ally during World War II.
    (D) communism seemed to be expanding in the region.
    (E) Cuba was helping North Vietnam.

15. Following the Revolution of 1979, Iran became

    (A) closely allied with the United States.
    (B) an Islamic theocracy.
    (C) ruled by the Sunni majority.
    (D) increasingly in support of women's rights.
    (E) increasingly tied to its neighbor Iraq.

16. Mao Zedong departed from orthodox Marxism by gathering support from

    (A) Urban workers
    (B) Disenchanted members of the merchant class
    (C) Rural peasants
    (D) The military class
    (E) Industrialists afraid of KMT policies

17. Indian nationalists hoped to achieve which of the following goals as a result of helping Great Britain during World War I?

    (A) Territorial expansion
    (B) British citizenship
    (C) Expansion of industrialization
    (D) Greater self government
    (E) Peace between Hindus and Muslims

18. The major goal of the Zionist movement was to

    (A) rebuild a homeland for Jews in Palestine.
    (B) expel the British from India.
    (C) gain independence for Israel.
    (D) seek revenge on the German people.
    (E) be recognized by the United States.

19. During the Russian Revolution of 1917, Lenin and the Bolsheviks least emphasized

    (A) Withdrawal from World War I
    (B) Redistribution of land
    (C) Abolition of religion
    (D) Redistribution of wealth
    (E) The importance of the working class

20. Which of the following was NOT a policy of Communist China?

    (A) Weaken family ties
    (B) Discourage Confucian traditions
    (C) Purge counterrevolutionaries
    (D) Encourage workers to strike
    (E) Collectivize agriculture

21. Which of the following is true of both the Mexican and Iranian Revolutions?

    (A) They were driven by a desire for a return to religious traditions.
    (B) Civil war between opposing groups resulted.
    (C) Foreign control and influence were lessened.
    (D) A democratic constitution was written.
    (E) The prior leadership returned after a period of disorder.

22. Biodiversity and global warming are both important examples of

    (A) Nationalists' issues
    (B) Persecution of indigenous people
    (C) Improved weaponry
    (D) Military dictatorships
    (E) Environmental problems

23. The independence movements in both India and Africa were led by the

    (A) Peasants
    (B) Educated elite
    (C) Communists
    (D) Military
    (E) White settlers

24. After the Cuban Revolution, Castro did all of the following EXCEPT

    (A) Collectivize farms
    (B) Centralize control of the economy
    (C) Seek alliances with the Soviet Union
    (D) Institute a nationwide election
    (E) Offer free education and medical services

25. Which of the following conclusions is best supported by the graph below?

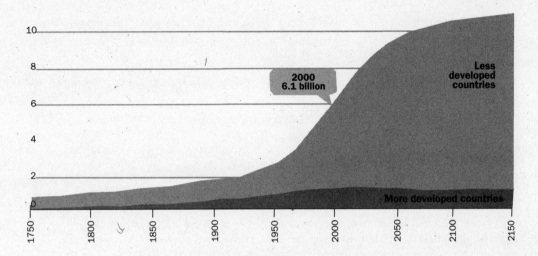

World Population Growth, 1750–2150

Source: United Nations, World Population Prospects,
The 1998 Revision; and estimates by the Population Reference Bureau

(A) More developed countries have had difficulty controlling their populations

(B) Less developed countries have become more politically influential due to population growth

(C) World population will more than double between 1970 and 2150

(D) Population growth in less developed countries is caused by economic prosperity

(E) Lack of health care has led to worldwide population growth

Document-Based Question

Directions: The following question is based on the accompanying Documents 1 to 4. (Some of the documents have been edited for the purpose of this exercise.)

This question is designed to test your ability to work with and understand historical documents. Write an essay that:

- Has a relevant thesis and supports that thesis with evidence from the documents.
- Uses all or all but one of the documents.
- Analyzes the documents by grouping them in as many appropriate ways as possible. **Does not simply summarize the documents individually**.
- Takes into account the sources of the documents and analyzes the authors' points of view.
- Explains the need for at least one additional type of document.

You may refer to relevant historical information not mentioned in the documents.

Based on the following documents, analyze the impact of the role of women on population growth in developing nations. Explain what additional kind of document(s) would help assess the impact of women on population growth in developing nations.

Document 1

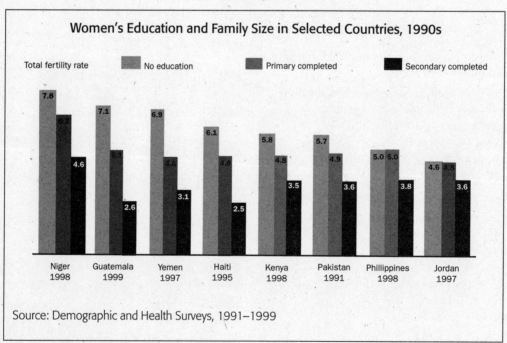

Document 2

Women's Age at First Marriage (years) and Family Size (TFR) in Selected Countries, 1990s

Country	Average age at first marriage	Total fertility rate
Chad	15.9	6.6
Yemen	16.5	6.5
Guatemala	19.4	5.0
Haiti	20.5	4.7
Jordan	21.5	4.4
Bangladesh	14.2	3.3
Egypt	19.7	3.3
Indonesia	18.9	2.8
Uzbekistan	20.1	2.8
USA	25.1	2.1

Source: Demographic and Health Surveys, 1991–1999; and Carl Haub and Diana Cornelius, 2000 World Population Data Sheet (Washington, DC: Population Reference Bureau, 2000)

Document 3

Demographic and Socio-Economic Indicators In India and the United States, Late 1990s

	United States	India	Kerala
Total fertility rate	2.1	3.2	1.8
Infant mortality rate	7	68	14
Life expectancy (male)	74	60	71
Life expectancy (female)	79	61	75
Female literacy	99	57	85
Contraceptive relevance (all methods)	76	48.2	63.7

Sources: Carl Haub and Diana Cornelius, 2000 World Population Data Sheet (Washington, DC: PRB, 2000); Registrar General of India; an National Family Health Survey

Document 4

An Example From India

Kerala is primarily rural and agricultural, as is most of India. The residents have low incomes. Yet in the early 1990s, women in Kerala were bearing about two children, on average. Between 1970 and 1992, Kerala's TFR dropped from 4.1 to 2.0 children per woman, the largest decline of any Indian state. By the end of the 1990s, the total fertility rate was down to about 1.8 children per woman. The infant mortality rate is also low, 14 deaths of infants under age 1 per 1,000 live births in a given year.

Why are the women in Kerala different? One obvious difference is their higher educational level. While most Indian women cannot read and write, 85 percent of women in Kerala are literate. The state government has assigned a high priority to ensuring that all residents have access to education.

In traditional Keralese culture, women can inherit land and wield some political power—a sharp contrast with other parts of India. And, while in most of India girls are considered a drain on family finances because their parents must pay a dowry to marry them off, Keralese women bring their families a brideprice. In Kerala, girls are considered an asset.

Source: http://www.prb.org

Change-Over-Time Question

Directions: Answer the following question: You should spend 5 minutes organizing or outlining your essay. Write an essay that:
- Has a relevant thesis and supports that thesis with appropriate historical evidence.
- Addresses all parts of the question.
- Uses world historical context to show change over time and/or continuities
- Analyzes the process of change over time and/or continuity.

Choose ONE of the following regions and discuss the changes and continuities of gender roles from 1914 to the present. Be sure to discuss changes as well as continuities.

Latin America
Russia
South Asia
China

Comparative Question

Directions: Answer the following question: You should spend 5 minutes organizing or outlining your essay. Write an essay that:
- Has a relevant thesis and supports that thesis with appropriate historical evidence.
- Addresses all parts of the question.
- Makes direct, relevant comparisons.
- Analyzes relevant reasons for similarities and differences.

> Discuss the similarities and differences between World War I and World War II, using ONE of the following points of comparison.
>
> Causes
>
> Effects on civilians
>
> Effects on colonial areas
>
> The global effects of the war

ANSWERS AND EXPLANATIONS

1. D

Economics was not a large factor in the tensions leading up to the Great War. Competition for empires and national rivalries between Germany and Britain were more important factors: The rise of nationalism had helped create a unified Germany after 1870. As a rising power, Germany wanted to rival Great Britain, and its aggressive military buildup threatened the existing balance of power in Europe. Imperialistic rivalries also created tension between Britain and France. Defensive alliances were created and helped to foster a sense of false security among the great powers. When the assassination in Sarajevo sparked a war between Austria and Serbia, it drew the other nations into the conflict.

2. E

Collectivization of farms is not typically of interest to fascists. Big business leaders tend to support fascist regimes because fascism promises to protect them from communism and it will also deal with labor organizations. Fascist regimes return the favor with strict controls on workers and other benefits for business owners. One facet of the business—regime relationship is the prohibition of all labor unions. This, in addition to military contracts, binds industry to the government. Fascist regimes exalt the nation above all else, and individual choice is discouraged. Young men are groomed for the military, and service to the state is the desired goal for all.

3. D

Within one year of entering the Great War, the United States promoted a list of war aims called the Fourteen Points. It was an idealistic postwar view that envisioned diplomacy replacing military might. Few of the points were realized, but many were used again after World War II to establish a more lasting postwar peace. The Potsdam Declaration was made late in World War II by the Allies. Likewise, the Four Freedoms were publicized as Allied war goals in 1942. The Treaty of Brest–Litovsk was made between Germany and Russia, after the Russian Revolution.

4. D

Without the membership of either the United States or Russia, the League of Nations was without strong leadership. The United States did not ratify the Treaty of Versailles, nor did it join the League of Nations. It was left to Britain and France to provide leadership to the League in Geneva, but they often could not agree on common issues. The establishment of the USSR as a communist regime after 1917 was a big change, but even the Soviets joined the League after a time and tried to fit into the constellation of European powers. Alliances prior to World War II were not the feature of diplomacy that they had been before 1914.

5. B

The European Union and the North American Free Trade Agreement were created to assist in the transfer of goods between nations. These trading blocs sought to stimulate business and to lead to consumer benefits, such as lower prices. NATO is not a trade association but rather a military alliance formed in 1949 to thwart communist expansion in Western Europe. APEC is a loose association of the countries in the Asia Pacific region; it hosts economic conferences every year. The G-7 was formed recently to allow major economic powers to share information on global problems. The OAS is an older combination of the nations in the American hemisphere not limited to trade concerns.

6. E

Trade competition between nations led to a decline in international business in the late 1920s. Many nations such as the United States established trade limits and barriers in the form of tariffs to protect domestic manufacturers. War debts were restructured in the 1920s, but these helped the nations of Europe to economically recover prior to the depression. It was the overproduction of agricultural goods that hurt farmers in the 1920s. The farming industry was in economic distress years before the equity market collapsed in New York. The rise of dictators in Europe took place both before and after the onset of the global depression. Certainly in Germany, the National Socialists (Nazis) were able to use the economic hard times to their advantage and gain support from the middle and lower classes.

7. E

One of the principals of developing both the League of Nations (after World War I) and the UN (after World War II) was the idea that peace-loving nations need to band together in times of crisis. This failed in the 1930s, and the peace collapsed. In 1950 and 1990, the UN applied collective security to the respective crises in Korea and Kuwait. The UN mandate to keep the peace is global and not limited to the situation in Europe. Détente was a feature of superpower relations during the Cold War in the 1970s and took place outside the UN's efforts to diminish the threat of World War III. Political debate does take place in the General Assembly, but no *one* political ideology is supposed to dominate. In 1950 and 1990, the UN had to gather troops to counter aggression in Korea and Iraq.

8. B

Industrial nations were hardest hit by the global depression of the 1930s. Britain and the United States were particularly hard-hit, along with Japan and Germany. Taxation was not a central cause of the depression in the 1930s. Government revenues did plummet after the depression struck, though, as the tax base shrank. Private banks, not governmental financial institutions, were the most vulnerable to failure during the depression if they were over-invested in the collapsing equity markets. Agricultural economies could survive on a subsistence level, but industrial nations experienced shocking rises in unemployment.

9. B

During the British years of control over the Indian subcontinent, there were many different domains. When Gandhi urged the British to quit India and give it home rule, he envisioned a large secular democracy. Muslims finally broke with him and demanded a separate Islamic nation. The partition of British India created an independent India and a divided Pakistan in the east and west. Britain had tried vainly to avoid partition, but finally announced it would leave India at a pre-announced time. This was a de facto recognition that British India would not remain in one piece politically. Gandhi campaigned tirelessly against partition and went on public fasts to protest against the need for a separate Muslim state. It was he, and not Jinnah (leader of the Muslim separatist movement), who was assassinated shortly after independence. The Punjab was the site of some of the worst violence during partition, but this was mostly between Hindus and Muslims.

10. C

The WTO is an adjunct part of the UN system and tries to oversee global trade. It has come under attack as a proponent of globalization, which some see as threatening jobs and displacing workers. Free-trade agreements such as the North American Free Trade Agreement (NAFTA) are created between sovereign states, not by the WTO. The WTO is part of the public sector and it does engage in buying and selling. The International Labor Organization (ILO) reports to the UN on labor issues. The WTO is a proponent of free trade and works against protectionist sentiments around the world.

11. C

The last two centuries have seen great movement of people from rural farmland to urban areas, where there are more jobs. This internal migration is one of the great trends in world history since the Industrial Revolution. Migrant workers who come from other countries would be an example of external migration. Shanty towns are a form of temporary, crude housing, usually associated with urban areas. Refugees fleeing to other countries would not be an internal phenomena. The economic status of the middle class does not define internal migration, which describes the physical movement of groups of people from one location to another.

12. B

Within the context of imperialism, empires have included many different ethnic groups and tribes. Taking ethnicity and tribalism into account has bedeviled politicians, as the world map has been redrawn many times through history. Africa was poorly segmented by the Europeans in the 1880s, and the Hapsburgs held many minorities within its empire until 1919. Nationalism did cause considerable problems in the Balkans as ethnic groups fought to establish their own countries, such as Croatia and Slovenia. Pan-Slavic solidarity did not stand the test of time as subgroups caused the disintegration of Yugoslavia after 1990. Ethnic and tribal tensions in Africa and the Balkans predate the founding of the UN and cannot be blamed on that international body. While undeveloped nations can use investment capital, this is not the root cause of ethnic and tribal tensions in Africa or the Balkans.

13. B

The fight for the rights of black Africans in South Africa was led by the African National Congress, or ANC. Its leaders were imprisoned and tortured during the white minority control of the government until 1992. Efforts by the outside world were largely thwarted by the white minority regime in South Africa until the end of apartheid. Blacks and their townships had no political power in white South Africa. Desegregation of the universities was not a major goal of blacks during apartheid. While there were black leaders who opposed the white regime, there was no "government" in exile that agitated abroad against Pretoria.

14. D

The Domino Theory was the fear that communism would continue to expand in Asia if its growth could not be halted. After the revolution in China in 1949 and the partition of Vietnam in 1954, communism seemed to threaten all of Southeast Asia. When the French left in the 1950s, the United States took more of an active role in trying to stabilize the region. Cold War tensions in Berlin were not directly connected to the situation in Southeast Asia. After losing Indochina in 1954, France was in no position to tell the United States what to do in Southeast Asia. The French Indochina War (from 1946) was funded largely by the United States. South Vietnam had not been a country during World War II. It was created in the multilateral settlement in 1954 at Geneva.

15. B

The overthrow of the Shah in Iran was led by Shiite clerics, some of whom had been in exile. After the revolution, the mullahs took control and instituted Islamic rule within the nation. Iran is mostly Shiite and women's rights were not championed in the 1979 revolution. The 1979 Iranian revolution was largely anti-American and resulted in the taking of the U.S. Embassy by a local mob. Iran–Iraq relations deteriorated immediately after the 1979 revolution and led to a gruesome border war in 1981.

16. C

Orthodox Marxist thought predicted that urban workers would revolt against their capitalistic masters and the world socialist revolution would begin in the cities. Mao Zedong adapted Marxist thought to the plight of the peasants in the countryside, and they were the vehicles by which Marxism was successful in overthrowing the Nationalists in 1949. The merchant class tended to support the Nationalists during the post-World War II revolution in China. The cadre of professional soldiers in China at this time was too small to constitute a class. Industrialists were the last group that would support Mao, as they had the most to lose in a socialist regime.

17. D

Through organizations such as the Indian National Congress, Indian nationalists had been fighting for greater self-government and believed from the British that their participation in the war would lead to that. India did not, however, achieve its independence until after World War II (in 1947).

18. A

The Zionist movement was created in the 19th century with the goal of creating a homeland for Jews in Palestine. This movement was furthered by the Balfour Declaration issued in 1917, giving British support to the Jewish homeland. This allowed for increased Jewish migration after the Holocaust and to the eventual UN recognition of the state of Israel in 1948.

19. C

Lenin's famous slogan, "Peace, Land, Bread," laid out his vision for Russia. Peace meant the desire to end Russia's involvement in World War I. Land meant a more equitable distribution of land to the peasant and working classes. Bread meant an end to the starvation and economic hardships of the Russian people. Though Lenin and the Bolsheviks later took power away from the Russian Orthodox Church, this was not something they emphasized to win the support of the Russian people.

20. D

After the communist victory in 1949, Mao's goals were to create an egalitarian society based on the power of the peasants. He did so by tying people to the state rather than to their families; by pointing out the backwardness of Confucian thought; by collectivizing agriculture; and by ridding society of the "bad" elements such as those considered to be counterrevolutionary. Through all these changes, it was important to maintain order, and therefore, the communist party would not encourage any worker strikes.

21. C

In Mexico, foreign companies owned much of the land and were reaping much of the profit. After the revolution, the new government made a strong effort to lessen foreign control of the economy. In Iran, the shah's government was seen as controlled by the West; after the revolution, an Islamic theocracy ruled, attempting to eliminate Western influence from the country.

22. E

Biodiversity has become threatened in the recent past because of the destruction of natural habits for many species and the depletion of natural resources. The earth's temperature has been rising as well (called global warming). These are major environmental problems facing the world today.

23. B

In both India and Africa, leaders emerged who had been educated in Europe and the United States. They used their experience and knowledge to return home and fight for the freedom of their own people. Gandhi in India was a British-educated lawyer, and Kwame Nkrumah received his education in the United States.

24. D

Although Castro had promised elections prior to the revolution, this was never carried out. To this day, Castro himself maintains power. True to a communist philosophy, however, he did collectivize farms, centralize control of the economy, and offer free education and medical services. His alliance with the Soviet Union caused much tension and conflict with the United States.

25. C

According to the chart, world population in 1970 was approximately 5 billion people. By 2150, it will exceed 10 billion. More developed countries had leveled off their population growths. It is unclear from the chart how much political influence less-developed countries will have due to population growth. Population growth is not necessarily caused by economic prosperity, since the less-developed nations have the greatest amount of growth, and improvements in health have led to a larger world population.

Document-Based Question: Sample Response

The developing countries around the world are experiencing the largest population growth even though they may seem the least equipped to deal with such a large population. According to the documents presented, there is a direct correlation between the education and marriage age of females and the number of children they conceive. In countries where women are educated and valued as important members of the society, birth rates are lower and the population is more under control.

When women are educated and marry older, they have fewer children. According to the graph of women's education and family size in selected countries in the 1990s, the more education a woman receives, the less likely she is to have a large family. For example, women in Niger with no education have an average of 7.8 children, while women with a completed secondary education have only an average of 4.6 children. As women become more educated, they seem to be more aware of the strain a large family can be. The purpose of this graph it to promote education of women as a means of reducing family size in developing countries.

According to the graph of women's age at first marriage (in years) and family size in selected countries in the 1990s, those women who wait longer to get married will have a smaller family. In Chad, for example, the average age at first marriage for women is 15.9 and the total fertility rate is 6.6. On the other hand, in the United States, the average age at first marriage is 25.1 and the total fertility rate is 2.1. This indicates that older women may be more in control of the family planning decisions or are simply older and therefore cannot have as many children as a women who is married in her teens.

Finally, the example from the Indian state of Kerala attempts to point out that when a culture values women, it empowers them, and it is those empowered women who can control family size. In Kerala, women bear only two children on average. This low birth rate can be explained by the fact that 85% of the female population is literate, and the state government funds their education. Also, women can inherit land, have some political power, and are not considered a drain on their family financially because they bring their families a brideprice when they get married. The purpose of this document is to prove that when women are valued in society, they can effect change in that society. It would be helpful to have some testimonial evidence from women themselves to see if they see the link between education, marriage age, and the size of families. It would be important to examine the reasons women may still feel pressure to have large families in developing countries.

As the world population continues to increase, these documents suggest that the best way to deal with the problem of a draining population is to empower women. When women can make some of their own choices, they will effect change. When women are educated, they will have fewer children, and population issues can be brought under control.

Change-Over-Time Question: Sample Response

Throughout most of Chinese history, the traditions of Confucianism have long influenced gender roles. However, the victory of the communists after the Chinese Civil War altered the roles of gender for the remainder of the 20th century. According to Mao, women held up half the sky and should be treated as such. The introduction of communism gave women new opportunities, both politically and socially. However, for many the traditional role for women as wife and mother remains, as well as the preference of having boys in the family.

After the communists won the civil war in 1949, many of the changes they implemented began to affect gender roles. The communists told women in the countryside that they should unbind their feet. In the new communist society everyone was needed to work, and the traditional idea of a women being confined and not working did not suit this new society. Also, in the factories, women and men were expected to work side-by-side. Mao also passed a new marriage law which forbade arranged marriages. Instead, women could choose their marriage partner. This law was met with much resistance, and even today many marriages in China are still arranged by one's parents.

While the women were working, the state-run nurseries watched over their children. Politically, though women could join the party, the party leadership remained mostly male. Later, during the rule of Deng Xiaoping, a onechild policy was initiated to slow down China's overwhelming population growth. Parents still preferred to have a boy and this can be seen in reported cases of female infanticide and the large number of female babies in orphanages.

Even though women were expected to work and to carry out traditional household responsibilities at the same time, the changes initiated during the Mao years did bring them new opportunities. Economic and political participation broadened their experience and altered the traditional Confucian gender roles of China.

Comparative Question: Sample Response

The First and Second World Wars were both the result of the accumulation of conflict that began in the 19th century. Nationalism, alliance systems, and acts of aggression all contributed to the start of these global conflicts. While WWI was more a result of growing tension and competition, WWII was caused by direct aggression.

Both wars were induced, at least partly, by the swelling of nationalist pride that began in the 19th century and endured into the 20th. The assassination of Franz Ferdinand and the conflict between Serbia and Austria-Hungry, for example, was a result of Serbian nationalism and was fueled by a longing for self-determination, another idea that took root and spread during this time. World War II was also begun by nationalism, especially that of the Germans. It was this German nationalism and desire for self-determination that fueled Hitler's campaigns to take over Europe. Both wars were sparked by the upset of the delicate balance of power in Europe. In WWI, tensions between the big powers of the time—Germany, Britain, Russia, and France—upset this balance. Likewise, the balance was tipped once again when Hitler's campaign began and the German "Reich" began to expand.

While WWI began with a conflict between small countries which then branched out through the tangled alliances of Europe to other, larger countries, WWII began with the big powers. WWI can be traced back to the rivalry between Austria-Hungary and Serbia. Over time, large powers such as Russia and Germany stepped in to defend their allies, and this enraged even more countries. The inception of WWI was therefore like a "ripple" effect—beginning quite small, and then expanding.

WWII was quite the opposite, beginning with the brutal campaigns and expansion of revisionist powers Germany and Japan. If WWI began with a ripple, WWII began with explosion. Large European powers got involved in WWI because they wanted to protect their allies, not because of direct acts of aggression against them. WWII was marked by such acts of aggression as the bombing of Pearl Harbor, the invasion of Poland, and the Rape of Nanking. While WWI began largely because of tension between countries that had been caused by competition for foreign markets and colonies, WWII was begun largely by fascism and a thirst for revenge. Hitler's attacks on Europe and the transformation of Germany into a dictatorship was made possible because the German people were vulnerable and scarred by the previous war.

These wars could be considered one continual conflict that was not properly resolved in the interim. The nationalism, alliances, and aggression that led to both wars points out that their roots were quite similar. The lesson learned is that the resolutions or lack thereof have shaped the way we make peace today.

| PART FOUR |

Practice Tests

HOW TO TAKE THE PRACTICE TESTS

This section of this book contains 2 practice tests. Taking a practice test gives you an idea of what it's like to sit through a full AP World History exam. You will find out which areas you're strong in, and where additional review may be required. Any mistakes you make now are ones you won't make on the actual exam, as long as you take the time to learn where you went wrong.

The 2 tests here are both full-length. They include 70 multiple-choice questions and 3 free-response (essay) questions. You will have 55 minutes for the multiple-choice section, a 10-minute reading period, and 120 minutes to answer the free-response questions.

Before taking a test, find a quiet place where you can work uninterrupted for 3 hours, and bring extra blank paper for your essays (you will get 16 pages for all three essays on the real exam). Time yourself according to the time limit at the beginning of each section. It's okay to take a short break between sections, but for the most accurate results, you should approximate real test conditions as much as possible. Use the 10-minute reading period to plan your answers for the free-response questions, but don't begin writing your responses until the 10 minutes are up.

Remember to pace yourself. Train yourself to be aware of the time you are spending on each problem. Take note of the general types of questions you encounter, as well as what strategies work best for them.

When you are done, read the detailed answer explanations that follow. These will help you identify areas that could use additional review. But don't only focus on the questions you got wrong. For those you got right, too, you can benefit from reading the answer explanation. You might learn something you didn't already know.

Before writing the free-response questions, you may want to review the material on essay writing found in chapter 1. Each essay has a different purpose and a different set of strategies for answering the question.

The sample free-response answers that follow in the answers and explanations are intended to help you understand how an informed student might approach the question.

Good luck!

HOW TO COMPUTE YOUR SCORE

Scoring the Multiple-Choice Questions

There are 70 questions on this section. To compute your score, calculate the number of questions you got wrong, then deduct $\frac{1}{4}$ of that number from the total number of correct answers. Unanswered questions neither earn nor lose points.

If you got 6 questions wrong and left 4 questions unanswered, you would deduct 1.5 (which is $6 \times \frac{1}{4}$) from 60 (the number of questions you answered correctly). Your score would be 58.5.

Test Score	Results
50–70	Excellent
40–49	Very good
30–39	Good
20–29	Fair
0–19 or less	Poor

Scoring the Free-Response Questions

The readers will have specific points that they will be looking for in each essay (called a rubric). The general rubrics for each of the three free-response essays can be found in chapter 1. Although you will not be able to accurately score your own essays, you can get a better idea of how to apply the scoring system to your own writing by reviewing the rubrics for each essay. Readers use the rubric as the guide for assigning points. Each free-response question is worth a certain number of points, and each point is awarded based on the answers that you provide. Each piece of information that they are able to check off in your essay is a point toward a better score.

Do not take any score on the practice test too literally. There is no way to determine precisely what your AP grade will be because:

- The conditions under which you take the practice test will not exactly mirror real test conditions.
- While the multiple-choice questions are scored by computer, the free-response questions are graded manually by faculty consultants.

For more information on the way that the College Board computes AP scores, refer to chapter 1.

Practice Test 1 Answer Grid

1. Ⓐ Ⓑ Ⓒ Ⓓ Ⓔ
2. Ⓐ Ⓑ Ⓒ Ⓓ Ⓔ
3. Ⓐ Ⓑ Ⓒ Ⓓ Ⓔ
4. Ⓐ Ⓑ Ⓒ Ⓓ Ⓔ
5. Ⓐ Ⓑ Ⓒ Ⓓ Ⓔ
6. Ⓐ Ⓑ Ⓒ Ⓓ Ⓔ
7. Ⓐ Ⓑ Ⓒ Ⓓ Ⓔ
8. Ⓐ Ⓑ Ⓒ Ⓓ Ⓔ
9. Ⓐ Ⓑ Ⓒ Ⓓ Ⓔ
10. Ⓐ Ⓑ Ⓒ Ⓓ Ⓔ
11. Ⓐ Ⓑ Ⓒ Ⓓ Ⓔ
12. Ⓐ Ⓑ Ⓒ Ⓓ Ⓔ
13. Ⓐ Ⓑ Ⓒ Ⓓ Ⓔ
14. Ⓐ Ⓑ Ⓒ Ⓓ Ⓔ
15. Ⓐ Ⓑ Ⓒ Ⓓ Ⓔ
16. Ⓐ Ⓑ Ⓒ Ⓓ Ⓔ
17. Ⓐ Ⓑ Ⓒ Ⓓ Ⓔ
18. Ⓐ Ⓑ Ⓒ Ⓓ Ⓔ
19. Ⓐ Ⓑ Ⓒ Ⓓ Ⓔ
20. Ⓐ Ⓑ Ⓒ Ⓓ Ⓔ
21. Ⓐ Ⓑ Ⓒ Ⓓ Ⓔ
22. Ⓐ Ⓑ Ⓒ Ⓓ Ⓔ
23. Ⓐ Ⓑ Ⓒ Ⓓ Ⓔ
24. Ⓐ Ⓑ Ⓒ Ⓓ Ⓔ
25. Ⓐ Ⓑ Ⓒ Ⓓ Ⓔ
26. Ⓐ Ⓑ Ⓒ Ⓓ Ⓔ
27. Ⓐ Ⓑ Ⓒ Ⓓ Ⓔ
28. Ⓐ Ⓑ Ⓒ Ⓓ Ⓔ
29. Ⓐ Ⓑ Ⓒ Ⓓ Ⓔ
30. Ⓐ Ⓑ Ⓒ Ⓓ Ⓔ
31. Ⓐ Ⓑ Ⓒ Ⓓ Ⓔ
32. Ⓐ Ⓑ Ⓒ Ⓓ Ⓔ
33. Ⓐ Ⓑ Ⓒ Ⓓ Ⓔ
34. Ⓐ Ⓑ Ⓒ Ⓓ Ⓔ
35. Ⓐ Ⓑ Ⓒ Ⓓ Ⓔ
36. Ⓐ Ⓑ Ⓒ Ⓓ Ⓔ
37. Ⓐ Ⓑ Ⓒ Ⓓ Ⓔ
38. Ⓐ Ⓑ Ⓒ Ⓓ Ⓔ
39. Ⓐ Ⓑ Ⓒ Ⓓ Ⓔ
40. Ⓐ Ⓑ Ⓒ Ⓓ Ⓔ
41. Ⓐ Ⓑ Ⓒ Ⓓ Ⓔ
42. Ⓐ Ⓑ Ⓒ Ⓓ Ⓔ
43. Ⓐ Ⓑ Ⓒ Ⓓ Ⓔ
44. Ⓐ Ⓑ Ⓒ Ⓓ Ⓔ
45. Ⓐ Ⓑ Ⓒ Ⓓ Ⓔ
46. Ⓐ Ⓑ Ⓒ Ⓓ Ⓔ
47. Ⓐ Ⓑ Ⓒ Ⓓ Ⓔ
48. Ⓐ Ⓑ Ⓒ Ⓓ Ⓔ
49. Ⓐ Ⓑ Ⓒ Ⓓ Ⓔ
50. Ⓐ Ⓑ Ⓒ Ⓓ Ⓔ
51. Ⓐ Ⓑ Ⓒ Ⓓ Ⓔ
52. Ⓐ Ⓑ Ⓒ Ⓓ Ⓔ
53. Ⓐ Ⓑ Ⓒ Ⓓ Ⓔ
54. Ⓐ Ⓑ Ⓒ Ⓓ Ⓔ
55. Ⓐ Ⓑ Ⓒ Ⓓ Ⓔ
56. Ⓐ Ⓑ Ⓒ Ⓓ Ⓔ
57. Ⓐ Ⓑ Ⓒ Ⓓ Ⓔ
58. Ⓐ Ⓑ Ⓒ Ⓓ Ⓔ
59. Ⓐ Ⓑ Ⓒ Ⓓ Ⓔ
60. Ⓐ Ⓑ Ⓒ Ⓓ Ⓔ
61. Ⓐ Ⓑ Ⓒ Ⓓ Ⓔ
62. Ⓐ Ⓑ Ⓒ Ⓓ Ⓔ
63. Ⓐ Ⓑ Ⓒ Ⓓ Ⓔ
64. Ⓐ Ⓑ Ⓒ Ⓓ Ⓔ
65. Ⓐ Ⓑ Ⓒ Ⓓ Ⓔ
66. Ⓐ Ⓑ Ⓒ Ⓓ Ⓔ
67. Ⓐ Ⓑ Ⓒ Ⓓ Ⓔ
68. Ⓐ Ⓑ Ⓒ Ⓓ Ⓔ
69. Ⓐ Ⓑ Ⓒ Ⓓ Ⓔ
70. Ⓐ Ⓑ Ⓒ Ⓓ Ⓔ

Part Four: Practice Tests | 245

Practice Test 1

Section I: Multiple-Choice Questions

Time: 55 Minutes
70 Questions

Directions: Each of the questions or incomplete statements below is followed by five suggested answers or completions. Select the one that is best in each case and then fill in the corresponding oval on the answer sheet.

1. Which of the following is true of both Mesopotamia and Egypt?

    (A) Both were organized into city–states.
    (B) Both were ruled by a military dicatorship.
    (C) In both, writing systems were used.
    (D) Both had monotheistic belief systems.
    (E) Mummification was important in both.

2. All of the following were characteristics of classical civilizations EXCEPT

    (A) Central government
    (B) Social stratification
    (C) Extensive trade
    (D) Organized bureaucracy
    (E) Democratic institutions

3. Buddhism and Christianity have which of the following in common?

    (A) Belief in one god
    (B) A hierarchal organization
    (C) An emphasis on missionary activity
    (D) De-emphasis on rituals
    (E) Selective salvation

4. Which of the following statements most accurately reflects a major difference between the fall of the Roman and Han Empires?

    (A) The effects of a decline in trade were more severe in Rome than in Han.
    (B) Only Rome suffered from major issues with government corruption.
    (C) While the Han had difficulty collecting taxes, the Roman Empire maintained an efficient tax collection system.
    (D) The spread of Buddhism had a large impact of the decline of Han, while Christianity had little impact on the decline of Rome.
    (E) Nomadic invasions impacted the Han more than the Roman Empire.

5. Dharma and karma are important concepts in which of the following two religions?

   (A) Judaism and Buddhism
   (B) Daoism and Confucianism
   (C) Hinduism and Islam
   (D) Buddhism and Hinduism
   (E) Christianity and Judaism

6. All of the following contributed to the Bantu Migration EXCEPT

   (A) Military conquest
   (B) Population pressure
   (C) Use of iron tools
   (D) Cultivation of bananas
   (E) Spread of agriculture

7. Which of the following statements best describes the political heritage of classical China?

   (A) Citizens are obligated to participate in the institution of government.
   (B) The emperor is to the state as the father is to family.
   (C) The leader with the strongest army will wield the power.
   (D) The emperor should be questioned by his people.
   (E) The leader is chosen by the wisest in the community.

8. Christianity spread to all of the following areas by 600 CE EXCEPT

   (A) Middle East
   (B) Western Europe
   (C) East Africa
   (D) Central Asia
   (E) East Asia

9. After the expansion of Islam into West Africa,

   (A) native animist beliefs disappeared.
   (B) the economy slowed.
   (C) a decentralized government developed.
   (D) civil war broke out.
   (E) trade increased.

10. According to Confucius, the most important role of the scholar–gentry class was to

    (A) help decide who would rule the nation.
    (B) found universities for teaching the young.
    (C) create a large bureaucracy.
    (D) rewrite the civil service exam every year.
    (E) promote harmony through the administration of the state.

11. Which of the following two religions have had the greatest impact on Japan through the centuries?

    (A) Daoism and Buddhism
    (B) Shinto and Buddhism
    (C) Animism and Hinduism
    (D) Christianity and Confucianism
    (E) Judaism and Daoism

12. In the time period 600 to 1450 CE, Dunhuang, Kashgar, and Samarkand were examples of

    (A) oasis towns on the Silk Road.
    (B) political capitals in East Africa.
    (C) economic centers on the Mediterranean Sea.
    (D) religious pilgrimage sites in South Asia.
    (E) port cities along the Indian Ocean.

GO ON TO THE NEXT PAGE

13. The collapse of empire was more severe in Western Europe than it was in the eastern Mediterranean or China because

    (A) only Rome lost political control of the empire.
    (B) continual waves of nomadic invasions made recovery difficult.
    (C) the increase in Rome's population made feeding the population difficult.
    (D) the Han dynasty in China was able to recover power.
    (E) the eastern Mediterranean developed feudalism, which restored order.

14. All of the following are true statements about Islam EXCEPT

    (A) Mohammed was the messenger of God
    (B) All are equal under the eyes of God
    (C) Muslims should pray five times a day
    (D) A clear line of succession was established after Mohammed's death
    (E) The hajj is the pilgrimage to Mecca

15. Which of the following had the most advanced naval technology in the time period 600 to 1450?

    (A) Western Europe
    (B) China
    (C) West Africa
    (D) Byzantine Empire
    (E) India

16. Which of the following empires existed more than five hundred years after the other four?

    (A) Han
    (B) Roman
    (C) Mauryan
    (D) Gupta
    (E) Song

17. All of the following were tributary states of China EXCEPT

    (A) Korea
    (B) Tibet
    (C) Vietnam
    (D) India
    (E) Japan

18. All of the following were advancements that occurred during the Tang or Song dynasties EXCEPT

    (A) First use of the compass
    (B) Invention of gunpowder
    (C) Printing press with movable type
    (D) Paper money
    (E) Decimal system

19. "The unexamined life is not worth living." This quotation was an important part of philosophy in which classical civilization?

    (A) China
    (B) India
    (C) Southeast Asia
    (D) Greece
    (E) Feudal Europe

20. The term *Dar al-Islam* refers to

    (A) areas that share a common Muslim culture as a basis for society
    (B) lands that are enemies of the Muslim religion
    (C) religious leaders influential in the community
    (D) conquered areas that refuse to convert to Islam
    (E) trade routes that link the Islamic world to the non-Muslim world

GO ON TO THE NEXT PAGE

21. The term *syncretism* refers to the

    (A) long-distance trade network that connected East and West.
    (B) combination of different forms of beliefs or practice.
    (C) political rejection of outsiders.
    (D) acceptance of new members into a social class structure.
    (E) monsoon winds that Malay sailors used to travel the Indian Ocean.

22. Which of the following is true of trade in the Indian Ocean during the time period 600 to 1450?

    (A) There was little to no economic interaction in the Indian Ocean
    (B) Europeans played a dominant role in the Indian Ocean
    (C) Due to nomadic invasions, economic activity slowed considerably
    (D) Chinese merchants were the only major participants in the trade
    (E) Trade flourished with a mix of East African, East Asian, South Asian and Middle Eastern merchants

23. The Ming dynasty halted the voyages of Zheng He because

    (A) the Chinese had a difficult time competing with European shipping technology.
    (B) the Chinese had an unfavorable balance of trade.
    (C) the voyages were expensive and the world beyond China was deemed of little value.
    (D) the ships had been greatly damaged during earlier expedition.
    (E) there was not enough demand for Chinese goods from the outside world.

24. Which of the following statements is an accurate comparison of the Aztec and Mongol empires?

    (A) Both groups expanded their empire by conquering and dominating neighboring areas.
    (B) The Aztecs collected taxes from their people, while the Mongols only demanded corvee.
    (C) The Mongols were far superior administrators than the Aztecs.
    (D) Trade was discouraged in both the Aztec and Mongol Empires.
    (E) Both the Aztecs and the Mongols were conquered by the Spanish.

25. The three statements below all refer to the

    - Works of Leonardo da Vinci
    - Importance of the Medici family
    - Wealth of Mediterranean Sea trade

    (A) Northern Renaissance
    (B) Protestant Reformation
    (C) Enlightenment
    (D) Italian Renaissance
    (E) Scientific Revolution

26. The religions Islam and Buddhism came into direct contact with each other during the time period 600 to 1450 in the region of

    (A) Western Europe
    (B) East Africa
    (C) Central Asia
    (D) Eastern Europe
    (E) Oceania

GO ON TO THE NEXT PAGE

27. In the time period 600 to 1450, the Mongols, Turks, and Vikings are all examples of

    (A) Large empire builders
    (B) Nomadic people
    (C) Large organized bureaucracies
    (D) Skilled horsemen
    (E) Muslims

28. Which of the following describes the major impact of the Crusades on Western Europe?

    (A) European political dominance in the Middle East aided their development of shipping technology.
    (B) The exposure to Eastern goods and technology led to an increase in trade.
    (C) The feudal system was strengthened as a result.
    (D) The loss of the Crusades set Western Europe back economically hundreds of years.
    (E) The status and powers of kings were permanently weakened.

29. The term *Middle Passage* refers to

    (A) the position of the Ottoman Empire in the middle of the European and Asian trade.
    (B) Zheng He's voyages between East Asia and East Africa.
    (C) the journey on slave ships from West Africa to the Americas.
    (D) the route crusaders took from Western Europe to the Middle East.
    (E) the voyage European immigrants took to the Americas.

30. The Colombian Exchange caused all of the following EXCEPT

    (A) The population of China increased.
    (B) The population of Native Americans declined.
    (C) American foods were introduced to Europe.
    (D) European diseases were introduced to the Americas.
    (E) African diseases were introduced to Europe.

31. All of the statements below refer to which empire in the time period 1450 to 1750?

    - Lucrative trans-Saharan trade
    - All emperors were Muslim
    - Islamic universities at Timbuktu

    (A) Ghana
    (B) Ottoman
    (C) Mughal
    (D) Songhay
    (E) Great Zimbabwe

32. The photograph of the Taj Mahal above is a representative of which type of architecture?

    (A) Hindu
    (B) Islamic
    (C) Byzantine
    (D) Chinese
    (E) Buddhist

GO ON TO THE NEXT PAGE

33. As the Ottomans dominated much of the Middle East and North Africa during the time period 1450 to 1750, which of the following empires dominated South Asia?

    (A) Safavid
    (B) Delhi Sultanate
    (C) Manchu
    (D) Mughal
    (E) Mongol

34. The women of the harem wielded power by

    (A) serving in administrative positions in the empire.
    (B) selecting the vizier.
    (C) influencing the sultan behind the scenes.
    (D) speaking in public on political matters.
    (E) serving as official leader if the sultan died suddenly.

35. Which of the following helped to contribute to the increase of the Atlantic slave trade?

    (A) Industrialization
    (B) Sugar plantations
    (C) Absolute monarchies
    (D) Laissez-faire capitalism
    (E) Enlightenment ideas

36. The list below refers to
    - Louis XIV
    - Philip II
    - Peter the Great

    (A) Enlightened despots
    (B) Revolutionary leaders
    (C) Absolute monarchs
    (D) Deposed leaders
    (E) Limited monarchs

37. All of the following statements are true about Japan during the time period 1450 to 1750 EXCEPT that

    (A) foreign trade was restricted by the government.
    (B) the shogun was the actual ruler.
    (C) Christians were persecuted.
    (D) the economy declined.
    (E) internal trade increased.

38. Between 1450 and 1750, European interest in American colonies was primarily motivated by

    (A) the need to escape the harsh European climate.
    (B) its ability to spread democratic beliefs to a new area.
    (C) the chance to make a large profit from cash crops.
    (D) the ease of travel to the Americas.
    (E) the importance of establishing military bases away from home.

39. A common feature of both Japanese and European feudalism was

    (A) Social mobility
    (B) Political participation by all classes
    (C) Strong centralized authority
    (D) Strict social structure
    (E) Christianity

40. Which of the following countries had global hegemony by 1800?

    (A) China
    (B) Great Britain
    (C) Russia
    (D) Japan
    (E) Portugal

41. Neoconfucianism refers to the

    (A) Rejection of Confucian beliefs during the Yuan dynasty
    (B) Blending of Buddhist and Confucian ideas
    (C) Spread of Confucianism to Japan
    (D) Use of Confucianism to monitor economic relations
    (E) Growth of Confucianism outside of China

42. Which of the following was NOT a policy of Russia's Peter the Great?

    (A) Increased foreign trade
    (B) Introduced Western style of dress
    (C) Improved technology
    (D) Extended serfdom throughout Russia
    (E) Used Western Enlightenment ideas in the government

43. A result of the political revolutions of the late 18th and 19th centuries was that they

    (A) spread Enlightenment ideas through Europe and the Americas.
    (B) strengthened European control over South America.
    (C) prevented the formation of the nation–state.
    (D) instituted Marxist ideas through Europe.
    (E) decreased the economic strength of European nations.

44. Which of the following was NOT one of the basic ideals of Enlightenment thinkers?

    (A) Popular sovereignty
    (B) Freedom of speech
    (C) Religious tolerance
    (D) Equality for women
    (E) Natural rights of man

45. All of the following were key principles of the formation of the United States EXCEPT

    (A) Written constitution
    (B) Federal government based on popular sovereignty
    (C) Equality for all
    (D) Three branches of government
    (E) Independence from Great Britain

46. Which of the following events aided the success of the Latin American independence movements in the 1800s?

    (A) German unification
    (B) The Sepoy Mutiny
    (C) Napoleon's invasion of Spain
    (D) The Industrial Revolution
    (E) The Emancipation Proclamation

47. All of the individuals below are examples of
    - Simon Bolivar
    - Miguel de Hidalgo
    - Jose de San Martin

    (A) Captains of industry
    (B) Spanish viceroys
    (C) Leaders of slave revolts
    (D) Revolutionary leaders
    (E) European imperialists

48. Dominant power in Latin America during the early 1800s lay in the hands of the

    (A) Peninsulares
    (B) Creoles
    (C) Middle class
    (D) Mestizos
    (E) Mulattoes

49. Which of the following BEST represents a key idea of Karl Marx?

    (A) The formation of trade unions would alleviate the problems of the industrial workers.
    (B) The abuses of the capitalist system would be solved only if the system were overthrown.
    (C) Democratic reforms would bring equality to the underprivileged.
    (D) Factory owners need to give workers a minimum wage and health insurance.
    (E) Collectivization of agriculture would increase production and allow for complete state control of the economy.

50. All of the following were results of industrialization EXCEPT

    (A) Improvements in working conditions
    (B) The ability to maintain the family unit as an economic unit
    (C) Greater opportunities for economic advancement
    (D) The ability to purchase cheaper manufactured goods
    (E) The ability to participate in leisure activities

51. All of the following statements describe developments in the Ottoman Empire in the time period 1750 to 1914 EXCEPT

    (A) Europeans were exempt from following Ottoman law.
    (B) Tanzimat reformers were inspired by Enlightenment thought.
    (C) The Young Turk Party promoted reforms like universal suffrage.
    (D) The Islamic leadership, or ulama, supported the liberal reforms.
    (E) Greece and Siberia achieved their independence.

52. The Berlin Conference of 1884–1885 resulted in the

    (A) division of Africa among European powers.
    (B) creation of spheres of influence in China.
    (C) redrawing of the map of Europe
    (D) colonization of India by the British
    (E) formation of the German state.

53. Which of the following accurately describes the changes for middle- and working-class European women in the time period 1750 to 1914?

    (A) Both middle- and working-class women achieved the right to vote.
    (B) Working class women labored in factories and middle-class women followed the cult of domesticity.
    (C) Middle class women were paid more than working-class women for similar jobs.
    (D) Working-class women were not as affected by the industrial revolution as middle-class women.
    (E) Both middle- and working-class women were confined to the home to perform domestic duties.

54. Social Darwinism refers to the belief that

    (A) scientific processes can address all issues formerly only answered through religious texts or authority.
    (B) industrialization will lead to the eventual revolution of the working class and an overthrow of the capitalist system.
    (C) the domination of European imperialists over subject peoples was an inevitable result of natural scientific principles.
    (D) a ruler has an obligation to protect the natural rights of his citizens
    (E) the earth is one of a group of planets that rotates around the sun which is in the center of the universe.

GO ON TO THE NEXT PAGE

55. The Indian National Congress and the Pan-African Congress were important examples of

   (A) Economic alliances between countries in the developing world
   (B) Nationalist organizations aimed at removing European control
   (C) International organizations with the goal of preventing Cold War conflicts
   (D) Non-government organizations aimed at bringing industrialization to Asian and African countries
   (E) Political alliances formed between developing nations in opposition to World War II

56. The Boxer Rebellion was to China what the Sepoy Mutiny was to

   (A) The Ottoman Empire
   (B) Japan
   (C) Korea
   (D) India
   (E) Africa

57. What late 20th-century problem in Latin America can be traced back to colonial times?

   (A) Urban crime
   (B) Uneven distribution of wealth
   (C) Agricultural overproduction
   (D) Theocratic rule
   (E) Low birthrates

58. Japan's expansionism in Manchuria and China in the 1930s coincided with

   (A) its rapid industrialization.
   (B) closer ties with the United States.
   (C) the growing influence of the League of Nations.
   (D) the declining power of Japan's emperor.
   (E) the re-arming of the British.

59. "For a Satyagraha brigade, only those are eligible who believe in ahimsa–nonviolence, and satya–truth. Satyagraha is a force that has come to stay. No force in the world can kill it."

   These are the words of

   (A) Winston Churchill
   (B) Siddhartha Gautama
   (C) Mohammed
   (D) Mohandas Gandhi
   (E) Mao Zedong

60. Which of the following statements is most accurate about the Russian and/or Chinese socialist revolutions?

   (A) Stalin was a devout follower of orthodox Marxism.
   (B) Mao directed his appeals to the rural peasantry rather than the urban proletariat.
   (C) Lenin believed in "war communism" above all else.
   (D) Trotsky emphasized peaceful coexistence with the West.
   (E) Mao was most successful in gaining support from educated elites.

61. Many developing nations struggle with

   (A) Low birthrates
   (B) Lack of natural resources
   (C) No foreign aid
   (D) Weak industrial base
   (E) Unmotivated working class

62. African and Asian nationalist movements in the 20th century were usually led by

   (A) Labor leaders
   (B) Urban factory workers
   (C) Aristocracy
   (D) Peasantry
   (E) The educated class

GO ON TO THE NEXT PAGE

63. The Treaty of Versailles did not forge a lasting peace because the

    (A) Central Powers would not concede defeat after the armistice.
    (B) Russians would not agree to the terms of the Treaty.
    (C) treaty was solely influenced by Woodrow Wilson's Fourteen Points.
    (D) United States wished to punish the Germans for starting the war.
    (E) Germans were forced to accept blame for the war and were severely punished.

64. Which of the following statements best defines genocide in the 20th century?

    (A) The trend toward liberalism in South Asia
    (B) The systematic murder of ethnic minorities
    (C) The rise of existentialist thought
    (D) The rapid industrialization of developing countries
    (E) The political conflict that leads to civil war

65. Islam is the main religious faith associated with which of the following nations?

    (A) Pakistan and Indonesia
    (B) Malaysia and Vietnam
    (C) Iran and South Africa
    (D) Bosnia and Romania
    (E) Madagascar and Sudan

66. A global effect of World War I was

    (A) the unwavering domination of European power worldwide.
    (B) a 20-year period of economic stability.
    (C) the rise of nationalist movements in colonial areas.
    (D) the spread of communist regimes in Western Europe.
    (E) the economic and political isolation of Japan.

67. Which of the following statements accurately compares India's and Cuba's role in the Cold War?

    (A) Both nations were supporters of the Soviet Union.
    (B) Both nations refused to choose sides.
    (C) Cuba was a supporter of the Soviet Union, while India remained non-aligned.
    (D) Cuba was a supporter of the United States, while India supported the Soviet Union.
    (E) Both Cuba and India were supporters of the United States.

68. Vladimir Lenin was to the Russian Revolution what Ayatollah Khomeini was to the

    (A) Zionist movement
    (B) Egyptian nationalist movement
    (C) Palestinian Liberation Organization
    (D) Iranian Revolution
    (E) Taliban in Afghanistan

69. Kwame Nkrumah, Jomo Kenyatta, and Franz Fanton are all examples of

    (A) Nationalist leaders
    (B) Communist leaders
    (C) Union leaders
    (D) Industrial capitalists
    (E) Dictators

70. Which of the following best describes the Israeli–Palestinian conflict in the latter half of the 20th century?

    (A) The international community ignored the issues of both sides.
    (B) Both sides had religious and historic claims to the same land.
    (C) The conflicts between European powers in the region continued.
    (D) The competition was over oil rights in the land.
    (E) Both sides have consistently refused to meet with each other.

IF YOU FINISH BEFORE TIME IS CALLED, YOU MAY CHECK YOUR WORK ON THIS SECTION ONLY. DO NOT TURN TO ANY OTHER SECTION IN THE TEST.

Section II

Part A
Mandatory reading period: 10 minutes
Suggested writing time: 40 minutes

Directions: The following question is based on the accompanying Documents 1–9. (Some of the documents have been edited for the purpose of this exercise.)

This question is designed to test your ability to work with and understand historical documents. Write an essay that:

- Has a relevant thesis and supports that thesis with evidence from the documents.
- Uses all or all but one of the documents.
- Analyzes the documents by grouping them in as many appropriate ways as possible. **Does not simply summarize the documents individually.**
- Takes into account the sources of the documents and analyzes the authors' points of view.
- Explains the need for at least one additional type of document.

You may refer to relevant historical information not mentioned in the documents.

1. Analyze the changing roles of women during communist revolutionary periods. Explain what **additional kind of document(s)** would help assess the changing roles of women.

   <u>Historical Background:</u> The Bolsheviks gained power in Russia in 1917, forming the Soviet Union. The Soviet Union, and specifically the Communist Party, remained in power until its collapse in 1991. In China, Mao Zedong and his Chinese Communist Party seized power in 1949. The Communist Party controls China up through the modern period.

Document 1

Source: V.I. Lenin, leader of the Bolsheviks and instigator of Communist Revolution in Russia, from articles in the official Soviet newspaper *Pravda*, 1920:

"It is essential that women workers take a greater part in the elections. The Soviet government was the first and only government in the world to abolish completely all the old, bourgeois, infamous laws which placed women in an inferior position compared with men and which granted privileges to men, as, for instance, in the sphere of marriage laws or in the sphere of the legal attitude to children. The Soviet government was the first and only government in the world which, as a government of the toilers, abolished all the privileges connected with property, which men retained in the family laws of all bourgeois republics, even the most democratic.

"The proletariat cannot achieve complete freedom, unless it achieves complete freedom for women"

Document 2

Source: Emma Goldman, an American anarchist deported to Russia in 1920, from her memoirs *My Disillusionment in Russia*, 1923:

"…the rations were distributed at the Commissary, but one had to fetch them himself. One day, while waiting my turn in the long line, a peasant girl came in and asked for vinegar. 'Vinegar! who is it calls for such a luxury?' cried several women. It appeared that the girl was Zinoviev's servant. She spoke of him as her master, who worked very hard and was surely entitled to something extra. At once a storm of indignation broke loose. 'Master! is that what we made the Revolution for, or was it to do away with masters? Zinoviev is no more than we, and he is not entitled to more.'"

Document 3

Source: Grigory Shegl, teacher at the Moscow Art Institute and artist, Official government poster 1931.

Caption: Say goodbye to kitchen slavery!

Let the new life begin!

Document 4

Source: Krupskaya, V.I. Lenin's wife and a leader within the Bolshevik Party, preface to Lenin's *The Emancipation of Women*, 1933:

"We in Russia no longer have the base, mean and infamous denial of rights to women or inequality of the sexes, that disgusting survival of feudalism and medievalism which is being renovated by the avaricious bourgeoisie ... in every other country in the world without exception."

Document 5

Source: Florence Ayscough, a Canadian sinologist who studied in Shanghai in the 1920s and 30s, quotations reflecting traditional and modern Chinese women, from her book *Chinese Women: Yesterday and Today*, 1937:

TRADITIONAL WOMEN

"To be unassuming, to yield; to be respectful, to revere, to think first of other people afterwards of herself, if she performs a kind of action, to make no mention thereof, if she commits a find, to make no denial; to endure reproach, treasure reproof, to behave with veneration and right fear; such demeanor is described as exemplify humility and adaptability...."

MODERN WOMEN

"'You'd better think it over and choose some other job. Driving tractors is no work for a slip of a girl like you.'

'Let me take the entrance examination anyway,' I said. 'If I fail, I shall have nothing more to say.'

I passed the examination. In the six years that followed I achieved my ambition of becoming a tractor driver, worked for a while as instructor to a women's tractor-drivers team, and became the vice-director of the Shuangchiao State Farm near Peking. That is still my work today."

Document 6

Source: Mao Zedong, Chairman of the Chinese Communist Party, excerpts from *The Selected Quotations of Mao Zedong* (Known as the *Little Red Book*):

A. *On Coalition Government*, April 24, 1945

"Protect the interests of the youth, women and children - provide assistance to young students who cannot afford to continue their studies, help the youth and women to organize in order to participate on an equal footing in all work useful to the war effort and to social progress, ensure freedom of marriage and equality as between men and women, and give young people and children a useful education...."

B. Introductory note to *Women Have Gone to the Labour Front*, 1955

"In order to build a great socialist society it is of the utmost importance to arouse the broad masses of women to join in productive activity. Men and women must receive equal pay for equal work in production. Genuine equality between the sexes can only be realized in the process of the socialist transformation of society as a whole."

Document 7

Source: Chinese poster used by the Chinese Communist Party (CCP), 1965:

Caption: Become a red seedling-Strike root, flower and bear seeds in the places the motherhood needs it most!

Document 8

Source: Shao Dangdi, Chinese grandmother and insurance agent, comments quoted in the American magazine *The New Republic*, March 2004:

"After Liberation, women were made very equal…. The government promoted women's equality, but also it was necessary for family survival: you couldn't live on a single income. Now, you can…. Work units were required to maintain a rough gender balance in all departments and at all levels…. Now the workplace is so competitive. There are too many educated young people vying for too few positions, so employers pick the men first."

Document 9

Source: Article in the official Chinese government's magazine *Women of China*, September 2004:

"Career women, a modern meaning in its earliest usage, referred to female workers in the spinning, filature and tobacco production industries. As more women received educations and the women's liberation movement shook the last part of the 19th century, female teaching school graduates were able to become primary school teachers or nursery governesses. Women also became medical practitioners. In the 1920s and 1930, women could become teachers, library workers, editors and/or translators, accountants, lawyers, clerks, writers, actresses, shop assistants, operators, typists, stenographers and post employees. All those positions required education and skills."

[**Note**: You will have 16 pages to write all three essays, so feel free to use additional paper.]

Part B
Suggested writing time: 40 minutes

Directions: You are to answer the following question. You should spend 5 minutes organizing or outlining your essay. Write an essay that:
- Has a relevant thesis and supports that thesis with appropriate historical evidence.
- Addresses all parts of the question.
- Uses world historical context to show change over time and/or continuities
- Analyzes the process of change over time and/or continuity.

2. Describe and analyze the effects of demographic and environmental changes, i.e. disease, animals, new crops, population on ONE of the following areas from 1450 to 1750. Be sure to discuss changes as well as continuities.

    The Americas
    China
    Europe
    Sub-Saharan Africa

_____
_____
_____
_____
_____
_____
_____
_____
_____
_____
_____
_____

Part C
Suggested writing time: 40 minutes

Directions: You are to answer the following question. You should spend 5 minutes organizing or outlining your essay. Write an essay that:
- Has a relevant thesis and supports that thesis with appropriate historical evidence.
- Addresses all parts of the question.
- Makes direct, relevant comparisons.
- Analyzes relevant reasons for similarities and differences.

3. Analyze the major similarities and differences between the spread of TWO of the following religions in the time period 1000 BCE to 600 CE:

    Judaism (Jewish Diaspora)
    Christianity
    Buddhism

Practice Test I: Answer Key

1. C
2. E
3. C
4. A
5. D
6. A
7. B
8. E
9. E
10. E
11. B
12. A
13. B
14. A
15. B
16. E
17. D
18. E
19. D
20. A
21. B
22. E
23. C
24. A
25. D
26. C
27. B
28. B
29. C
30. E
31. D
32. B
33. D
34. C
35. B
36. C
37. D
38. C
39. D
40. B
41. B
42. E
43. A
44. D
45. C
46. C
47. D
48. A
49. B
50. D
51. D
52. A
53. B
54. C
55. B
56. D
57. B
58. A
59. D
60. B
61. D
62. E
63. E
64. B
65. A
66. C
67. C
68. D
69. A
70. B

ANSWERS AND EXPLANATIONS

1. C

Mesopotamia used cuneiform as its form of writing and Egypt used hieroglyphics. Mesopotamia was organized into city-states, but Egypt was organized into kingdoms. Egypt's government was more centralized than was Mesopotamia's. Both cultures were polytheistic, not monotheistic. Mummification was an important religious practice in Egypt, though not in Mesopotamia.

2. E

Classical civilizations had all of the choices except democratic institutions. Although Greece and Rome had some elements of democracy, this was not a characteristic of most classical civilizations. The citystate of Athens had a direct democracy in which only citizens could vote and the republic of Rome had a government that elected its officials to govern. These democratic institutions were limited to a minority of the populations and were both relatively short-lived.

3. C

Both Buddhism and Christianity successfully spread because of its missionary activity. Since in both religions all could join and all were considered spiritually equal, each spread extensively. Unlike Buddhism, Christianity believes in one God. Christianity is considered a hierarchical religion, but not Buddhism. Both Christianity and Buddhism have rituals important to their practice and both belief systems offer universal salvation.

4. A

In both empires, a decrease in trade occurred. However, the Roman Empire was more interdependent than the Han. As a result, the decrease in trade badly damaged the Roman Empire economically, while the Han was more self-sufficient. Both empires dealt with issues of government corruption and had difficulty collecting sufficient taxes. The spread of Christianity, it has been argued, did cause a decrease in the feelings of loyalty to the Roman state, but Buddhism did not significantly spread to most of China until after the fall of the Han. Nomadic invasions damaged both empires, but the continuation of waves of nomadic invasions continually damaged the Roman Empire after it fell.

5. D

Hinduism and Buddhism both believe in the concepts of dharma and karma. Dharma is one's duty or role in life, and karma is what happens as a result of how well one does with his/her dharma.

6. A

The Bantu were a group that originated in West Africa. This agricultural society experienced population growth which initiated migration. The use of iron tools and the cultivation of bananas allowed the Bantus to migrate further and spread agriculture. Although the Bantus may have had conflict with groups they encountered as they migrated, military conquest was not a motivation to migrate.

7. B

According to Confucius, the basis of the state is the family. Since the ruler is the head of the state, he should model proper behavior for the state just as the father would model proper behavior for the family.

8. E

Christianity had some influence in all of the areas by 600 CE except East Asia. Christianity came to have some influence in East Asia, but not until after 600 CE. Trade routes, missionaries, and conquest in the classical period aided the spread of Christianity to the Middle East, Western Europe, East Africa, and Central Asia.

9. E

As a result of the spread of Islam into West Africa, the volume of trade along the trans-Saharan trade routes increased. Relationships were established with Muslim merchants and those relationships led to more trade. Although Islam did spread to West Africa, native animist beliefs were often incorporated into the new belief system. The economy grew rather than slowed, and a more centralized form of government developed. Centralized governments often kept order in their kingdoms, and thus decreased conflict.

10. E

Confucius believed that the civil servants taken from the scholar class would run the country for the emperor and would promote harmony in the empire. They would have no role in determining who the ruler would be, or in other duties.

11. B

Shinto and Buddhism have been the two most visible religions in Japan over the last thousand years. Shinto is native to Japan, while Buddhism came via China in the 6th century. Fewer than one percent of Japanese people are Christian. Daoism is native to China and not historically widespread in Japan.

12. A

Dunhuang and Kashgar are located in modern-day western China, and Samarkand is located in Central Asia. These cities grew as a result of the Silk Road trade, supporting merchants and markets and aiding in the spread of religious beliefs, such as Buddhism.

13. B

After the fall of Rome, nomadic invasions continued, making it very difficult for the area to recover. As a result, a decentralized form of government developed which provided protection for its inhabitants. Both Rome and the Han lost political control of their respective empires. Rome's population decreased as a result of the spread of disease. The Han Empire did not recover power. The eastern Mediterranean did not develop feudalism; it stayed unified and became known as the Byzantine Empire.

14. A

After the death of Mohammed conflict arose over the succession of the next leader. Two groups—the Sunnis and Shias—emerged with conflicted ideas. The Sunnis believed that the wisest in the community should lead and the Shias believed that the leader should be a direct descendent of Mohammed.

15. B

During the time period 600 to 1450, China had developed advanced naval technologies, such as the compass and more advanced ships. During the Ming dynasty, massive ships were built and sent out to make voyages throughout the Indian Ocean. These ships were far superior to any used by other countries at that time.

16. E

The Song dynasty existed from 960 to 1279 CE in China. The other empires had all fallen by 600 CE.

17. D

China dealt with its neighboring areas by establishing a tributary relationship, in which the tributary states would have to recognize the superiority of China. Korea, Tibet, Vietnam, and Japan all had some form of a tributary relationship with China at some point in its history, but India never did.

18. E

The Tang and Song dynasties are known for their economic and technological advances; however the decimal system was developed in India during the Gupta Empire.

19. D

This quote is attributed to Socrates and is representative of the Greek philosophical stress on the importance of the individual.

20. A

Dar al-Islam refers to the lands that were culturally influenced by the religion of Islam. When the political organization of Islam declined, the influence of Islam continued in this cultural area. By the year 1450, Dar al-Islam stretched from Western Europe to Eastern China.

21. B

As religions spread, they often incorporated or blended with native beliefs. This process is known as syncretism. As Christianity spread to Western Europe, it took on pagan ideas, such as the timing of certain holy days. In Africa, as Islam spread, it incorporated certain cultural practices of the Native Africans. In China, Buddhism incorporated Daoist and Confucian ideas as it spread.

22. E

During the time period 600 to 1450, trade in the Indian Ocean flourished. It connected East China with East Africa and the many areas in between.

23. C

The ships of the Ming dynasty were far superior to any others on the sea, but the voyages were very expensive and the trade that was generated was deemed of little value. The emperor cancelled the missions under pressure from Confucian scholars and instead focused on internal stability and defending the northern border from a possible Mongol return.

24. A

The Aztecs and the Mongols built their empires by conquering and dominating their neighbors. Both collected taxes. The Mongols were not particularly efficient administrators; instead they often relied on their conquered people to administer the empire. Trade flourished in both areas. Only the Aztecs were conquered by the Spanish.

25. D

Leonardo da Vinci, the Medicis, and the Mediterranean sea trade all relate to the Italian Renaissance, the cultural rebirth that began in the late 14th century.

26. C

These two religions came in contact along the trade routes of Central Asia. Buddhism had spread to the region earlier from India through the Silk Road. Islam spread to Central Asia beginning in the 8th century and often overtook Buddhism as the dominant belief system.

27. B

All three groups were nomadic peoples who moved into neighboring areas. The Mongols and Turks were empire builders, but not the Vikings. The Turks later developed an organized bureaucracy in the Ottoman Empire, but the Mongols and Vikings were not known for their bureaucratic expertise. While the Mongols and Turks were both skilled horsemen, the Vikings were more known for their seafaring skills. The Turks and some Mongols converted to Islam, but the Vikings did not.

28. B

As a result of the Crusades, Western Europe was reintroduced to the goods and technology of the Middle East. This led to an increase in trade and an increase in interaction with the outside world for Western Europe.

29. C

The Middle Passage was the journey that African slaves took from the coast of West Africa to the Caribbean and the Americas. This journey took months and was characterized by brutal conditions which caused the death of some Africans en route.

30. E

Although European diseases, like smallpox, spread to the Americas causing the death of millions of Native Americans, African diseases did not spread to Europe as a result of the Colombian Exchange. New foods were introduced from the Americas to Europe and to China which led to population increase.

31. D

In the time period 1450 to 1750 the kingdom of Songhay controlled West Africa during which these developments occurred. Ghana was also a kingdom in West Africa, but it fell before 1450. The Ottoman Empire dominated the Middle East and North Africa. The Mughals dominated India. Great Zimbabwe developed power in East Africa.

32. B

The Taj Mahal was built during the Mughal Empire as a tomb for the Emperor Shah Jahan's wife. The Islamic-style architecture can be seen in the use of the dome and minarets.

33. D

During the time period 1450 to 1750, the Mughals conquered and ruled India. The Safavids ruled over Persia. The Delhi Sultanate ruled the northern part of India beginning in the 11th century. The Manchus ruled China. The Mongols ruled an empire throughout much of Asia in the 1300s and 1400s.

34. C

The women of the harem included the wives and concubines of the Ottoman sultan. Although their movement outside the harem was restricted, they often exhibited great influence over their husbands. By advising the sultan or pushing forward their choice for the next sultan, the women of the harem could exert significant influence.

35. B

The sugar plantation greatly increased the Atlantic slave trade because growing sugar was very labor intensive. In order to make a significant profit, plantation owners needed cheap labor to cultivate the sugar. The popularity of this cash crop led to a large increase in the demand for slaves in the Americas.

36. C

All three of these rulers were European absolute monarchs in the time period 1450 to 1750. The rulers often claimed their power came by divine right, and that their rule was to be unquestioned.

37. D

During the time period 1450 to 1750, Japan was ruled by the Tokugawa Shogunate which heavily restricted foreign trade. The shogun ruled and the emperor was a figurehead. After gaining some initial conversions, the government banned the Christian missionaries and persecuted those who had converted. During this period of restricted foreign trade, internal trade increased and the economy prospered.

38. C

The ability to make large profits in cash crops drew many Europeans to the Americas in the hope of making their fortunes.

39. D

Under both Japanese and European feudalism a strict social structure reinforced the system. Those born as serfs or peasants remained as such throughout their lives, as well as those lucky enough to be born as lords or daimyos.

40. B

By 1800 Great Britain had emerged as the dominant world power. The industrial revolution and the building of an overseas empire led to Great Britain's power.

41. B

Neo-Confucianism developed during the Tang dynasty in response to the growing popularity of Buddhism in China. The incorporation of Buddhist beliefs and Confucian ideas became very influential in China and Japan.

42. E

Peter the Great wanted to Westernize Russia by increasing foreign trade, Western style of dress, and technology. In order to maintain social stability and appease the noble class he extended serfdom throughout Russia, but Peter was an absolute monarch who did not use Enlightenment ideas in the government.

43. A

The political revolution in the Americas and Europe led to a spread of Enlightenment ideas throughout these areas. As a result, Spanish and Portuguese power in South America decreased. Many nation states were inspired by the ideas of the Enlightenment. Industrialization had a large impact on the spread of Marxist ideas and the political revolutions of the 19th century and Europe continued to grow in economic strength.

44. D

Enlightenment thinkers believed in the right of people to choose their government (popular sovereignty), freedom of speech, religious tolerance, and natural rights of man, but often ignored the rights and equality of women.

45. C

Though the American state claimed that all were created under God, the reality was that the Constitution did not recognize the equality of women or slaves.

46. C

While Napoleon was building his European empire in the early 1800s, he invaded both Spain and Portugal and deposed their rulers. This weakening of Spain and Portugal allowed the Latin American colonies to successfully fight for their independence from the European powers.

47. D

Simón Bolívar and José de San Martín led the revolutionary movements for independence in South America. Miguel de Hidalgo was a priest who led a peasant movement in Mexico.

48. A

The peninsulares, or those born in Europe, had the dominant power in Latin America in the early 1800s. The Creoles, descendents of Europeans, led independence movements in hopes of establishing power for themselves.

49. B

Marx wrote that the only way for the working class to overthrow the capitalist system was through a revolution. After the revolution, the proletariat would own the means of production.

50. D

The family unit had been an economic unit prior to industrialization, but was not so afterwards. As a result of industrialization, the prices for manufactured good significantly decreased. As a result, the working class could now afford these goods. The improvement in working conditions occurred after government reforms demanded them. Some people were able to economically advance more than they could before industrialization. The middle and upper classes had time to participate in leisure activities.

51. D

Reforms and changes in the Ottoman Empire were often resisted by the ulama, or religious leadership. The incorporation of more Western ideas often undermined the authority of the ulama.

52. A

The Berlin Conference was a meeting of European powers called in order to avoid war. The European powers agreed to ground rules for the colonization of Africa and as a result the map of almost all of Africa was carved up by European powers.

53. B

As working class women entered the factories, middleclass women were often influenced by the ideal of the cult of domesticity. This ideal preached that the goal for women was to create a perfect household for their husbands and children.

54. C

Based on Charles Darwin's theories of evolution and survival of the fittest, Social Darwinism believed that Europeans had evolved to a higher level than those they were conquering. This was used as a justification for European imperialism.

55. B

The Indian National Congress was a group of educated Indians formed with the permission of the British in the late 19th century. This group helped to lead the nationalist movement in India under the leadership of Mohandas Gandhi. The Pan-African Congress first met in 1919 after World War I. It stressed African unity and helped to create nationalist movements, which came to eventually defeat the European colonial powers.

56. D

The Boxer Rebellion was an anti-foreign rebellion in China in 1900 that was forcefully put down by European powers. The Sepoy Mutiny occurred in 1857 in India, when sepoys (Indian troops who served the British army) rebelled after learning that animal (cow or pork) fat was being used to grease ammunition cartridges for rifles. This offended both

Hindu and Muslim sepoys. The mutiny was forcefully put down by the British, who then assumed full control of India as a colony.

57. B
Since the days of Spanish colonization, Latin America has had a small percentage of people controlling most of the wealth. To this day, the landed elites dominate political and military life. The area has historically had high birthrates, and until recently, a tendency toward right-wing military governments.

58. A
Japan's rapid industrialization created a need for more and more of the raw materials that it lacked. It moved into Korea and later northeast China to get these materials. The successful annexation of Manchuria in 1931 weakened the prestige of the League of Nations and encouraged the militarists who were intensely loyal to the Emperor.

59. D
Mohandas Gandhi, later known as the Mahatma, believed in the forces of nonviolence and truth. He used these in the struggle against the British until India's independence in 1947.

60. B
Mao departed from classical Marxist theory, which suggested that revolution would begin among dissatisfied urban workers. He saw the potential of revolution among the millions of downtrodden Chinese peasants.

61. D
Lack of capital and a weak industrial base held many nations back from developing. Many poor nations have no lack of foreign aid or natural resources, but cannot find the money or technology needed to industrialize.

62. E
Asian nationalists (such as Ho Chi Minh) and African nationalists (such as Jomo Kenyatta) were well educated—even professionally trained in Europe—before becoming leaders in the colonies from which they came. Peasants were not able to communicate their political wishes, and if any aristocracy existed, they were often in league with the ruling colonial regime.

63. E
The European allies were looking to punish Germany after World War I, and even though American president Woodrow Wilson promoted "peace without victory" in his Fourteen Points, his wishes were largely ignored. Germany was forced to accept blame for the war and pay large war reparations. This crippled the German economy and allowed for the rise of a fascist regime seeking to restore glory to the country.

64. B
In the 20th century, the act of genocide was carried out against many minority groups. Examples are the Armenians in Turkey in 1915 and the Jews in Eastern Europe during World War II.

65. A
Pakistan and Indonesia are both primarily Muslim nations.

66. C
As a result of the weakening of European power after World War I and the strengthening of the ideas of self-determination, nationalist movements rose in colonial areas such as Asia and Africa.

67. C
During the cold war, Cuba, a communist nation, was a strong supporter and ally of the Soviet Union, much to the disappointment of its neighbor, the United States. India, on the other hand, was one of the leaders of the non-alignment movement in which nations refused to cater to one side or the other in the cold war.

68. D
Lenin led the Bolsheviks to power in the Russian Revolution in 1917, and Ayatollah Khomeini led the Iranian Revolution in 1979. The latter revolution resulted in the creation of an Islamic fundamentalist state.

69. A
Kwame Nkrumah was a nationalist leader in Ghana. Jomo Kenyatta was the nationalist leader in Kenya, and Franz Fanton led nationalist uprisings in French-controlled Algeria.

70. B
Both the Palestinians and the Israelis claim religious and historic ties to the same land. The international community has often been involved in attempting to help settle peace. European powers do not control this area anymore. Both sides have sat down to meet with varying degrees of success over the years.

Part A: Document-Based Question: Sample Response

Communist revolutions offered new economic opportunities for women in Russia and China. Previously, women had been very restricted to traditional roles in both societies, but after the communist regimes came to power, women were hailed as an economic necessity. It was preached that a true socialist revolution would only occur if equality of the sexes also occurred. The reality of these changes, however, was not so promising.

In Russia, women had been relegated to very traditional roles, but after the communists came to power, were hailed as the builders of a new Russia. The leader of the Bolsheviks, V. I. Lenin, wrote in the official Soviet newspaper that it was essential for women workers to take a greater part in elections. He also noted that the Soviet government was the first in the world to offer women more freedom: "The proletariat cannot achieve complete freedom, unless it achieves complete freedom for women." His position as the leader of the government heavily influenced his point of view. The article purports to glorify and praise all the Soviet government had done for women in comparison to the "bourgeois republics."

Emma Goldman, an American anarchist who was deported to Russia in the 1920s, writes about an instance in the ration line, when a young girl tries to get a luxury item—vinegar—for her master, and the other women there remind her that he isn't entitled to it any more than they. The story demonstrates how women are beginning to stand up for themselves and no longer accepting a lowly position. Lenin's wife, Krupskaya, herself a leader in the Bolshevik Party, reported that Russia no longer denies women their rights like every other country in the world. This excerpt is taken from the introduction to Lenin's book *The Emancipation of Women*; her purpose is clearly to glorify the change taking place for women in Russia. An official government poster also glorifies the new position of women as it tells them to "say goodbye to kitchen slavery." The purpose of this poster is to motivate women to enter the workforce and participate in the building of a new and strong Russia. The changing roles of women in Russia would be more thoroughly analyzed if there were documentary evidence from a woman not politically connected, whose life had been transformed as a result of the revolution. It would also be helpful to have statistical evidence which analyzed the economic conditions of women before and after the revolution to judge whether their lives had improved.

Similarly in China, the revolutionary government encouraged women to enter the workforce and help build a better and stronger nation. Florence Ayscough, a Canadian sinologist, notes that traditionally women were to be unassuming and humble, but now women could stand up for themselves and seek out better economic opportunities. The Chairman of the Chinese Communist Party, Mao Zedong, wrote in his *Little Red Book* that women must be on equal footing as men in the workforce and should have the freedom to choose their own marriage partners. His purpose seems to be to motivate women to become productive members of society, but it would be important to know to what degree these ideas were carried out. Were women really able to choose their own marriage partners, or did family pressure and tradition win out?

A government poster also encourages women to participate in the economic strength of China. It shows an idealized woman happy as she works in the field to build a new China. Shao Dangdi, however, is quoted in an American magazine in 2004 as saying that while women and men had equal footing in the workplace after the revolution, such is no longer the case. Now, in a more competitive workplace, men are often hired over women. According to this article, the capitalist changes occurring in China seemed to be hurting the economic roles of women. Written in the same year in an official Chinese government magazine, an article notes that the more women have gained rights to education, the greater their economic opportunities have been. It would be helpful to hear from a woman who lived through the transition to the communist government to see if her economic role was truly transformed, and then to see if the capitalist changes of today are adding to or taking away from her economic opportunities.

There is no denying that women in Russia and China had greater economic opportunities as a result of their countries' communist revolutions. They entered the workforce and were hailed by the party as crucial members of society. It is harder to ascertain to what degree traditional values remained and how capitalist changes to these societies will further revolutionize the role of women.

Part B: Change-Over-Time Question: Sample Response

As a result of the encounter with the Americas following Columbus's voyages in the late 15th century, the Americas were dramatically impacted by demographic and environmental changes. Demographically, the spread of disease led to a major decline in the native population, the migration of Europeans changed the social structure of the area, and the importation of African slaves transformed the society both socially and economically. Environmentally, the introduction of new crops and animals transformed the land and drastically changed the way people lived.

Before 1492, the Americas were a land settled by a diverse population. In Mexico, the Aztecs controlled a diverse empire, and in South America, the Incas had conquered their own large empire in the Andes Mountains.

With the arrival of the Europeans, major demographic and environmental changes occurred. New diseases began to appear in the native population, particularly, smallpox. Since the natives had no prior immunity to this disease, the results were devastating. The Europeans, on the other hand, had been exposed to the disease back home and were not as severely affected. The Aztec empire lost 95 percent of its population within a century, and in this weakened state, was easily controlled by its Spanish conquerors.

Between 1500 and 1800, 100 million people died from the spread of smallpox to the Americas. The new plantation economy set up by the Europeans, however, established a system of forced labor, and since so many natives were dying, the African slave trade was extended across the Atlantic Ocean to fulfill the demand for labor. The slaves, along with the native and European populations, made up a new social structure in American society—one based on race. The peninsulares, settlers from Spain or Portugal, made up the highest class (the Creoles were their descendants). Intermarriage led to new classes: the mestizos (a mix of native and European) and the mulattoes (a mix of African and European). The full-blooded natives and Africans made up the lowest class.

Environmentally, America had been transformed. New crops and animals never previously seen were introduced, altering the environment, economy, and diet of the people. In particular, animals such as horses, cattle, pigs, sheep, goats, and chickens were introduced. The Americas did not have any large draft animals, so the introduction of these animals helped to transform farming. Additionally, sugar cultivation was introduced; forests were cleared and plantations were set up to grow this profitable cash crop. However, native crops like corn, potatoes, and tobacco continued to be important economic commodities in the Americas. Additionally, natural resources like silver were mined in the mountains of Mexico and Peru using native forced labor. The profits from these resources greatly benefited the Spanish crown, but little benefit was seen by the native people.

The time period 1450 to 1750 was a time of dramatic change for the Americas. As the world was becoming more closely integrated, the Americas were brought into the global trade network. Demographically the population was dramatically changed by the destruction of the native population and the introduction of Europeans and Africans. Environmentally, the introduction of new crops and animals and the mining of natural resources, like silver, transformed the landscape of the Americas forever.

Part C: Comparative Question: Sample Response

Between the years 1000 BCE and 600 CE, new religious ideas began to arise from different civilizations, and a few were able to spread so vastly that they came to be widespread global movements. The introduction of long-distance trade during this period aided this religious growth. Christianity and Buddhism rose to be dominant world religions and their spread altered them significantly in similar ways. These religions had drastically different impacts on the Roman and Mauryan Empires, which they came to influence, respectively.

The spread of religion during the classical period took place mostly by way of the Silk Road, which spanned from China all the way to the Mediterranean world. Buddhism, originating in India, was able to reach much of China, Japan, Korea, Sri Lanka, and all of the Indian subcontinent. Oasis cities along trade routes became Buddhist centers, where missionaries found many willing converts. Likewise, Christianity found its converts by promising salvation in heaven. Christianity, originating in Jerusalem and coming to dominate the Roman Empire, faced more difficulty as it spread, as its missionaries were not tolerated or embraced. In fact, many were persecuted. Persistent diligence prevailed however, and the success of Christianity is still relevant in today's world.

With the spread of religion came the branching of religion. Buddhism was popular and accessible because it could assimilate to many cultures. Out of traditional Buddhism came the Theravada School (influential in Southeast Asia) and the Mahayana School (influential in China). Furthermore, Buddhism sometimes collaborated with Confucianist principles and Shinto deities. In Southwest Asia, Christians became ascetics and rejected materialism. Both Christianity and Buddhism began as reforms of pre-existing religions (from Judaism and Hinduism, respectively), but both spread and branched to be important distinct religions, which could fit the lifestyles of different peoples.

A religion can only truly grow to be a global movement when it infiltrates the government and affects aspects of life apart from spirituality. In the Mauryan Empire, Ashoka's conversion to Buddhism had a great effect on his people. Peace was encouraged throughout the empire; Ashoka practiced cultural pluralism and allowed conquered people to keep their own traditions, and the citizens were truly unified under a cultural authority. In great contrast was the influence Christianity had on the Roman Empire. Before the popularization of the religion by zealous missionaries and the conversion of the Emperor Constantine, Christians had been persecuted. But when Christianity grew to be the dominant religion of the area, it was the non-Christians who suffered persecution. Though some emperors declared divine right, ultimately government authority was weakened as people looked to God and salvation for their strength. The economy became unsteady, as churches and church officials were exempt from taxes. Buddhism seemed much less controversial in India and actually succeeded in unifying the Mauryan Empire and its people. Conversely, Christianity caused chaos, upheaval, and disunity, and it contributed to the fall of the Roman Empire.

While Christianity and Buddhism did come to dominate the classical era by growing and spreading far beyond their centers of origin, they also greatly influenced the governments of which they became a part. Even today, they play a significant role in world history. When religion becomes a driving political force, the results can be overwhelming and sometimes tragic.

Practice Test 2 Answer Grid

1. Ⓐ Ⓑ Ⓒ Ⓓ Ⓔ
2. Ⓐ Ⓑ Ⓒ Ⓓ Ⓔ
3. Ⓐ Ⓑ Ⓒ Ⓓ Ⓔ
4. Ⓐ Ⓑ Ⓒ Ⓓ Ⓔ
5. Ⓐ Ⓑ Ⓒ Ⓓ Ⓔ
6. Ⓐ Ⓑ Ⓒ Ⓓ Ⓔ
7. Ⓐ Ⓑ Ⓒ Ⓓ Ⓔ
8. Ⓐ Ⓑ Ⓒ Ⓓ Ⓔ
9. Ⓐ Ⓑ Ⓒ Ⓓ Ⓔ
10. Ⓐ Ⓑ Ⓒ Ⓓ Ⓔ
11. Ⓐ Ⓑ Ⓒ Ⓓ Ⓔ
12. Ⓐ Ⓑ Ⓒ Ⓓ Ⓔ
13. Ⓐ Ⓑ Ⓒ Ⓓ Ⓔ
14. Ⓐ Ⓑ Ⓒ Ⓓ Ⓔ
15. Ⓐ Ⓑ Ⓒ Ⓓ Ⓔ
16. Ⓐ Ⓑ Ⓒ Ⓓ Ⓔ
17. Ⓐ Ⓑ Ⓒ Ⓓ Ⓔ
18. Ⓐ Ⓑ Ⓒ Ⓓ Ⓔ
19. Ⓐ Ⓑ Ⓒ Ⓓ Ⓔ
20. Ⓐ Ⓑ Ⓒ Ⓓ Ⓔ
21. Ⓐ Ⓑ Ⓒ Ⓓ Ⓔ
22. Ⓐ Ⓑ Ⓒ Ⓓ Ⓔ
23. Ⓐ Ⓑ Ⓒ Ⓓ Ⓔ
24. Ⓐ Ⓑ Ⓒ Ⓓ Ⓔ
25. Ⓐ Ⓑ Ⓒ Ⓓ Ⓔ
26. Ⓐ Ⓑ Ⓒ Ⓓ Ⓔ
27. Ⓐ Ⓑ Ⓒ Ⓓ Ⓔ
28. Ⓐ Ⓑ Ⓒ Ⓓ Ⓔ
29. Ⓐ Ⓑ Ⓒ Ⓓ Ⓔ
30. Ⓐ Ⓑ Ⓒ Ⓓ Ⓔ
31. Ⓐ Ⓑ Ⓒ Ⓓ Ⓔ
32. Ⓐ Ⓑ Ⓒ Ⓓ Ⓔ
33. Ⓐ Ⓑ Ⓒ Ⓓ Ⓔ
34. Ⓐ Ⓑ Ⓒ Ⓓ Ⓔ
35. Ⓐ Ⓑ Ⓒ Ⓓ Ⓔ
36. Ⓐ Ⓑ Ⓒ Ⓓ Ⓔ
37. Ⓐ Ⓑ Ⓒ Ⓓ Ⓔ
38. Ⓐ Ⓑ Ⓒ Ⓓ Ⓔ
39. Ⓐ Ⓑ Ⓒ Ⓓ Ⓔ
40. Ⓐ Ⓑ Ⓒ Ⓓ Ⓔ
41. Ⓐ Ⓑ Ⓒ Ⓓ Ⓔ
42. Ⓐ Ⓑ Ⓒ Ⓓ Ⓔ
43. Ⓐ Ⓑ Ⓒ Ⓓ Ⓔ
44. Ⓐ Ⓑ Ⓒ Ⓓ Ⓔ
45. Ⓐ Ⓑ Ⓒ Ⓓ Ⓔ
46. Ⓐ Ⓑ Ⓒ Ⓓ Ⓔ
47. Ⓐ Ⓑ Ⓒ Ⓓ Ⓔ
48. Ⓐ Ⓑ Ⓒ Ⓓ Ⓔ
49. Ⓐ Ⓑ Ⓒ Ⓓ Ⓔ
50. Ⓐ Ⓑ Ⓒ Ⓓ Ⓔ
51. Ⓐ Ⓑ Ⓒ Ⓓ Ⓔ
52. Ⓐ Ⓑ Ⓒ Ⓓ Ⓔ
53. Ⓐ Ⓑ Ⓒ Ⓓ Ⓔ
54. Ⓐ Ⓑ Ⓒ Ⓓ Ⓔ
55. Ⓐ Ⓑ Ⓒ Ⓓ Ⓔ
56. Ⓐ Ⓑ Ⓒ Ⓓ Ⓔ
57. Ⓐ Ⓑ Ⓒ Ⓓ Ⓔ
58. Ⓐ Ⓑ Ⓒ Ⓓ Ⓔ
59. Ⓐ Ⓑ Ⓒ Ⓓ Ⓔ
60. Ⓐ Ⓑ Ⓒ Ⓓ Ⓔ
61. Ⓐ Ⓑ Ⓒ Ⓓ Ⓔ
62. Ⓐ Ⓑ Ⓒ Ⓓ Ⓔ
63. Ⓐ Ⓑ Ⓒ Ⓓ Ⓔ
64. Ⓐ Ⓑ Ⓒ Ⓓ Ⓔ
65. Ⓐ Ⓑ Ⓒ Ⓓ Ⓔ
66. Ⓐ Ⓑ Ⓒ Ⓓ Ⓔ
67. Ⓐ Ⓑ Ⓒ Ⓓ Ⓔ
68. Ⓐ Ⓑ Ⓒ Ⓓ Ⓔ
69. Ⓐ Ⓑ Ⓒ Ⓓ Ⓔ
70. Ⓐ Ⓑ Ⓒ Ⓓ Ⓔ

Practice Test 2

Section I: Multiple-Choice Questions

Time: 55 Minutes
70 Questions

Directions: Each of the questions or incomplete statements below is followed by five suggested answers or completions. Select the one that is best in each case and then fill in the corresponding oval on the answer sheet.

1. Which of the following correctly matches the river with the civilization that developed around it?

    (A) Nile: India
    (B) Yellow: Egypt
    (C) Tigris and Euphrates: Mesopotamia
    (D) Indus: China
    (E) Ganges: Greece

2. The Twelve Tables and Hammurabi's Code are important examples of

    (A) Written laws
    (B) Trade agreements
    (C) Political treatises
    (D) Religious doctrines
    (E) Social structures

3. In a patriarchal society,

    (A) the leader holds absolute power.
    (B) power resides with the men.
    (C) religious leaders dominate politics.
    (D) trade is severely restricted by the government.
    (E) social mobility exists.

4. Which of the following statements accurately compares Hinduism and Islam?

    (A) Both religions believe in the importance of idol worship.
    (B) Hinduism de-emphasizes rituals, while Islam places greater emphasis on rituals.
    (C) Both religions believe in a powerful creator god.
    (D) Islam provides a strict social structure, while Hinduism has greater social mobility.
    (E) Hinduism was spread by missionaries, while Islam was a religion passed down through the family.

5. Which of the following correctly matches the founder or prophet with his religion or philosophy?

    (A) Jesus : Islam
    (B) Confucius : Daoism
    (C) Siddhartha Gautama : Zoroastrianism
    (D) Mohammed : Christianity
    (E) Abraham : Judaism

GO ON TO THE NEXT PAGE

6. All of the following actions represent filial piety EXCEPT

   (A) Taking care of one's parents when they are ill
   (B) Showing love, respect, and support for one's parents
   (C) Honoring one's ancestors by carrying out sacrifices after their death
   (D) Respectfully pointing out errors one's parents make to help them improve
   (E) Ensuring that one has a male heir

7. All of the following statements describe important global developments during the time period 8000 BCE to 600 CE EXCEPT

   (A) In response to the growth in trade, systems of currency were developed.
   (B) The use of metallurgy allowed people to make stronger and more efficient weapons and tools.
   (C) The formation of nomadic empires led to the increase in trade along the Silk Road.
   (D) As civilizations developed, so did the need to keep records and communicate further; therefore, systems of writing developed.
   (E) Cities rose in which job specialization could occur and larger populations could be maintained.

8. Harrapa and Mohenjo–Daro were examples of

   (A) Oasis towns along the Silk Road
   (B) Greek city–states
   (C) Port cities along the Mediterranean Sea
   (D) Indus river valley cities
   (E) Commercial centers of the kingdom of Ghana

9. The Roman Emperor Constantine influenced the spread of Christianity in the way that the Mauryan Emperor Ashoka influenced the spread of

   (A) Judaism
   (B) Confucianism
   (C) Hinduism
   (D) Zoroastrianism
   (E) Buddhism

10. Which of the following statements most accurately compares the role of women in Christianity and Buddhism?

    (A) In both religions, women had an opportunity to follow an alternative life in the monastery.
    (B) In both religions, men were considered spiritually superior.
    (C) Christianity attracted many female converts initially, while Buddhism attracted very few.
    (D) Buddhist women were forbidden from reading the sacred prayers, but Christian women were encouraged to read the Bible.
    (E) In both religions, women often held important leadership positions.

11. Which group in Confucianism can best be equated with the Brahmins in Hinduism?

    (A) Merchants
    (B) Scholar–gentry
    (C) Peasants
    (D) Rulers
    (E) Monks

GO ON TO THE NEXT PAGE

12. Which of the following statements best describes the significance of the Bantu migration?

    (A) The migration allowed for the opening up of the trans-Saharan trade and the spread of Islam to West Africa.
    (B) As the Bantus migrated, they spread their agriculture, culture, and language throughout Africa.
    (C) The migration eliminated hunter and gather communities from Africa and established an economy solely based on agriculture.
    (D) Christian missionaries often followed the Bantus as they migrated, spreading their religion and Western values throughout Africa.
    (E) The Bantus used the monsoon winds to migrate from Southeast Asia to East Africa, bringing the banana, which could be easily cultivated in Africa.

13. "He (the superior man) does not mind not being in office; all that he minds about is whether he has qualities that entitle him to office. He does not mind failing to get recognition; he is too busy doing the things that entitle him to recognition." (Analects IV.14)

    The above quote from the Confucian Analects stresses the idea that

    (A) The emperor is close to the gods and should be treated as such.
    (B) Proper behavior and respect for parents must always be considered.
    (C) The real leader focuses on work, rather than recognition.
    (D) A superior man always receives praise for a job well done.
    (E) Recognition comes and goes, but a superior man always has his family.

14. All of the following represent significant global developments during the time period 600 to 1450 CE EXCEPT

    (A) Trade and interaction were at their height during Pax Mongolia, the period when peace and order were established in the vast Mongol empire.
    (B) One of the worst epidemic diseases in history—the Black Plague—spread during this period, due to the movement of people and their increased interaction.
    (C) Religions such as Islam, Christianity, and Buddhism preached the equality of all believers, and all three spread with the help of merchants and/or missionaries.
    (D) Major technological developments such as the compass, improved ship building technology, and gunpowder helped to shape the development of the world.
    (E) European kingdoms reigned supreme as the dominant power during the time period, entering and then taking over the profitable Indian Ocean trade.

15. Which of the following ruled the Middle East and North Africa at the same time that the Tang dynasty ruled China?

    (A) Delhi Sultanate
    (B) Abbasid Caliphate
    (C) Ottoman Empire
    (D) Songhay Empire
    (E) Egyptian kingdom

16. A significant consequence of the Mongol invasions was that

    (A) northern China was converted into steppe land for Mongol nomads.
    (B) western Europe took over 200 years to fully recover from the Mongol invasions.
    (C) Trade and communication along the Silk Road flourished.
    (D) Mongol rule in India helped to incorporate the areas into the Indian Ocean trade network.
    (E) the Mamluks brought Islam to the Mongols and served as co-rulers of the Mongol kingdom of Egypt.

17. Ibn Battuta, Marco Polo, and Rabban Sauma are all examples of

    (A) religious missionaries who helped to spread their religions along the Silk Road.
    (B) travelers who were able to travel great distances and record their journeys.
    (C) political diplomats who served the Mongol khan in various parts of the empire.
    (D) merchants who profited from the open flow of trade during the Pax Mongolia.
    (E) explorers who sailed to the Americas and claimed land for European kingdoms.

18. Which of the following statements most accurately compares the leadership of the Roman Catholic Church and Eastern Orthodox Church?

    (A) The pope was the head of both the Roman Catholic and Eastern Orthodox Churches.
    (B) Local lords made religious decisions for the Roman Catholic Church, while the patriarch guided the Eastern Orthodox Church.
    (C) The pope was the spiritual head and leader of the Roman Catholic Church, while the Emperor and Patriarch were co-heads of the Eastern Orthodox Church.
    (D) Both religions allowed local communities to make religious decisions for them, as long as the head of the church was consulted first.
    (E) The king, in Western Europe, and the emperor, in Eastern Europe, ruled over their respective churches.

19. All of the following statements accurately describe the Chinese impact on Japan EXCEPT

    (A) Use of civil service exam
    (B) Importance of filial piety
    (C) Spread of Buddhism
    (D) Culture practice of the tea ceremony
    (E) Concept of the Heavenly Emperor

20. All of the statements below refer to which of the following?
    - Mansa Musa's pilgrimage to Mecca
    - Trans-Saharan trade route
    - Tolls collected on trade in gold and salt

    (A) Ghana
    (B) Mali
    (C) Songhay
    (D) Ethiopia
    (E) Great Zimbabwe

GO ON TO THE NEXT PAGE

21. By 1450, Buddhism had spread to all of the following EXCEPT

    (A) Tibet
    (B) China
    (C) Japan
    (D) Korea
    (E) Philippines

22. Which of the following statements accurately compares the role of the Turks in India and in the Middle East?

    (A) In both areas, an organized force invaded and took over the existing empires.
    (B) The Turks formed the Delhi Sultanate and took control in India, while Turks gained power in the Abbasid Caliphate through military positions and power.
    (C) The Abbasids were easily defeated by Turkish invasions, while in India, the Turks had trouble establishing political control.
    (D) The Turks who invaded India converted to Hinduism, while the Turks who invaded the Middle East converted to Islam.
    (E) In both areas, the Turks were successfully driven out by the native populations, preventing them from establishing any permanent political control.

23. The Mongols were successful in creating the world's largest empire because

    (A) their military forces always outnumbered the opposition forces.
    (B) the spread of the Black Plague had significantly weakened the settled populations.
    (C) the civilizations that were conquered often had weak or declining political power.
    (D) the use of political negotiations eased the transfer of land into Mongol hands.
    (E) their belief in Islam appealed to many of their conquered peoples.

24. West Africa was greatly influenced by the trans-Saharan trade in the way that East Africa was influenced by the

    (A) Atlantic Ocean trade
    (B) Mediterranean Sea trade
    (C) Silk Road trade
    (D) Indian Ocean trade
    (E) Pacific Ocean trade

25. All of the following accurately describe the exchange of agriculture or technology during the time period 600 to 1450 EXCEPT

    (A) The magnetic compass originated in China and spread to Europe via the Indian Ocean trade.
    (B) Sugarcane originated in southwest Asia and spread to Europe as a result of the interaction during the Crusades.
    (C) Gunpowder originated in China and spread to Persia, the Middle East, and eventually Europe, by way of the Mongols.
    (D) The Black Plague originated in the Mongol Empire and spread to the Middle East and Europe via the Silk Road trade.
    (E) Smallpox, originating in Europe, spread to the Americas and caused the destruction of the Native American population.

GO ON TO THE NEXT PAGE

26. Which of the following statements accurately compares the Incan and Roman Empires?

    (A) Both emperors claimed to be descendents of the sun god.
    (B) Both empires built effective road systems which aided communication and trade throughout their empires.
    (C) The Incan empire had a tradition of representative government, while the Roman empire claimed divine right.
    (D) Both Empires declined due to nomadic invasions and a significant decrease in trade.
    (E) The Roman Empire incorporated diverse people, while the Incan Empire was homogeneous.

27. Which of the following is an accurate list of important trading cities in the time period 600 to 1450?

    (A) London, Baghdad, Delhi
    (B) Venice, Samarkand, Changan
    (C) Paris, Brussels, Cairo
    (D) Timbuktu, Rio de Janeiro, Beijing
    (E) Rome, Constantinople, Mecca

28. The self-sufficient economic system that developed in Western Europe during the time period 600 to 1450 is known as

    (A) Industrialization
    (B) Mercantilism
    (C) Manorialism
    (D) Capitalism
    (E) Communism

29. All of the following statements regarding the Black Plague and its impact are accurate EXCEPT

    (A) The Black Plague spread from southwest China along trade routes.
    (B) The devastating disease killed most victims within a few days.
    (C) In Western Europe, workers demanded higher wages and peasants rebelled, leading to a decrease in serfdom and a weakening of the feudal system.
    (D) Anti-Semitism increased as Jews—used as scapegoats—were accused of poisoning the wells.
    (E) In the Middle East, many Muslims abandoned their faith and blamed Muslim clerics for not being able to contain the disease.

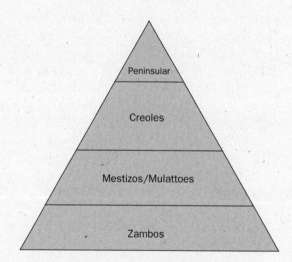

30. The chart above represents the social class structure in

    (A) Feudal Japan
    (B) Feudal Europe
    (C) Mughal India
    (D) The Incan Empire
    (E) Spanish America

31. The purpose of the encomienda system was to

    (A) eliminate the Native American population.
    (B) prevent the Atlantic slave trade from increasing.
    (C) supply Europeans with a steady supply of labor.
    (D) give Native Americans economic opportunities.
    (E) aid industrialization in the Americas.

32. Which of the following was NOT exchanged from the Americas to Europe?

    (A) Tobacco
    (B) Tomatoes
    (C) Cattle
    (D) Potatoes
    (E) Corn

33. Which of the following most accurately describes the treatment of the Chinese by the Manchus?

    (A) Chinese were forbidden from engaging in trade with the outside world.
    (B) Chinese men were forced to wear their hair in a queue (ponytail).
    (C) Chinese women were encouraged to marry Manchus.
    (D) Confucian scholars were removed from government positions.
    (E) Chinese women were forbidden from binding their feet.

34. Which of the following statements most accurately describes the silver trade in the time period 1450 to 1750?

    (A) Chinese demand for silver drove the trade.
    (B) Spain was unable to attain the needed supply of silver.
    (C) The Ottoman Empire served as the middleman in the trade.
    (D) The Ming dynasty was strengthened due to the inflation of silver.
    (E) Silver mines in South Africa produced most of the world's silver.

35. During the time period 1450 to 1750, England rose as a dominant power in the Indian Ocean primarily because

    (A) the English had defeated their major competitor, the Chinese, in the Opium War.
    (B) of the use of joint-stock companies, allowing private investors to take risks and benefit from trade in the Indian Ocean.
    (C) the Ottoman Empire had great difficulty retaining its position as the dominant power in the Indian Ocean.
    (D) the Portuguese voluntarily withdrew their economic interests in the region.
    (E) the Mughal Empire financially supported the trading posts established by the English.

36. The Mongols and the Ottomans shared all of the following characteristics EXCEPT

    (A) Gunpowder technology
    (B) Administrative expertise
    (C) Steppe diplomacy
    (D) Interest in distant trading partners
    (E) Autocratic leadership

37. Dynastic decline was apparent in the Qing regime of 19th century China for all of the following reasons EXCEPT

    (A) A decline in foreign trade
    (B) Famine and mass migrations
    (C) Corruption and intrigue within the royal court
    (D) Rebellions against the dynasty
    (E) Rising lawlessness and banditry in the provinces

38. The wearing of a veil by women of the Islamic faith was

    (A) adopted from the Persians.
    (B) proclaimed by the prophet.
    (C) an Ottoman import after the 15th century.
    (D) common only in Arabia.
    (E) proscribed in the Qur'an.

39. From 1500 to 1850, those able to keep out the intrusion of the West were the

    (A) Mesoamericans
    (B) Sub-Saharan Africans
    (C) Indians of South Asia
    (D) Japanese
    (E) Chinese

40. Which of the following places or empires had a road system similar to the Tang dynasty's?

    (A) Rome and Persia
    (B) Moscow and Kiev
    (C) Athens and Persia
    (D) Egypt and Babylon
    (E) Japan and the Mughals

41. Which of the following is the most accurate statement about the Atlantic slave trade between 1450 and 1750?

    (A) Slaves were brought to Europe to work in the mines.
    (B) All slaves were brought safely to the New World.
    (C) The trade was part of a larger triangular trade pattern.
    (D) Most slaves were brought to work on rice plantations in North America.
    (E) Most slaves were taken from the Saharan area.

42. Mao Zedong launched the Cultural Revolution in China in order to

    (A) strengthen Confucian education in China.
    (B) increase China's military assistance to North Vietnam.
    (C) prepare for an attack on Taiwan.
    (D) strengthen his power base and discredit his rivals.
    (E) preserve ancient Chinese artifacts.

43. The earliest monotheistic religion was

    (A) Christianity
    (B) Zoroastrianism
    (C) Buddhism
    (D) Islam
    (E) Judaism

GO ON TO THE NEXT PAGE

44. In the 20th century, many newly independent African states

   (A) were able to industrialize quickly.
   (B) were plagued by ethnic tensions owing to the inherited colonial boundaries.
   (C) remained on good terms with their colonial masters.
   (D) refused to take part in the United Nations.
   (E) successfully embraced democracy as the best form of government.

45. The goal of the non-alignment movement in the 1960s was to

   (A) replace the United Nations.
   (B) remain neutral during the cold war.
   (C) concentrate on domestic reforms.
   (D) convince the United States to supply military aid.
   (E) increase political freedom at home.

46. A result of the competition for African colonies in the 19th century was

   (A) More rapid decolonization
   (B) The Berlin Conference of 1885
   (C) More cordial relations among European powers
   (D) The reunification of Italy in 1870
   (E) The colonization of Ethiopia

47. The Spanish were able to conquer the Incan empire in part because

   (A) there was internal strife among the leadership.
   (B) incan animistic religious beliefs existed.
   (C) other native groups helped them in the defeat.
   (D) no silver was found in South America.
   (E) the Andes region has a flat topography.

48. All of the following describe major global developments that occurred between 1450 and 1750 EXCEPT

   (A) The Colombian Exchange of goods, disease, and cultures spread throughout the world.
   (B) Improvements in and the spread of shipping technologies and gunpowder weapons allowed European countries to begin their dominance of the world.
   (C) The inclusion of the Americas in the global trade network allowed a truly global economy to develop.
   (D) Industrialization spread throughout Europe, changing the pace of work, the prices of goods, and the family unit.
   (E) African people were forcibly transported across the Atlantic Ocean to fill the demand for forced labor on plantations.

49. During the time period 1750 to 1914, the developments below occurred in the

   - Taiping Rebellion
   - Opium War
   - Self-Strengthening Movement

   (A) Japan
   (B) Korea
   (C) India
   (D) China
   (E) Vietnam

50. In the late 19th century, the growth of Japan as a world power was facilitated by

   (A) Democracy and liberal reforms
   (B) Industrialization and military strength
   (C) Cultural isolation and decentralization
   (D) International protection and aid
   (E) Communism and totalitarianism

GO ON TO THE NEXT PAGE

51. Which of the following is an accurate description of the relations between Belgium and the Congo in the 19th and early 20th centuries?

    (A) The two areas had an open trade agreement that was mutually beneficial.
    (B) The Congo won its independence from Belgium.
    (C) Belgium took advantage of the people and natural resources of the Congo.
    (D) Congo rulers fought bloody wars with the Belgian Royal Army.
    (E) Belgium attempted unsuccessfully to take over the Congo.

52. The emancipation of the serfs in Russia in 1861 caused which of the following to happen?

    (A) Serfs won political rights and were exempt from any taxes for land they received.
    (B) Most serfs went on to successful careers as industrial capitalists.
    (C) Few serfs moved to cities to work in the factories.
    (D) Most serfs remained desperately poor.
    (E) All landlords refused to recognize the serfs' freedom and ignored the emancipation.

53. Which of the following most significantly influenced both Italy and Germany in the 19th century?

    (A) Communism
    (B) Fascism
    (C) Democracy
    (D) Zionism
    (E) Nationalism

54. All of the following describe major global developments in the time period 1750 to 1914 EXCEPT

    (A) With the development of industrialization, the world became truly interdependent.
    (B) The way that people worked, lived, traveled, related to their families, communicated, and identified themselves changed for many people.
    (C) The industrialized nations, in search of raw materials and new markets, often colonized areas to protect economic interests.
    (D) The institution of slavery remained unchallenged throughout the period and the plantation system dominated the economy of much of the world.
    (E) Enlightenment ideals such as equality, freedom of speech, and freedom of religion became very influential in many parts of the world.

55. One effect of the West's cultural influence on Meiji Japan was that

    (A) Japanese literature was affected by European models, and writers experimented with Western verse.
    (B) Christianity replaced Buddhism and Shinto as the most popular religion in Japan.
    (C) the Japanese rejected Western fashion and hairstyles.
    (D) Confucian values were eliminated in Japan.
    (E) devotion to the emperor was replaced with loyalty to one's political party.

GO ON TO THE NEXT PAGE

56. All of the following are examples of the new leisure opportunities enjoyed by the middle class in the late 19th century EXCEPT

    (A) The bicycle
    (B) Newspapers
    (C) Television
    (D) Theater
    (E) Professional sports

57. Which of the following methods did Mohandas Gandhi (India) and Kwame Nkrumah (Ghana) use in their struggle for independence from the British?

    (A) Civil disobedience
    (B) Hunger strikes
    (C) Military force
    (D) Guerilla warfare
    (E) Terrorism

58. All of the following areas experienced acts of genocide in the 20th century EXCEPT

    (A) Rwanda
    (B) Kosovo
    (C) Armenia
    (D) Cambodia
    (E) India

59. Attaturk of Turkey and Peter the Great of Russia shared a

    (A) Commitment to Islam
    (B) Goal of westernization
    (C) Desire to spread democratic values
    (D) Hope of achieving a warm-water port
    (E) Desire for a communist revolution

60. All of the following accurately describe outcomes of World War I EXCEPT

    (A) Germany was economically and politically devastated. It had lost millions of men in the fighting and was forced to pay huge reparations to the Allies.
    (B) Japanese concessions in the treaties led to a surge of nationalism in China, and a cultural and intellectual period known as the May Fourth Movement.
    (C) The use of the atomic bomb set up a technological stalemate known as the cold war, in which the Soviet Union and the United States were the two dominant world powers.
    (D) In exchange for their help against the Central Powers, Arabs had been promised independence, but their land was carved into French and British mandates.
    (E) India fought on the side of the British and had been promised great self-government after the war, but little change occurred. This encouraged a surge in nationalism.

61. All of the following describe global developments of the time period 1914 to the present EXCEPT

    (A) The world's population grew from one billion people worldwide to over six billion.
    (B) During the cold war, a major goal was to avoid world destruction from the use of nuclear weapons.
    (C) The introduction of communist governments in various parts of the world challenged traditional social structure models, attempting to empower the working and peasant classes.
    (D) From the airplane to the atom bomb, the discoveries in math, science, and technology revolutionized how we live and communicate.
    (E) The nation-state first appeared and became a new concept of political identity.

GO ON TO THE NEXT PAGE

62. NATO, OPEC, EU are all examples of

    (A) Nonalignment movements
    (B) International organizations
    (C) Political parties
    (D) Stock exchange symbols
    (E) Charitable organizations

63. The apartheid system in South Africa can be described as

    (A) a series of restrictive laws enacted with the goal of maintaining the separate societies of black and white.
    (B) the collaboration between black and white South Africans in the effort to remove British colonial rule.
    (C) the economic system which industrialized South Africa and focused on the mining of diamonds and gold.
    (D) the political party that encouraged widespread democracy and participation throughout South Africa.
    (E) the organization that fights the spread of AIDS in South Africa by encouraging Western nations to donate cutting-edge medicines.

64. All of the items below were policies during the rule of
    - Five-Year Plans
    - Collectivization
    - The Great Purge

    (A) Mao Zedong
    (B) Vladimir Lenin
    (C) Joseph Stalin
    (D) Karl Marx
    (E) Deng Xiaoping

65. Since the 1980s, many countries in Latin America have moved politically toward

    (A) Communism
    (B) Representative democracy
    (C) Fundamentalism
    (D) Totalitarianism
    (E) Anarchism

66. In the Balfour Declaration of 1917, the

    (A) United States supported the Palestinians' right to settle their homeland and govern as they chose.
    (B) British government committed to support the creation of a homeland for Jews in Palestine
    (C) Russians declared the right to occupy the Middle East region in order to prevent the spread of capitalism to the area.
    (D) Germans occupied the former Ottoman Empire, claiming the need for "Lebensraum" for German people.
    (E) Ottoman Empire refused to recognize the independence of Palestine and forced the territory to remain part of the empire.

67. Which two religions had continuous conflicts in India in the latter half of the 20th century?

    (A) Christians and Hindus
    (B) Buddhists and Muslims
    (C) Sikhs and Buddhists
    (D) Hindus and Muslims
    (E) Christians and Muslims

68. Perestroika and glasnost were both policies that influenced

    (A) Decolonization in Africa
    (B) The fall of the Soviet Union
    (C) The Arab-Israeli conflict
    (D) The war on terror
    (E) Ethnic conflict in Yugoslavia

GO ON TO THE NEXT PAGE

69. The statements below all describe which type of political system?
    - A single party in charge of all government
    - Ultra-nationalism and glorification of the state
    - Militarism and glorification of war as the ultimate expression of power

    (A) Democracy
    (B) Absolute monarchy
    (C) Anarchism
    (D) Fascism
    (E) Utopianism

70. In both the French Revolution (18th century) and Russian Revolution (20th century),

    (A) communism resulted.
    (B) democracy was achieved.
    (C) a reign of terror occurred.
    (D) the monarch returned to power.
    (E) the international community cooperated.

Part Four: Practice Tests
Practice Test 2

Section II

Part A

Mandatory reading period: 10 minutes
Suggested writing time: 40 minutes

Directions: The following question is based on the accompanying Documents 1–6. (Some of the documents have been edited for the purpose of this exercise.)

This question is designed to test your ability to work with and understand historical documents. Write an essay that:

- Has a relevant thesis and supports that thesis with evidence from the documents.
- Uses all or all but one of the documents.
- Analyzes the documents by grouping them in as many appropriate ways as possible. **Does not simply summarize the documents individually.**
- Takes into account the sources of the documents and analyzes the authors' points of view.
- Explains the need for at least one additional type of document.

You may refer to relevant historical information not mentioned in the documents.

1. Describe and analyze the economic and social effects of the Spanish conquest of the Americas after 1492. Explain what type(s) of **additional kinds of document(s)** would help describe and analyze the impact of the Spanish conquest of the Americas.

   <u>Historical Background</u>: Following Christopher Columbus's encounter with the Americas in 1492, waves of Spanish conquistadors arrived, hoping to stake their own claim on the "New World."

Document 1

Source: Hernando Cortes, Letters from Mexico, August 12, 1521:

On leaving my camp, I commanded Gonzalo de Sandoval to sail the brigantines (ships) in between the houses in the other quarter in which the Indians were resisting, so that we should have them surrounded, but not to attack until he saw that we were engaged. In this way they would have surrounded and so hard pressed that they would have no place to move save over the bodies of their dead or along the roof tops. They no longer could find any arrow, javelins or stones with which to attack us; and our allies fighting with us were armed with swords and bucklers, and slaughtered so many of them on land and in the water that more than forty thousand were killed or taken that day.

Document 2

Source: Bernardino de Sahagun, a Franciscan friar who was instrumental in preserving information about Aztec culture, *General History of the Things of New Spain*, 1519 to 1521:

After the previously mentioned hardships that befell the Spaniards in the year 1519, at the beginning of the year 1520 the epidemic of smallpox, measles, and pustules broke out so virulently that a vast number of people died throughout this New Spain. This pestilence began in the province of Chalco and last for sixty days. Among the Mexicans who fell victim to this pestilence was the lord Cuitlahuactzin, whom they had elected a little earlier. Many leaders, many veteran soldiers, and valiant men who were their defense in time of war, also died.

Document 3

Source: Antonio Vasquez de Espinosa, a Spanish friar and missionary who sought to convert the Indians to Christianity, describes the silver mines of Potosi:

Theses Indians are sent out every year under a captain whom they choose in each village or tribe, for him to take them and oversee them for the year each had to serve; every year they have a new election, for as some go out, others come in. This works out very badly, with great losses and gaps in the quotas of Indians, the villages being depopulated; and this gives rise to great extortions and abuses on the part of the inspectors toward the poor Indians, ruining them and thus depriving the chief Indians of their property and carrying them off in chains because they do not fill out the mita assignment…

So huge is the wealth which has been taken out of this range since the year 1545, when it was discovered, up to the present year of 1628, which makes 83 years that they have been working and reducing its ores, and that merely form the registered mines, as appears from an examination of most of the account in the royal records, 326,000,000 pesos have been taken out.

Document 4

Juan Ginés de Sepæûlveda (1490–1573), a scholar and apologist for the Spanish treatment of the Indians in the Americas:

Turning then to our topic, whether it is proper and just that those who are superior and who excel in nature, customs, and laws rule over their inferiors, you can easily understand . . . if you are familiar with the character and moral code of the two peoples, that it is with perfect right that the Spaniard exercise their domination over those barbarians of the New World and its adjacent islands. For in prudence, talent, and every kind of virtue and human sentiment they are as inferior to the Spaniards as children are to adults, or women to men, or the cruel and inhumane to the very gentle, or the excessively intemperate to the continent and moderate . . .

Document 5

Bartolomé de las Casas, Dominican friar, *A Short Account of the Destruction of the Indies*, 1542:

As we have said, the island of Hispaniola was the first to witness the arrival of Europeans and the first to suffer the wholesale slaughter of its people and the devastation and depopulation of the land. It all began with the Europeans taking native women and children both as servants and to satisfy their own base appetites; then not content with what the local people offered them of their own free will (and all offered as much as they could spare), they started taking for themselves the food that natives contrived to produce by the sweat of their brows, (which was in all honesty little enough) ... Some of them started to conceal food they had, others decided to send their women and children into hiding, and yet others took to the hills to get away from the brutal and ruthless cruelty that was being inflicted on them. ...

Document 6

Source: Engraving by Flemish engraver Theodor de Bry taken from a 16th-century Dutch edition on the *A Short Account of the Destruction of the Indies* by Bartolome de las Casas:

[**Note**: You will have 16 pages to write all three essays, so feel free to use additional paper.]

Part B
Suggested writing time: 40 minutes

Directions: You are to answer the following question. You should spend 5 minutes organizing or outlining your essay. Write an essay that:
- Has a relevant thesis and supports that thesis with appropriate historical evidence.
- Addresses all parts of the question.
- Uses world historical context to show change over time and/or continuities
- Analyzes the process of change over time and/or continuity.

2. Choose ONE of the trade routes and analyze the changes and continuities of the role and influence of that trade route from 600 to 1750. Be sure to discuss changes as well as continuities.

   Trans-Saharan
   Silk Road
   Indian Ocean
   Mediterranean Sea

Part C
Suggested writing time: 40 minutes

Directions: You are to answer the following question. You should spend 5 minutes organzing or outlining your essay. Write an essay that:
- Has a relevant thesis and supports that thesis with appropriate historical evidence.
- Addresses all parts of the question.
- Makes direct, relevant comparisons.
- Analyzes relevant reasons for similarities and differences.

3. Analyze the major similarities and differences of the economic and political effects of TWO of the following social class structures from 600 to 1750 CE.

   Hindu Caste System
   European Feudalism
   Japanese Feudalism
   Spanish American social structure
   Traditional Confucian social structure

Practice Test 2: Answer Key

1. C
2. A
3. B
4. C
5. E
6. D
7. C
8. D
9. E
10. A
11. B
12. B
13. C
14. E
15. B
16. C
17. B
18. C
19. A
20. B
21. E
22. B
23. C
24. D
25. E
26. B
27. B
28. C
29. E
30. E
31. C
32. C
33. B
34. A
35. B
36. B
37. A
38. A
39. D
40. A
41. C
42. D
43. E
44. B
45. B
46. B
47. C
48. D
49. D
50. B
51. C
52. D
53. E
54. D
55. A
56. C
57. A
58. E
59. B
60. C
61. E
62. B
63. A
64. C
65. B
66. B
67. D
68. B
69. D
70. C

ANSWERS AND EXPLANATIONS

1. C

The Tigris and Euphrates Rrivers surround the areas known as the Fertile Crescent which developed into the Mesopotamian civilization. The Nile was in Egypt,; the Indus and Ganges were in India, and the Yellow River was in China.

2. A

The Twelve Tables were the written laws of the Roman Republic, and Hammarabi's Code from Mesopotamia was the first written collection of laws. Both were influential in the development of future laws.

3. B

A patriarchal society is one in which men hold the dominant power. Many traditional societies were patriarchal.

4. C

Both Islam and Hinduism believe in a powerful creator God. In Islam, Allah is the one true God. In Hinduism, Brahma is the creator god. While idol worship is practiced in Hinduism, it is forbidden in Islam. Hinduism has a stronger emphasis on rituals than Islam. Hinduism's social structure is stricter than Islams. Islam is the religion that was spread is by missionaries.

5. E

Abraham is considered the founder of Judaism. He is also important in Christianity and Islam. Mohammed is the key prophet in Islam. The philosophy of Daoism is attributed to Laozi. Zoroaster is the founder of Zoroastrianism. Jesus is believed to be the son of God in Christianity.

6. D

Filial piety is a Confucian belief that stresses respect for one's parents. One should never do anything that causes one's parent worry. Parents should be honored and not questioned, even if it is respectfully.

7. D

The great nomadic empires, namely the Mongols, were not a significant global development until the late 13th and 14th centuries, after the referenced time period.

8. D

Both of these cities were part of the Indus civilization, which was not discovered until the 1920s.

9. E

Ashoka was a emperor of the Mauryan dynasty in India who converted to Buddhism after fighting a bloody battle. He encouraged the spread of the religion by building roads and sending out missionaries throughout India and beyond.

10. A

In both Christianity and Buddhism, women could live the life of a nun. For women living in a patriarchal society, this was an alternative to a more traditional life of wife and mother. In both religions, women were considered spiritually equal to men. Both religions attracted female converts, but women were rarely in leadership positions.

11. B

The Brahmins in Hinduism are the highest caste of priests and scholars. In Confucianism, the highest and most well-regarded class is that of the scholar-gentry. The people in this class often studied Confucian teachings and attained jobs in the government after passing the civil service exam.

12. B

The Bantu migration which began in approximately 3000 BCE resulted in the spread of agricultural techniques and technology throughout much of Africa. It did not, however, eliminate hunting and gathering from Africa. Additionally, Bantu culture and language spread throughout the continent.

13. C

The quote taken from the Confucian Analects states that a true leader is not overly concerned with recognition. A true leader focuses on the work itself.

14. E

From 600 to 1450, Europe was not a global world power; instead the area was in a period of recovery and restoration. After 1450, Europe began to get directly involved in the Indian Ocean trade, which helped it to become a world power.

15. B

The Tang dynasty ruled China in the 7th–10th centuries. At that same time, the Abbasid Caliphate ruled most of the Middle East and North Africa. The Delhi Sultanate ruled northern India in the 11th and 12th centuries. The Ottoman Empire ruled the Middle East and North Africa, but not until the 14th century. The Songhay Empire ruled West Africa in the 15th and 16th centuries, and the Egyptian kingdom dates back to the Foundations period.

16. C

The Mongols conquered the world's largest empire and in doing so, allowed the exchange of goods, culture, and technology to occur. The period, known as Pax Mongolia, witnessed a surge in trade and communication along the Silk Road.

17. B

Ibn Battuta was a Muslim scholar who traveled extensively in West Africa, the Middle East, and the Indian Ocean. Marco Polo was an Italian merchant who traveled from Venice to the Mongol Empire along the Silk Road. Rabban Sauma was a Nestorian Christian who traveled to Europe from the Mongol Empire on behalf of the Mongol khan. All three of these travelers recorded their journeys, which has helped to provide first-hand accounts of the history of the 13th and 14th centuries.

18. C

The Roman Catholic Church and the Eastern Orthodox Church split officially in the 11th century, though they had been growing apart for centuries. The pope remained the spiritual head and leader of the Roman Catholic Church, and the patriarch and the Byzantine emperor served as co-rulers of the Eastern Orthodox Church.

19. A

While Confucian ideas were very influential in Japan, the civil service exams were never adopted. Important government jobs were hereditary positions.

20. B

The kingdom of Mali, which ruled West Africa in the 13th and 14th centuries, gained great wealth from the tolls collected from the gold and salt traded along the trans-Saharan route. The religion of Islam was also very influential: The emperor Mansa Musa had converted to Islam and went on a pilgrimage to Mecca with an entourage of thousands.

21. E

Buddhism was influential in Tibet, China, Japan, and Korea by 1450, but it had not traveled as far as the Philippines.

22. B

The Turks who invaded India organized themselves into the Delhi Sultanate, which dominated most of northern India. In the Middle East, however, the Turks were often hired as mercenaries in the Abbasid army. Over time, their military power grew, and the sultan, ruler of the Turks, soon wielded more power than the caliph.

23. C

The Mongols were a powerful military force, but they never outnumbered the people they conquered. It was actually quite the opposite. What did help the Mongols conquer such large armies was that the civilizations they invaded were often declining in power. Some Mongols did convert to Islam, but that was something they learned from the conquered people.

24. D

The trade from the Indian Ocean greatly influenced East Africa. The wealth from the trade led to the rise of powerful city-states such as Sofala and Kilwa. These states are often referred to as Swahili city-states after their language, which was a blend of Bantu language and Arabic. In the 900s, Islamic merchants traded gold, slaves, and ivory for pottery, glass, and textiles from Persia, India, and China. As the trade increased, so did the wealth of the city-states. Much like Ghana and Mali, these powerful city-states were governed by kings who taxed and controlled the trade. They built stone mosques and public buildings, and the ruling elite dressed in silk from China.

25. E

Smallpox was devastating to the American population, but not until after their encounter with Europeans in 1492.

26. B

The road systems that were built in these large empires greatly facilitated trade and communication. The Incan king alone claimed to be a descendent of the Sun God. The Roman republic did have a form of representative government. Both empires were brought down, partly by invasions, but the drop in trade was more significant in Rome and in the Incan empire. Both empires were made up of diverse people.

27. B

Venice was an important trading city along the Mediterranean Sea, Samarkand was an important oasis town along the Silk Road, and Changan was considered the start of the Silk Road trade in China. London, Paris, Brussels, Rio de Janeiro, Beijing, and Rome were not significant trading cities at that time.

28. C

Manorialism was the economic system used in much of Europe during the time period 600 to 1450. This system revolved around the manor, where serfs farmed the land and lords oversaw their work. The system was self-sufficient; anything needed was available on the manor, and as a result, outside trade was limited.

29. E

Since Islam does not have the hierarchical structure that Christianity has, there was no group of priests on which to place blame. So, unlike many Christians who felt abandoned by the church, Muslims (and Islam) were not significantly challenged during the Black Plague.

30. E

The social structure of Spanish America was based on race. At the top were the peninsulares, who had come directly from Europe. At the bottom were the zambos, who were a mix of Native American and African.

31. C

The early Spanish settlers in the Caribbean had a need for significant labor recruitment. The encomienda system gave Spanish settlers the right to demand labor in the mines and fields of native peoples. These laborers were worked hard and punished severely.

32. C

With the exception of cattle, all of the products were transferred from the Americas to Europe during the Colombian Exchange. Cattle went from Europe to the Americas, which at the time did not have large draft animals.

33. B

In order to separate the Chinese from themselves, the Manchus insisted that Chinese men wear their hair in a queue. This hairstyle involved shaving the top of the head and a long braid in the back. The ultimate sign of rebellion by the Chinese would be to cut off one's queue.

34. A

The great Chinese demand for silver drove the silver trade. The silver was supplied largely by Mexico, Peru, and Japan. The Spanish served as the middlemen transporting the silver to China. The Ming dynasty actually experienced serious problems with inflation as a result of the large influx of silver that flowed into China.

35. B

Unlike Portugal, whose government financed all of its expeditions in the Indian Ocean, Britain used joint-stock companies, in which investors—not the crown—funded the expeditions.

36. B

While the Ottomans were known for their administrative expertise, the Mongols were quite inefficient administrators who often relied on those they conquered to administer the empire.

37. A

China experienced an increase in foreign trade in the 19th century, though not necessarily a willing rise. The increase was often at the insistence of European powers. For example, the British participated in a lucrative opium trade with the Chinese in exchange for Chinese goods such as tea.

38. A

The Islamic tradition of veil wearing was actually adopted from Persian women. Nowhere in the Quran does it state that women must be veiled.

39. D

During the rule of the Tokugawa Shogunate, the Japanese closed their doors to outside interaction, and as a result, successfully avoided the intrusion of the West.

40. A

As in the Tang dynasty, the Roman and Persian Empires both had extensive road systems. This encouraged trade and facilitated communication throughout the empires.

41. C

The Atlantic slave trade was part of a larger triangular trade network in which slaves were brought from Africa to the Americas. Cash crops were brought from the Americas to Europe, and goods such as gunpowder weapons were brought from Europe to Africa.

42. D

In the 1960s, Mao Zedong initiated the Cultural Revolution in an effort to revolutionize China. The goal was also to raise his own status above that of the Communist party and purge the party of his enemies. A group of teenagers known as the Red Guards rampaged cities, ordered the destruction of temples, and closed schools. The military was eventually needed to suppress the anarchy they had created, and the country ended up losing a generation of educated people.

43. E

Judaism is the earliest monotheistic religion. The Hebrews, or Jews, believe that they had a covenant with God, as his chosen people. In order to keep the covenant, Jews are asked to believe in only one God and follow the 10 Commandments.

44. B

As many African nations achieved their independence, they did so along the colonial borders established during imperialism. Unfortunately, the Europeans did not consult the Africans in drawing up these borders, and oftentimes, conflicting tribes or ethnic groups were at the borders of the same countries. This has led to conflict in many new nations.

45. B

The goal of the nonalignment movement was to remain neutral in the cold war and not get dragged into the conflict between the United States and the Soviet Union. Nations such as India supported this movement, in hopes of standing on its own.

46. B

As European competition heated up, the potential for conflict seemed imminent. In response to this rising tension, German Chancellor Otto von Bismarck called the Berlin Conference. Delegates (none of which were African) were invited to establish the ground rules for colonization of Africa, and it was decided that any European state could establish an African colony after it had notified the others.

47. C

To conquer the Incan empire, the Spanish used advanced military technology. In addition, however, they allied themselves with native groups, many of whom were suffering from the effects of the smallpox epidemic.

48. D

Industrialization was a global movement, but it did not begin until after 1750.

49. D

The Taiping Rebellion (1850s) hoped to introduce reform to China. Internal disputes within the Taipings finally helped the Qing dynasty to defeat them, but it was a desperate 10-year struggle that exhausted the imperial treasury. Aggressive British traders began to import opium into China, and a customs dispute in Guangzhou led to the first Opium War in 1839. This resulted in two humiliating defeats for China and a series of disadvantageous treaties which gave Britain and other European nations commercial entry into China. In the 1860s and 1870s, with government-sponsored grants, local leaders promoted military and economic reform in China using the slogan, "Chinese learning at the base, Western learning for use." These leaders built modern shipyards, railroads, and weapon industries, and founded academies focused on the study of science. It was a great foundation, but the Self-Strengthening Movement only brought change to the surface. It also experienced resistance from the imperial government, in particular, the Empress Dowager Cixi.

50. B

During the Meiji period in Japan, the government-sponsored industrialization and military build-up allowed Japan to rise as a world power. This was evident in Japan's victory in the Russo–Japanese War in 1904–05.

51. C

The ruler of Belgium, King Leopold II, took control of the large area in central Africa known as the Congo. The native people were forced to supply him with rubber, and were subjected to brutal consequences if they did not cooperate.

52. D

In 1861, Czar Alexander II abolished serfdom, and the government compensated landowners for the loss of land and serfs. The serfs gained their freedom and their labor obligations were gradually cancelled. They won very few political rights and had to pay a redemption tax for most of the land they received. Few serfs prospered and most were desperately poor. The emancipation led to little increase in agricultural production, as peasants continued to use traditional methods of farming. It did, however, create a large urban labor force for the newly industrialized empire.

53. E

Both Italy and Germany were formerly decentralized areas. In the 19th century, they were unified into new nations, thanks to a rise in nationalism, military victories, and political planning.

54. D

Slavery was indeed challenged during this period. Many 19th-century liberals in Europe and North America supported the abolition of this institution, as it openly conflicted with the Enlightenment ideals of liberty and equality. The slave trade ended officially in Great Britain in 1807, and in the United States in 1808—though a secret slave trade continued through much of the century. The emancipation of the slaves took much longer: British colonies emancipated slaves in 1833, French colonies in 1848, the United States in 1865, and Brazil in 1888.

55. A

As Japan was opening up to the industrialization of the West, it was also heavily influenced by Western culture. Japanese literature was affected by European models, and so writers began to experiment with Western verse. Architects and artists created large buildings of steel with Greek columns much like those seen in the west. Many Japanese also copied Western fashion and hairstyles. In spite of these powerful influences, though, Japan also continued to emphasize its own values.

56. C

As wages increased and work hours decreased in the industrial age, people were given new opportunities. A larger middle class led to an increase in the importance of leisure. The use of advertising communicated a sense of 'needing things' to people. The bicycle, for instance, became the "must-have" item of the 1880s. Newspapers, theaters, and professional sports all became popular in this new era of leisure and consumption. The television, however, was not introduced until the mid-20th century.

57. A

Both leaders used civil disobedience, like strikes or non-cooperation, in their fight for independence from Great Britain.

58. E

India did not experience genocide in the 20th century, though ethnic conflict between Muslims and Hindus took place (and continues today).

59. B

Both rulers wanted to westernize and modernize their countries. Though Turkey was a Muslim country, Attaturk saw Islamic institutions as backward and introduced Western ideas and institutions. He wanted to take power away from religious authorities. Peter the Great was strongly opposed to democratic reforms, but did dream of westernizing and establishing a warm-water port.

60. C

The use of the atomic bomb was an outcome of World War II, not World War I.

61. E

The concept of the nation-state gained initial prominence in the 19th century with the unification of Italy and Germany, and the independence movements in North and South America. It continued to be an important political organization in the 20th century.

62. B

The North Atlantic Treaty Organization, the Oil Producing and Exporting Countries, and the European Union are all international organizations formed to achieve common goals with other nations.

63. A

Apartheid means separateness. In order to maintain its power, the minority white government enacted laws to separate blacks and whites in South Africa. Under this system, 87% of the territory was designated for white citizens, with the remaining part for black citizens.

64. C

Stalin instituted his Five-Year Plans in hopes of increasing industrial and agricultural productivity. Individual farms became collectivized, and those who refused collectivization were killed. The Russian people experienced tremendous oppression during Stalin's Great Purges of the 1930s. Thousands were tried and executed, and millions imprisoned.

65. B

Many Latin American countries have struggled politically and economically in the 20th century, but since the 1980s, many have been moving politically toward representative democracy.

66. B

Following World War I, the British held a mandate in Palestine, but had made conflicting promises to the Palestinian Arabs and the Jews. In the Balfour Declaration of 1917, the British government committed to support the creation of a homeland for Jews in Palestine, and allowed Jews to migrate to Palestine during the mandate period. The Arab Palestinians, on the other hand, saw British rule and Jewish settlement as forms of imperial control.

67. D

Hindu and Muslim conflict dates back hundreds of years in India, but the conflict worsened after independence was granted to India and Pakistan (the Muslim-dominated area led by Muhammad Ali Jinnah). This division led to a mass migration of Muslim and Hindu refugees and terrible violence. Tension still exists today.

68. B

When Gorbachev came to power in 1985, he introduced a policy of perestroika ("restructuring"), which was the beginning of a market economy with limited free-enterprise and some private property. His policy of glasnost ("openness") encouraged people to discuss the strengths and weaknesses of the Soviet system. These changes and the weakness of the Soviet economy facilitated the fall of the Soviet Union.

69. D

Fascism, which was used by Hitler (Germany) and Mussolini (Italy), is a form of ultra-nationalism with an absolute leader and strong central government running the show.

70. C

The French Revolution suffered a reign of terror under the leadership of Robespierre. The Russians experienced their own reign of terror, or Great Purge, under the rule of Stalin.

Part A: Document-Based Question: Sample Response

The European encounter with the Americas had a devastating impact both socially and economically on the native populations. Economically, the natives were taken advantage of and forced to perform labor. Socially, they were deemed inferior and were brutalized by the European conquistadors.

Economically, the natives suffered a huge loss of population and were pushed into forced labor. Bernardino de Sahagun, a Franciscan friar, reported the devastation that occurred to the native population as a result of smallpox. This excerpt from General History of the Things of New Spain demonstrates sympathy for the plight of the natives. He wrote that in "1520 the epidemic of smallpox, measles, and pustules broke out so virulently that a vast number of people died throughout New Spain." This major loss of population severely weakened the people and allowed them to be easily defeated and economically dominated by the Europeans. Additionally, the natives were forced to labor for the Europeans. Antonio Vasquez de Espinosa, a Spanish friar and missionary, described the silver mines of Potosi. He describes how the natives were forced to work for the mines and they were often carried off in chains to their labor. Espinosa, a missionary interested in converting natives to Christianity, seems to be sympathetic and angry about their treatment. While the native were tolling away in the mines, the Spanish were getting incredible wealthy. In the period of Espinosa's investigation over 300 million pesos of silver were taken out of the mines. What is missing here is the voice of the native. It would be helpful to have a primary source that describes the economic situation before the encounter and a contrasting view after the encounter to truly judge the significance of the change.

Socially, the arrival of Europeans was equally devastating. The natives were viewed as inferior to the Europeans, enslaved, and brutalized. Hernando Cortes, a Spanish conquistador, describes his conquest of Mexico in 1521. In it he describes how easily the natives were conquered and that other native groups aligned with the Spanish to aid in their defeat. Cortes's purpose in writing these letters is to glorify his own missions. Juan Gines de Sepulveda supplies a justification for the treatment of the native people, writing that the natives were clearly inferior in character and morals. He equates them with children, women, and the cruel and inhumane. Sepulveda's purpose is to justify the treatment of the natives by lowering them to a level beneath their European conquerors. Not all Europeans, however, were convinced that the natives deserved this inferior treatment. Dominican friar Bartolome de las Casas, wrote in A Short Account of the Destruction of the Indies in 1543 of the devastation and depopulation that the natives were suffering. His purpose was the get the attention of the Spanish king so he would end the abuses taking place. Las Casas did meet with some success when new laws were passed protecting native peoples, though enforcing the laws was a difficult matter. It would be helpful to have some documentary evidence on the effects of las Casas's book, perhaps a copy of the new laws or the testimony of a native before and after the laws were passed. Finally, an engraving by Flemish engraver Theodor de Bry shows the brutal Spanish burning a group of native people alive. This engraving was included in a Dutch edition of las Casas' book, and was meant to illustrate the atrocities committed by the Spanish.

Economically and socially the Americas were transformed by the Spanish conquest following 1492. The native American population suffered extremely negative consequences of forced labor and social inferiority, while many Spanish profited and rose to new levels of social significance.

Part B: Change-Over-Time Question: Sample Response

The Silk Road was the thriving trade route through much of the period 600 to 1750. From 600 to 1450, it served as the major thoroughfare for the exchange of goods, technology, and culture. From 1450 to 1750, trade along the road began to decline as the seaborne trade of the Indian Ocean took a higher prominence in global trade.

By 600 CE, the Han dynasty had fallen in China, and a period of disorder followed, but China was eventually reunited by the Sui and then the Tang dynasties. The Tang and later Song dynasties revived trade along the Silk Road with the Islamic world. Buddhism spread, as did paper and gunpowder along the trade routes. Oasis towns like Kashgar and Samarkand grew and thrived because of the active trade route. When the Mongols conquered China and much of Asia, the Silk Road flourished even more, as the safety and security of the Pax Mongolia allowed for safe travel along the oasis towns of the Silk Road. Travelers such as Ibn Battuta and Marco Polo used these trade routes to travel extensively during this period. Continually, Europeans were receiving Asian goods after their long journeys on the Silk Road and paying high prices for them.

By 1450, however, the overland trade route became less important as more focus turned to the seas. The Indian Ocean, which had been an important trade route previously, became a key trading zone. Europeans, who had previously been receiving their Asian goods via the Silk Road were now traveling around Africa to the Indian Ocean to trade these Asian products themselves. The new global trade network, with the inclusion of the Americas after 1492, was more driven by sea trade and as a result, the trade along the Silk Road began to decline.

The Silk Road was a dominant trade route throughout the time period 600 to 1450. The political stability and safety during this time period aided this thriving trade route. However, after 1450 the Europeans entered the Indian Ocean to get Asian goods for themselves via the sea trade. The rise of Europe and its involvement in global trade led to the decline in the Silk Road trade.

Part C: Comparative Question: Sample Response

Social structures serve the purpose of bringing stability to society. They set established roles and responsibilities in an effort to have a more organized and productive society. The social structures of traditional Confucianism and European feudalism had similar economic impacts in stabilizing society. Politically, however, Confucianism helped to create a more centralized society, while European feudalism maintain a localed decentralized society.

Economically, both Confucianism and European feudalism helped to create financially stable societies. In feudalism the serfs were the lowest class and were bound to the land. This provided a laboring class of people who were not permitted to leave, therefore promoting economic stability. Economically, feudalism encouraged a self-sufficient system in which land was the primary form of wealth and extensive trade was not necessary. In Confucianism, the peasants were also a stable class of workers in this agriculturally based society. Additionally, merchants were considered lower than peasants because they didn't produce anything; rather they were parasites who lived off the labor of others. Consequently, a merchant may have been economically wealthy, but considered socially low. The social/gentry class, like the European lords, controlled the land in which the peasants or serfs labored.

Politically, the impact of these social structures differed. Confucianism praised the emperor as the father of the people who set the example for the state, much the same way that the father sets the example for the son. Additionally, government positions, according to Confucius, should be based on merit. This led to the creation of the civil service examination system, in which students took exams based on Confucian thought to achieve government jobs. Although only the landed gentry class could afford to be educated for such an exam, the opportunity for advancement did exist. Feudalism, on the other hand, was solely based on heredity. Lords inherited their land from their fathers and the land was passed down by generation. In feudalism, the king gave land to the lords in exchange for military service. This arrangement created a decentralized form of government where the king gave away much of his power (the land) to the noble class.

The stability of both Confucianism and feudalism changed over time. However, both systems successfully created stable societies for China and Europe with economic production based on agriculture. Politically they differed, as Confucianism encouraged a more centralized government under the rule of the wise emperor, and feudalism created a decentralized political system in which power was distributed to the noble class.

Glossary

The AP World History course focuses on the "big picture" of history. It is not critical that you memorize names, dates, or events, yet the knowledge of certain world history vocabulary terms can be crucial in framing the analysis of world history. The terms presented here come primarily from the words used by the College Board to describe the important content material in AP World History.

GENERAL TERMS

Civilization: This term can be a loaded issue of historical debate. Who is civilized and who is not? Strictly speaking, a civilization is settled and agricultural. Thus it is able to produce surplus food that can support an elite class. At times, however, the term has been used to separate those cultures considered advanced from those that did not "measure up," especially during the time of European imperialism.

Demography: The study of population dynamics. Demographics is important in the study of world history because population dynamics provide evidence of important historical trends, such as disease pandemics, and migrations.

Diffusion: The spread of items from one place to another. In world history, the phrase *cultural diffusion* is used to describe the spread of ideas, such as religions and products, as with trade.

Gender: Describes the social roles that men and women adopt. Different cultures at different times have vastly different notions of gender roles. Even within a given society, gender roles may differ between different social groups, such as between the elites and the peasantry.

Historiography: The study of the way that historians write history. In one sense, it is the history of history. A person examining historiography would look at the way that a Marxist historian, for example, would frame the historical record differently than a person with an imperialist perspective.

Interregional: The connections between different regions of the world. Trade connections, for example, between South Asia and East Africa are an example of interregional contacts.

Migration: The movement of people from one area to settle in another area. Migrations can be voluntary or forced, such as with slavery.

Patriarchy: A social system in which the father is the head of the family or a system in which men dominate the social structure.

Periodization: The division of historical time into different periods. AP World History, for example, divides the course into five different periods of history. How history is divided is a matter of great debate since it by nature sets up different dates as the critical division points.

Technology: The way in which people adapt their knowledge to tools and inventions. The concept of technology in AP World History represents a major theme of the course.

8000 BCE to 600 CE

Animism: A type of religious belief that focuses on the roles of the various gods and spirits in the natural world and in human events. Animist religions are polytheistic and have been practiced in almost every part of the world.

Caste System: The social system of the Aryans divided people into four castes, also known as Varnas. This caste system had a profound impact on the development of the Hindu religion. Each of the four main castes had specific roles to fulfill in society.

Classical: Represents a period of great cultural significance in society before the modern age. In a limited form of usage, classical refers to the age of Athens in ancient Greece and to the time of the Roman Republic and Empire. The term classical, however, can also be applied to non-Mediterranean cultures, such as the Qin Dynasty of China.

Filial Piety: A form of respect shown by children to their parents. Filial piety is a crucial concept in Confucian thought, and can also be seen in the respect and veneration shown to elders and ancestors.

Monotheism: The religious belief in one God. Judaism, Christianity, and Islam all represent monotheist religions.

Neolithic Revolution: The term "Neolithic" means "new stone age." During the early years of the Neolithic period, which corresponds to the starting point of the AP World History course of 8000 BCE, humans discovered agriculture and settled into fixed communities.

Nomadic: A way of life in which people do not have a settled home but rather move from place to place in order to support their livelihood. Pastoral nomads move in order to find places for their animals to forage; hunter-gatherer nomads seek out new areas for finding and hunting food.

Pastoral: Refers to a group that herds domesticated animals for their livelihood. Often pastoral people are also nomadic.

Polygamy: A cultural trait in which one person is married to more than one spouse at a time.

Polytheism: Religious belief in more than one god. The ancient Greeks, for example, practiced polytheism.

Silk Roads: The trade routes that linked the Mediterranean area of the Roman Empire with the Chinese Qin Dynasty. Silk textiles and other precious trade goods traveled across the silk roads about 2000 years ago. Later, the Silk Roads flourished under the Mongol period of the 13th century.

600 to 1450 CE

Caliphate: Caliphs were the political—and to a certain extent religious—successors of Muhammad. The term in Arabic means "deputy." Four noble caliphs following Muhammad were themselves succeeded by the caliphs of the Umayyad and Abbasid Empires.

Crusades: Military invasions during the Middle Ages by the Christians of Western Europe with the objective of capturing the Holy Land from Muslims. Christian crusader states were established along the eastern Mediterranean coast until later Muslim counter-attacks reconquered the area. The Crusades were also responsible for increasing the cultural and economic integration of Southern Europe with the rest of the world.

Dar al-Islam: A term meaning "house of Islam" in Arabic. The Dar al-Islam is the expanse of the Islamic world. In the centuries that followed the death of Muhammad, Dar al-Islam stretched from the Iberian Peninsula of Western Europe to the far islands of Southeast Asia.

Feudalism: A social and political system in which lords are granted landed estates by a monarch in exchange for their loyalty, especially in military matters. Feudalism existed during the Medieval period in Western Europe and also in Japan during the age of the Shoguns.

Indian Ocean Trade System: A network of trade established between the Indian subcontinent and the Swahili trade cities of Eastern Africa. Ocean-going merchants from the Arabian Peninsula used the regular patterns of the monsoon winds to travel back and forth carrying cargoes of textiles, spices, and precious metals. The domination of the Portuguese in the Indian Ocean during the 16th century ended the previous dynamics of this trade system.

Manorialism: A type of social structure in which a lord has control over the labor on his agricultural estate. Typically serfs were bound to the land and required to work for the lord.

Missionary: A person who spreads his or her religious belief to others. In several of the major world religions, such as Buddhism, Christianity, and Islam, missionaries were vital in the spread of the faith.

Pandemic: A widespread outbreak of disease. Disease pandemics, such as the bubonic plague of the 14th century and the smallpox pandemic in the Americas after contact with the Europeans, caused global transformations.

Papacy: Referring to the authority of the Roman Catholic Pope, who is seen as the spiritual successor to Saint Peter. During the Medieval period, the papacy had great religious and some political power over almost all of Western Europe.

1450 to 1750

Absolutism: A style of government that came about in Europe during the 17th century. Absolute monarchs generally ruled a highly centralized state by concentrating power in their own hands. State-run armies, religions, and economic policy often supported the absolutist state. Louis XIV of France represents what many historians consider to be the epitome of absolutism.

Coercive Labor: Any labor system that involves force, such as various forms of slavery, serfdom, and indentured labor. Almost all civilizations relied on some form of coercive labor up to the 19th century.

Columbian Exchange: The biological exchange that occurred as a result of European involvement with the Americas following Columbus's voyage. Diseases, animals, and plants were transmitted from the Old World to the New World, vastly changing both.

Empire: A political unit in which groups of people, often in different countries, are controlled by a single ruler. Imperial systems are by nature expansionist.

Enlightenment: An intellectual movement centered in Western Europe during the 18th century. The Enlightenment focused on rational thought, order, and logic. These concepts had widespread impacts, such as on the American Revolution and the emancipation of slavery.

Harem: Strictly defined, a harem is the place within a Muslim palace where women were housed. Harems also refer to the women, typically concubines, who are attached to a powerful political ruler.

Neo-Confucianism: A movement to return to traditional Confucian values that occurred especially during the Song Dynasty.

Reformation: The religious movement for reform of the Roman Catholic Church during the 16th century. The Reformation led to the creation of new Protestant Christian churches that sought authority separate from the Pope.

Renaissance: The period of intellectual and artistic "rebirth" that occurred first in Italy during the 14th and 15th centuries. During the Renaissance, many elite people sought inspiration in the ideals of classical times and focused on the ideas of humanism and individualism.

Scientific Revolution: A major period of change in scientific thought that occurred in Europe beginning in the 16th century. The scientific revolution was characterized by the use of observation and experimentation using the rational tools of the scientific method.

1750 to 1914

Bourgeoisie: The middle class in European industrial society. During the French Revolution, the social group of mostly wealthy professionals and businessmen, who helped lead the initial phases of the revolution, were known as the bourgeoisie. Later Karl Marx would consider the bourgeoisie to be the social class most responsible for the capitalist exploitation of industrial society.

Colonialism: Rule by one country over another country. In colonialism raw materials and markets of the colony are often used to enrich the mother country.

Communism: A political philosophy best represented by the thinking of Karl Marx during the 19th century. In communism a violent revolution is needed in order to overthrow capitalism and create a society based on social equality.

Emancipation: The liberation of a group of people from the control of other people. Typically emancipation relates to the liberation of people under a coercive labor system, such as slavery or serfdom. Emancipation may also refer to female emancipation, in which women achieve rights equal to those of men.

Ideology: A system of ideas or ways of thinking that guides the decisions of a group of people. Ideology generally involves issues of politics, but it also has economic, social, and cultural implications.

Imperialism: The process by which mostly European countries established political and economic control over other parts of the world starting in the 16th century and reaching its height in the 19th century.

Industrialism: The development of a complex economic system using the factory system of production. Industrialism is one of the main characteristics of a society becoming modernized.

Marxism: A system of political and economic thought developed first by Karl Marx in the mid-19th century. Marxism emphasizes class struggle as the dominant aspect of social change and historical transformation.

Nationalism: A political belief that people should have pride and loyalty to their nation and/or ethnic group. Often in nationalism people see their own nation as having special aspects that separate and elevate their people in relation to people of other nations.

Social Darwinism: An intellectual movement that used Charles Darwin's biological ideas of natural selection and the "survival of the fittest" to human societies. European Social Darwinists of the 19th century saw other parts of the world as weak and thus justifiably exploited.

1914 to the Present

Apartheid: A governmental policy of racial separation that arose in South Africa during the middle of the 20th century. It was dismantled in the 1990s when black South Africans gained political representation.

Cold War: The period of conflict between the United States and its allies, and the Soviet Union and its allies. The cold war began soon after World War II and ended in the last years of the 20th century.

Consumer Society: A society, especially in modern times, that expresses itself through the process of consumption of material goods. Issues such as the globalization of corporate brands and the role of multinational corporation, in countries around the world are both indicators of the diffusion of the values of consumer society.

Decolonization: The process by which former colonies became independent. Countries in South Asia and much of Africa became independent through decolonization during the middle of the 20th century.

Deforestation: The elimination of vast numbers of trees by logging operations as in Brazil and Indonesia or by individuals for firewood and construction material as in Haiti. Deforestation can have dramatic local environmental impacts, such as soil erosion. Widespread deforestation has been linked to broader ecological issues of a global nature.

Demographic Transition: The shift to both lower birth rates and lower death rates, thus leading to stable population dynamics. Demographic transitions occur with countries that experience modernization, and the advantages of modern medicine and lower child mortality.

Developing World: Parts of the world that have an economic system in which the process of industrial development is not advanced. Much of Africa, Asia, and Latin America is part of the developing world.

Fascism: A political system that emerged in Europe following World War II. Fascism combines ideas of extreme nationalism with authoritarian rule to oppose both liberal democracy and communism. Mussolini's Italy was the first fascist country.

Feminism: A social and political movement that views women as equal to men. Feminists demand equal rights and the elimination of patriarchal control.

Genocide: The planned, systematic killing of a group of people. The Nazi genocide of the Jews and other groups is known as the Holocaust. The 20th century also witnessed other acts of genocide, such as against the Armenians at the beginning of the century and in Rwanda at the end of the century.

Globalization: The process by which national boundaries become increasingly less important, as a result of economic, social, and cultural interactions between parts of the world.

Guerrilla War: A style of warfare that emphasizes irregular fighting units that use surprise attacks and unconventional methods.

Multinational Corporation: A company with operations in a variety of different countries. The late 20th century, with its rapid move toward globalization, saw a rise in influence of multinational corporations.

Non-Aligned Nations: Countries that remained neutral during the cold war conflict between the United States and the Soviet Union. For years, India was the symbolic leader among the non-aligned nations.

Pacific Rim: Those areas that surround the Pacific Ocean. The term is typically used to describe the new economic influence of the nations of East and Southeast Asia.

Popular Culture: Cultural issues of common identity that bind a group of people together. Film, music, and sports are all important aspects of modern popular culture. In recent years, popular culture has become increasingly globalized.

Third World: Strictly speaking, the Third World was the term used during the Cold War to describe those countries that were not part of Western allies of the United States or allies of the Soviet Union. Generally, it is applied to countries of the developing world, especially in Latin America, Africa, and Asia.

Urbanization: The process involved in the growth of cities and the areas surrounding them. Typically, urbanization occurs as part of the processes of industrialism and modernization. People migrate from rural areas or from other countries into rapidly growing urban centers so that they can take advantage of economic opportunity.